Female-to-Male Transsexualism

Historical, Clinical and Theoretical Issues

Leslie Martin Lothstein, PhD

Routledge & Kegan Paul
Boston, London, Melbourne and Henley

First published in 1983
by Routledge & Kegan Paul plc
9 Park Street, Boston, Mass. 02108, USA,
39 Store Street, London WC1E 7DD,
296 Beaconsfield Parade, Middle Park,
Melbourne, 3206, Australia, and
Broadway House, Newtown Road,
Henley-on-Thames, Oxon RG9 1EN
Printed in the United States of America
Copyright © Leslie Martin Lothstein 1983

Library of Congress Cataloguing in Publication Data

Lothstein, Leslie Martin, 1942–

Female-to-male transsexualism.
Bibliography: p.
Includes index.
1. Sex change.   2. Transsexuals — Psychology.
3. Women — Mental health.   I. Title.   [DNLM: 1. Transsexualism.   WM 610 L882f]
RC560.C4L65 1983   616.85'83   83–3254

ISBN 0–7100–9476–0

dm

To

ROSE

Contents

Foreword by Milton Eber   ix

Acknowledgments   xiii

1 Introduction to the problem of female transsexualism   1
     The female transsexual: Barbara   1
     Perspectives on the female transsexual   2
     Female transsexualism and the mental health profession 4
     Myths concerning the female transsexual   5
     Unanswered questions   14
     The female transsexual as experiment   15
     Barbara's letter: a woman's distress signal   16
     The Case Western Reserve Gender Identity Clinic: the
     project   17

2 Historical, psychological, and medical issues   19
     Historical instances of women who impersonated men   19
     The medical-psychological perspective   21
     Summary   47

3 Diagnostic issues   50
     Historical issues of diagnosis in female transsexualism 50
     Contemporary issues in the diagnosis of female trans-
     sexualism   57
     Summary   84

4 The phenomenology of female transsexualism: clinical
   cases   86
     The Case Western Reserve Gender Identity Clinic   86
     Female transsexuals: the group   90

Contents

The impulsive psychopath: Barbara/Brian   95
The picaresque saint: Randi/Randy   110
The crazy kid next door: Patricia/Pat   133
The misfit: Donna/Douglas   146
Methods of investigation   159

5   Psychobiological issues in female transsexualism   164
Background   164
Female transsexuals with undiagnosed biological
    conditions   165
Cerebral pathology   167
EEG measures   167
Increased androgen levels   170
Chromosomal-hormonal factors   172
H-Y antigen studies   177
Overview   179

6   Psychological issues and theories of female transsexualism   181
Female core gender identity   181
Abnormal female development: the roots of female
    transsexualism   197
Theoretical approaches   208
A proposed theoretical framework for female trans-
    sexualism   233
Conclusions   244

7   Psychological and biological treatment of the female
transsexual   255
The psychological evaluation of self-diagnosed female
    transsexuals   255
Psychological approaches   260
The transition to maleness   280
Hormone therapy for female transsexuals   281
Surgical treatment for female transsexuals   291

8   Overview and future prospects   302

Appendix: prevalence and sex ratio of female transsexualism   308

Bibliography   312

Index   331

Foreword

Consider the plight of a clinician facing for the first time a patient wishing for a surgical sex change. A brief historical review of some of the difficulties inherent in this type of clinician/patient encounter is an appropriate starting point. It was not until the mid-1960s that there was agreement on what to call such a patient; the term transsexual was gaining general acceptance at that time. No uniform standards of care for the hormonal and surgical sex reassignment of these patients were available prior to 1979, when care guidelines were prepared and disseminated by a national interdisciplinary committee. Standard descriptive criteria for the psychiatric diagnosis of transsexualism were first made available in 1980 with the publication of the American Psychiatric Association's *DSM* III. And it is with the publication of this book that the clinician is offered for the first time a systematic, comprehensive, psychodynamic exploration of the major diagnostic and treatment issues of this clinical phenomenon. While focused on the female patient, it addresses most of the significant problems concerning transsexualism as a whole.

Drawing from eight years of intensive work with over 200 patients (fifty-three women) as Co-Director of the Case Western Reserve University Gender Identity Clinic, Dr. Lothstein chose as his focus the female because she is even less well understood than the male, and the apparent upsurge in female requests for surgical reassignment creates an immediate need for clarification of crucial treatment issues. Although the CWRU multidisciplinary clinic is one in which surgery is available, Dr. Lothstein and his staff zealously applied a variety of sophisticated psychological and psychoanalytic concepts and techniques in their efforts to understand and treat these patients. Among the findings reported in this volume are the following:

1. Most patients had significant chronic adjustment problems and 40 per cent were considered severely disturbed.

2. A psychotherapeutic approach is the treatment of choice, and the majority of patients improved significantly from this method, choosing a non-surgical solution to their gender dysphoria.

3. A pure form of psychoanalytic psychotherapy is not successful; confrontational and educational techniques need to be combined with more traditional methods.

4. Group therapy used adjunctively facilitated the patient's engagement in the therapeutic process.

5. Hospitalization needs to be utilized to deal with suicidal crises and other episodes of dyscontrol.

6. Surgical reassignment is considered to be a last resort for some patients, but surgery and psychotherapy are not regarded as mutually exclusive.

7. Some patients are only able to engage in psychotherapy after surgery and to seek solution of conflicts which, after all, are untouched by anatomical reconstruction.

With impressive scholarship, Dr. Lothstein traverses a difficult technical terrain, integrating material from such diverse fields as neurology, endocrinology, genetics, electroencephalography, surgery, behavioral psychology, family dynamics, traditional psychoanalytic concepts, object relations theory, and the psychology of the self. In his commitment to a global approach to the transsexual phenomenon, no stone is unturned, no obscure piece of evidence is ignored. Yet, his is clearly a psychoanalytic enterprise and his creative thrust is directed toward conceptualizing the transsexual patient as essentially a person with marked intrapsychic and interpersonal conflicts best understood from the vantage point of contemporary psychoanalytic theory. Kohut's self psychology has had a particularly significant impact on his thinking and leads to one of his key hypotheses regarding the patient's core disturbance. At the risk of greatly oversimplifying his elegant and detailed formulation, Dr. Lothstein regards transsexualism as a disorder of the self. The preoedipal self-object environment of the female patient is one in which the developing female gender-self (his original concept) is insufficiently mirrored by a mother whose own psychological conflicts make her intolerant of her daughter's burgeoning femininity. This failure to provide age-appropriate mirroring to sustain and promote this aspect of the developing self can give rise to devastating disintegration anxiety. The child thus threatened may turn to an important male figure (father, grandfather, older brother), a figure who is idealized, and identify with him, forming an archaic merger in which the object is massively internalized. In other words, the female child defensively and globally identifies with a male figure to share in his perceived strength and to attain the affirming, admiring responses which mother can only now confer. This is a challenging hypothesis worthy of further psychoanalytic investigation.

A major portion of the book is devoted to detailed case histories. Here we experience the compassionate intensity of Lothstein as a clinician and the evocativeness of his writing style. The case history has a rich tradition in psychology and psychoanalysis, but for those who might question this method of scientific discourse the author offers an eloquent defense of its validity. These histories stand up well against the plethora of autobiographical accounts of the transsexual experience now available in the popular press, which can be self-serving in their frankness, often concealing more than they reveal. Lothstein's cases illuminate the transsexual phenomenon — the sadness, the struggles, the defeats, the desperate search for survival. He demonstrates the importance of intergenerational influences, the multiple factors leading to a common pathway, the use of primitive defenses, and the erratic life styles of his patients. Specific attention is directed to separation-individuation conflicts and the threats to mother's psyche of the daughter's nuclear female gender-self. We come to understand each patient as a person, not as a circumscribed clinical entity, and to empathize with her struggle for self-affirmation. At the same time we respect the dedicated efforts of the therapist and vicariously experience his doubts, anxieties, and occasional small triumphs.

This volume is considerably more than a treatise on the diagnosis and treatment of a clinical disorder. The author's probing intelligence examines and clarifies many complex clinical and theoretical areas: development of female sexuality; origins of gender identity; psychology of mother–daughter interactions; intergenerational influences on psychopathology; clinical value of in depth projective psychological assessment; integration of classical psychoanalysis, object relations theory, self psychology, and other important contemporary psychoanalytic contributions; validity of the single case study methodology;

design and implementation of a research- and treatment-oriented gender identity program. And this is only a partial list.

Those who feel more comfortable with precise definitions, discrete categories, and simple explanations will be disappointed. Dr. Lothstein provides none of this. For him the transsexual patient can only be understood through study of the complex interplay of biological, psychological, and social forces. What brings a self-diagnosed transsexual patient to our offices and clinics is the end result of multiple converging pathways. He makes clear that the incongruity of identity and anatomy so disturbing to the patient is a symptomatic coalescence of extraordinary intricacy. The patient must be treated intensively and extensively; the therapist must have considerable tolerance of ambiguity as well as tolerance of complexity. There are no precise predictive criteria that will help differentiate those patients who might ultimately be candidates for surgery, but this volume persuades us with its data and clinical case illustrations that the psychological should precede the surgical.

Dr. Lothstein, a rare combination of creative, committed clinician and scholarly researcher, presents in this book a model of applied clinical psychology that should serve as an inspiration to the experienced psychologist as well as the neophyte. His work is testimony to the vitality of psychoanalytic concepts and techniques. Mental health professionals or anyone wishing to fully understand the transsexual patient will find much to be mined from this rich lode. Psychoanalytically oriented researchers will find herein many valuable hypotheses as well as an extremely useful model for the investigation of this disorder. Above all, this volume is a long awaited and much needed guide for the beleaguered clinician.

Milton Eber, Ph.D.
University of Miami School of Medicine

Acknowledgments

Over the past few years I have had the rare opportunity to meet periodically with a number of serious scholars, who are above all compassionate human beings, from the Harry Benjamin Gender Dysphoria Association, who have devoted a large part of their professional lives to the task of understanding and helping the transsexual. These individuals, including Richard Green, Paul Walker, Donald Laub, Ira Pauly, and Norman Fisk, have helped me to transform my primitive ideas of transsexualism into a sophisticated way of thinking about the issues. I want especially to thank Richard Green for encouraging me to continue my investigations at the moment when I felt most ill-equipped to do so; I cannot thank him enough.

There are, however, two men who have probably played the most important role in the development of my thinking about transsexualism: Robert Stoller and John Money. While I have only recently met John Money, it was through my readings that I first became acquainted with his serious and important scholarship on the subject of transsexualism. The reader will recognize the threads of his work throughout my book. Robert Stoller, however, has been my personal mentor. When I first became acquainted with his research on transsexualism, I was still a graduate student in philosophy. It was probably not ironic that the last book I read as a graduate student in philosophy became the focus of my clinical academic career as a psychologist. While I have not always agreed with his conclusions, I share his clinical interests in psychoanalysis and always believed that his methods and scholarship in transsexual research were the model to emulate. Over the past year he has been my critic and guide: dutifully reading every word of the manuscript, providing me with support and encouragement while helping to refine my ideas and temper my style. I cannot thank him enough for extending his personal warmth and clinical acumen to my project; I am forever indebted to him.

On a daily basis I had the opportunity to work with many colleagues from the Case Western Reserve Gender Identity Clinic. I wish to thank all of them for their efforts in helping to sharpen my thinking and providing the structure for developing a gender clinic so that I could engage in my clinical research on transsexualism. I would like to give special thanks to Aaron Billowitz and the staff of Metropolitan General Hospital for their spiritual and financial support of the clinic. To Stephen Levine, my colleague and friend, I owe a special debt. He has been one of my best (and severest) critics and also my greatest source of support. Thanks, Stephen.

I want to express my gratitude to Marvin Wasman and Douglas Lenkoski for providing a rich and open atmosphere of inquiry in the Department of Psychiatry at CWRU so that I, and my colleagues, could undertake our research. I am also grateful for their continued support throughout my sabbatical so that I could be free of financial burdens while writing this book.

I owe special thanks to Milton Eber, with whom I have enjoyed an especially good working relationship. Over the years he has listened patiently to my ideas and provided an important source of criticism of my work. Because I value his scholarship, clinical sensitivity, and intellectual insight I asked him to serve as a reader for this manuscript. I cannot fully express my gratitude for his help in refining my ideas and guiding my thinking (ever so skillfully) so that the final product was more professional. I also want to thank Harvard Medical School for providing me with a clinical position at Cambridge City Hospital so that I could pursue my research (especially Charles Ducey for being so understanding of my need for free time to complete my research). I am especially grateful to the staff of the Countway and Widener Libraries for helping me in my research. I also wish to thank Lilian Levine, librarian at the Allen Memorial Medical Library in Cleveland, who assisted me throughout my sabbatical year by securing books and papers which I needed to complete my research.

I would also like to express gratitude to the following people who have helped me to understand better the clinical and conceptual issues of transsexualism: Jon Meyer, Howard Roback, Carol Steinmann, Terry Buck, Deborah Heller, Tom Brod, and Jeffrey Lowery. My clinical indebtedness to Irwin Kremen, Elaine Crovitz, Mary Huse, Bob Carson,

Robert Schnitzer, Irene Stiver, Lenore Behar, Maurice Schilling, and Ray Greenberg can never be fully expressed. To Carol Baker, of Routledge & Kegan Paul, I wish to express my thanks for her interest in and enthusiasm for my ideas and for helping to bring this work to publication.

I want especially to thank my brother Arthur, who has provided continual support and interest in my work. His philosophical perspective and critical approach to original texts have profoundly influenced my own scholarly style. Throughout my sabbatical year I was provided the comfort, support, and love of two wonderfully generous and special women – Rose and Doris. I can never express enough caring and love for these two women.

Above all I want to express my love and appreciation for my wife Mary Anne, who not only provided me with her love and warmth but also her careful and scholarly reading of my manuscript, which, in the midst of taking care of our three children, was no small task. Finally to Ted, Dan, and Jessica, thanks for being so loving and understanding while I struggled through the various phases of this book.

For permission to quote from previously published works, thanks are due to the publishers and authors listed below. Full bibliographic details of works cited are given in the Bibliography. To Sigmund Freud Copyrights Ltd, The Institute of Psycho-Analysis, and The Hogarth Press Ltd for permission to quote from volume 19 of *The Standard Edition of the Complete Psychological Works of Sigmund Freud*, translated and edited by James Strachey; to International Universities Press, Inc., New York, for permission to quote from *Infantile Origins of Sexual Identity*, 1981, by H. Roiphe and H. Galenson; to the *International Journal of Psycho-Analysis*, and to A. Frances, M. Sacks, and M. Aronoff, for permission to quote from their article "Depersonalization: a self-relations perspective," 1977; to the *International Journal of Psycho-Analysis* and to Elizabeth M. Kohut and Ernest Wolf, for extracts from "The disorders of the self and their treatment: an outline," 1978, by H. Kohut and E. Wolf; to Plenum Publishing Corp., New York, and to Robert Stoller for permission to quote from "Etiological factors in female transsexualism," *Archives of Sexual Behavior*, 1972; to Plenum Publishing Corp. and I. Pauly for permission to quote from "Female transsexualism: Part I," *Archives of Sexual Behavior*, 1974; to *The Psychoanalytic Quarterly* for quoted material from "Parental influence in unusual sexual behavior in children," Edward M. Litin et al., 1956; and to the *American Journal of*

Psychotherapy and Ethel S. Person for permission to quote from E. Person and L. Ovesey, "The transsexual syndrome in males: I, Primary transsexualism," 1974. Material from *Emergence: A Transsexual Autobiography* by Mario Martino, copyright © 1977 by Mario Martino and harriet, is used by permission of Crown Publishers, Inc., New York. The case history presented in chapter 7 originally appeared in my article "Psychotherapy with patients with gender dysphoria syndromes," and is reprinted with permission from the *Bulletin of the Menninger Clinic*, vol. 41, no. 6, pp. 563–82, copyright 1977, The Menninger Foundation.

Chapter 1

Introduction to the problem of female transsexualism

The female transsexual: Barbara

Several years ago I received the following letter from a self-diagnosed female transsexual:

Dear Dr. Lothstein,

My name is Barbara and I am interested in speaking with you or someone at the clinic about myself.

I am 23 years old and physically I am a girl, but inside I am a male. I have felt this way since I was quite young and it has been very painful. I have discussed my gender problem with many professional individuals, but nothing has actually happened. I've been in contact with Transition Midwest, but since their clinic is so far I haven't really spoken to them. I also contacted a female to male transsexual and it was very nice talking to him, but only talking [sic] helps so much. I am very depressed and guilt ridden.

My guilt feelings stem from my experience in College. I attended a Christian college in Ohio as an Art Communications and Psychology major. My last year there I finally opened up to someone about my problem and I should not have. I was a sinner, they said. And I was born a girl and that's what I should be. They told me to pray to God to take these feelings away, but they never disappeared.

I was asked to leave the college because they thought I was gay. I never even became involved with anyone, but because I was attracted to women, they believed I was. I know I am not a latent homosexual or a transvestite, but a transsexual. I feel male and I am. But my guilt and the fact that I don't want to be diagnosed as a freak has hurt me. I need to talk to someone who can understand me and

1

accept me. I feel as though I am stuck in a time warp or a gender
warp and I want to accept myself and like myself and not feel guilty.
   I am very interested in talking to someone from your Clinic if it
is possible.
   Thank you for reading my letter and I hope to hear from you
soon.

Barbara L.

Over the last eight years I have read many letters from women like
Barbara who, because of their transsexual feelings, have experienced
intense personal anguish, suffering, and humiliation. At the very least
their gender pathology has confused most observers. Barbara's depiction
of herself as being "stuck in a time warp or gender warp," and "diagnosed
as a freak" is a perception shared by many female transsexuals. Until
more is known about the phenomenon of female transsexualism patients
like Barbara will continue to experience intense personal anguish as
they will be stigmatized by segments of their society (who mislabel
them as homosexuals), and neglected and misunderstood by mental
health practitioners.

Perspectives on the female transsexual

While there are some individuals who envy and revere the woman
who wishes to change sex (perceiving the female transsexual as liberated
from traditional stereotypical sex roles), there are others who simply
view the female transsexual as psychotic. For a few individuals, however,
there is a mystique surrounding the transsexual which has even led one
grant foundation to fund an exotic research project to investigate a
possible relationship between transsexualism and the transmigration of
souls after death! (*Omni*, 1981). These diverse views of the female transsexual reflect our society's confusion about and fascination with bisexuality (views which are couched in a male-centered cultural paradigm).
   Many of the controversial issues of female transsexualism have
stemmed from sensational news stories which have generally stirred up
strong public reactions and prematurely polarized thinking about rather
complex social-psychological issues. The result has been that society's
attention has been turned away from a rich appreciation of the psychological problems of female transsexualism to the more elusive moral,

2

religious, and bioethical issues. In some cases women who have changed their sex to male have become embroiled in litigation so that they could return to their work or families, certain segments of society having decided that, having changed their sex, those women were no longer morally fit to continue carrying out their jobs (see Grossman, 1974; Voyles vs. Davis, 1975) or to take custody of their children (see Christian vs. Christian, 1973).

As more and more women request sex reassignment surgery (SRS), the moral, religious, and bioethical issues of female transsexualism are becoming an important source of social debate. For example, is it moral to allow a woman who changed her sex to continue to teach in the public schools? Wouldn't she have a corrupting influence on a child's views of sex roles, gender identity, and sexual preference? Should a woman be allowed to retain custody of her children after sex change? Would sex change render a female transsexual incompetent to raise children according to prescribed social standards? Could the labor force absorb a female transsexual in a male role without threatening the very fabric of men's and women's "work" and work relationships? What about the religious implications of sex change? If a transsexual woman married another woman in the guise of a man, would such a marriage be legal, ethical, moral? (see Frances vs. Mark, 1974). What about the role of medicine in allowing the wife of a female transsexual to be artificially inseminated in order to have a family? None of these are moot issues. Indeed, everyone who has had clinical contact with a female transsexual has broached some, or all, of these issues. The phenomenon of female transsexualism not only challenges traditional ways of thinking but also seems to imply a revolutionary understanding of maleness, femaleness, and societal sex roles. Indeed, from the point of view of social and biomedical ethics the problems of female trans-sexualism are like an uncharted landscape. In comparison with male transsexualism less is known about female transsexualism. While this lack of information probably stems from society's male-centered paradigms (in which femaleness is devalued and degraded), it may also express society's unconscious hostility towards and confusion at female transsexualism: the female transsexual posing a serious threat to a male-centered society by implying that one solution to female subjugation would be to change sexes! The possibility that a female could obtain a real penis through surgery underscores the vulnerability of accepting a male-centered view of the world.

The female transsexual also seems to pose a threat to some feminists who have, at times, taken a strong stand against female transsexualism. Indeed, some lesbian groups have felt betrayed by the female transsexual's rejection of her female body, viewing female transsexualism not as a psychological disorder, but as an ideological issue in which political-economic issues were at stake. Caught between the Scylla of heterosexuality and the Charybdis of homosexuality, the female transsexual has indeed been trapped in a time or gender warp; a netherland of confusion, misunderstanding, isolation, and alienation. In effect, having been stigmatized and psychologically removed from ordinary social interaction, the female transsexual has also been unable to receive psychological help from mental health professionals who did not have the conceptual tools to formulate an appropriate diagnostic schema for evaluating and treating her condition.

Female transsexualism and the mental health profession

⚡ Until 1980 the American Psychiatric Association did not even include transsexualism as a clinical condition worthy of study. When transsexualism was finally included as a disorder there was no attempt to separate male from female transsexualism. Consequently, there were no guidelines for evaluating, diagnosing, and treating female transsexualism as a distinct clinical entity. If the disorder of transsexualism was ever mentioned in the major psychology and psychiatry texts, it was either given short shrift or the focus, however brief, was on male transsexualism. Moreover, there was no book devoted solely to the subject of female transsexualism. Harry Benjamin, who pioneered research into transsexualism, noted that "sometime in the future she [the female transsexual] may merit a book devoted to her alone" (Benjamin, 1966). In effect this volume represents the first attempt to organize the body of literature on female transsexualism and to devote an entire book to the condition of female transsexualism.

Mental health professionals not only had difficulty deciding about diagnostic issues in transsexualism, but they had considerable difficulty addressing the issue of treatment. This probably had less to do with personal biases than with ignorance about the condition. However, their failure to research the condition appropriately meant that the transsexual was not provided with adequate counseling or was not referred for appropriate treatment. As a result, the transsexual's sense of failure, guilt, and depression was increased. Indeed, the lack of a sound knowledge base for diagnosing and treating female transsexualism has perpetuated the female transsexual's suffering. Consequently, most clinicians have either approached the evaluation of female transsexualism with a preconceived view of their problems or employed cultural paradigms which further stigmatized the transsexual.

While most clinicians today are familiar with homosexuality as a life style and a clinical phenomenon, few clinicians have actually had direct patient contact with female transsexuals. For those of us who have devoted a part of our clinical practice to the diagnosis and treatment of transsexuals, we have been privy to innumerable instances in which our patients' real psychological problems have been ignored, as they have been berated, lectured, and exhorted by clinicians to give up their transsexualism. Some people like our letterwriter, Barbara, had been viewed as sinners who were in need of salvation.

At the other end of the spectrum were those clinicians who vigorously supported the patient's requests for surgery — at times reacting with an enthusiasm for sex reassignment surgery that went beyond even the patient's goals. Many of these clinicians seemed to view transsexualism not as an emotional disorder but as an ideological issue, involving an alternative life style, and a freedom for the individual to pursue a variant of her female sexuality.

Myths concerning the female transsexual

Because most female transsexuals were self-diagnosed, they often presented their transsexualism as a kind of *fait accompli*, a condition which had a truth of its own. The situation was complicated by the fact that female transsexuals often appeared more knowledgeable about their condition (and at the same time more blind to it) than most of their counselors. In fact, while a number of articles on female transsexualism have been published in the world literature, very little is actually known about the disorder. Indeed, there has been no available body of knowledge, no source book, to which a clinician (or the female transsexual) could turn to learn about the disorder. Consequently, much of our knowledge about female transsexualism is based on myths: myths which evolved out of our lack of knowledge about the condition and which have continued to subjugate our clinical thinking and treatment of female transsexuals by raising half-truths and fictions to the status of "clinical facts" and then exerting a pervasive influence over our clinical practice. In order to understand the problems of clinical intervention in female transsexualism, it is important that we first clarify the myths of female transsexualism (which will be addressed throughout this book). I am using the word myth in a restricted sense, meaning "a notion based more on tradition or convention than on fact; a received idea" or "one of the fictions or half-truths forming part of the ideology of society" (*American Heritage Dictionary*, 1979). While the myths I am outlining have not been embraced *in toto* by any one school of thought, they do represent the distilled views of a number of diverse clinicians who represent different theoretical points of view on female transsexualism. In most cases these myths evolved from clinical anecdotes and fragments of speculative thought about female transsexualism and not from a systematic study of female transsexualism. I have labelled these views myths in order to call attention to their essential non-scientific character and to question them as established truths.

Myth 1: Female transsexualism does not exist as a disorder, or if it does, it is so rare that it is not worth investigation

Compared with other psychological disorders female transsexualism is rare. However, it is certainly not a rare disorder when compared with male transsexualism. This myth is probably the result of a combination of factors including half-truths, misinformation, and prejudiced beliefs. Recent evidence of the prevalence, incidence, and sex ratio of trans-sexualism demonstrates that female transsexualism is an important and growing clinical phenomenon (see Appendix); it is certainly worthy of investigation.

Until recently transsexualism was viewed as a male phenomenon for several reasons, including: (1) the fact that most gender clinics had been set up to provide clinical services for only the male transsexual; (2) the majority of transsexuals who applied for sex reassignment surgery were male (a possible artifact since female transsexual surgery was not possible until very recently); (3) most transsexual researchers were males who possibly exerted a bias in their focus on male transsexualism;

(4) social pressures made it easier for the female transsexual to establish a social niche; (5) it has been historically more acceptable for males versus females to admit of sexual dysfunctions and to seek out help for their disorders. The most critical reason why female transsexualism has been ignored clinically probably relates to the current social and political status of female sexuality, in which puritanical beliefs regarding female sexuality still have a pervasive influence on clinical practice. In addition, most sexual researchers are male, and their male-centered views (sometimes labeled as homocentric or patricentric) have probably been communicated to women who have been discouraged from applying to the gender clinics.

The clinical evidence clearly suggests that female transsexualism, while not reaching "epidemic proportions" as some researchers have suggested, is certainly not a rare phenomenon versus male transsexualism. But why study it? Why should clinical effort be spent on studying a disorder which is neither prevalent nor life-threatening? Why is female transsexualism worth investigating? Simply stated, the investigation of female transsexualism leads us to understand better such diverse clinical phenomena as (1) how normal gender role and identity may develop and also go awry; (2) how such issues as primary femininity, female core gender identity, and sexual identity are established; (3) how female gender diffusion may occur as part of other forms of psychopathology, e.g. schizophrenia, narcissistic and borderline personality disorders. While this list is not inclusive, it points to the fact that an investigation of female transsexualism, rather than being frivolous, touches on most of the central issues of female psychology. It seems, therefore, that Myth 1 may exert an unfair and unreasonable constraint on research into female sexuality, and needs to be abandoned.

Myth 2: Female transsexualism is a new phenomenon having no historical antecedents and being the product of media exploitation of fads regarding interest in anything sexual

In Chapters 2 and 3 the historical, cross-cultural, literary, mythological, medical, and psychological antecedents of female transsexualism are reviewed. The data are compelling. Female transsexualism is, as one researcher suggested, "un mal ancien" (Vague, 1956); a disorder which has its roots in ancient civilization; is mentioned in the Bible

(Deuteronomy 22:5); has cross-cultural and anthropological significance; and was first noted as a possible psychological disorder in the nineteenth century. The fact that the media have exploited the sensational aspects of female transsexualism is interesting but irrelevant to its historical roots. Clearly we are not dealing with a fad but a phenomenon which is documented throughout western civilization and across many non-western cultures.

Myth 3: Female transsexualism is solely a physiological disorder, related to chromosomal, genetic, and endocrinological influences

It has been widely believed that the disorder of female transsexualism can be explained entirely by an appeal to a purely physiological hypothesis. In Chapter 5 the bases for this belief are examined and critically explored. Such issues as the effect of prenatal hormones on brain development and gender behavior, cerebral pathology, EEG disturbances, chromosomal-genetic-hormonal factors, and recent studies on H-Y antigen are explored. While there is some evidence implicating a physiological basis for some female gender disorders, the basis for believing Myth 3 arises from two sources: evidence from studies on intersexual disorders and hermaphroditism (often confused with transsexualism), and the need of female transsexuals to resolve their personal guilt by attributing the disorder to an underlying physiological cause. Moreover, the conclusions of a recent study on homosexuality which popularized the notion that homosexuality was an inborn condition have been used by transsexuals to explain their condition (Bell et al., 1981). Once this myth is dispelled, researchers will be able to tease out the physiological versus psychological components of a given patient's female transsexualism. In Chapter 5 these issues will be thoroughly explored.

Myth 4: All female transsexuals are clinically psychotic and delusional about their gender identity

The view that all female transsexuals are psychotic is false. However, while only a small percentage of female transsexuals (between 5 per cent and 15 per cent) are overtly psychotic or schizophrenic, this is

8

significantly larger than that found in the general population. The majority of female transsexuals are not delusional about their gender identities. They know that they are biological females; they know the status of their physical sex. Rather, they *wish* to become males. Throughout the book the myth of the female transsexual's psychosis is unraveled and her "delusional" beliefs in her maleness are explored.

Myth 5: All female transsexuals are normal apart from their gender pathology; female transsexuals are more stable than male transsexuals

On the other hand, there is another group of clinicians who, in contrast to those clinicians who adhere to Myth 4, believe that female transsexuals are more stable than their male counterparts. This belief is critically explored in Chapter 3 and is viewed as the most prevalent myth about female transsexualism. The myth is founded on a belief which has little empirical basis and one that is, at best, moderately patronizing. It has led to confusion among female transsexuals (regarding their normality) and mistreatment and mismanagement of their condition. This myth has also had a deleterious effect on the clinical enterprise.

The view that female transsexuals are normal apart from their gender pathology is also a myth. Female transsexuals live in a world which, for the most part, stigmatizes them and excludes them. Every day the female transsexual has to negotiate a false self in her social world. The psychological and emotional cost of such impersonation is enormously stressful. Consequently, she must learn to manage false social realities and live in constant fear of exposure. At best, ordinary living is emotionally draining and filled with suffering. Most female transsexuals also have serious personality disorders and while not psychotic, they have subtle thought disorders which affect their sense of reality and their ability to relate to others. In addition to their personality disturbances many female transsexuals exhibit a wide range of other psychiatric symptoms: including depression, anxiety, panic attacks, and severe psychosomatic complaints. Until the full extent of their psychological disabilities is recognized, adequate diagnosis and treatment of their emotional disorders will not be provided.

Myth 6: All female transsexualism can be explained by appeal to a unitary theory: theories as diverse as psychoanalysis, object relations theory, behaviorism, learning theory, information systems, and family systems theory

With apparent disregard for clinical experience, and ignoring the diversity of female gender pathology (erroneously labeling a number of different disorders as female transsexualism), investigators have offered various unitary hypotheses to explain female transsexualism. While each of these theories offers a partial explanation of the phenomenon, many of the investigators have presented their partial explanations as the whole truth, thereby abrogating new insights by transsexual researchers. The most prominent view, that all female transsexuals are stigmatized homosexuals, is, at best, an exaggeration of a partial truth. In addition, many clinicians have prematurely accepted the view that female trans-sexualism has a typical female transsexual dynamic; that is, the family in which father masculinizes his daughter, who then replaces him in the family by rescuing a depressed helpless mother from his withdrawal and aggression. This view is at best an oversimplification of a family dynamic found among some female transsexuals. In Chapter 4 these views, which have dominated clinical thinking, are critically explored. The clinical data in Chapter 4 contraindicate a unitary explanation of female transsexualism.

Myth 7: Female transsexualism is a sexual disorder

The view that female transsexualism is a sexual disorder is also shown to be a myth. Logically it is not a sexual disorder at all but a gender disorder. Throughout this book I argue that female transsexualism is primarily a disorder of the self-system (see Brod, 1981) involving an early childhood developmental arrest, disturbances in ego functions, and stemming primarily from borderline personality and narcissistic disorders. The *Diagnostic and Statistical Manual of Mental Disorders* published by the American Psychiatric Association in 1980 (*DSM* III) defines borderline personality disorder as one in which

the essential feature is a personality disorder in which there is instability in a variety of areas, including interpersonal behavior, mood, and self image . . . Interpersonal relations are often intense and unstable, with marked shifts of attitude over time. Frequently there is impulsive and unpredictable behavior that is potentially physically self damaging. Mood is often unstable, with marked shifts from normal mood to a dysphoric mood or with inappropriate, intense anger or lack of control of anger. A profound identity disturbance may be manifested by uncertainty about several issues relating to identity, such as self-image, gender identity, or long term goals or values.

Moreover, individuals suffering from a borderline personality disorder have primitive and rigid defenses, which often impair their reality testing; have a frantic need to be with people and cannot stand being alone; have permeable ego boundaries; and may experience transient psychotic episodes and regressive behaviors which are of schizophrenic proportions. The disorder is characterized by its stable instability. Investigators have suggested that it is a severe developmental disturbance, consolidating during one of the various subphases of separation-individuation (occurring between ages 1 and 3).

Borderline personality is not a disorder that only sexologists and sex therapists should be interested in, but a psychological disorder which all clinicians should be learning more about. As a result of the interface between one's subjective experience of a gender (gender identity) and the social expression of gender identity (gender role), the female transsexual's gender role is influenced by, and molded by, her society and culture. In this sense female transsexualism is also a social condition which has political, ideological, and sociological meaning.

Myth 8: All gender clinics offer equivalent psychological care to the female transsexual, including following strict standards of care

As a result of media presentations it has appeared as if the almost forty gender clinics throughout the western hemisphere have been established along similar lines to serve the needs of the female trans-sexual. The perpetuation of this myth has continued to provide an aura of hope for the female transsexual that she can be psychologically evaluated in a competent manner when, in fact, such a possibility is quite rare.

In actuality a number of diversely trained clinicians, with varied levels of training, different educational backgrounds, and extremely varied abilities in assessment and psychotherapeutic skills, are involved in these gender identity clinics. In most cases the term clinic is misleading since only one or two people may be involved. Some gender clinics are no more than surgical centers which provide surgery on a fee-for-service basis. Often the "thorough" evaluation that is advertised is nothing more than a one-day, three- to eight-hour evaluation in which the person's psychological status is sorely neglected.

My experience suggests that the female transsexual is more than likely to be provided only minimal psychological evaluation. Moreover, she is likely to be served inadequately by almost all of these clinics, depending on who evaluated and eventually treated her. Not only does each clinic differ on what it can offer, but the treatment between clinicians in the same clinic may be dramatically different. Moreover, while the Harry Benjamin Association has written up a proposal for *Standards of Care* (Walker et al., 1980), there are no universally accepted standards of care for the female transsexual and no obligation by any clinic or clinician to embrace those endorsed by the Harry Benjamin Association.

Myth 9: Sex reassignment surgery is the treatment of choice for the female transsexual; psychotherapy is useless in treating the female transsexual

For over three decades this myth has influenced clinical thinking. It was a myth perpetuated by surgeons who believed that they were reducing the transsexual's suffering by providing her with sexual surgery. It was also a myth perpetuated by reported psychotherapy failures, in which lengthy psychotherapeutic treatments failed to change the female transsexual's gender identity back to female. In actuality there were few, if any, reports which actually demonstrated psychotherapeutic failures. It was a myth perpetuated by the patients themselves, who vigorously sought surgery, threatened suicide unless surgery was provided, and formed political self-help groups to lobby for surgery.

In Chapter 7 I explore these issues and demonstrate that, while surgery may be beneficial to a few select patients, the evidence clearly suggests that psychotherapy and not surgery is the treatment of choice for female transsexuals. An inspection of the personnel involved in the assessment of female transsexuals at the various gender clinics suggests that the majority of them have little or no training in the methods of descriptive psychiatry, psychoanalytic psychopathology, or intensive long-term psychotherapy. The majority of gender clinicians represent a variety of occupations, including social workers, job counselors, cosmeticians, body builders, endocrinologists, surgeons, lawyers, and ministers.

Myth 10: Female transsexualism is not a psychological disorder but an alternative life style

Given current cultural paradigms, female transsexualism cannot be viewed simply as an alternative life style. Women who identify as transsexuals experience an urgent, compulsive, unrelenting wish to rid themselves of their breasts and inner female organs. They are obsessed with wearing men's clothing, enacting a male role, and being socially accepted as men. They deny being homosexual and insist on dating feminine heterosexual women. Most of these women are driven to have surgery and are obsessed with the idea of having a penis. It is not as if they have a choice.

All female transsexuals experience a sense of urgency to change their gender roles. They believe that only when they act out their inner male wishes will they experience a sense of calm and completeness. Their actions and wishes suggest that they are not choosing an alternative life style but are compelled by their obsessions to become male. By all current standards their compulsions, urges, anxiety, depression, and obsessions must be viewed as evidence of a profound psychological disorder.

As a social phenomenon female transsexualism does, however, involve living an entirely different life style. But the life style is highly obligatory, involves considerable stigmatization, and cannot be freely chosen. As part of her obligatory life style the female transsexual constantly lives with the fear of exposure and the risks of being harassed as an impostor. If she wants to pass as a male, the female transsexual must not only "look" male but must change all of her important documents to male (that is, birth certificate, social security card, school records, driver's license, insurance forms, passport, occupational or professional licenses, medical records, property deeds, securities, etc.). Changing one's name (which is the simplest procedure) is only the first step in changing one's public identity. There is also clinical evidence which suggests that enacting a male social role does not fully alleviate the female transsexual's anxiety and depression. Indeed, many female transsexuals are profoundly stigmatized by various elements in society which are homophobic. Once they are mislabeled as homosexuals or sexual deviants, they are further isolated from needed support systems.

Until proven otherwise, female transsexualism must be viewed as a psychological disorder. However, this does not justify the unnecessary labeling and stigmatizing of the female transsexual. Hopefully, as a byproduct of my investigation into female transsexualism, the field will become demythologized and the subject of female gender identity disorders opened up to new inquiry.

Unanswered questions

Over the years I have been impressed that, no matter how hard one tries to raise questions concerning female transsexualism, the doors are quickly shut. In 1976 I initially raised the problem for our own gender clinic by insisting that one of us pursue the issue of female gender problems in a serious vein. At first no one expressed interest. Eventually two clinicians, one a woman, showed some interest but lacked the spark to follow through on their work. Two years later as co-director of the clinic I insisted that we set aside two meetings a month to discuss the topic of female transsexuals. The enthusiasm soon waned, and by the second session the clinic staff abandoned the effort.

Why is there so much resistance to learning about female transsexualism? Is there something inherent in the female transsexual's quest that silences our curiosity? Does the female transsexual's psyche arouse something dreadful within each of us that says, "hands off"? Have male researchers ignored the topic because they view a woman's desire to become a man as natural, and therefore a trivial phenomenon to investigate? Or have male researchers ignored this aspect of female sexuality, just as they have ignored other problems of female sexuality, because of their homocentrism? Boswell (1980) and Bullough (1976) firmly believe that these issues relate to the historical fact that men have been in a position of authority.

From another perspective clinicians may have played down the significance of female transsexualism because female transsexuals seem to suffer less apparent anguish than their male counterparts. This probably stems from several factors which relate to society's acceptance of tomboyism and the fact that when girl children (who have historically enjoyed a low social status) mimicked boys they were often treated better. Since women in our society are allowed a greater latitude of dress and freedom of gender role expression than men, they are less likely to be singled out, harassed, and stigmatized than are their male counterparts. Few people are shocked or surprised to see a woman dressed as a man. A woman may be viewed as "too aggressive" or "too tough" but she is not usually harassed, ridiculed, and shamed for crossdressing as a man (unless her crossdressing is accompanied by boisterous, obnoxious behavior which brings her to the attention of various authorities). It may be that our cultural permission for women to crossdress has made it seem that female transsexuals' conflicts are trivial and not serious enough for scientific investigation. I hope to show that female transsexualism is neither a trivial nor an unimportant clinical phenomenon, but one that needs to be seriously studied.

The female transsexual as experiment

Above all, the transsexual, as Stoller (1975) reminds us, is society's naturalistic experiment on the bedrock of human bisexuality. The transsexual is also society's constant reminder of how the goals of civilization (power, wealth, success, position) have bifurcated the human self-system, splitting off the opposing male and female elements in the personality (leaving each of us fragmented, incomplete, and yearning for wholeness). The female transsexual also reminds each of us that "normalcy" (in terms of gender roles) does not reside in the enactment of stereotypical male and female roles, but in the fusion of those elements of psychosexual bisexuality: that is, involving such experiences as tenderness, aggressiveness, caring, independence, warmth, and assertion that lead to psychological androgyny. It is not ironic that at a time in history when women's liberation has become such a focal issue, psychological research should be focusing on psychological androgyny as one of the measuring rods of "normalcy" in sex or gender roles.

By acting out her bisexuality, the female transsexual is alternately admired, hated, envied, feared, loved, and despised. Above all, there is the mystique about the female transsexual. The female transsexual has also been viewed as courageous, challenging social stereotypes and transcending society's cultural paradigms of gender roles. Various segments of our society are also curious about the range of transsexual adaptations (including the issue of surgery and genital metamorphosis), standing in awe of the transsexuals' merging of gender roles and dismayed by their failure to meet certain cultural expectations of masculinity and femininity. In the final analysis it is the confusion about female transsexualism which has leant credibility to the myths.

Barbara's letter: a woman's distress signal

I would like, for a moment, to return to the letter from Barbara which stimulated this discussion. Barbara is one of the hundreds, perhaps thousands of self-labeled female-to-male transsexuals who experience profound anguish and personal suffering over their gender problems. Some women like Barbara apply directly to gender identity clinics for some form of psychological or surgical intervention to ameliorate or cure their gender problems. The fact that over the past decade the number of women applying for sex reassignment surgery has steadily increased needs to be examined. One explanation for this phenomenon may relate to the women's liberation movement and the struggle over sexual parity, some women trying to achieve parity through sexual transformation. Indeed, new freedoms also bring anxieties.

Barbara's letter testifies to the intense feelings of rejection and personal suffering that she underwent as a result of the church's treatment. However, those of us in the gender field are also aware of the large number of clergy, of all faiths, who would have responded compassionately and, at times, with good clinical common sense in helping women like Barbara get professional help. But her letter attests to the primitive way in which people who are different in some respect are treated in our society. These are not simply psychological issues, and do not go away by interpretation. They are political and ideological issues often couched in religious and moral language, which suppress individual differences, oppress some sexual minorities, and perpetuate human suffering. These are not issues which are resolved by administering hormones or providing sex reassignment surgery (SRS).

The Case Western Reserve Gender Identity Clinic: the project

The ideas put forward in this book are based on clinical data collected over the last eight years (1974 to 1982) from over 200 male and female transsexual patients (fifty-three of whom were women). All of those patients were evaluated and treated for transsexualism by approximately twenty different clinicians. As co-director of the clinic, I also had the opportunity to implement a research project on the intensive psychotherapy of self-diagnosed transsexuals. Each year we averaged about ten staff members (with a core group of four clinicians). Our staff included a wide variety of trainees who served for one-year traineeships. While we had no outside funding, the majority of the staff was on full-time salary (in a number of academic areas outside of the gender area) and chose to devote their research time to the study of transsexualism. All work was on a voluntary basis, with full support from the Department of Psychiatry. We were an interdisciplinary group of clinicians, with various educational levels and different training interests. We met weekly for almost eight years to discuss our clinical cases and to try to understand everything we could about gender identity pathology. Because of our diverse clinical careers, our different clinical interests, and our lack of funding, our record keeping was, initially, not as systematized as it might have been. However, our aim was never simply to look at numbers but at the richness of clinical material available from each of our patients. The one rule we had about our evaluations was that no one would be refused evaluation and treatment. Unfortunately, this rule changed two years ago (1980) as staff limitations forced us to refer some patients outside the clinic. Such a practice would be an inestimable loss for a gender clinic just starting out.

Because of my own training background in intensive psychoanalytically oriented psychotherapy, and my interest in treating severely disturbed, character-disordered patients in psychotherapy, I made a decision to attempt to employ a modified form of intensive psychoanalytically oriented psychotherapy with all of my transsexual patients. I have never regretted that decision, and, hopefully, neither have my patients. I approached each patient's problems with an open mind as to the outcome of therapy, always keeping in mind the social-medical interface of their problems and their personal goals. I learned a good deal about female transsexuals because I have rarely been overly intrusive, encouraging all patients to use psychotherapy towards accomplishing their own goals (which at times may have led to surgery), and allowing the evolution of the clinical material they permitted me to hear to influence and change my perceptions of their condition.

The case histories in Chapter 4 were not chosen randomly. They represent those cases with which I had the most clinical contact. I do not presume to maintain that my analyses of the case histories are purely objective. Also I do not believe that my interpretations are value-free or that such a stance is possible or necessary for achieving objectivity. My interpretations are just that: constructions which facilitated my work with the patients and led to a better understanding of their gender conflicts. Perhaps other constructions would yield different results. I am not opposed to thinking that there are alternative ways of construing the female transsexual's reality. On the other hand, I have had ample opportunity to share my ideas with professional colleagues at national and international meetings. I can only surmise from their encouragement of my psychotherapy research program into transsexualism that my ideas are generally shared.

I am concerned that, as a male, my ideas about one form of female sexuality may be overly determined by my own unique perspective, a perspective which has political, ideological, and theoretical biases. I trust that each reader will arrive at his or her own conclusions as to how my unique perspective as a male influences my understanding of female transsexualism. Most importantly, I wish to stress the importance of engaging in long-term, intensive evaluations (including extensive psychological testing and long-term psychotherapy) of the female transsexual, an argument which will be evident throughout this book.

It is my hope that this book will serve many purposes, but above all that it will stimulate further inquiry into problems related to female sexuality, specifically female transsexualism, and will break down the psychological barriers to investigating this intriguing phenomenon by exploring case material in depth, and so expose the various myths which have handicapped the clinical enterprise.

Chapter 2
Historical, psychological, and medical issues

Historical instances of women who impersonated men

Historical, literary, and mythological examples

There is considerable historical (Warnes and Hill, 1974; Bullough, 1975, 1976), literary (Weigert-Vorwinkel, 1938; Kubie, 1974), and mythological (Green, 1969) evidence suggesting that women have successfully impersonated men, crossdressed as men, and wished to change their sex. Vague (1956) has described the phenomenon of female gender role and identity disturbances as not of recent origin but "un mal ancien."

Bullough (1976) describes the Amazon women who at the age of eight had their right breasts burned off so that they could fire a bow with greater accuracy. Boswell (1980) also cites several examples from Roman civilization; for example, Martial, who "describes a lesbian who can outdrink and outeat any man, plays at male sports, wrestles, can lift heavier weights than a man, and who 'puts it to' eleven girls a day; [and] Lucian [who] portrays Megilla as shaving her head and boasting that she is 'a man in every way'." He also cites a practice in the Muslim world "of dressing pretty girls to look like pretty boys by cutting their hair short and clothing them in male attire."

Some of the more exotic historical examples of women who impersonated male roles (with varying degrees of success) have been described by Bullough (1976). His examples include, "an English army surgeon . . . who at his death was found to be a woman; Charles Parkhurst, a stage-coach driver in the West who on his death was found to be a female"; Lucy Ann Slater, alias the Rev. Joseph Lobdell, "who regarded herself as a man, and married a woman"; John Coulter, who was successfully married for twenty-nine years "without her wife realizing her husband was a female"; Murray Hall, a Tammany Hall politician who "lived as a man for 30 years so successfully that her daughter did not know her father was a woman"; Sophia Hedwig, who in the 1880s actually had surgery performed in order to enhance her transition to maleness; and finally David Cook, "who was picked up for draft evasion only to be exposed as a woman." Ellis (1936) described the case of Nicholai de Raylan (a male impersonator) who, as secretary to a Russian Consul, married two women who believed him to be a man.

De Savitsch (1958) noted that "in some women, like George Sand, transvestism may be limited to the adoption of a masculine name only." In other women, like Joan of Arc, the inner yearnings to be a man were focused on her wearing of male clothing. Indeed, Mary Walker "became the first American woman to be commissioned an Army Surgeon and the only woman expressly granted Congressional permission to wear man's clothing" and who "in spite of considerable hostility and ostracism . . . continued to dress and act as a man." There was also the story of Pope John VIII (also known as Pope Joan), who, impersonating a man, became Pope and, it was rumored, died in 855 C.E. during childbirth in front of a crowd of people. Henry Fielding (1960) also wrote a novel entitled *Female Husband*, which was based on a true story of a woman who impersonated a man and married several "unsuspecting women." Finally, there was the autobiography of Radclyffe Hall, which described "the tragedy of a girl with transvestic homosexual instincts being born to parents who desired a son" (Hall, 1929).

Overview

These historical instances of female gender role and identity disturbances provide a glimpse into what appears to have been a more common medical-psychological problem. However, physicians either failed to recognize the significance of those problems or the phenomenon was, indeed, too rare or exotic to warrant serious attention. Pauly (1974a) and Roback et al. (1976), however, believed that the lack of interest in female gender role and identity disturbances probably stemmed from a pervasive homocentric bias among historians and researchers (who were predominantly male). However, the recent phenomenon of large numbers of females applying for sex reassignment surgery (SRS), combined with a rise in consciousness regarding women's issues, has led to the recognition by the health care professions that these problems deserve serious attention. This change in priorities has also led to a recognition by the medical-psychological community of the importance of female gender role and identity disturbances.

In order to understand the key concepts and problems involved in the evaluation, diagnosis, and treatment of female gender role and identity disturbances, it is necessary to place these problems in their correct historical medical-psychological perspective. Such an undertaking will provide the reader with the necessary framework for posing those basic questions that need to be addressed, so that a comprehensive schema for evaluating, diagnosing, and treating women with gender role and identity disturbances can be formulated.

The medical-psychological perspective

I have chosen to review the literature chronologically in order to present the material in the same way that clinicians would, or should, have read it. The reader can then follow the developmental issues as they would have appeared to the clinician who researched the literature.

The German influence (1870-1930)

The first complete description of a female who wanted to change sex was reported by Westphal in 1870. Westphal described several cases (including one female) whom he labeled as having "contrary sexual feelings" ("die konträre Sexualempfindung"). The women (Frl. N.), who was thirty-five years old, was living with her sister when she contacted Westphal in May 1864. She described feeling like a man ever since early childhood. At age 8 she was sexually attracted to another woman. The patient was described as a large woman with masculine features but otherwise normal female physiology. Her family history was quite impoverished. Her father had committed suicide after living a guilty and melancholy life. The mother died of a breast ailment during pregnancy. The patient was in and out of mental hospitals and only wished to be changed into a man ("Ich . . . möchte gern ein Mann sein."). In addition to her gender dysphoria, the patient had several somatic disorders, including headaches. She was also constantly aware of being observed by others. Westphal also hinted at the possibility of a paranoid condition and a latent homosexual attachment to her sister. He did not, however, expand on these issues.

In 1922 Hirschfeld described the first clinical cases of what we today label as female transsexualism. The following year, Stekl (1923), describing a case of female transsexualism, conceptualized the patient's wish for sex change as involving a shift from a *Hässlichkeitskomplex* to a *Schönheitskomplex*. He also related her condition to an *Electra-komplex*. The German adequately describes the intense inner self-hatred that these patients felt towards their bodies, and their goal of transformation into beautiful and pretty creatures.

Working at the Institute of Sexual Science in Berlin, Germany, Hirschfeld directed a clinic for studying transvestism. While his first report on a female transvestite (who desired to change sex) was reported in 1922, it was with the publication of *Die Transvestiten: Eine Untersuchung über den Erotischen Verkleidungstrieb* (1910) that the term "transvestite" came into vogue and a clinical resource was available for investigating gender role and identity disorders. Benjamin, a colleague and friend of Hirschfeld, reported that Hirschfeld's work was "destroyed by the Nazis . . . in their march to power [1933] . . . [because] the Institute's confidential files were said to have contained too many data on prominent Nazis" (Benjamin, 1966, p. 25).

Hirschfeld described the phenomenon of women with intense gender envy and "intense love of uniform" who took "part in the war as active soldiers." He stated that "during World War I many such women felt very happy because they were able to live 'normally' wearing men's boots, caps of office, tunics, and trousers, etc. " When these women were dressed in men's clothing they felt relaxed and natural; in women's clothing they felt imprisoned. Some of these women lived married lives while impersonating men. One "woman transvestite worked for years as a postman without anyone even suspecting her true sex; another worked for ten years in a factory as a packer." Hirschfeld also reported two suicides of female transvestites. One involved a woman impersonating a "Captain Tweed," who in 1904 slit her throat. Because she had commanded a transatlantic ship and been institutionalized in a sailor's home (due to illness), no one suspected that "Captain Tweed" was a woman. A second case in 1909 involved a headwaiter, Michael Semeniak, who committed suicide (by taking poison) when "he" feared being exposed as a woman. Hirschfeld's cases of female transvestism suggested a continuum of female gender pathology, in which crossdressing as a man could not be explained by a unitary hypothesis.

Cross-cultural influences (1940–80)

In 1949 Cauldwell reported on the case of a woman who desired to become a man. He labeled the disorder "psychopathia transsexualis" and thereby introduced the term "transsexual" into the clinical literature. With some degree of chagrin, Pauly (1974a) noted that it took almost twenty-seven years from the time of Hirschfeld's initial report of female transsexualism until Cauldwell's presentation in 1949. Pauly (1974a) stated that, "the interest in female cases of transsexualism as determined by publications in the literature, has lagged about a decade behind that for male cases."

Redmount (1953) was the first clinician to describe a case of female transsexualism in depth. He reported on a case of a 33-year-old woman who "had assumed a male role all of her life." She had a severely deprived early developmental history, viewed her father as a "mean tyrant" and was relieved by his murder (she was twelve) because "he was mean to my mother and all of the kids." The woman claimed that after an appendectomy at age 17, the physician told her that "she had internal male organs but that they were in some way diseased or injured and were removed." There was no corroboration of her report. After the mother's death from cancer, the woman became quite distressed, and three years later (age 26) was admitted to a mental hospital and discharged with the diagnosis of psychopathic personality with homosexual and suicidal preoccupations. The patient had twice been married to females (one of whom had a child by a previous marriage). Throughout her life she was regarded as a freak. She also had a poor work history.

This case history is a pivotal one in that most of Redmount's conclusions about the dynamics of the case have been accepted and supported by other investigators (oftentimes with little or no mention of Redmount's contribution to our understanding of female transsexualism). Redmount's conclusions were that, "The patient's assumption of the male identity appears to represent both a defense of herself and a way of relating to the idealized mother whom she needed. Establishing

23

herself as male . . . like father . . . she could offer herself as a protective substitute in relating to potentially supportive but vulnerable figures like the idealized mother." Redmount also noted how difficult it was for the woman to impersonate the male role and argued that "the problem of maturation in this role seems to have introduced new insecurities into her life." The importance of this case focused on two factors. The first factor was Redmount's recognition of the psychodynamic triad in female transsexualism: an abusive father with whom the patient identified; a warm supportive mother who needed to be rescued (the patient reported that mother "was the only friend I had. When I lost her I had none."); and a daughter who attempted to rescue her mother and protect her from the father's onslaughts. The second factor was Redmount's opinion that the patient was severely disturbed psychiatrically (a factor which had not been reported in the majority of clinical case reports of female transsexuals). The patient also seemed to have a thought disorder focusing on her magical belief that if she cut off her arm (which she attempted during adolescence) she could then "kiss her elbow and become a boy."

By 1953 it was clear that female transsexualism was not isolated to a few rare cases. After the celebrated Christine Jorgenson case, Hamburger (1953) reported that 108 women sent him letters from all over the world requesting SRS. The age distribution ranged from 15-55, with the ratio of females requesting information being 1:4. Only one of the women reported being married and six were divorced. All the women reported homosexual desires and none mentioned having attractions to men. Twenty-three per cent of the women reported having masculine features which they thought contributed to their views of themselves as male. Hamburger concluded that "in women who feel like men the wish for a change of sex does not seem to manifest itself or become dominant until the person in question falls in love with another woman; this happens in the great majority of cases."

Barahal (1953) presented a lengthy case of a 22-year-old woman who requested SRS whom he diagnosed as being transvestitic. The patient was illegitimate and had "never seen her real father and only recently had learned who he was." The mother, succumbing to the gossip of the local villagers, "rejected the patient very early in life, and began to board her with various friends and relatives." Barahal listed at least nine major changes and moves in the patient's life up through age 14. The patient had a ninth grade education. Since early childhood "she had an ungovernable desire to be a boy and had insisted on wearing boy's clothing." The analysis, which was reported up through the 154th session, was partially conducted while the patient was hospitalized. The case study was important because of the detailed presentation of the patient's therapy (in a session-by-session format). Barahal concluded that there was a close "relationship between her insatiable drive for masculinity and her early relationship to her mother or mother substitutes." The patient was seen as viewing the woman's role as "disadvantageous and dangerous." Indeed, the patient was molested by several men, including a relative, and, as a woman, perceived herself as being vulnerable to male aggression. The mother repeatedly told the patient that had she been born a boy she could have cared for her mother in a more protective manner. The patient learned that "in order to obtain her mother's love she had to be a boy." Early in life the patient was seen as competing with men "for the love of the mother, even to assuming a man's attire." Barahal concluded that "female transvestism, therefore, is not a manifestation of homosexuality but of a drive for masculinity."

Barahal was the first clinician to consider the preoedipal attachment of the child to its mother as a possible determining force in the evolution of a gender identity disturbance. He also supported Redmount's findings (though he did not cite him) that the female transsexual's mother needed to be protected, while encouraging an unconscious male fantasy in her daughter to take over the husband's role. In addition, Barahal suggested that early childhood separations and losses may have compromised this woman's ego development and led to her ego diffusion and/or gender identity confusion (especially in her magical thinking that dressing in male clothing made her a "real" male). Barahal also suggested that non-conflictual learning processes in early childhood may be a causal agent in the development of adult gender identity and role disturbances.

McCully (1963) reported on the projective test findings of a 32-year-old Catholic woman who wished to change her sex. The patient, the youngest of two female siblings, had an early identification with males (age 5) and was a tomboy during latency. She described her father as "a volatile person who was sometimes physically abusive" to her. When the patient was nine her mother died and she was sent to boarding school. At this time she felt isolated from her peers and she became "absorbed with the idea that something was wrong with her genitalia."

She had a sundry work history including one job on a farm where she dressed as a boy. Even as a young child the patient was aware of her homoeroticism. Later as an adult she reached orgasm through masturbation with the "belief that she had testicles inside her groin." McCully noted that she was quite convincing in her male role.

A mental status exam revealed that the woman's thinking was circumstantial and concrete. Moreover, she was depressed, tense, and had insomnia, declared that she was a psychic, was mildly paranoid, but revealed no evidence of an overt thought disorder. McCully was incredulous that there were no florid signs of schizophrenia (reflecting a pervasive clinical bias that transsexuals were either psychotic or schizophrenic). He interpreted the patient's male wishes (in the light of her aversion to female sexuality) as a "kind of reaction formation against deeply repressed feminine qualities." McCully also noted that the patient employed primitive defenses (including splitting, projection, denial, and grandiosity). McCully suggested that the patient suffered little anxiety because "she concretized her problem and projected it onto society." In the light of current thinking, the diagnostic issues of the case could best be explained along the lines of a borderline personality disorder.

Philippopoulos (1964) reported on a case of transvestism in a 17-year-old girl who was treated in psychotherapy 3–4 times a week for 6 months (112 sessions). The case resulted in a complete reversal of the patient's gender identity conflicts and transvestism. Philippopoulos noted that the patient was born "the only daughter of an urban family who lived in a provincial town in northern Greece." The patient served the role of a go-between for the parents and often watched helplessly as the father beat his wife in a drunken rage. The mother cursed the patient, stating, "Accursed be the hour when I delivered you a girl . . . if you were a boy I should, at least, have the hope that you would grow up one day and avenge me." The mother dressed the patient in boy's clothes, stating, "even long trousers are worth more than a thousand girls." During adolescence the patient was identified as a tomboy and impersonated a boy. Eventually the mother demanded that the patient give up her male role "because it was now time to become a woman." Mother brought her daughter to a physician to cure her of her maleness. Philippopoulos, reporting on a follow-up of the patient five years post-therapy, stated that she was now living and working as a female. He speculated about the "overdetermining attitude which the mother played on a purely conscious level in the genesis of transvestism."

With the publication of Benjamin's *The Transsexual Phenomenon* (1966) a new era of research into the spectrum of gender identity disturbances began. This was the first major clinical book to go beyond the single case study and present data on a large number of individuals (n = 172) who had requested evaluation for sex reassignment surgery (whom he labeled "transsexuals"). Of this group twenty (12 per cent) were women. While Benjamin focused primarily on the male transsexual, he noted that "sometime in the future she [the female transsexual] may merit a book devoted to her alone."

The focus of Benjamin's research was on gathering macro-psychological data on a large group of transsexual patients so that their various cases could be compared and general issues extracted (to facilitate clinical decisions and management regarding the care of the transsexual patient). An endocrinologist by profession, but primarily a person with compassion for the transsexual's plight, Benjamin is considered the pioneer investigator into the transsexual phenomenon. While his research was, at times, on shaky methodological grounds, Benjamin had a knack for short-term counseling and understood the difficulties in recommending the transsexual for psychological treatment.

Benjamin's conclusions were derived from a retrospective study in which he interviewed large groups of male and female transsexuals. He did not employ a standardized interviewing technique and depended entirely on the patient's honesty through self-reports and responses to questionnaires. He also rated his patients (and classified them as being transvestite and transsexual) using a modified scaling approach popularized by Kinsey et al. (1948).

In his portrayal of the female transsexual, Benjamin's style was that of a physician-sociologist, focusing on such broad issues as: the patient's symptomology; sex life; etiology; physical data; social position; surgery; and counseling. He assumed that the prevalence of female transsexualism was greatly underestimated (secondary to the females's reluctance to openly avow her problems). Female transsexuals were noted to have a strong wish for sex change; a conviction that they were males trapped in female bodies; a hatred for their breasts and genitals; a propensity for falling in love with feminine, heterosexually oriented women; a wish to be a husband and father; a dislike for lesbians and an anti-homosexual attitude. Most of the female transsexuals in his study had been married, and several had children.

Benjamin suggested that the etiology of female transsexualism involved early childhood conditioning, and constitutional-predispositional factors. He seemed to believe that one day researchers would uncover an innate biological factor underlying transsexualism. He noted that in all cases the sense of being male first appeared during the oedipal period (age 5) and that many of the patients were first born (whose mothers may have wanted a son). Physiological data were unremarkable. However, Benjamin always recommended a thorough medical screening of each patient, including a physical exam, and chromosomal-genetic and hormonal tests. However, none of his medical investigations demonstrated a physiological explanation for the women's transsexualism.

The twenty female transsexuals seemed to represent all social classes and a wide variety of occupational types. Benjamin was clearly antipsychoanalytic and viewed psychotherapy that aimed at total rehabilitation of the patient's gender as useless. He was, however, quite enthusiastic about the use of surgery and hormones, claiming that fifteen of the women who had androgen therapy "greatly benefited." However, one woman who had undergone surgery was reported to have converted back to the female role.

Benjamin reported that seven of the eight patients who had genital surgery had a satisfactory outcome. Some had even married and were leading relatively stable lives. The only case history presented in any depth (a patient referred to as Joe) appeared in the Appendix. The patient, a post-surgical transsexual, had a history of early childhood gender identity confusion, suicidal acting out, and a two-year psychiatric treatment which failed to correct her gender problems. Joe's early childhood was not reported. She did, however, reveal a chronic longing for a penis. She also reported being encouraged (even at an early age) by mother, the maternal grandmother, and occasionally father, to crossdress in male attire. The patient was described as married (in her male role) and leading a happy life.

In 1967 Gittleson and Dawson-Butterworth investigated the relation between female schizophrenia and subjective ideas of sex change. Their findings suggested that female schizophrenics, as opposed to nonschizophrenic controls, had a greater incidence of genital hallucinosis and delusions, in addition they had a higher frequency of ideas of being in the process of, or of becoming, or of having become a neuter or a man. They did not compare their findings with a control group of transsexuals.

Simon (1967) reported on a case of a 37-year-old female who was married, had two children, and presented with a wish for sex change. He labeled her condition "transsexualism." The patient, an immature childlike individual, was reportedly quite volatile and profoundly suicidal. She also had a chronic history of pelvic pain and had been hospitalized for a total of four years on an inpatient psychiatric service, "usually for symptoms of acute anxiety, depersonalization, and threatened suicide." During latency she developed a strong attachment to her father and became inseparable from him. At this time (age 8) she was also molested by a middle-age man. The patient eventually left home, married, and had two children (a girl and then a boy). As an adult she often took alcohol as self-medication. After one of her hospitalizations she was placed in intensive psychotherapy. The therapy goals, which aimed at converting her to heterosexuality, failed. The patient then began dressing full-time as a man. Eventually, she had her ovaries removed (which did not abrogate her pelvic pain). After surgery the patient began living with a woman in a marital-type relationship.

Money and Brennan (1968) reported on the gender identity of six female patients whom they labeled as transsexuals. Indeed, five had undergone a mastectomy and hysterectomy. Three patients had also begun surgery for the construction of an artificial penis. The patients were older than their male counterparts (i.e. male transsexuals in their program) with the average age being 37.5 years (range 32–51), and were of bright normal intelligence (IQ range 97–131). As a group, these female patients reported early childhood histories of tomboyism, interest in boys' games, and a desire for high levels of physical activity and exertion and rough-and-tumble play. On psychological tests they identified with traditionally masculine interests; they denied being interested in or identifying with stereotypically feminine orientations. All the patients hated their breasts and wished to have them removed. The authors argued that the female patients lacked a "typical" maternal interest in childbearing and were defective in this area. Unfortunately, little information was provided about their family backgrounds, early childhood development, or relationships with parents. This study, like Benjamin's, was a departure from the single case study method. While Money and Brennan provided data on larger numbers of patients, their study suffered from an oversimplification of complex issues. The study was, however, important: by presenting larger groups of patients, it had a wider data base from which to draw conclusions. Money and Brennan concluded that female transsexualism was a unitary psychological disorder of unknown etiology.

In a continuation of their previous study, Money and Brennan (1969) reported on additional information on their female transsexual subjects and included one additional case. The women were evaluated on several measures: WAIS IQ, vocational ability, and motivation. The women were seen as being superior in verbal versus numerical or space form abilities. Money and Brennan concluded that, "if verbal skill is a feminine trait, then they show accepted female cognitive patterns." They argued that "these seven patients did not exhibit a stereotypically masculine intelligence-test pattern of response." Moreover, they showed high achievement and tended to achieve vocationally (which the authors related to a "compensation for their psychosexual disability"). One can certainly take issue with their notion of a universal male-female cognitive gender difference, which has been shown to be either a statistical artifact or too small to be conceptually relevant (Hyde, 1981).

Vogt (1968), using the clinical case approach, reported on five cases of female transsexuals (three adolescents and two young adults). His findings suggested that the patients generally came from modest backgrounds; in three of the homes there was no father figure, with the mother being the most important person; all had a history of tomboyism and a preference for boys games and activities; with one exception they were all of average intelligence (one patient was of superior intelligence); and there was evidence of neurotic features in most cases. This last point needs to be underscored, since the case histories included anxiety and agoraphobia, hypochondria, a factitious bleeding disorder, feelings of panic, psychiatric hospitalization, institutionalization at a school for maladjusted girls, alcoholism, imprisonment, morbid jealousy and violence, and psychosomatic disorders that required hospitalization. In spite of this lengthy list of psychological and psychiatric symptoms and apparent social maladjustment, Vogt viewed their social-surgical outcomes as satisfactory! No explanation was given for the contradiction between Vogt's subjective appraisal of the patients' positive outcomes and the observations which suggested severe maladjustment.

With the publication of Green and Money's *Transsexualism and Sex Reassignment* (1969), clinicians were provided with the first sourcebook for evaluating, diagnosing, and treating people with profound gender identity disturbances (i.e. diagnosed transsexuals). Only two of fourteen chapters, however, focused on female transsexuals, and one of those (Money and Brennan, 1969) had been previously published (two other chapters of the remaining eighteen focused on surgical aspects, which I will discuss later).

The contribution by Pauly was represented by a series of articles on female transsexualism which he published over a decade (Pauly, 1963, 1974a, b). After reviewing the literature Pauly presented four case histories of female transsexuals (one of whom was Mexican-American). While he felt that it was too early to pinpoint the etiology of female transsexualism, he did speculate on its possible pathogenesis:

> During childhood there is an identification with a strong, masculine father figure. This father-daughter relationship is not an excessively close one, as is the case between mother and son in male trans-sexualism. The mothers are perceived by their daughters as weak or ineffectual, or less admirable than father, in much the same manner that fathers of male transsexuals are perceived by their sons. A protective attitude toward mother develops with all the dynamics of a reverse oedipal situation (Pauly, 1969, p. 86).

Pauly also speculated that sometime in the future researchers may discover a neuroendocrine hypothesis to explain some of the variants of these conditions.

Pauly stated that "female transsexuals seem better adjusted in their male roles . . . [and that] they demonstrate less psychopathology [than male transsexuals]." This view exerted a strong influence on subsequent investigators (some of whom seemed to have taken Pauly too literally, confusing adjustment in the male role and a more repressed–constricted–inhibited style with being "normal" and without apparent psychopathology). Pauly concluded that a combination of supportive counseling, testosterone therapy, and surgery should be considered. He believed that "until further evaluation suggests contrary results, one must accept sex reassignment surgery as the only available means of alleviating the suffering of the transsexual individual" (1969, p. 87).

Léger et al. (1969), reviewing the literature on transsexualism, noted that: "The majority of the cases reported in the literature focus on male transsexualism; [and that] observations of female transsexualism are quite rare." They presented a case history of a young woman, Anny, who was referred to them for evaluation for hormone therapy and SRS. A picture of Anny in male clothing accompanies the article. On clinical interview Anny appeared intact, lacking any apparent anxiety, and affecting a very masculine image. While she was having little difficulty meeting other women in her male role (Anny denied being homosexual), her family situation was becoming intolerable as her parents actively objected to her SRS wishes.

Léger et al. (1969) reported that Anny's condition was chronic, relating back to early childhood. The patient was ten years younger than her older brother, and as far back as she could remember she had wanted to be a boy. She preferred to play ball or other boys' games and refused to play with dolls. Anny stated that she even viewed herself as male in her dreams. While she was willing to be candid about her SRS wishes, the authors suggested that she was less than candid about her family life. Most of the information came from the parents, who were quite distressed. They reported that Anny stuffed a towel in her pants to simulate the appearance of a penis; she also bound her breasts.

The case was quite typical of female transsexuals. Here was a young woman with no apparent physical basis for her transsexualism. She had a normal female anatomy and was a genetic, chromosomal female. The most pertinent information about the patient's condition came from the psychological tests. Results from the Minnesota Multiphasic Personality Inventory (MMPI), Rorschach, and Thematic Apperception Test (TAT) were presented. The findings suggested a tendency towards dissimulation, paranoid traits, poor reality testing (her F + % on the Rorschach, which measures reality testing, was only 57%, the norm being about 80%), impulsive behavior, narcissism marked by conflicts with her mother, jealousy towards her brother, and a depressive attitude. In summary they concluded that Anny evidenced a "personality marked by profound anguish, a bad social adaptation, poor reality testing, a dissociative tendency, and a search for security in the adoption of a male role." They concluded that the psychological testing was indispensable in uncovering her underlying psychosis.

Warner and Lahn (1970) reported on a case of a 28-year-old white Catholic South African woman. The patient was the fourth of four siblings, having an older brother and two older sisters, and was virtually an only child because of the age gap. Three years prior to her birth, the mother had aborted a male fetus and the husband had put pressure on her to become pregnant again in order to have another male child. When the patient was born she was rejected by the mother "and cuddled and adored by father." At two years of age the patient's brother was removed from the home and "hospitalized for cardiac and pulmonary diseases and remained away until the patient was eight." With the brother's return, the family was quite chaotic and the patient began to fantasize about being a boy. Indeed, the prodigal son was "showered by mother's affection" only to have his skull fractured by father, who threw a rock at him to keep him from assaulting and drowning the patient! Around age 11 a series of deaths, surgeries, and hospitalizations left the patient fearful of penetration "of her body by enemata or thermometers." She began to believe that she had had a penis which had been surgically removed during an appendectomy. When she was 15 her parents divorced. During her teens her father was twice remarried and divorced. During this time the patient made a serious suicide attempt and was told by mother that "she was sorry she had kept the patient alive." Throughout early adulthood the patient suffered from anxiety attacks and was alcoholic and assaultive. Hospitalized for depression, she was placed on anti-psychotic (Stelazine) and anti-depressant (Elavil) medication. The patient rejected long-term hospitalization.

Psychological testing revealed "a picture of a passive, timid, emotionally inhibited individual of bright normal intelligence, rigidly naive and uninsightful." It was concluded that the patient's wishes for surgery represented identification with the aggressor and "smothering fantasies related to heterosexuality." Some of the factors which may have contributed to her cross-gender identification were listed as: "the father's wish for a boy; early identification with father; rejection by and longing for mother who favored the patient's brother with whom the patient identified as an aggressor, and of whom she was afraid; early fear of heterosexuality and smothering as well as a frightening primal scene experience." The authors also wondered about the development of "an encapsulated delusion around the patient's heterosexuality" (citing the formula for individuals who have a dread of homosexuality: "If I love a man/woman I must be a woman/man"). The patient's wish for SRS was interpreted as a "quasi delusional defense against psychosis." With apparent disregard for the case history material, Warner and Lahn concluded that female transsexuals are more dependent, less disturbed and psychopathic; have a lessened need to demonstrate their masculine characteristics; and have less psychopathology. Unfortunately, the clinicians did not present the patient's psychotherapy in depth.

Christodorescu (1971) presented the case of an adopted, adolescent female transsexual (age 18) whose adoptive mother was described as a psychopath (who had been separated from her mother from ages 1 to 10). The patient had a turbulent early childhood and a history of tomboyism (with crossdressing beginning actively at age 11). She was reportedly raped at age 13 by an older male (recalling the penetration with disgust). The patient was described as sentimental, faithful in her love affairs, having impulsive–hysteroid reactions to frustrations, and being easily discouraged by setbacks. She had consolidated a masculine identification. Psychotherapy was viewed as having been of little success in orienting her back to a female role and identity. Christodorescu was the first clinician, however, to state that "a patient's claim for a sex-conversion operation is not a sufficient criterion for a diagnosis of transsexualism."

Ihlenfeld (1972), a co-worker of Benjamin's, was responsible for extending the idea that female transsexuals are better adjusted than male transsexuals. He reported that they "find moving into the opposite sex role much less of a social problem than does the male." The female transsexual was also viewed as less demanding, fulfilling her obligations, and posing few management problems. Ihlenfeld's equation between passing well in the male role and being viewed as better adjusted psychologically (fostered by Pauly, 1969) has subsequently led some clinicians to think of the female transsexual as being without psychological distress and as "normal." As I will show, this view has compromised the psychological treatment programs of many self-diagnosed female transsexuals.

By 1972, Stoller, who had all but neglected female transsexuals in his 1968 publication *Sex and Gender*, reported on ten female transsexuals. In that study Stoller reported that the mothers of these patients were generally removed from the family (usually by depression). The fathers, who were viewed as substantial people, refused to support their wives in their suffering. They did, however, send in their daughter as a substitute or "surrogate" husband. Stoller noted that even as girls these women were unfeminine, their masculine behavior encouraged by both parents "until the islands of masculine qualities coalesce into a cohesive identity." Stoller's views corroborated earlier investigators who noted that the female child had a need to rescue an endangered, motherly woman by enacting a surrogate husband role. Stoller also noted that while the patients' attractions to other women began in early childhood, all of them disavowed being homosexual. They viewed their sexual orientation as heterosexual and were attracted to heterosexual, feminine women who were maternal and enjoyed male bodies. Stoller believed that the fathers' pleasurable reactions to their daughters' emerging masculinity fostered that masculinity. In this sense Stoller stressed the importance of family and psychodynamics in the etiology of female transsexualism.

However, in contrast to male transsexualism, which Stoller saw as growing "from a nonconflictual learning process on the order of imprinting, conditioning, shaping, and identification," female transsexualism was seen as growing out of conflict, cumulative trauma, and defensive psychological processes.

In 1973, at the Second Interdisciplinary Symposium on Gender Dysphoria Syndrome at Stanford University Medical Center, Pauly attempted to provide a composite picture of the average female transsexual patient who was being evaluated at gender identity clinics throughout the world. Some of these ideas stemmed from an earlier, unpublished paper which he had presented in 1963 at the American Psychiatric Association meeting. He reported the following findings: female transsexualism was primarily a psychological disorder; females reported a preference for the male role beginning around age 7; sexual attraction towards females was reported around age 13, with sexual contact with females initiated around age 18; passing as a male began about age 19; requests for SRS were initiated about age 25; and the women obtained SRS between 28–30 years of age. There seemed to be a chronological progression through various phases leading to the evolution of a new gender role and identity.

Pauly reported that 56 per cent (n = 25) of female transsexuals made suicide attempts, and all reported being seriously depressed at one time (whereas 69 per cent were found to be mild to severely depressed on examination). While a smaller number of women were married (19 per cent) and had children (16 per cent), approximately 50 per cent dated men and had intercourse with men. All of the female transsexuals considered themselves heterosexual. Unfortunately, there was no breakdown of statistics according to race, education, etc. This is important since Stoller had pointed out that up to 1972 all the female transsexual patients were white and middle class (with the exception of one of Pauly's patients who was Mexican-American). Stoller (1972) wondered whether this could be the result of "a sampling error or the result of sociological factors."

In 1974 Pauly published two articles on female transsexualism which have served as the major resource for researchers and clinicians (Pauly, 1974a, b). In those articles he reviewed the world literature on female transsexuals which consisted of descriptions of eighty cases. The cases were all reanalysed *post hoc* using a 102-item instrument (which was not presented). Additionally, he provided a substantial bibliography for future researchers.

Citing prevalence studies of female transsexuals in Sweden and the USA, Pauly reported that for women over 15 years of age the incidence of the disorder was 1/103,000 and 1/130,000 respectively, while ratios of male-to-female transsexualism were 3:1 and 1:1. Pauly noted that during the 1960s there was an increasing number of females requesting SRS (see Appendix on incidence of female transsexualism).

Pauly's analysis suggested that female transsexuals perceived their mothers as needing protection from their fathers. Indeed, the transsexuals' mothers were viewed as cold, rejecting, emotionally disturbed, and unavailable. The patients were also seen as masculine, identifying with their fathers (who were viewed as large, masculine, alcoholic, physically abusive, and assaultive men). A large number of the women were raised in rural settings, and with the exception of one Mexican-American, all were Caucasian.

The women reportedly first became aware of their cross-gender wishes around age 7 (range 2–13 years). They were disgusted by their breasts and female genitalia and envied boys their genitals. Many of the women prided themselves on being the toughest kid. Puberty was traumatic, with the onset of menarche and the development of breasts shattering their hopes of ever being male. All of the women denied being homosexual and chose feminine women as their lovers.

Pauly concluded that "the breasts are the most obvious insignia of femaleness and the first point of surgical attack." His views have been substantiated by other investigators who concurred that the majority of female transsexuals who had a mastectomy did not go on to have phalloplasty; it was primarily their breasts which they wanted removed.

In his second study, Pauly (1974b) focused on the psychological and psychiatric status of these same patients. However, since the analysis was *post hoc* it must be regarded with a certain amount of scepticism. Pauly reported that on various IQ measures the female transsexuals scored above average (the mean IQ scores of 105 are highly unreliable since no standard test was administered). The majority of patients came from lower socioeconomic classes and had at least a high school education. Only one of the thirty-five patients was thought to be schizophrenic; six patients (24 per cent) were seen as delusional (with the delusions focusing on their belief that they were of the opposite sex). Pauly distinguished between ideas of sexual metamorphosis, confused psychosexual identification, and gender confusion as related to diverse psychiatric conditions such as psychotic states, schizophrenia or transsexualism. He concluded that female transsexuals are neither psychotic nor delusional "and certainly not schizophrenic in the majority of cases reported." He also reported that "on most of the psychological measures, female transsexuals seem to be better adjusted, freer of paranoid trends, and more realistic in their appraisal of what is possible for them [than male transsexuals]." He did, however, report that 34 per cent of them had personality disorders, and that depression was a primary problem (with 17 per cent making suicide attempts). Pauly cited Baker and Green's (1970) study in which a female transsexual reportedly committed suicide ten years post-surgery. A review of the literature revealed only one other case in which a woman attempted to mutilate her breasts or genitals (see Späte, 1970), a phenomenon which was quite rare among female transsexuals.

While Pauly noted that biological factors such as chromosomal disorders and physical disease (e.g. Stein-Leventhall syndrome) may play a role in the activation of a female gender identity disorder, he believed that the etiology of female transsexualism, while not fully known, was probably related to "certain intrafamily dynamics in the development of female transsexualism." These dynamics involved the transsexual-to-be identifying with a physically assaultive father who was unavailable to his weak, emotionally withdrawn wife, and having a need to rescue the mother from him (playing the role of a surrogate husband). In effect, the family dynamic, first reported by Redmount, has remained unchallenged up to the present time.

Bloch (1975), discussing "the cases of . . . four children [two of whom were girls] who adopted an opposite sexual identity," provided an alternative explanation of the family dynamic to that of Pauly. The girls, aged 4 and 5, were treated by Bloch in psychoanalysis. Bloch argued that the analyses of all four children elucidated the moment that they evolved a wish to change sex. These wishes were all related to "defensive fantasies which protect[ed] the child against the parent's wish for infanticide . . . [in which] the assumption of a different identity defends [her] against the actual threat of infanticide." Bloch argued that in each case the children believed that "only a change of sex could secure the threatening parent's love and thus save [her] life . . .: In a desperate attempt to save [her] life at a specific moment of what [she] experienced as acute danger [s]he therefore transformed [her]self." The defensive maneuver was seen as serving a twofold purpose: repressing the parent's murderous rage and threat of infanticide, and maintaining "the illusion that it is possible to receive love." The affirmation that one is a member of the other sex was interpreted as a defensive flight into an assumed identity to protect the boundaries of the self from annihilation and achieve the twofold purpose given above. The form-ulation, based on clinical psychoanalysis, provided an in depth look at the speculative pathogenesis of the wish to become the opposite sex. It was difficult, however, to assess how universal this dynamic was for all children with gender identity disturbances (no less for adult females with gender identity disturbances). It was also difficult to know if there was any relationship between these childhood gender identity problems and adult transsexualism.

Roback et al. (1976) reported on the psychopathology of ten female sex-change applicants, whom they contrasted with two control groups of females: an outpatient psychiatric group and a surgery group. (The MMPI was used as the criterion of psychopathology.) They concluded that while the ten female sex-change applicants had "more than the usual psychological debilities," their MMPI scores contraindicated a severe neurosis of psychosis. These findings corroborated those of Rosen (1974) in demonstrating the relative "psychological well being of female-to-male transsexuals." The latter conclusion must be viewed with caution, as the sample size was small and the authors used only a single measuring instrument (the MMPI). While they failed to find that "stark reality impairment necessarily underlies transsexualism," they did show that these patients were not free of psychological deficit.

Davenport and Harrison (1977) presented a case history of a 14-year-old girl who wished to change sex. She received two years of individual and milieu therapy (she was hospitalized for twenty months and seen three times a week by a male therapist). The therapy was viewed as a success in that the girl abandoned her cross-gender wishes and resumed her female role. This was one of the few cases presented in which a gender identity change was successful. The girl was described as a tomboy who, during adolescence, was withdrawn from her family and peers. She had two siblings, and her mother was described as having a lifelong depression (including a postpartum depression after the patient's birth for which she was psychiatrically hospitalized). The patient also received psychotherapy at age 3 (in a child guidance clinic). She was referred and treated for head banging, hair pulling, and excessive demands for maternal attention. The patient's history suggested a needy, clinging, dependent child who was desperately reaching out to a mother who was empty, depressed, and unavailable.

The patient was also viewed as having a severe constriction of her thought processes, and a misconception that SRS would turn her into a "perfectly normal boy." The major issue in her therapy was that of separation–individuation. Once she began to get angry at her father there was a noticeable improvement in all areas of her psychic functioning. The parents, however, seemed to support her male identity by "sometimes act[ing] as though they wished she were not a girl." From her therapy it emerged that her fantasies of being a boy increased at times when she felt "rejected and depressed, and thus [that] being a boy would bring her attention and approval." The patient's main focus of rebellion against her parents centered on her wearing male clothing, which also had a "magical sexual quality, i.e. clothes make the man." The combination of a constriction of thought, repression of feelings, and an extremely moralistic attitude was part of what clinicians meant when they said these patients were "healthy."

Martino, a female-to-male transsexual who ran a counseling clinic for other female transsexuals, summarized his findings:

Drawing on our counseling experience with roughly one hundred persons, we considered a characteristic profile of the female-to-male transsexual in the 1960s.

Our mean age was twenty-seven years, our height was five feet six inches, our weight was one hundred forty-four pounds. The dominant ethnic groups were Irish, Italian, and German, in that order – with the English, Puerto Rican, Blacks, Polish, French, Greek, Spanish, Swedish, and Welsh following. Only one each were Canadian, Chinese, Colombian, Cuban, Danish, Hungarian, Indian, Rumanian,

Russian, or Turkish. Three percent claimed more than one nationality. Eighty-seven percent were from patriarchal families, thirteen percent from matriarchal ones. Sixty percent came from families not too closely knit, twenty from "the usual," twenty from warm and loving families.

Religion was practiced by seventy-three percent. Fifty-seven percent were Roman Catholic, thirty-four percent were Protestant.

Forty had high school diplomas, eighteen were in B.A. and B.S. programs, eleven had Master's degrees, six were in master's programs, six had less than high school education, two had Ph.D. degrees.

Occupations ranged from unskilled labor to college professorships.

Postoperatively, ninety-four percent were forced to change residence because of community non acceptance. Seventy percent of sex-reassigned persons wanted to move to the suburbs, twenty percent preferred the city.

Ninety-nine percent thought of themselves as true transsexuals. All had agreed that the mate should be told before marriage. Ninety percent wanted to marry "the old fashioned girl." Only five percent of the wives had engaged in a lesbian relationship before meeting the female-to-male transsexual. Only six percent frequented gay bars preoperatively (1977, pp. 242–3).

Martino also pointed out that 23 per cent of the female sex change patients "were in the medical and paramedical fields; half of them in nursing." While it is difficult to assess the meaning of this data, it seemed that Martino's group reflected a special group of female trans-sexuals who sought help from a non-traditional setting. In this sense his findings provided a fresh insight into the wider spectrum of female gender patients who were not evaluated in gender clinics and university hospital programs.

Green (1978) published a preliminary report on the sexual identity and orientation of thirty-seven children (age range 3–20 years) raised by homosexual and transsexual parents. Nine of the children were raised by female-to-male transsexuals. Green noted that four of these children did not know that their "father" or "stepfather" was trans-sexual. Six of the children were girls and three were boys. Only one of the girls was labeled a tomboy, whereas none of the other children (while growing up) were described as either a sissy or tomboy. Seven of the nine children had clearly gone through established lines of gender identity development, the boys describing themselves as masculine and heterosexual, and the girls describing themselves as feminine and heterosexual. Two other children were too young (a boy aged 8 and a girl aged 7). Green's study challenged theorists to rethink some of the basic assumptions about patterns of identification and family influence on the sexual preference and the gender identity of children. Some of the methodological limitations of the study included the lack of a control group and a too brief follow-up period. Green's conclusions, that the children revealed conventional sexual identity development in rather "unconventional families," must be viewed cautiously. Green's findings not only go against the grain of current psychoanalytic and learning theory, but also of common sense. He correctly identifies his study as a "preliminary report."

In response to Pauly's (1969) comments that he was unaware of any reported cases of suicide, successful or attempted, by female-to-male transsexuals (see the case of Baker and Green, 1970), Herschkowitz and Dickes (1978) did report on one such case. The patient was apparently granted surgery in order to prevent further suicide attempts. However, four years post-surgery she was hospitalized secondary to a serious suicide attempt. The surgery had not resolved this woman's object relations dilemma, and post-surgery she could neither attract women nor function adequately as a male (i.e. achieve erection and penetration).

Fleming and Nathans (1979) reported on a case study of a 23-year-old female transsexual with whom art therapy was used in order to understand the central issues behind her transsexual wishes. The patient had a lifelong gender identity problem and always considered herself to be a male (but more to the point, "a reincarnation of a Greek god"). In all other areas of thinking her reality testing and orientation were intact. As the art therapy progressed, "the drawings revolved around the major themes of absolutism and negative identity, physical transformation, rites of passage, and the quest for identity." The patient's conflicts were viewed as couched within the framework of adolescent development.

In a second paper, apparently dealing with the same patient, Fleming and Ruck (1979), employed a Jungian framework, described the patient's dilemma as "a mythic search for identity," in which "transsexualism can be seen as expressive of the theme of the union of opposites." In a critique of that paper, Redfearn (1979) distinguished between mythic symbolism and psychotic delusions "of an overactive mythology" and concluded, "there must be some strain attached to living as a god among people who are regarding one as a lunatic."

Ehrhardt et al. (1979) compared lesbians (n = 15) and female-to-male transsexuals (n = 15) in behavioral patterns of childhood and adolescent development. All information was gathered from interview data. There were no differences between the two groups on the following indices: tomboy behavior, doll play, maternal rehearsal. The female transsexuals differed significantly from the lesbians on such measures as crossdressing (80 per cent prevalence for the female transsexuals and 0 per cent for the lesbians); gender identity confusion in adolescence (there was none reported for the lesbian group); and hatred towards one's breasts and menarche (70 per cent for the female transsexuals and 10 per cent for the lesbians). The authors argued that the differences between the two groups helped to determine both clinical-diagnostic and management issues.

Uddenberg et al. (1979) reported on the parental contact of twenty-four transsexuals (twelve male, twelve female) as compared to a control group. On all measures the transsexuals reported poorer relationships with their parents, suggesting to the researchers that a disturbance in the parent-child relationship was a contributing factor in the etiology of transsexualism.

Fleming et al. (1980) compared the scores of seventy-two transsexuals (fifty-five male and seventeen female) on the Bem Sex-Role Inventory (BSRI). The females were noted to have scored primarily as masculine sex typed (n = 6) or androgynous (n = 6). The females' scores, when compared with Bem's male and female norms, showed some interesting results. The "distribution of [the females] across the four BSRI categories did not differ significantly from Bem's normative college student male distribution, but was marginally different from that of Bem's females." The transsexuals' scores were also compared to those scores reported in the clinical literature. The female transsexuals' Bem scores were congruent with their clinical interview material, where they clearly stated that their gender role was male and their gender identity, masculine.

Shtasel (1979) presented a case of a 25-year-old black female teacher who had requested SRS. This was the first reported case of a black female transsexual. The patient was the youngest of twelve siblings; she had very warm feelings for her mother and no feelings for father. As a girl she was a tomboy and at age 12 fell in love with another girl of her own age. In sex play with boys she had only felt disgust. There was no reported crossdressing. At age 17 she had had her first date with a woman but could not tolerate the social disapproval involved. She was manifestly anti-homosexual. From late adolescence on she had begun to assume she was a male, and by early adulthood to wonder whether sex reassignment surgery (SRS) might not be a solution to her gender problems. Eventually her partner objected to her wishes for SRS and the patient acknowledged the fact that her partner never viewed her as a male (a crushing reality to the patient).

Shtasel believed that the patient's wishes for SRS stemmed from her aversion to homosexuality, and the patient's homophobia was treated behaviorally with systematic desensitization. We are told that the therapy was a success and that the patient was eventually able to give up her cross-gender wishes and accept her homosexuality.

The existence of anti-homosexual attitudes among a subgroup of transsexuals had been labeled by Meyer (1974) as stigmatized homosexuality, or, for some transsexuals, a cause of their gender dysphoria. Shtasel, citing Pomeroy (1975) noted that, "Some homosexuals, because of societal proscription, have developed such phobic reactions regarding expression of homosexual interests that they believe themselves transsexuals and would rather give up their gender than face a life of homosexual behavior."

In conclusion Shtasel suggested that patients requesting SRS should be treated primarily (and at times exclusively) for their phobic reactions to homosexuality before any drastic hormonal or surgical methods were implemented. While Shtasel offers sound advice, this case was rather uncomplicated and seems to be a variant of female transsexualism. Indeed, the disorder of female transsexualism seems far too complex to be reduced to a unitary homophobic explanation.

Strassberg et al. (1979), using the Tennessee Self Concept Scale, reported that on this measure seventeen female "candidates for sex change surgery (average age 23.71 years) varied appreciably in self-concept and adjustment, and as a group are indistinguishable from psychiatric controls." They found that "between one fourth and one third of the [female] applicants for sex change surgery are seriously psychologically disturbed." This was one of the few clinical reports that evidenced any serious psychological distress among female transsexuals. One might well ask why this self-designated group of transsexuals was so candid about their distress. Whatever the explanation, the finding of Strassberg and his colleagues must be seriously considered.

Lothstein (1980a), reporting on thirty-seven adolescent gender-dysphoric patients, ten of whom were teenage girls (average age 16.8) found that 75 per cent of the girls were diagnosed as having severe character disorders while the other 25 per cent were diagnosed as schizophrenic. Two of the girls eventually had surgery once they reached the age of 21 (after five years of evaluation and therapy). Eight of the ten females were intensively evaluated. While these patients seemed more stable, less impulsive, and more reflective about their gender conflicts than their male counterparts (and also more willing to participate in psychotherapy), they certainly evidenced serious psychopathology in their own right. Given the flux of the adolescent self-system, and the apparent success of psychotherapy, it was suggested that "psychotherapy may be the best technique to help adolescents with their psychosexual conflicts."

Sorensen and Hertoft (1980) summarized the literature on trans-sexualism and made a plea for the "careful phenomenologic elucidation of the condition . . . as a necessary precondition" for diagnosis. They also characterized the literature as suggesting that "the psyche of the female transsexual . . . [is] less deviating than that of the male, and it has often been thought that she adapted herself better . . . than did the transsexual male." The female transsexual's libido was noted to be less weak than had first been thought, but "more unambiguously homo-sexually directed than the libido of the transsexual man." The authors promulgated the following ideas on female transsexuals:

1 female transsexualism begins in early childhood;
2 crossdressing usually begins before puberty;
3 tomboy behavior is evident even during adolescence;
4 there is a protecting attitude towards the mother and other women;
5 there is a dissociation from the father (who is also imitated);
6 the adopted sex role is stereotyped and caricatured;
7 the female's sex role is not as caricatured as it is for male trans-sexuals;
8 female transsexuals are domineering towards women;
9 generally they are involved in homosexual activity;
10 from an etiological standpoint female transsexualism resembles homosexuality;

11 transsexual women play an active and domineering part in sexual relations;

12 they do not usually allow their partners to make contact with their genitals;

13 they only allow genital contact if their partner views their clitoris as a penis;

14 sex/gender roles are not exchanged between the partners (as in ordinary homosexual activity);

15 their libido is quite low;

16 transsexual women are impulsive (e.g. their social histories often include criminality and alcoholism);

17 many female transsexuals exhibit a tendency towards overt aggressive behavior;

18 most female transsexuals exhibit depression;

19 as a group they are less psychologically disturbed than transsexual males;

20 they are often viewed diagnostically as impulsive characters with sociopathic tendencies;

21 their social integration is often judged to be better than their male counterparts.

Sorensen and Hertoft viewed this list as descriptive of the phenomenology of female transsexualism. They believed that the main differences between male and female transsexuals relate to "the female's closer affinity to homosexuality than the male's." The female transsexual was viewed as having a need to "create a perfect illusion of the always potent, active, and domineering male." They also noted the discrepancy between the notion that the female transsexual was better adjusted socially and psychologically than her male counterpart, and the fact that she was often viewed as impulsive (with a history of criminality, alcoholism, and a label of sociopath and impulsive character).

In essence, the female transsexual was viewed as having a more alloplastic defense system than the male's autoplastic defense system. In conclusion, Sorensen and Hertoft felt that "the transsexual female . . . seeks to subdue [an] insecure gender identity by obtaining ego-satisfaction in adoption of strong outer attitudes and actions. She takes on a caricatured masculine attitude . . . is genitally fixated and preoccupied with sexual display." While they saw the necessity of "delimiting the transsexual syndrome phenomenologically," they

45

recognized that this was more difficult to do for females than for males. Derogatis et al. (1981) tested twenty female transsexuals and 143 heterosexual controls on the Derogatis Sexual Functioning Inventory. The results indicated "hypermasculine gender role definitions and fantasy themes among the transsexual group with decrements in terms of sexual information and range of sexual experiences. The transsexual females revealed moderately dysphoric affect profiles but were unremarkable in terms of psychological symptoms." While the study did introduce a standardized clinical instrument for evaluating large numbers of patients, it suffered from oversimplifying complex issues by employing restrictive categories. Moreover, there was no way to control for the female transsexuals' need to distort their autobiographies so that they would be viewed as better candidates for surgery.

Bernstein et al. (1981), checking the files of 163 gender-dysphoric patients who applied for sex change (thirty-two of whom were women), compared them with a matched control group on the variable of parental losses. They concluded that, of the twenty-seven who had lost a parent, the wish for sex change either first appeared after the death or was intensified by the death. Of this group, 33.7 per cent of the total female transsexual applicants (compared with 34.3 per cent of the total male applicants) had lost one or both parents, including one mother, four fathers, and in five cases both parents had died. The authors noted that there was an "unusually high incidence of father loss by gender-disordered patients" and suggested that the role of the father and parental death may play a crucial role in the release of the female transsexual's desire for sex change.

Lothstein and Roback (1981) reported on a study of five black females who applied to the CWRU Gender Identity Clinic for SRS. They compared their findings with data on the national incidence of black female transsexualism (being gathered in an ongoing study by Roback). The results indicated that 3 per cent of the CWRU patients were black females (n = 5), compared to 1.1 per cent of the national sample (representing nine clinics). A detailed clinical study of the five CWRU patients was provided, including patient characteristics; psychological test results; clinical interview material; and diagnoses. The finding of pernicious psychopathology among this group – three patients were diagnosed as schizophrenic and two as having borderline schizophrenic characters – raised the issue of the incompatibility of being a black female and also being transsexual. It was speculated that black women may somehow be "innoculated" against severe gender identity pathology and only exhibit such pathology as a consequence of a schizophrenic illness or borderline schizophrenic state.

Levine and Lothstein (1981) reported on the preliminary diagnostic findings of eighteen female patients requesting SRS. Eleven of the patients (60 per cent) had profound psychological disturbances; two patients were psychotic and several suffered from severe psychosomatic disorders. While a schema for diagnosing female gender identity disturbances was put forward, the authors also proposed substituting the term "gender dysphoria syndromes" for "transsexualism." This diagnostic schema was based on two factors: the onset of the disorder and the level of adaptation which the patient achieved. Primary and secondary gender dysphoria were described. It was suggested that "surgery should not be considered the only, or the best treatment for the syndrome . . . [and that] psychotherapy can help many patients, especially those with secondary gender dysphoria."

Summary

In this section I have reviewed some of the historical themes of female transsexualism and provided some vignettes of instances of women who impersonated men. My purpose was to place female transsexualism within its appropriate historical perspective so that it may be viewed as "un mal ancien." Moreover, once female transsexualism has been provided with an historical framework, the reader may begin to appreciate how various concepts emerged and how the processes of evaluation, diagnosis, and treatment for female transsexualism evolved.

Next I reviewed the medical–psychological perspective on female transsexualism, showing how, for the past two centuries, physicians and psychologists have recognized the existence of a female gender identity disorder for which they have struggled to find a name. A review of the major literature in English, French, and German highlighted the international aspects of the disorder.

What clearly emerged were several lines of investigation which characterized the different branches of the basic sciences and the social sciences which have attempted to study female transsexualism. Each of these lines of investigation has involved distinct methodological approaches: the single case study; large group approach; clinical interview;

psychotherapy and analysis; the use of objective questionnaires; and psychological testing. Lacking systematic control groups and universally accepted measuring instruments, the conclusions of the various studies are difficult to compare. Yet, one is able to discern certain themes, patterns, and similarities among the various presentations of female gender disorders. In addition, each of the various specialties has analysed the data from a unique perspective.

Physicians, focusing on the pathological issues of female trans-sexualism, have employed an illness model in their investigations. They have also concentrated their efforts on learning about the effectiveness of hormones and surgery in the treatment of female transsexualism. On the other hand, clinical psychiatrists and psychologists, using several different models, have focused their attention on the diagnostic and psychotherapeutic issues in female transsexualism. Employing such diverse theoretical frameworks as psychoanalysis and learning theory (and using either the single case study or large group approach), they have attempted to understand the pathogenesis of female transsexualism.

Sociologists, studying the ways in which the female transsexual negotiates her social reality through male impersonation and "passing," have focused on the relativity and diversity of gender roles, depicting female transsexuals by such macro-molecular variables as criminality, social position, number of close friends, assumption of social-sexual role *vis-à-vis* their partner, etc. Sexologists, using similar methodological approaches to those of the sociologists, have also focused their attention on macro-molecular variables, but with an emphasis almost entirely on the sexual *Lebenswelt* of the women.

While each of these lines of inquiry provides an insight into the disorder of female transsexualism, there has been no attempt to bring all of the insights under the aegis of a coherent theoretical framework. Moreover, there has been a consistent pattern in which investigators have taken an idea about female transsexualism and, on the basis of scanty evidence, converted it into a truth or a theory (e.g. the idea that female transsexuals are more "stable" than their male counterparts). The most recent efforts to provide a "careful phenomenologic elucidation of the condition" have focused on bringing together "insights" from the various lines of inquiry and presenting them as a coherent pattern of female transsexualism. The real thrust of this phenomenological approach is to focus on hard data versus speculative inquiry.

There is a growing body of literature on female transsexualism, one which reflects the increasing numbers of female patients who are requesting evaluation for "transsexualism," and the interests of clinicians and researchers who wish to learn more about this phenomenon. This literature also reflects the confusion of the various investigators who, trying to make sense out of the wealth of data, have failed as yet to present a unified and coherent body of knowledge which can be used to construct an adequate working theory of female transsexualism. It will be the task of this book to provide a coherent analysis of the phenomenology of female transsexualism (as a clinical disorder), to explore critically some of the working assumptions of female transsexual research, and to provide a viable framework for evaluating, diagnosing, and treating female transsexuals.

Chapter 3
Diagnostic issues

Historical issues of diagnosis in female transsexualism

Krafft-Ebing's contribution

Physicians began recording case histories of female transsexualism in the early part of the nineteenth century (Friedreich, 1830; Westphal, 1896). It was not, until the publication of Krafft-Ebing's *Psychopathia Sexualis* (1894) that these disturbances were recognized as being worthy of medical investigation. In that study Krafft-Ebing reported nine cases in which women were treated for gender identity and role disorders. Because those cases were recorded in the last century, prior to the introduction of medical-surgical techniques which made sexual surgery a reality, they provide us with rich clinical material on female transsexualism untainted by modern media exploitation of transsexualism. Moreover, those cases provided a baseline for studying the modern analogues of female gender identity and role disturbances.

The first case involved a 29-year-old woman who was regarded as having a simple reversal of sexual feeling. This woman, who came from a family "having bad nervous taint," initially began wearing men's clothing in order to earn a living. She also impersonated a man in order to attract women lovers and to secure work as a male. However, she periodically switched back to her female role. The second case involved a woman in her mid-thirties who was reportedly in a "stage of transition to change of sex delusion." The woman had a childhood history of tomboyism, interest in wearing boys' clothes, and feelings of mortification "at being a woman." It was observed that "she gave the impression of being a man clad in female garb." At one point she began to experience delusions about her body; specifically she "was horrified to notice her breasts disappearing." After an undisclosed illness she realized that "her former period of life spent as a woman seemed strange to her [and] . . . she could no longer play the role of [a] woman." Indeed, she returned to her husband and children and "assumed the role of the man in her house." Krafft-Ebing noted that "she now became reconciled to her change of sex, brought about by her severe illness."

The remaining seven cases were reported under the heading "congenital sexual inversion in women." These were not simply cases of female homosexuality, but all involved impersonation of the male role, wearing of male clothes, dreaming and imagining oneself in the male role, and early childhood experiences in which the woman revealed a preference for stereotypically male toys, games and roles (behavior we would label tomboyism). In addition, all the women recalled being homoerotically attracted, at first to other girls and then to older women. While it may have seemed compelling to explain these patients' "male identity and role" disorders as stemming from a stigmatized homosexual condition, it was also clear that, for some of the women, their "sexual inversion" was ego syntonic and acceptable. In none of the cases, however, was there a fear of turning into the opposite sex, or a request for sexual surgery.

In the next seven cases (average age 27.57 years, range 23–36 years) the women reportedly experienced a broad range of gender pathology associated with their homosexual orientation. One woman stated that "I felt like a man . . . at twelve I had a mania to pose as a boy." In another case the woman "preferred playing at soldiers and other boys' games: she was bold and tomboyish" and dreamed about herself in the male role. In the third case the woman wished to become a soldier. She also lived and worked as a man for a number of years "with such a natural skill that, as a rule, she was able to deceive people concerning her sex." Another woman received a police certificate allowing her to "go about in male attire."

In yet another case a woman came to Krafft-Ebing's attention after she was discovered by her fiancée to be impersonating a man. The patient had a lifelong gender identity and role conflict. As a child she had played at "robbers" (taking the boy's role). She felt convinced that "her genitals could not be right"; and "she bewailed the fact that she was not born a man, as she hated feminine things and dress generally." In yet another case a woman was described who frequently crossdressed in male attire, and also had a childhood history of preferring boys' games and toys. She was regarded by her relatives as having "sexually changed" approximately two years after she refused a proposal of marriage. The patient "looked upon herself as a man."

The last and most picaresque case also involved deception. In 1889 Dr. Krafft-Ebing evaluated a young woman posing as a Count, who swindled "his" father-in-law in business, and "entered into matrimonial contracts" impersonating a man. The patient, assuming the identity of a certain Count Sandor, turned out to be " no man at all, but a woman in male attire, Sarolta (Charlotte), Countess V." As a child the patient's father had raised her as a boy (the father cannot, however, be accused of having a double standard since he also raised his son as a girl!). In addition, the patient's mother supported her male wishes and allowed her daughter to openly impersonate a man. The result was that the woman "had an indescribable aversion for female attire – indeed, for everything feminine." In fact, for more than ten years she impersonated the male role, to the point of stuffing handkerchiefs in her trousers to give the impression of a scrotum and penis. Eventually she petitioned the courts and was granted permission to live as a male in society without harassment. "The 'countess in male attire', as she was called in the newspapers, returned to her home, and again gave herself out as Count Sandor."

While these cases reflected a broad range of gender pathology, they did share certain common themes. The patients revealed a spectrum of male impersonation behaviors, and all of them reported an early childhood history of gender identity and role confusion. As children they believed themselves to be boys, identified with boys' behavior, played boys' games, engaged in heightened physical activity and rough-and-tumble play, and had a high energy level. With one exception, none of the other patients was overtly delusional; that is, they did not actually believe that they were boys or were turning into boys; rather, they wished to become men (i.e. they knew they were biological females: they were not delusional about their sex). In one case, however, the precipitant for the patient's gender role reversal was the onset of an acute psychosis. In all the other cases the patients' childhood cross-gender beliefs reflected their underlying wishes to become males.

As the women entered adolescence, their gender dysphoria intensified. While some of them occasionally crossdressed and fantasized about being men, others impersonated men and lived and worked as men. These behaviors continued throughout adulthood. Some of the women explained their behavior as a conscious deception meant to attract women as sex objects (since they felt that as females they would be rejected by heterosexual women), or to obtain better jobs. Additionally, some of the women hated their female bodies (especially their breasts and genitals) and felt as if they were impostors when dressed in feminine attire. Whether some of them expressed an overt wish for a penis or SRS is unknown. By current standards, most of these women would have been diagnosed as transsexual and a few of them might today have been referred for SRS. The main issue, however, was that SRS was not prescribed because society was not ready to accept such dalliances, and the medical-surgical technology was unavailable.

Krafft-Ebing labeled all the women's gender conflicts as examples of "sexual inversion" (what is labeled today as homosexuality). He interpreted their wishes to become men as an outgrowth of their "aberrant" homosexuality and their determination to sexually attract females. His recommendation for the treatment of this disorder was for the physician to "combat . . . homosexual [attitudes] and encourage . . . heterosexual feelings and impulses" (while also discouraging masturbation). Because of the satisfaction that their symptoms afforded them Krafft-Ebing noted that these women were difficult to treat. He felt, however, that their "salvation" was important and that if all else failed hypnosis should be tried.

In spite of Krafft-Ebing's reports, there was little clinical interest in regarding female gender identity disorders in their own right. It was clear, however, that these women could not simply be diagnosed as transvestites or fetishists. Their wishes to become men and their behavioral transvestism reflected a craving to live out a male life style (which went beyond a purely erotic interest). Moreover, it was apparent that Krafft-Ebing was dealing with a complex psychodynamic and behavioral disorder which was multifaceted and multidetermined.

Freud's serendipitous contribution

In 1911 Freud published his account of the Schreber case, in which one of the patient's initial symptoms in his personality decompensation was a delusion that he was changing sexes and becoming a woman. The case, which subsequently became a classic in psychiatry, associated *change of sex* fantasies with homosexuality, delusions, and psychosis (a view later popularized by Meerloo (1967), who believed that transsexual wishes were delusional and that one was collaborating with the transsexual's psychosis by offering SRS as a form of treatment). The question of psychosis in transsexualism will be discussed later.

Freud's analysis of the Schreber case was not originally presented as a possible explanation for transsexualism. However, it has subsequently become an important resource for transsexual researchers interested in the differential diagnosis of transsexualism from homosexuality, transvestism, and psychosis. In this sense, Freud's contribution to our understanding of a possible psychotic element in transsexualism was quite serendipitous. Stoller (1975), commenting on the Schreber case, stated that, "At the center of the clinical picture is the transsexual desire: Schreber's sex is changing. He gradually comes to feel, at first with paranoid fright and later with megalomanic voluptuous pleasure, that he is being supernaturally influenced so that his body is changing to female and that he shall procreate a new race." Schreber's ego dystonic fear of turning into a woman allows us to understand the regressive aspects of the transsexual wish and the defensive maneuvers involved in achieving (for the male transsexual) "a state of oneness" with the mother. Unfortunately, none of Freud's cases involving ideas of sex change involved females.

Hirschfeld's contribution: the transvestite

With the publication of Hirschfeld's *Die Transvestiten* (1910) the medical field was provided with the first in depth study of crossdressing (now labeled transvestism) in which a woman's enactment of a male life style and her wish to become a male were documented. Bullough (1976) noted that "Hirschfeld, who was both a homosexual and a transvestite" was convinced by "his own sexual inclinations" that transvestism was not a perversion. Hirschfeld's convictions, however, were not generally accepted by other researchers. Indeed, most psychoanalytic studies have focused entirely on the fetishistic (Fenichel, 1953; Segal, 1965; Bak and Stewart, 1974), or perverse (Sperling, 1964; Gershman, 1970) aspects of transvestism while denying that female transvestism even exists. However, Hirschfeld did provide clinical examples of female transvestism and documented the erotic aspects of crossdressing for some women. More recent psychoanalytical investigations have directed their attention to the "transitional phenomena" (Person and Ovesey, 1974a; Volkan, 1979) and the symbolic aspects (Limentani, 1979) of transvestism.

Hirschfeld's introduction of the new term "transvestism," literally, to crossdress, to describe a form of cross-gender role impersonation (that is, wearing the clothes of the opposite sex) did not solve the diagnostic problems. Moreover, his labels such as "clothing transvestite," "name transvestite," pregnancy transvestite," "partial transvestite," seemed quite confusing. It was unclear if these different behavior labels implied a unique psychodynamic precursor or even a qualitatively distinct clinical disorder. The term transvestite neither explained the phenomenon under investigation nor was it entirely descriptive of the wide range of gender patholody that was often masked by wearing the clothes of the opposite sex. Indeed, some of his transvestite patients would now be regarded as exhibiting a wide spectrum of gender disturbances including perversions, fetishism, transvestism, sado-masochism, homosexual transvestism, butch homosexual transvestism, and transsexualism.

In spite of advances in sex research, there was still no universally acceptable diagnostic label to apply to those female patients with a lifelong gender identity and role disorder, whose anguish and suffering led them to the conviction that sex change was the only viable treatment modality.

A disorder in search of a name

Hirschfeld's term "transvestite" (whose spelling, e.g. trans-vestite, transvestitism, was often as confusing as the term) was used so differently (depending on the theoretical orientation of the clinician or researcher) that it could be applied to a diversity of clinical phenomena. For behavioral psychologists and sociologists (Garfinkel, 1967; Bogden, 1974; Feinbloom, 1976) it referred to a style of dress and preference; a behavioral role portrayal that related to themes of "passing," "role transition," and "stigmatization theory." For psychodynamically oriented clinicians, "transvestism" came to be viewed as both an impulse and defense against castration anxiety (coupled with the use of massive denial) and a primitive belief in, and identification with, the phallic woman (Segal, 1965).

Lacking a diagnostic schema, clinicians attached many different labels to gender identity and role disturbances. The list seemed endless and testified to the prevalence of the phenomena under investigation. Some of the terms used were: "genuine transvestism" (Hamburger, 1953); "metamorphosis sexualis paranoica" (Hirschfeld, 1922); "contrasexism" (Westphal, 1869); "psychopathia transsexualis" (Cauldwell, 1949); "eonism" (Ellis, 1936); "sex role inversion" (Brown, 1964); "true transsexual" (Stoller, 1968); "paranoia transsexualis" and "psychosexual inversion" (Pauly, 1965). As late as 1951 many clinicians still used the term "transvestism" to identify patients with profound gender pathology who requested SRS (Hertz et al., 1961).

Benjamin's contribution: "transsexualism"

The term "transsexual," which was coined by Cauldwell (1949), was clinically introduced by Benjamin (1966) to differentiate diagnostically two ` distinct disorders: transvestism from transsexualism. The term transsexualism was applied to those patients with a lifelong gender identity disorder who, in addition to crossdressing (which was tradition-ally associated with fetishism and transvestism), identified completely with the opposite sex, believed that they were trapped in the wrong body, and wanted surgery to correct that disorder. These ideas have come to be identified with the *core* features of transsexualism. Patients who suffered from transsexualism believed that by changing their bodies (that is, undergoing sex reassignment surgery) to match their cross-gender feelings they could become whole persons. The new term transsexualism, however, did not immediately clear up the conceptual problems of diagnosis. Moreover, even through the 1950s, several clinicians continued to use the term transvestism interchangeably with the new term transsexualism, creating a state of virtual diagnostic chaos. The fact that some clinicians believed that a transvestite could evolve into a transsexual only confused the matter further.

There was also considerable disagreement within the medical-psychological community concerning the usefulness of the term trans-sexual. Indeed, Benjamin (1966) used the term in at least three different ways. Using a sex orientation scale (modeled on the work of Kinsey et al., 1953) Benjamin described crossdressing along a continuum of transvestism (type 1, pseudo; type 2, fetishistic; and type 3, true) to transsexualism (type 4, non-surgical; type 5, moderate intensity; type 6, high surgical intensity). The non-surgical transsexual was seen as wavering between transvestism and transsexualism (with the term transsexualism being equated with a desire for SRS, although Benjamin noted that the true transvestite may also find SRS attractive). Type 5 and type 6 transsexuals were seen as making the most demands for SRS (with SRS being indicated for the type 6 transsexual). Benjamin presented the typology as typical for male transsexuals. No attempt, however, was made to rework the typology for female transsexuals.

Benjamin's schema suggested a continuum of sex and gender role "disorientation and indecision." He stated, however, that "If these attempts to define and classify the transvestite and the transsexual appear vague and unsatisfactory, it is because a sharp and scientific separation of the two syndromes is not possible. We have as yet no objective diagnostic methods at our disposal to differentiate between the two." If this was the case for males, it was especially true for females with gender role and identity disorders (whom diagnosticians either conceptually avoided or related to homosexual "disorders," Stoller, 1975).

Contemporary issues in the diagnosis of female transsexualism

The debate over the term "transsexual"

While the scientific community debated the usefulness of the term "transsexual," the media and the lay community accepted it unequivocally. And within a short period of time, whether they liked it or not, the scientific community was stuck with the term. There was, however, some concern over the implied equation of the diagnosis of transsexualism with SRS (especially given the fact that SRS was an experimental surgical procedure which was not universally accepted). Here was a disorder in which the patient told the doctor what her diagnosis was and how to treat it. Consequently, these patients became known as self-diagnosed transsexuals. They also insisted on being treated solely with hormones and surgery. Many clinicians who were unfamiliar with the condition of transsexualism simply accepted the patient's account of her disorder. Reacting to the patient's anguish and pleas for help, many of these clinicians tried to help the female transsexual seek out a medical solution to her condition (especially when the patient insisted that prior psychotherapy had failed).

57

Kubie and Mackie (1968) recommended "eschewing the term 'transsexual' completely because it implied that many of the problems related to gender transmutations have already been clearly faced, studied, and solved which they have not." Stoller (1968) also wondered whether the term "transsexual" (like the term "transvestite") was less a diagnosis than a symptom of a more profound underlying disorder. Meyer (1974) suggested that the term be used only for those who had undergone the operation. Others debated over the spelling of "transsexual" (Money, 1974).

Some clinicians (Benjamin, 1966; Stoller, 1968; Person and Ovesey, 1974a) believed in the concept of a *primary, true,* or *pure* transsexual. The search for a *true* or *primary* type of transsexualism seemed to be an attempt to identify which of the self-labeled transsexual patients applying for SRS would benefit from SRS. Other investigators noted that patients applying for SRS were a diverse group of clinical variants suffering from a broad spectrum of gender, personality, and developmental disorders (Socarides, 1970; Meyer, 1974; Money, 1974).

As the number of applicants for SRS grew, so it became apparent that patients were requesting SRS for a variety of gender identity and role disorders. The diagnosis of transsexual became synonymous with SRS. What did these requests mean? Why would non-transsexuals even request SRS? The situation was made more complex by the proliferation of patients requesting SRS and the increasing numbers of clinics set up to evaluate and treat self-labeled transsexuals. The burgeoning literature on transsexualism also suggested that the wish for SRS might be a diagnostic factor in its own right and independent on the diagnosis of transsexualism. It appeared as if many individuals with a chronic, but latent gender identity or role conflict could, under intense stress, come to believe that a change of sex could cure their problems. Clearly, this group of patients was significantly different from Stoller's depiction of the true male transsexual. Moreover, as transsexual issues were sensationalized and oversimplified by the media, many patients came to see a solution to their human suffering in terms of sex reassignment surgery.

It has become common knowledge that some effeminate homosexuals might, at the instigation of fellow homosexuals, or under the stress of a personal relationship that was threatened with collapse, be persuaded to undergo SRS (only to regret it later). Other patients labeled sexual psychopaths, sadists, masochists, psychotics, schizophrenics, or as having organic pathology, might also request SRS during a period of intense stress (functional or organic) and might experience a personality deterioration or decompensation (Newman and Stoller, 1974; Person and Ovesey, 1974a; Eber, 1980). Such individuals have been labeled as *non-transsexuals* or *secondary transsexuals*. But in light of a lack of consensus about the meaning of the term transsexualism, do these categories tell us any more than that the person should not be referred for SRS? Apparently so, since at least one gender identity clinic team (Laub and Fisk, 1974) has suggested that some non-transsexuals (i.e. non primary or true transsexuals) might benefit from SRS (Fisk, 1978). To the interested clinician, no less to the curious lay observer, the diagnostic situation in transsexualism must appear confusing at best.

Gender dysphoria syndrome: a compromise diagnosis?

In response to the phenomenon of large numbers of patients requesting SRS, Fisk (1973) introduced the diagnosis *gender dysphoria syndrome*, which he felt would more accurately describe the phenomenon being clinically investigated. This diagnosis was elaborated on by Laub and Fisk (1974) and later by Meyer and Hoopes (1974). It was defined as "a descriptive term, encompassing selective clinical situations or a set of psychosocial symptoms and/or behaviors that have been reported by a group of deeply troubled and often desperate patients seeking gender reorientation, including sex conversion." Fisk noted that "by conceptualizing our patients as having gender dysphoria syndrome, we have obviously liberalized the indications and requirements for sex conversion surgery." In other words, it appeared as if the diagnosis gender dysphoria syndrome was self-serving, replacing the term transsexualism in order to justify the referral of non-transsexuals for SRS. The situation was not only confusing, but when carefully considered, appalling. Moreover, changes in diagnostic labeling seemed to apply to male transsexuals only.

Diagnostic confusion: the APA's DSM contributions

Neither of the first two *Diagnostic and Statistical Manuals of Mental Disorders* (*DSM* I and II) published by the American Psychiatric Association (1952, 1968) made reference to those gender identity disorders which we now label as transsexualism. Since this was a major reference guide for mental health clinicians, the failure to classify gender identity disturbances contributed significantly to the confusion over the diagnosis. Moreover, the debate over diagnosis suggested a kind of philosophical nominalism: that is, for some clinicians, unless the disorder had a name, it simply did not exist. But naming a disorder is not equivalent to providing an explanation for it.

In 1980 *DSM* III was published. The disorder of "transsexualism" was not only given formal recognition, but other gender identity disorders were also recognized. These disorders were categorized under the heading "psychosexual disorders." Gender identity was defined as "the sense of knowing to which sex one belongs, that is, awareness that 'I am a male' or 'I am a female'." There was a clear effort by the authors of *DSM* III to provide a category for a number of gender identity disorders for which clinicians had no diagnostic criteria. *DSM* III defined gender identity as:

> The private experience of gender role, and gender role is the public expression of gender identity. Gender role can be defined as everything that one says and does including sexual arousal, to indicate to others or to the self the degree to which one is male or female.
>
> Disturbance in gender identity is rare, and should not be confused with the far more common phenomena of feelings of inadequacy in fulfilling the expectations associated with one's gender role. An example would be an individual who perceives himself or herself as being sexually unattractive yet experiences himself or herself unambiguously as a man or woman in accordance with his or her anatomic sex (*DSM* III, p. 261).

Three types of gender identity disorders were also classified: (1) transsexualism, 302.5x; (2) gender identity disorder of childhood, 302.60; (3) atypical gender identity disorder, 302.85. In deciding to use the designation "transsexual" as opposed to "gender dysphoria syndrome," the authors of *DSM* III chose the most commonly accepted, widely used term for describing patients with severe gender pathology who met certain criteria (described below). Some individuals with severe gender pathology could also be classified under the following *DSM* III diagnoses: transvestism (302.30) and fetishism (302.81), listed under the paraphilias; borderline personality disorder (301.83), listed under the personality disorders; identity disorder (313.82), listed under disorders characteristic of late adolescence. It was not made clear why the diagnosis of gender identity disorder of childhood was not included under the section on "disorders usually first evident in infancy, childhood, or adolescence." The *DSM* III criteria for diagnosing transsexualism included the following core features:

1 sense of discomfort and inappropriateness about one's anatomic sex;
2 wish to be rid of one's own genitals and to live as a member of the the other sex;
3 the disturbance has been continuous (not limited to periods of stress) for at least two years;
4 absence of physical intersex or genetic abnormality;
5 not due to another mental disorder such as schizophrenia.

In addition, the small x which is found at the end of the code for transsexualism (302.5x) was for recording the prior sexual history:

1 = asexual
2 = homosexual (same anatomic sex)
3 = heterosexual (other anatomic sex)
0 = unspecified

An individual (male or female) who met all of the above criteria was diagnosed as transsexual. The denotative criteria for *DSM* III diagnosis, however, do not imply a form of treatment for a specific disorder. However, the connotations of a diagnosis of transsexualism always imply the possibility of hormonal or surgical treatment. In this sense the term "transsexual" is a loaded one in that it implies an experimental form of intervention or treatment. An overview of some factors which *DSM* III listed as characteristic of transsexualism includes the following:

1 the age of onset varied form early childhood to adulthood and was related to prior sexual history;
2 there were usually co-existing personality disturbances;
3 the course of transsexualism was chronic and unremitting;
4 social and vocational impairments were associated features;
5 depression, suicide attempts, and attempts at genital mutilation were evident;

6 while an early disturbed parent–child relationship was noted as typical, no familial pattern was identified.

Although some mention of female transsexualism was made, there was no attempt to set up specific criteria for diagnosing female trans-sexuals. It was, however, hinted at in the manual (and evident in the literature), that in many ways male and female transsexualism are qualitatively distinct disorders. Indeed, two propositions regarding female transsexualism were raised. The first stated that: "Individuals who have female-to-male transsexualism appear to represent a more homogeneous group than those who have male-to-female transsexualism. That is, they are more likely to have a history of homosexuality and to have a more stable course, with or without treatment." The second proposition suggested that evidence of "childhood masculinity in a girl-child increases the likelihood of transsexualism."

These two propositions have played such an important role in the diagnosis of female transsexualism that they need to be explored at length. In spite of the inadequacies of the term transsexual, its wide acceptance, both in the professional and lay communities, compels us to accept the term as descriptive of the *core features* of the various gender identity and role disorders described over the past 150 years. In order to insure ease of communication, I have chosen to adhere to the *DSM* III criteria for diagnosing transsexualism. Whenever the term transsexual is applied to a female with gender identity pathology it will always embrace at least the five core features designated by *DSM* III.

Proposition 1: the so-called "stable" course of female transsexualism

The first proposition, focusing on the prior history of homosexuality and the stability of the female transsexual, has been reported consistently throughout the literature. Because this proposition has exerted such an overriding influence on clinicians who evaluate and treat transsexuals it needs to be carefully examined, especially since there has been a recent upsurge in SRS for females. In the example that follows I have chosen to present the case history of a female with a long-standing gender identity disturbance who was referred to our clinic for trans-sexual evaluation. The patient had been followed through evaluation, psychotherapy, SRS, and the post-operative course for over eight years. She was one of the first female transsexuals to be evaluated prior to the establishment of the CWRU clinic, and was always regarded by our clinicians as the most "stable" of our patients. I hope to use the case to explicate the meaning of the patient's "stability" and its effects on her diagnosis, evaluation, and treatment.

Case history: Tina/Tim

Tina, a 27-year-old white female, was referred by her family doctor for a transsexual evaluation. At the time of the referral she was enrolled in college. Tina was living with her girlfriend and working as a security guard impersonating a male. From the standpoint of social-vocational adjustment she was viewed as quite successful, having lived and worked as a male successfully for several years.

Tina's character was that of a passive-dependent, unassertive, somewhat withdrawn individual who encouraged caring and maternal/paternal responses (especially from her therapist). In her interpersonal interactions Tina was mildmannered, polite, friendly, and almost ingratiating. Moreover, she was totally understanding of our need to intrude into her life and volunteered to cooperate fully in any way possible. Tina's use of intellectualization camouflaged an underlying guarded quality to her self-system (which only surfaced intermittently). In this sense she was unlike so many transsexuals who are described as impulsive, paranoid, histrionic, and demanding, posing severe management problems to their often beleaguered therapists.

From early childhood Tina identified as a male, preferring to engage in rough-and-tumble play, having a high energy level, and wanting to wear boys' clothes and become a boy in every way. She typically avoided girls' play and activities, shunning all doll play and avoiding emotional displays.

Tina had an older brother with whom she had little contact. She dismissed as irrelevant any role he might have played in her cross-gender wishes. Tina's father (a factory foreman) and mother (a housewife) were described by the patient as constituting an unremarkable middle-class family who were devoid of any major psychopathology. Her denials about the possible influence of her family on her condition reflected a tendency she had of glossing over things and covering over important areas of conflict through the use of conscious suppression, denial and control.

Tina stated that she was generally accepted by her peers and had no unusual relationship problems. During the fourth grade her teacher was, however, upset enough about her gender role behavior that she actively encouraged Tina to act more female. In junior high school Tina began dressing in unisex clothing and was mildly rebellious, having disciplinary problems in school. During this time she managed to keep her grades up. In the tenth grade her male feelings intensified as she struggled with her unacceptable homosexual feelings. She had a strong erotic interest in other girls but could not tolerate being viewed as a homosexual. Subjectively she viewed herself as a man who was erotically interested in other women. She also had a strong need for the girls she was attracted to to view her as a man. To that extent she typically avoided lesbian girls and dated only heterosexually oriented girls. However, her illusion broke down and she became quite depressed at having to play a charade of male impersonation. Indeed, her depression intensified around menstruation but never reached suicidal proportions.

Although Tina discussed her gender conflicts with her parents, the home situation became intolerable such that she had to move out of the house and live with a friend in order to graduate from high school.

Tina was fourteen when she first kissed a girl and fifteen when she began to engage in overt homosexual activity (by her assessment her behavior was heterosexual). At age eighteen Tina fell in love with another woman and entered into a three-year monogamous relationship. Their sex life was active and satisfying, helping to form a bridge to a more enriching personal friendship. Tina's girlfriend stated that she viewed Tina as a male and did not consider herself to be homosexual.

When Tina dressed in male clothing she felt confident, assertive, strong, invulnerable, and secure. Her crossdressing was not fetishistic (in a dynamic sense) in that she did not eroticize the clothing. Indeed, she denied ever becoming so aroused by crossdressing that the act alone led to masturbation.

Tina has bright normal to superior intellectual abilities and evidenced considerable emotional stability. Superficially her judgment appeared intact, and aside from her idiosyncratic gender behavior, there were no obvious signs of manifest ego impairment, psychosis, or schizophrenia. The most striking fact about Tina was how likeable she was. Indeed, everyone wanted to take her side and facilitate her role change to male.

The concept of stability in Tina's transsexualism

From a strictly *DSM* III standpoint Tina met all the criteria for a diagnosis of transsexualism. She exhibited a profound sense of gender discomfort and believed that she should have a male body. Indeed, she wished to be rid of her breasts and to have phalloplasty. Her disturbance was chronic and she had lived full-time as a male for over three years. She was erotically attracted to females and had had several relationships with women. While she refused to label these relationships as homosexual, her behavior and fantasy suggested (from my standpoint) a homoerotic preference. There was no evidence of a physical intersex or genetic disorder; nor was there overt evidence from clinical interviewing of another mental disorder. Tina's past history and current behavior were less chaotic and impulsive than for most male transsexuals. At first glance her case seemed to illustrate the first proposition concerning female transsexuals: that they had a prior homosexual history and a stable course to their disorder.

I have no doubt that Tina would have been judged as a "true" or "primary" transsexual, if not as a good candidate for surgery at most gender clinics. Indeed, within a short time after evaluation she would have been referred for hormone treatment or SRS; one may well ask, however, what "stable" means with reference to a transsexual disorder. What does it mean to call someone's disorder "stable" when the person craves to have her sex changed and threatens to commit suicide unless this is done? From a psychological perspective "stable" seems to refer either to the patient's subjective view or to the therapist's evaluation of her "successful" level of adaptation and coping style, including social-vocational adjustment, and an absence of sociopathy (embracing such complicating social factors as arrest record, prostitution, and drug addiction). The assessment of "stability" may also refer to those psychological factors which are embedded in the evaluation process: that is, cooperative behavior; a lack of impulsivity; an ability to delay gratification; and the capacity for frustration tolerance. It was for these reasons that female transsexual patients were viewed as less difficult to work with than their male counterparts. Moreover, the absence of a manifest affective disorder, in conjunction with an apparent lack of what Kernberg (1975) has called "non specific ego weaknesses" (capacity to bear anxiety, tolerate frustration, and delay gratification), made these patients seem as if they were "stable" aside from their gender dysphoria.

Once Tina was conceptualized by the treatment team as an example of a "stable" female transsexual, her assessment and treatment were predetermined. In a personal communication Jon Meyer has described a woman like Tina whom the Johns Hopkins gender clinic deemed to be their most stable and reliable patient. After SRS she became impulsively disorganized, promiscuous, and generally out of control. How are we able to account for such discrepancies between what was observed during the evaluation of a female transsexual and her subsequent behavior? I hope to be able to answer this question in the course of my inquiry.

In order to review the assessment process I will present a reconstruction of the patient's diagnostic evaluation (which I observed and recorded but with which I was not directly involved). This analysis will help us to better understand the process of how decisions regarding diagnosis and treatment of female transsexuals are made by a multidisciplinary gender identity clinic. The clinic at Case Western Reserve University Medical School, in the Department of Psychiatry consists of approximately ten interdisciplinary clinicians who have met weekly for more than eight years to evaluate, diagnose, and treat patients with gender identity disorders.

The diagnostic process: the example of Tina
Tina was initially evaluated at the Cleveland Metropolitan General Hospital gender identity clinic. (She was evaluated there prior to the organization of the CWRU gender identity clinic, which combined the staff and facilities of University Hospitals of Cleveland and Cleveland's Metropolitan General Hospital.) After an initial intake Tina was referred to the surgeon for a physical exam. The patient, who was 22 years old, was then seen by a male social worker for evaluation. The social worker also interviewed Tina's parents and her lover. It was noted that her family situation was quite chaotic and that she had recently physically attacked her father. Tina's behavior was interpreted in terms of her gender dysphoria (as if the disorder provided its own rationale and source of explanation for her behavior). In conclusion, the social worker noted that "whether or not Tina has more of a homosexual,

or a trans-sexual orientation, remains somewhat unclear. She does not demonstrate any pathology in other areas of her life. In fact, she appears to be coping with life rather effectively and possesses a good measure of personal maturity . . . it is unclear whether or not she desires the operation to function as a male or to justify her 'homosexual' behavior or to reverse a rejection of her femininity by her parents."

An MMPI which was administered revealed an 8-4/4-8 profile (with scale 5 being the third highest). The consultant, who was not a member of the gender identity clinic, summarized his findings by stating: "I would expect [the profile] to be associated with a female homosexual [and] in any case the point would be that there is not gross pathology here beyond the sex role identification problem." He recommended that "we do not find indications for a need for psychiatric consultation." However, as part of the evaluation procedure the patient was assigned to a therapist (in this case a male psychiatrist) who saw her for a prolonged evaluation period.

Seven months later the psychiatrist, who saw the patient approximately once a week for four months, stated: "I consider the patient to be a true transsexual, that is a person who identifies in all respects (except physical sexual characteristics) with sex opposite his [sic] biological one . . . the patient shows many strengths and there is no history of significant psychopathology or *sociopathic* [my emphasis] behavior." He recommended that she be started on hormone therapy.

The designation that Tina was stable seemed to mean several things: she kept her psychotherapy appointments and was rarely late or cancelled appointments; she met all her obligations at the clinic and paid her therapy and medical bills; she followed the regimen outlined by the treatment team and neither challenged that treatment regimen nor went to another clinic; she had a passive-dependent personality; she graduated college and obtained high grades; she lived with the same female for over a year; and she was attempting to relate to her parents in what was judged to be a "mature" way. From a strictly psychological standpoint almost everyone who interviewed her saw her as devoid of major psychopathology. The fact that she was *not* diagnosed as sociopathic, and that she was a likeable, friendly woman were probably the deciding factors in regarding her as "stable".

Psychological tests: the uninvited guest
A review of Tina's files revealed that while she had been administered a

full battery of psychological tests they had not been fully utilized in the clinical decision-making process.

Talks with colleagues at other gender identity clinics revealed that complete psychological testing was rarely obtained because it was viewed as either too expensive or irrelevant to the diagnosis and treatment of transsexualism. In retrospect, both objections were really based on the fact that most gender clinics did not have *any* psychodynamically trained psychologists to administer or interpret such tests. In addition, one colleague stated that since the diagnosis of transsexualism could not be made on the basis of the Rorschach test there was no reason to administer that test. However, some clinicians have maintained that one can diagnose transsexualism from the "draw-a-person" test, the idea being that if the patient draws the opposite sex figure first s/he has a possible transsexual gender disorder. While such anecdotal arguments are common, and have even spawned research (Machover, 1949; Fleming et al., 1979), the conclusions are, at best, specious. No single psychological test ought to be used to diagnose a specific disorder. Moreover, the use of psychological tests to diagnose transsexualism is of doubtful value, since the very possibility of a clinical diagnosis of transsexualism has been called into question. Psychological testing involving a wide range of clinical assessment instruments may, however, facilitate overall personality assessment and diagnosis by providing important clinical material from areas not generally tapped by clinical interview alone. For some disorders, like the borderline personality condition (which has often been viewed as the basic structure of the transsexual's personality) psychological testing is central to confirming the diagnosis (Gunderson and Singer, 1975).

Tina's first battery of psychological tests
Tina was psychologically evaluated one year after she was placed on hormone therapy and one year after SRS. The projective test material provides a clinical picture of the patient that is not available from any of the clinical interview data. While I did not administer the tests I have provided my own independent interpretation of the results.

On the Wechsler Adult Intelligence Scale (WAIS) the patient scored a verbal IQ of 119, a performance IQ of 116, and a full scale IQ of 119. Her scores suggested that she was functioning in the bright-to-normal range of intellectual abilities. There was considerable inter-test scatter among all subtests, and a significant amount of intra-test scatter on the verbal tests. This scatter suggested considerable variability and inefficiency in her thinking and the possibility of ego defects, especially in those ego functions related to attention, effortful concentration, and organization of thought. While not overtly psychotic, her thinking could become disorganized under stress. Her high intelligence, coupled with her high comprehension subtest score on the WAIS, also suggested her capability for utilizing knowledge of social mores and conventions in a manipulative manner.

On the Thematic Apperception Test (TAT) Tina's stories were logical and coherent, contraindicating an overt psychotic thought disorder. While she tended to utilize fantasy and daydreaming as major defenses, she was able to organize the themes of the pictures without resorting to gross reality distortion. However, her object relationships were somewhat disturbed. She tended to characterize relationships as overidealized and viewed women as unfulfilling, untrustworthy, and guilt-provoking. There was the suggestion that she avoided angry feelings because of their perceived destructive potential. Men were also overidealized. Moreover, Tina equated the physical expenditure of energy and high activity level with maleness and identified with both aspects. There was, however, no evidence of her preoccupation with sexual surgery and there was a conspicuous lack of attention to gender-related themes (both of which are of interest).

While Tina's Rorschach test elicited only fifteen responses (below the norm of twenty), the number of movement responses (a measure of tension, anxiety, and conflict) and the use of multiple determinants suggested that she was experiencing a considerable amount of inner turmoil and anguish. Indeed, she seemed to be attempting to control and defend against unacceptable sexual and aggressive impulses which were seeking self-expression beyond her control. Her defensive struggle was not entirely successful. At times her massive use of denial and projection could interfere with her judgment and reality sense. While she evidenced the capacity for realistic perceptions, and was not overtly psychotic, her thinking was, however, subject to intrusion and distortion from her affectively laden impulses. Indeed, at times her thinking could appear confusing and perplexing. She appeared to have a subtle, but generally non-intrusive, thought disorder. None of this was evident on clinical interview (unless one viewed the symptoms of transsexualism as manifestly "crazy").

As a woman Tina felt vulnerable, weak, strange, odd, unconventional, and overwhelmed by her dependency needs and her yearnings to surrender to another woman in a passive way. Her feelings of discomfort as a woman also stemmed from her fear of being penetrated, intruded upon, or becoming the object of aggression. Indeed, as a woman she perceived herself as small, hopeless, ineffectual, and overwhelmed. Her "male" personality element, while acting as a kind of talisman (via the symbolic power she associated with the penis), was also formless and at times ego-alien. The split between her male and female elements was experienced as ego dystonic. She seemed to believe that only as a man could her dependency needs be met. In effect, she was enmeshed in a profound personality conflict from which there seemed no escape. In an attempt to resolve this conflict she had conceptualized a solution that was at best primitive – to become a man and thereby omnipotently resolve all her conflicts.

Tina also seemed to be struggling with an underlying depression which was defended against by her homosexual excitement. Indeed, she was preoccupied with homosexual imagery which she found both exciting and frightening. At times she seemed to defend against these impulses by resorting to phallic images which had a magical soothing quality. Her response to card 9 of the Rorschach ("looks like a real strong flower," combined with a sexual theme) suggested that she was still trying to integrate the phallic elements into her personality without resorting to the drastic measure of sex change. It was also suggested that she could be quite guarded and at times paranoid. This paranoid style and the use of primitive psychological defenses — denial, splitting, omnipotence, projection, projective identification — helped to defend against her inner feelings of fragmentation of self which threatened to overwhelm her ego.

Tina's sexuality and the primitive nature of her impulses seemed to disorganize her. By the end of the Rorschach test she became overwhelmed by the color (symbolizing her impulses and affects), and was unsuccessful in *unifying* the images. Her need to unify concepts and percepts suggested that she experienced herself as fragmented and in need to unification. Moreover, feeling vulnerable to any form of criticism, she lacked self-cohesion, her narcissism also seemed damaged, and her self-esteem was impaired. Her goal orientations, however, were somewhat intact and she was motivated to graduate college and enter a profession.

Tina also had the potential for a rich fantasy life, and a varied imagination. To the observer she appeared absorbed in daydreaming. She did, however, also evidence conflict-free areas of her ego which were able to develop independently of her gender conflict. Unfortunately, Tina was not administered a complete battery of psychological tests prior to being placed on hormone therapy. However, the testing suggested that the hormones had not eradicated her psychic conflicts. Indeed, she was experiencing heightened conflicts over her gender role and identity and was struggling to protect her self from being overwhelmed and destroyed by outside forces. The conflicts she manifested could not be resolved by hormonal or surgical treatment.

Tina's defensive structure allows us to see why she could be viewed as "stable" and could provide rather "stable" responses to the objective psychological tests – for example, on the MMPI, which assessed her interpersonal style and character structure. She had erected a bland facade to control her inner excitement and confusion. Her paranoid defensive system manifested an intermittently guarded style character-ized not by impulsive, hostile outbursts and attacks (secondary to feeling criticized and hypersensitive to any stimuli), but rather by a friendliness and politeness, a Madonna-like silence, and a controlled outer facade (reflecting her paranoid need for omnipotence and control). This style was prompted by her intensely perceived passive strivings and yearnings which she feared would never be met if she were too aggressive.

It was clear that Tina was not free from emotional turmoil. If we assumed that the clinicians who viewed her (almost two years prior to the tests) as "healthy" and "stable" were correct, then one conclusion might be that the hormone therapy was disrupting that quiescence and that the future would be bleak for Tina (especially if her depression surfaced). If that were the case, then male hormones might be shown to have a deleterious effect on the psychological life of female trans-sexuals. There was, however, no crucial test for this hypothesis.

In summary, the findings suggested a bi-modal clinical picture. On clinical interviewing and objective psychological testing Tina appeared "stable" and free of serious psychopathology. Intensive psychological testing, however, suggested that she had a subtle but non-intrusive thought disorder and the capacity to regress under stress. The overall clinical picture suggested a mild borderline personality disorder.

Tina's psychological testing post-SRS

The second battery of psychological tests was administered a year after SRS. Initially, Tina kept up her facade, but eventually became quite depressed. She admitted that she had lied to her therapist about how satisfied she was with the phalloplasty because she did not want to "let him down." The battery of psychological tests were re-administered (at my request) when Tina (now calling herself Tim) was judged to have successfully overcome both her depression and her regret at the surgery (almost a year later).

On the WAIS, Tina scored a verbal IQ of 119, a performance IQ of 120, and a full scale IQ of 120. These scores were congruent with her previous intellectual testing scores. While there were some elevations of her subscores, the examiner attributed some of this to Tina's familiarity with the tests through personal experience and her having recently taken a college-level course on psychological testing. However, she revealed the same basic pattern of inter- and intra-test scatter, and her thinking was still viewed as inefficient. Her score on the picture completion subtest of the WAIS was significantly elevated from her past score. The nature of the task on this subtest was to identify "missing parts" of pictures. Tina's responses suggested that she was more vigilant about her environment and, now having a penis, might be evidencing less castration anxiety. There was also the suggestion that she was moving from a more fantasy-dominated life to one in which action and acting out played a greater role.

Tina's TAT stories suggested that she was now more conscious of the themes suggested by the first Rorschach. She was feeling more estranged and alienated from people and despairing of ever having good interpersonal relations. Tina implied that her decision to have SRS might have been a bad one; post-surgery she felt more like a misfit. Her feelings of estrangement from people intensified. She was more aware of how she isolated her affect and employed rationalizations, and was growing increasingly depressed and coming to view her SRS as having failed to provide her with a means of personal salvation. Above all, Tina seemed preoccupied with her relationship with father. She felt that he infantilized her. She was frightened of his strength (that is, her perception of his strength) and power over her (which suggested an unresolved transference relationship to her therapist). Apparently SRS had abrogated her defensive identification with the aggressor. In effect, her real penis was not as powerful as her imaginary one. However, on the surface, Tina stated that she valued her new penis and verbalized satisfaction with the surgery. In spite of her ambivalence her therapist viewed her surgery as a success. The second Rorschach, however, revealed a breakdown in Tina's control system. While she did provide twenty-three responses, her F + % was 57 per cent (normal value, 80% < F + % < 90%), suggesting that her reality testing could, at times, be markedly impaired. Her extended F + % was, however, within normal limits (EF + % = 87%) and supported the initial findings of a subtle but intrusive thought disorder, which had a variable effect on her cognitive performance. At times she could appear organized and "stable," but at other times the word "stable" could hardly describe her state of disorganization and near fragmentation (all of which were actively contained by Tina's paranoid omnipotent control strategies, and concealed by her "tranquil" pose, or what I would now label her "blank self" defense). This defense has been described by Giovacchini as part of a transference relationship in "as-if" and pseudo "as-if" personalities who either had been treated as if they did not exist, were struggling to achieve identity, or experienced themselves as emotionally void ("a defensive superstructure to protect . . . against self-hatred and disruptive rage" (Giovacchini, 1975)).

Tina's responses suggested that she experienced herself as a strange, defective person, a creature with features who had a disturbed body image and an impaired self-concept. The anguish and turmoil evidenced in her previous testing were still there, but her depression was now surfacing, as was her potential for acting out. Her main concerns now focused on her inability to establish ego boundaries: objects and relationships tended to blur into or merge with each other; her images of self and other were vague and impressionistic. Moreover, her responses suggested an individual with a reservoir of fantasy and a vivid imagination which could, however, be harnessed in the service of her intellect. Her object relationships, which appeared superficially intact, were in fact impaired, being governed entirely by her passive-dependent, clinging-masochistic personality. On the Rorschach her human percepts were seen either as silhouettes or as poorly formed.

Of particular interest was Tina's use of transparent barriers to protect herself from intrusion. She perceived figures leaning on and reflected in a mirror, and "an odd animal standing on a plexiglass floor . . . and . . . a person looking up through the floor." While distancing her from a perceived threat, these responses also suggested a voyeuristic component of her object relationships by which she could participate with the feared and exciting object. There was also the suggestion that Tina needed to erect a primitive persona in order to conceal her true self and protect the inner core of her personality. On the other hand, SRS had apparently unleashed an exhibitionistic and narcissistic part of the self that had hitherto lain dormant. Her phallic exhibitionism and narcissism surfaced after her penis was surgically constructed. She seemed obsessed with looking and being looked at. The excitement of being observed was also frightening and led to her erecting a depersonalized defense. She oscillated between a need to be exposed and a need to be concealed. There was also the suggestion that she was adopting a more masochistic sexual role. Her defenses too were more thinly veiled and she could not protect herself from her surfacing sexual and aggressive impulses (which reflected what Kohut (1977) has called "byproducts" of a fragmenting or disintegrating self).

Tina's main defenses seemed to be splitting, denial, omnipotence, projection, projective identification, fantasy, and acting out. These rigid defenses allowed for her controlled, organized clinical self-presentation which others labeled as "stable." However, her use of denial had partially broken down and she seemed more vulnerable to primary process thinking. While she feared her aggressive impulses, she also nurtured them as a self-protective force against being intruded upon. In a magical way the new phallus was internalized as a symbolic shield which protected Tina from annihilation. Whereas the wish for a penis had previously held symbolic meaning, now Tina had a real penis. While the existence of the phallus signified the potential for aggression (which could both protect and destroy her), it also symbolized her separation conflict from her father, whom she now feared.

While one could now view Tina as more psychologically aware and available for psychological intervention, none of the dilemmas she faced at the prior testing situation had been resolved. Indeed, it appeared as if her conflicts had been exacerbated. More than ever she needed psychotherapy (a view borne out by her continued need to relate to her psychotherapist, and by a comment from one of her acquaintances that "Tina seemed more disturbed than ever").

Problems in Tina's "transsexual" diagnosis
How might one account for the discrepancies between the results of the clinical interview, which agreed with the patient's self-reports that Tina

was stable and rehabilitated post-SRS, and the results of the psychological testing? Was this an example of a *folie à deux* between therapist and patient? Or were the results of the psychological testing being taken too seriously?

The evaluation process, we may recall, was also not without some element of clinical disagreement. While the social worker was confused as to whether Tina was "homosexual" or "transsexual," the psychiatrist was convinced she was a "true transsexual." The shift from a state of confusion regarding Tina's gender identity to a certain belief that she was a "true transsexual" was made almost entirely on the basis of clinical interview material. This move also involved a shift in pronouns in which the evaluators now called the patient "he." The MMPI report, which I can only regard as inadequately interpreted, and the recommendation – "ill-advised" – against psychological intervention may have been guided more by the consultant's prior conceptions of homosexuality and transsexualism than by the clinical facts. At that point in Tina's evaluation no one requested complete psychological testing.

Tina's diagnostic evaluation posed some interesting yet common problems in the diagnosis of female transsexualism. The evaluation suggested how differing clinical views are resolved less out of an appreciation for the clinical data than out of deference to one's clinical biases and to the opinion of the primary or referring clinician. Above all, the question of whether Tina was a good candidate for SRS dominated the clinical inquiry. Tina's lack of noxious personality traits, coupled with the fact that she was not sociopathic, always reinforced the idea that she was a good surgical candidate. No one raised the question that her "health" and "stability" might suggest that she be provided more intensive psychotherapy in lieu of gender reassignment. One might argue that if the clinicians were interested in supporting her "health" and "stability," then SRS would have been contraindicated. The paradox is that gender clinics are usually organized in such a way as to find true transsexuals to refer for SRS and that the "healthier" female gender patients are the ones referred for SRS.

In the process of arriving at Tina's diagnosis and subsequent treatment, two clinical procedures seemed crucial: (1) Tina's immediate evaluation by the surgeon (a communication which surely supported the patient's fantasy that SRS was a viable solution to her problems, thereby increasing her demands for SRS); and (2) Tina's referral for hormone therapy (which may have communicated the therapist's hopelessness with regard to reconstructive psychotherapy). The implication was that, if therapy was useful at all, it could only be adjunctive to SRS, not curative in and of itself. Of interest was the fact that two males, the psychiatrist and the social worker, with different levels of education and training, had entirely different views of the case, with the medically trained clinician treating the patient's complaints medically.

The lack of appreciation that psychological testing could shed light on Tina's clinical condition was rather remarkable given the important role that psychological testing has traditionally played in the diagnostic process (Schafer, 1948) and the value it had for some members of the clinic. Two papers on the psychological testing of transsexuals supported the view of the importance of utilizing testing in the evaluation process (McCully, 1963; Hill, 1980). In trying to account for this discrepancy, I was struck by several lines of development among transsexual researchers. The most striking fact was that here we have a primary psychological disorder, transsexualism, which was being treated mostly by individuals with little or no psychiatric/psychological training, some of whom did not even have the clinical training to pose the necessary questions. This was not, however, the case in Tina's evaluation (which made the process all the more confusing).

Several extrinsic factors may also influence the diagnostic process. The initial reports of psychotherapy failures (without the parameters of "success" ever being operationalized) may have reinforced the idea among some clinicians that any form of psychotherapeutic approach to the transsexual was at best naive. There is also a cadre of gender clinicians who espoused a transsexual ideology which implied that anyone who refused to treat transsexuals medically–surgically was prolonging their suffering and persecuting them. The Hippocratic Oath has seldom been so willfully stretched and injudiciously applied as by the medical practitioner who used it to rationalize his/her justification for intervening in a medically aggressive way (so as not to prolong suffering) in the treatment of female transsexuals. I am not suggesting that a small number of select patients may not benefit from SRS; rather the rationale for medical-surgical intervention had been stretched far beyond its scientific basis and was in need of a new support system. It seemed, to turn on a Kierkegaardian phrase, that I was witnessing a "teleological suspension of the clinical" even among sophisticated clinicians.

Proposition 2: tomboyism and transsexualism

The second proposition stated in the *DSM* III criteria for female transsexualism was that evidence of "childhood masculinity in a girl-child increases the likelihood of transsexualism." While this proposition was being supported as a viable hypothesis by *DSM* III clinicians, one might well ask what the evidence was for such a claim. Are there "masculine" girls who grow up to be transsexual? What exactly is meant by "childhood masculinity" in a girl child "increases the likelihood of transsexualism"? How much "masculinity" makes adult transsexualism predictable? These are not moot questions since parents and pediatricians need to be informed about the nature of risks in childhood if appropriate interventions and referrals for treatment are to be made.

Although no serious-minded clinician would take issue with the idea that adult behavior has childhood antecedents, it was quite another matter to argue *ex post facto* that a disorder present in adulthood must also have been present in childhood (in the same way). Rekers et al. (1977) cite no fewer than eight studies in which "clinical and research evidence indicates that gender identity problems in childhood are strongly predictive of sexual orientation disturbance in adulthood and transsexualism in particular." A review of these studies revealed that none of the children were followed into adolescence (no less adulthood). The researchers assumed that these children were experiencing exactly what adult transsexuals had described; that is, adult transsexuals reported that as young children they had experienced severe gender identity and role conflicts. None of the researchers seemed to entertain the possibility that the childhood and adult disorders might be two separate diagnostic entities. It appeared, therefore, that almost all the evidence for proposition 2 came from two sources: studies of children with gender identity and role disturbances, and studies of adult transsexuals who recalled that as children they had exhibited gender identity and role disturbances. Until recently there have been no longitudinal studies following children with gender identity and role disturbances through adulthood. It seemed that evidence for the second proposition was not based on empirical data but on a speculative hypothesis. A review of the literature was quite sobering.

In point of fact, it was not until 1979, when the results of a longitudinal study on gender identity disorders was published, that an intelligent answer to the question could be provided (Money and Russo,

1979). In effect, the results of that study disproved proposition 2 as it related to boyhood antecedents of male transsexualism. Unfortunately, there were no studies which dealt with girlhood antecedents of female transsexualism.

In their longitudinal study of male children, Money and Russo (1979) reported on the findings of nine of eleven boys who as children were recognized as having severe gender identity and role disorders. The boys were studied up through their young adulthood. In order to qualify for their study the boys had to meet the following criteria: "exceptional interest in dressing in girls' clothing; avoiding play activities typical of boys and preferring those of girls; walking and talking more like girls than boys; and stating overtly the wish to be a girl." It was discovered that as adults "all are known to be homosexual or predominantly so. None is known to be either a transvestite or transsexual, though one formerly began the real-life test for transsexualism and quit after 6 weeks."

The results, though preliminary, suggested that for boys with an early childhood gender role and identity disturbance, there was a strong possibility that they would become homosexuals but *not* transvestites or transsexuals. In the light of these findings, the proposal of Rekers and his colleagues (1977) for a dual theory of childhood gender identity and role disturbances which is predictive of adult gender disorders needs to be reconsidered. In that study they had delineated two childhood gender disorders: a "gender identity disturbance" which was predictive of adult transsexualism, and a "gender behavior disturbance" which was predictive of adult transvestism. Their hypotheses were certainly called into question by Money and Russo's findings.

The hypothesis that tomboyism was predictive of transsexualism was also derived from studies of gender-disordered girls who expressed an interest in dressing in boy's clothing, avoided playing with girls and girls' games (preferring those of boys), had a high energy level and enjoyed physical activity, walked and talked more like boys, and who expressed a wish for a penis and to grow up and be a boy (Green, 1967, 1974). Tomboyism in girls was less stigmatizing, with the result that girls did not suffer the intense social and emotional rejection, humiliation, and shame experienced by boys with gender identity and role disorders – who were stigmatized and labeled as sissies. Consequently, girls were regarded as having an easier time giving up their gender-disordered behavior as they entered adolescence. Moreover, adults seemed less rejecting of tomboys, seeming at times to support them in their "male" quests. And a girl who wanted to wear male clothing could dress in unisex clothing without the social ridicule and shame a boy would experience when dressed in girls' clothing.

Female childhood identity disorders

The Diagnostic and Statistical Manual of Mental Disorders (1980) not only perpetuated the myth of proposition 2 but also added to the confusion. Under the heading "Psychosexual Disorders" *DSM* III listed "Gender Identity Disorder of Childhood" (302.60). For some reason the authors now chose to delineate a male and female component to this disorder (which they should have done for the adult disorders as well). Childhood gender identity disturbances were viewed as having the following features:

> The essential features are a persistent feeling of discomfort and inappropriateness in a child about his or her anatomic sex and the desire to be, or insistence that he or she is, of the other sex. In addition there is a persistent repudiation of the individual's own anatomic attributes. This is not merely the rejection of stereotypical sex role behavior as, for example, in "tomboyishness" in girls or "sissyish" behavior in boys, but rather a profound disturbance of the normal sense of maleness or femaleness. . . . For females the age of onset is also early, but most begin to acquiesce to social pressure during late childhood or adolescence and give up an exaggerated insistence on male activities and attire. A minority retain a masculine identification and some of these develop a homosexual arousal pattern. . . . Females who later develop this disorder have mothers who were apparently unavailable to them at a very early age, either psychologically or physically, because of illness or abandonment; the girl seems to make a compensatory identification with the father, which leads to the adoption of a male gender identity. . . . In a small number of cases, the disorder becomes continuous with transsexualism (pp. 264–5).

Several points need to be examined. First, the term "tomboyism" seemed to take on a new meaning. The authors of *DSM* III appeared to be using the word colloquially whereas it had a specific meaning for all the researchers on childhood gender identity disturbances. Second, the comment that "the disorder becomes continuous with Transsexualism" must be viewed as gratuitous. Indeed, in a personal communication with Richard Green he has stated that there was no evidence that a childhood gender identity disturbance is predictive of transsexualism (but it was strongly indicative of future sexual orientation, that is, homosexuality). Clearly, while there was some evidence that child and adult gender identity disorders are continuous, there were no longitudinal studies showing that children with gender disorders necessarily grow up to become transsexuals (see Eber, 1982).

The prevalence and incidence of childhood gender identity disturbances are unknown. Some practitioners, however, have estimated an incidence of one case in every 100,000 children (Rekers et al., 1977) or similar to that reported for adult gender identity disorders. This is probably a conservative figure.

The *DSM* III diagnostic criteria for childhood gender identity disturbances separated the male and female components. The criteria for female childhood gender identity disturbances were reported to be as follows:

A Strongly and permanently stated desire to be a boy, or insistence that she is a boy (not merely a desire for any perceived cultural advantages from being a boy).
B Persistent repudiation of female anatomic structures, as manifested by at least one of the following repeated assertions:
  1 that she will grow up to become a man (not merely in role);
  2 that she is biologically unable to become pregnant;
  3 that she will not develop breasts;
  4 that she has no vagina;
  5 that she has, or will grow, a penis (pp. 265–6).
C Onset of the disturbance before puberty.

Unfortunately, there was no attempt to delineate each of the above issues along developmental lines. Indeed, there are considerable cognitive and emotional differences among children between the ages of 1 and 12 (both inter- and intra-agemate groupings). None of these differences was taken into account by the *DSM* III diagnostic schema; a crucial finding, since profound gender identity and role disturbances have been noted even during the second year of life (Galenson et al., 1973; Rekers and Lovaas, 1974).

Clinical acceptance of the second proposition (which is not warranted by the facts) would have important consequences for the treatment of girls with childhood gender identity disturbances, especially since we are in the midst of a revolution in sexual roles and stereotypes which is having the most dramatic effect on women in our society. Whatever the relationship between a child and adult's gender identity or role disturbance, the treatment of choice should *always* be psychotherapy, and if possible treatment should begin in childhood. Once the child enters adolescence the opportunity for acting out and gaining support from deviant subcultural peer groups changes the shape of the disorder, thereby necessitating an entirely different psychotherapeutic approach to the treatment of female transsexualism. While it is true that most girls outgrow tomboyism and psychological intervention is not necessary, the reverse is true for girls with severe gender identity disturbances.

In summary, while there was no evidence that childhood gender identity and role disturbances would necessarily lead to adult transvestism or transsexualism, these disorders were serious enough to warrant psychological intervention and were predictive of later adult homosexuality. One cannot rule out future longitudinal studies which could demonstrate a causal link between adult and child gender identity and role disorders.

Problems in diagnosis: an overview

The diagnosis of transsexualism has also been influenced by behavior therapists, who have played a pivotal role in most gender identity clinics. While behaviorists have successfully treated some transsexual patients, they have also promised more than they could deliver, at the same time avoiding some of the moral issues around treatment itself by ignoring the wider issues about society's role in transsexualism. Moreover, by setting up psychoanalysis and psychotherapy as straw men the behaviorally oriented clinicians have made it seem as if dynamically trained clinicians had nothing to offer the female transsexual but continued failures in the psychotherapeutic sphere (a point also maintained by Benjamin, 1966). Since behaviorists were not trained to give projective tests, no less to appreciate the importance and usefulness of projective testing, it was not surprising that they viewed projective testing as, at best, irrelevant.

Sociologists have also contributed to our misunderstanding of diagnostic issues in transsexualism. The insightful contributions of sociologists to understanding the phenomenon of role transition and the female's passing in the male role have been eclipsed by their confusion of the transsexual phenomenon with the wider issues of cultural relativism, sex role parity, and "equal rights" for sexual minorities. By failing to recognize the psychological underpinnings of transsexualism (which needed to be addressed by psychological methods of treatment), sociologists thereby reinforced the notion that transsexualism was simply a variant sexual behavior which was more a social than a psychological problem. The sociologists' perspective, however, has sharpened our awareness of the phenomenon of passing; stigmatization of the transsexual; the role progression from homosexuality, transvestism, to transsexualism; and theories of symbolic interactionism as they relate to society's homo- and trans-sexual phobias.

Finally, the refusal by some psychoanalysts to appreciate the non-delusional aspects of transsexualism and to understand the relation of preoedipal and developmental issues to transsexual symptomology, have led to further problems in diagnosis. Too many female transsexual patients have initially been referred to analysts only to be labeled as psychotic and refused adequate treatment. However, there have been a number of scholarly analysts (Sperling, 1964; Stoller, 1968; Limentani, 1979; Volkan, 1979) who have challenged conceptual biases and opened up the field of transsexualism to serious inquiry.

All of these professions have contributed to the continued failure by mental health specialists to adequately diagnose and evaluate the female transsexual patient. It was not surprising, then, that the intersection of biases of so many traditions has paralyzed thinking in the diagnosis of female transsexualism, and led to a lack of awareness of the importance of intensive psychological testing and psychotherapy in the overall evaluation and treatment plan for the female transsexual.

Even with regard to such universally accepted mental disorders as schizophrenia and neurosis, different clinicians may disagree on a patient's diagnosis. While some clinicians have challenged the use of clinical interviewing alone in differential diagnosis, there has also been disagreement among psychologists about the validity of their measuring instruments and which tests one should use in a clinical examination.

Moreover, when the data of psychological tests are used for predictive purposes, beyond their intended role as assessment instruments, it is unlikely that the clinician will be able to make predictions beyond chance.

How, then, are clinicians with diverse levels of training and different educational backgrounds, using diverse clinical assessment approaches and instruments, able to arrive at the diagnosis of "true transsexual" with such a degree of certainty? The issues are no less complex when one considers the fact that it was not until the spring of 1980 that the diagnosis of transsexualism was even included in the American Psychiatric Association's *Diagnostic and Statistical Manual of Mental Disorders* (*DSM* III), even taking into account the APA's abandonment of psychodynamics in favor of descriptive symptomology.

Clinical psychiatric diagnosis must be viewed as an ongoing process involving the interplay of many factors over a long period of time. While no one factor should have ultimate ascendancy, neither should one omit data crucial to the diagnostic process (such as the results of psychological testing). The analysis of Tina's "transsexual" diagnosis illustrated a central problem in the diagnosis of the female transsexual: the curious omission of relevant information which might have altered the entire course of her diagnosis and treatment. From my perspective, the results of psychological testing and intensive psychoanalytically oriented psychotherapy (Lothstein, 1977b; Lothstein and Levine, 1981) provided some of the most pertinent clinical information on the phenomenology of Tina's female "transsexualism." This issue will assume even greater significance as we investigate those cases of female transsexualism in which the "stability" of the patient is not a primary "given."

Prior to *DSM* III only a few select clinicians had widespread clinical experience with so-called transsexuals, and even fewer had experience with female transsexuals. Becoming an expert in transsexualism meant that one had to apprentice oneself to a clinician whose practice included large numbers of patients with gender identity and role disturbances, familiarize oneself with the literature on transsexualism, and perhaps interact with those diversely trained and educated clinicians who met every two years to discuss their work in the evaluation, diagnosis, and treatment of transsexualism. Most transsexual research has been conducted within the context of a gender identity clinic (which was often attached to a surgery program). In some cases, the director of the clinic was the surgeon. However, even in those instances where the clinic director was neither a surgeon nor a physician the assumption that some transsexual patients could benefit from SRS was widely held.

One may ask what does constitute a clinically competent evaluation of a patient with a severe gender identity and role disturbance, and who is a self-labeled female transsexual. The fact that the female patient seems to diagnose her own transsexualism should not deter the clinician from providing the patient with a complete and thorough psychological and medical evaluation.

The fact that many patients refuse to pay for such an evaluation has probably been the greatest single obstacle to their receiving appropriate help. In some cases the patients may have been coached to reject the help of the mental health professionals (who themselves may back off from a transsexual evaluation because they do not feel clinically competent to diagnose transsexualism).

It is not surprising, then, that a search of the literature on the psychological testing of transsexuals revealed only a few in depth reports (McCully, 1963; Hill, 1980). In order to evaluate the female transsexual patient competently, the clinician needs to have received extensive training in projective testing, and be well versed in several areas of theory, including self psychology; psychoanalytic psychopathology; object relations theory; behavior and learning theory. The task of evaluation/treatment must be approached from a broad-based psychobiological and psychodynamic perspective.

In the chapter on theory I will show how my clinical research with female transsexuals has led me to conceptualize their problems not in terms of sexual disorder but in terms of a profound psychological disturbance of their self-system. For this reason the utilization of a purely sexological approach to treatment misses the core problem of the female transsexual.

Summary

In this chapter I have presented some of the historical issues of diagnosis in female transsexualism. Drawing on the insights of Krafft-Ebing, Freud, Hirschfeld, and Benjamin, I discussed the major issues regarding the need to recognize clinically the existence of the diagnosis of transsexualism.

Focusing on the new diagnostic nomenclature for transsexualism as discussed by *DSM* III, I called into question the whole diagnostic process for transsexualism. Specifically, I challenged two major propositions regarding female transsexualism which have profoundly influenced clinical thinking: the first related to the so-called stability of the female transsexual; the second related to the continuity between childhood and adult manifestations of female transsexualism. Both propositions turned out to be false.

Using the case of Tina as an example, I dissected the diagnostic process and showed how important clinical decisions were made, while important data which might have altered the course of Tina's diagnosis were not taken into account. I argued that this is a common practice among gender identity clinicians who evaluate female transsexuals — this practice needs to be changed.

My discussion of the current thinking on childhood gender identity and role disturbances suggests that research in this area is still quite primitive.

In the following chapter I will present clinical material from fifty-three women who applied to the CWRU gender identity clinic for a transsexual evaluation, and case material on four female transsexuals in depth. The data will provide the basis for establishing a foundation and framework for a comprehensive theory of female transsexualism.

Chapter 4
The phenomenology of female transsexualism: clinical cases

In the introductory chapter I pointed out how our thinking about female transsexualism has been guided by a number of myths which have been elevated to the status of "truths." In Chapters 2 and 3 some of these myths were explored critically through an historical analysis of the phenomenon of female transsexualism. So far, our explorations have revealed that female transsexualism is not a unitary phenomenon but a number of diverse gender disorders involving profound psychological impairment, and a final common pathway — a request for sex reassignment surgery.

In this chapter I will describe the Case Western Reserve University research project on gender identity disorders and then present, (1) the group data for all fifty-three women who were evaluated for transsexualism; and (2)   four in depth case histories of women who were extensively evaluated and treated for their "transsexualism." All the women in our study viewed themselves as transsexuals and believed that sex reassignment surgery would cure their gender problems. It is hoped that the clinical case material presented in this section will facilitate our understanding of the phenomenon of female transsexualism. Finally, I will critically explore the various methods of investigation employed so that the reader will have a better understanding of how our methods of inquiry influence our findings.

The Case Western Reserve Gender Identity Clinic

It has been almost a decade since I was asked to evaluate my first transsexual patient. Indeed, my initial involvement with transsexual research began quite fortuitously. By chance a colleague, Dr. Stephen

Levine, asked if I would evaluate psychologically an aging heterosexual man who wanted to change his sex. Our mutual psychological-psychiatric explorations with this patient led to the formation of a study group on patients with gender identity problems. We were both interested in how transsexualism related to the larger issues of ego identity and the formation of the self. Moreover, we were curious to discover if there was a relationship between early childhood issues of sexual identity and the later establishment of core gender identity. All of these issues seemed to be related to the more fundamental one of how one developed self and gender identity from both a normal and an abnormal perspective.

Shortly after announcing to our colleagues that we were interested in evaluating transsexuals (in 1974), we were inundated with referrals, and learned that another hospital in Cleveland was also screening patients for transsexual surgery. In the course of the next two years we formed an alliance between Case Western Reserve University's Department of Psychiatry and an affiliated county hospital, Cleveland Metropolitan General. By the fall of 1975 we joined both staffs to form the Case Western Reserve University Gender Identity Clinic.

The gender clinic consisted of approximately ten interdisciplinary clinicians, including psychiatrists, clinical psychologists, a social worker, a nurse-sociologist, and trainees from various disciplines, who met weekly for $1\frac{1}{2}$ hours to present new cases and evaluate and treat, in long-term individual and group therapy (using various theoretical and treatment strategies), patients who were self-labeled transsexuals. In addition, we established a medical liaison which included two endocrinologists, an internist, and three surgeons. While the medical staff did not routinely attend our clinic meetings, they were considered part of the diagnostic team. At various times a number of lawyers also assisted our patients with their legal difficulties.

All of our patients went through a similar evaluation process. A typical evaluation included the following procedures:

1 The patient contacted our social worker, who screened the patient's complaints and, if necessary, set up an appointment with the patient.
2 The patient was interviewed by the clinical social worker for a minimum of one hour. The social worker filled out a referral form on the patient (including demographic data, insurance, and psychological type questions).

87

3 The patient filled out the Minnesota Multiphasic Personality Inventory (MMPI) and a Self Administering Questionnaire which I devised. This included a social history questionnaire; sentence completion test; kinetic draw-a-family test; modified Bender Gestalt test; the Yale Preliminary Test of Intelligence; and selected items from the Wechsler Adult Intelligence Scale and the Wechsler Memory Scale.

4 The patient was given a brochure explaining our program: the services offered; the expenses to be incurred; and the obligations that patients were required to meet before they could be considered for surgery. For several years our evaluation costs were modest — free for indigent patients, and on a sliding fee scale for others. Eventually, we established an evaluation fee of approximately $250.00. This modest charge covered all of the above work plus a minimum of five more hours of evaluation by opposite-sexed clinicians and the staff of his/her case.

5 The case was presented at one of the weekly meetings and assigned to a primary and a secondary clinician (if possible they were of opposite sexes).

6 The primary clinician interviewed the patient and his/her significant family members, friends, and spouse or partner. Usually four hours of interviewing were involved.

7 The patient was then interviewed for approximately one hour by the secondary clinician, whose main role was to provide a second opinion — usually one from the perspective of an opposite-sexed clinician.

8 The case was then presented to the clinic committee and discussed at length (usually one session was needed).

9 The results of the conferences were presented to the patient. Acceptance into the clinic meant that the patient had to become engaged in long-term intensive psychotherapy (individual and group) with one of the therapists usually being the primary clinician. No time limit was placed on the therapy, though the patients were generally in therapy for several years.

10 During the treatment phase the therapists periodically reported on their patients and updated any changes in patient status.

11 Once the minimum time for hormonal or surgical referral was passed, it was up to the primary clinician to decide when, or if, to present his/her patient to the clinic committee for

hormonal or surgical treatment.

12   Prior to presentation for hormone treatment the patient was referred for a full battery of psychological testing.

13   The clinic scheduled a time to discuss the patient's request for hormone therapy. If approved, the patient was referred to our internist and endocrinologist, who were advised of our decision to approve the patient for hormone therapy. It was up to the physician, however, to make the final judgment. If there were any medical contraindications for the use of hormones, it was the physician's responsibility to explain this to the patient.

14   The patient continued in psychotherapy and was periodically examined by the endocrinologist.

15   When the therapist and patient arrived at a decision that surgery was recommended, the therapist presented the case to the clinic committee. If the committee agreed that surgery might be indicated, the patient was required to meet with the entire clinic committee and to present her/his case. The interview usually lasted one hour.

16   The committee met for an unspecified amount of time to consider the patient's request for sex reassignment. In some cases it was granted directly. In other cases more tests were recommended to facilitate our decision-making.

17   The patient was appraised of the clinic's decision. If surgery was indicated the patient was referred to the surgeon for an evaluation. Once again, if the surgeon found anything that contraindicated surgery, the final decision to operate rested with him/her.

18   The patient had to agree to respond to our need to have her/him available for interviewing and filling out follow-up questionnaires throughout the post-operative period, and for an indeterminate amount of time after surgery.

19   The patient was provided specific counseling around the issue of surgery; the nursing team was prepared for the patient's entry on to the general surgical ward; and the primary clinician followed the patient throughout the course of hospitalization.

20   After surgery the patient continued in psychotherapy and the primary clinician periodically reported to the clinic about the patient's condition. In addition, a schedule was set up for interviewing the patient and filling out the post-operative questionnaires.

21 Throughout the evaluation it was the responsibility of the primary clinician (who was usually the individual or group therapist) to act as liaison for the patient, helping in her/his social and environmental adjustment (e.g. with legal, family, and medical difficulties).

While this list may seem overwhelming, our clinic committee viewed it as containing the bare minimum requirements for providing a comprehensive evaluation and treatment program for the self-labeled transsexual. Because we lacked funding, and functioned out of at least two hospitals, we were never able to set up a central filing system. In some cases important data on a patient were lost. By the third year of operation we systematically recorded patient information on a standardized intake sheet, and also recorded systematic information on a standardized psychological form constructed by Dr. Levine. These sources of information were periodically used by researchers in reviewing our diagnostic intake procedures.

Throughout the evaluation process we periodically reviewed our work with each patient and upgraded both our understanding of the patient's problems and his/her diagnosis. When feasible each of our patients was given a psychiatric diagnosis, a personality diagnosis, a psychometric diagnosis (on the MMPI), and a psychological diagnosis based on a full battery of psychological tests. Many patients had multiple diagnoses in each category. In some cases we disagreed among ourselves as to what the patient's final diagnosis should be. This variability in diagnosis reflected several different interacting processes including: the need not to label a person prematurely as a transsexual (nor to use that as the sole diagnosis); our different levels of training; our different theoretical orientations; our various commitments to diagnostic nomenclature; and our willingness to tolerate ambiguity by entertaining multiple diagnoses which reflected changes in the patient over a period of time.

Female transsexuals: the group

Over an eight-year period fifty-three female transsexuals were evaluated for sex change surgery. This group comprised forty-eight whites and five blacks (9 per cent of the total). The data reported below came from numerous sources, including clinical interview material, psychological testing, and the patient's written material. Given the nature of our clinic's emphasis on providing good clinical care, and the idiosyncracies of various clinicians and patients, we were unable to collect systematic data for all of the patients. However, all of the percentages reported below included 100 per cent response for demographic information and at least 80 per cent for interview-oriented questions.

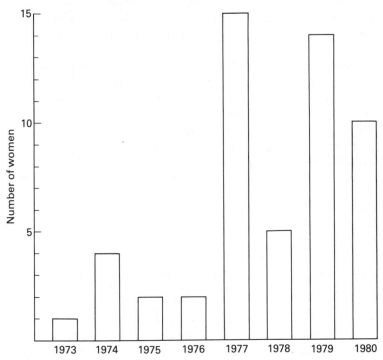

Figure 4.1 *Female transsexual applicants to CWRU (per annum)*

At the time of intake the average age of the patients was 23.7 years (range 14 to 43 years). During the same time we evaluated 147 males, or a ratio of about 3:1 males to females. It was clear that over the years an increasing number of females were applying to our clinic for sex reassignment surgery (see Figure 4.1). By 1980 we were seeing about eleven new women patients a year. In a study presented by the Stanford University gender identity clinic (Dixen, 1981), of 767 applicants 288 (38 per cent) were women (average age 27.3 years). This study suggested a male: female ratio of 1.6:1 respectively. While earlier reports had suggested a ratio of anywhere from 10:1 to 6:1 males to females, it was clear that the male:female ratios were reaching parity as more and more females applied for transsexual evaluation.

Because of our gender clinic's location in the inner city of Cleveland, the majority of our patients came from lower socioeconomic classes (Hollingshead IV and V; see Hollingshead and Redlich, 1958). However, about 30 per cent of the patients were not from the lower socioeconomic groups, and a number of patients came from out of state or from suburban and rural areas.

Many patients had already assumed male names prior to being evaluated by our clinic, including such nicknames as "Bird," "Moose," "Wild Boy," "Sucker," "Snoopy," and "Frenchy." One patient referred to herself as "Bob-Mom," thereby fusing her male and female identities. The psychodynamic aspects of a female transsexual's decision to choose a new name have been related to several factors, including separation-individuation difficulties, problems with object relations, a need to resolve conflict over one's self-identity, etc. (Althof, 1980). In a preliminary paper presented on the sociological and psychological characteristics of thirty-nine of these patients, it was reported that "a larger proportion of females had a second name at the time of referral" (Shen and Jones, 1981).

The women in our group had an average of an eleventh-grade education, though five of them had graduated from college, one had a postgraduate degree, and three had associate degrees. Approximately one third of the women were unemployed and on some form of relief. Those who were employed had a range of jobs including X-ray technician, word processing specialist, clerk, jockey, dishwasher, school teacher, barmaid, security guard, mechanic, Internal Revenue Service employee, truck driver. One woman admitted to being a prostitute functioning within the lesbian community.

Seven patients (13 per cent) were first born; six patients (11 per cent) were last born; and two (3 per cent) were only children. There were no clear-cut birth order effects. However, the patients did come from large families, averaging about 3.5 children per family. About one quarter of the patients who admitted to any religious affiliation said they were Catholic. Two patients were Jewish, and two other patients came from families in which one of the parents was Jewish. There were no Oriental or Hispanic women in the study.

While the majority of the women stated that they began crossdressing around age 5, at least twelve patients (23 per cent) began crossdressing in adolescence (range 12–19 years). Because of the nature of data gathering it was often difficult to know what this meant for the patient. Clearly, some forms of crossdressing and thoughts of becoming a man did not occur until a woman was well into adolescence. Three patients (approximately 6 per cent) stated that they became aroused sexually while crossdressing. For most of the women crossdressing was relaxing and made them feel natural and at ease. Once in male clothing their anxiety decreased and their confidence increased.

Almost half of the patients reported early childhood histories in which child abuse, including violence and neglect, was common and losses, separations, and abandonments the norm. Four patients reported being physically abused by both parents, while at least twelve women (23 per cent) reported incestuous experiences, including two who gave birth to their own fathers' babies. The actual level of incest was probably underreported. Moreover, at least 62 per cent of the patients ($n = 33$) reported early childhood situations in which abandonments, divorces, affairs, deaths, physical injuries, and poverty played an important role in the instability of their families and in the poor organization of their social relationships.

Only two of the women had experienced delayed menses; one reporting extremely regular but painful menses. One woman described herself as asexual, two women never had sexual relationship with anyone, while the majority of women had their first voluntary sexual relationship with another woman. When responding to sexually oriented questions, half the patients reported that in their sexual fantasies (or day and night dreams) they viewed themselves as male. Approximately half the group reported also having some sexual experience with men. In this sense they did not follow the so-called homosexual pattern described in the research.

Seven woman (13 per cent) reported a bisexual pattern of sexual functioning. At least nine of the woman had married and four had children. In two of the cases the children were being reared by other relatives and were unavailable for interview. The other two patients had three children, one of whom (a boy aged 10) had a severe character disorder and was in treatment; another boy (16) had spent three years in a state hospital for paranoid schizophrenia, and his sister, while quite young (aged 5), seemed to be hyperactive and possibly hypomanic (having an affective disorder).

Almost half of the women were suicidal at one point in their lives. Some of them had made serious suicide attempts: by taking pills, throwing herself in front of a car, attempted hanging, and slitting wrists and throat. In spite of these suicidal gestures and attempts only one of the women actually killed herself. Indeed, of the 200 patients (including 147 men and fifty-three women) only one man's suicide attempt succeeded — he shot himself in the stomach. In that case the patient had never made the full transsexual switch. Approximately one quarter of the female patients had also been psychiatrically hospitalized, and a few had had multiple hospitalizations.

Of the fifty-three women, full psychiatric diagnoses were obtained for forty-six. The other seven patients had MMPI diagnoses, but they had not remained in treatment long enough for a thoroughgoing diagnosis to be established. Most of the diagnoses resulted from a consensus opinion of our clinic staff. There were some cases, however, in which a patient's diagnosis represents my reinterpretation of the clinical material. This was necessitated because some primary therapists who had initially refused to diagnose a patient for fear of their being stigmatized, eventually "diagnosed" her as "normal," provided that she did not reveal any overt psychosis or bizarre behavior (apart from a wish for sex reassignment). While I could not accept such a labeling schema, my eventual diagnostic label was, in most cases, closer to the results of psychological testing than to those of clinical interviewing. Table 4.1 summarizes these findings. Using my schema, about 40 per cent of the patients were diagnosed as either psychotic, borderline, or schizophrenic.

Clearly, it would be beneficial if we could reconstruct a composite picture of the average female transsexual. The data, however, suggest that female transsexualism is the outcome of many different converging paths, no single one of which can be isolated and depicted as the essence of female transsexualism. On the other hand, what emerges is anything but a "stable" picture of those females who identify as transsexuals. Indeed, we are presented with a picture of family life in which disorganization, chaos, and overstimulation were common occurrences. Some of these families exhibited outright violence, engaging in child abuse and incest. A majority of the women described their early childhoods as characterized by themes of abandonment, loss, separation, and death. Most of the women had little love for their parents (though there were exceptions); were generally depressed, and experienced considerable

Table 4.1 *Psychological testing diagnoses of 53 female transsexuals*

Passive aggressive	3
Impulsive narcissistic personality	6
Character pathology (undifferentiated)	4
Character neurosis	10
Schizoid/paranoid	4
Borderline personality	10
Psychotic	1
Schizophrenic	9
No available diagnosis	6
Total	53

emotional turmoil and severe personality disturbances. Many of them also seemed to have chronic adjustment problems, and almost 40 per cent could be described – by any standards – as having profound psychological distress.

A group psychological profile never gives us the necessary details to identify any single member. For this reason it is imperative to look closely at the lives of individual women who grew up to identify as female transsexuals. What problems did they face? What patterns emerged which might shed light on the etiology of their disorder? It is hoped that the following case histories will provide answers to some of these questions. The cases are presented in order to provide a more intensive view of how a variety of women, throughout their life cycles, choose a certain kind of gender adaptation to their chronic gender dysphoria. While all of the cases have been altered to protect the identities of the patients, nothing of significance has been omitted which would alter one's understanding of these cases.

The impulsive psychopath: Barbara/Brian

It was hard to believe that the cocky, self-assured "male" sitting in the waiting room was really a biological female. Introducing herself as Brian, she demanded hormones and surgery and stated: "I'm a man trapped inside a woman's body. I'm in desperate need to match my body with my mind, the real me inside. I will not be a complete person, I am just a freak until then." At her side was an attractive, feminine-appearing woman whom she introduced as "my wife, Alice."

For the past two years Barbara (age 28) had assumed a male identity, dressing full-time as a male and living and working as a male. She sported a ducktail hairdo, dressed in an exaggerated male style, and related to everyone as a man. Recently she had taken the name Brian and was in the process of getting a legal name change. She was currently raising her two children (Richard, 13; Arlene, 2) and living with her "common law wife."

Throughout her interviews Barbara had a broad smile on her face. She appeared confident, optimistic, and garrulous, fielding all questions magnificently and always having an answer. On the surface Barbara seemed unconflicted about her "maleness." She was, however, puzzled by my questions. Claiming that I was the first person who did not accept her story at face value, she felt I mistrusted her or, at least, misunderstood her. She was right. As I learned more about her life style and family history, my initial scepticism was vindicated.

Barbara was a middle child. Her sister Frances, four years older than Barbara, had been born out of wedlock. When Barbara was four county welfare removed Frances from the home. After an unsuccessful placement in a juvenile center, Frances was placed in a series of foster homes until the age of 16, when she returned to the family. Frances was reportedly abused by mother, and was also an unmanageable child. Barbara stated that Frances crossdressed as a male, was actively homo-sexual, and also had a wish to be a man. There was also the suggestion that Frances and Barbara were sexually involved with one another. Barbara described her sister as having abandoned her Italian Catholic roots and as being currently married to a black man and living a bisexual, promiscuous, chaotic life.

Susan, the youngest of the three sisters, was born just about the time Frances was removed from the home. As for each of the siblings, no one knew who her real father was. Susan's birth coincided with the apex of the family's chaos. Mother, who completely rejected Susan (while embracing Barbara as her favorite child), firmly sowed the seeds of Susan's hatred, jealousy, and envy, such that Susan has openly sworn to seek vengeance and kill Barbara. During an interview, Susan viciously attacked Barbara's homosexual life style. Her behavior suggested a volatile, homophobic, unstable person, who was bent on vengeance.

Indeed, at the mere mention of the word homosexual, her eyes flashed and she became irrational and paranoid.

Barbara remembered very little of her early childhood. She was told that her father, of Italian ancestry, had abandoned the family prior to her birth (but there are no records that mother ever married the man). Mother, an impulsive, paranoid, disorganized woman, told Barbara that during her pregnancy with her she prayed for a boy and was depressed and disappointed when she delivered another girl baby. Mother's pregnancy with Barbara was unplanned; the "husband," a chronic alcoholic, reacted to the pregnancy by beating his wife viciously. Immediately after the birth the "father" abandoned the family. Barbara's birth was uneventful and she was named after mother's sister, a warm, indulgent, overly dependent woman who enjoyed nurturing hurt animals and caring for strays (traits which became important parts of Barbara's personality).

Barbara recalls being told she was an active, friendly, lovable, cuddly, but demanding baby. Her earliest memories included cutting her thumb at age 2; feeling sad when Frances was removed from the home; and witnessing an accident in which her stepfather sawed off two of the fingers on his left hand. She also recalled that mother was chronically drunk and often stayed away from home for days. When Barbara was a year old a new man moved into the house. He would soon become her stepfather and assume full responsibility for raising her. A passive-dependent, emotionally empty, emasculated man, he was Barbara's source of protection against her mother.

Barbara's mother came from a family in which child abuse, neglect, and alcoholism were rampant. The intergenerational problems were clear cut. The maternal grandmother, like the mother, was a chaotic, disorganized, alcoholic woman; she abused her daughter (Barbara's mother) and abandoned her, dying when the mother was 10. The maternal grandfather, an ineffectual man, never remarried and lived with his daughter until he died of tuberculosis when Barbara was 9 years old.

Mother was the oldest of four siblings in a family which included two boys and a girl. The siblings were described as being "at each other's throats"; the family relationships were characterized by intense jealousies, rivalries, and sadomasochistic interactions. Mother had been designated as the "tough," "mean" sibling, a tomboy who was always ready for a fight, and who was violently anti-homosexual. Barbara described her mother as always ready to throw a punch. She was a nagging, complaining woman who shouted obscenities and behaved erratically and eccentrically. While the mother refused to talk to anyone at our clinic, her phone conversations, letters, and meetings with the nurses suggested that she had an undiagnosed paranoid schizophrenia. She was an intrusive, impulsive, dangerous woman who periodically stormed into her daughter's house and took over the family, insisting on bathing her adolescent grandson and inspecting his bowel movements. At times Barbara had to call the police to have mother removed from the house. Mother would then stand on the street shouting up obscenities to her daughter (calling her a "whore," "cunt," and "lesbian").

Throughout Barbara's childhood, mother had a series of tandem relationships which exposed Barbara to confusing sexual and aggressive experiences. Mother virtually abandoned Barbara to the stepfather and was either out partying with men, engaged in alcoholic binges, or at work (where she was employed as a salesperson). Barbara recalled feeling constantly abandoned by mother, but also feeling the need to cling to her. The stepfather, Alan, became Barbara's core parental object.

Alan, a janitor by trade, was an emotional and physical cripple. He was deaf, alcoholic, impotent, and partially disabled (having sawn off two fingers). Barbara was, however, deeply attached to him. While Alan raised Barbara as his own child, he related to her as a boy, calling her by a male name and referring to her as "my son." He not only encouraged Barbara's masculine strivings, but may have envied them. In spite of his faults Barbara admired and respected him, modeling her "maleness" after the stepfather. It was not until Barbara was 16 that she was told that Alan was not her real father. When Alan died Barbara was suicidally depressed and began to entertain transsexual wishes, which suggested that his death was a major stressor and precipitant of her wishes to become a man.

Barbara's biological father was reportedly a violent, abusive man whom mother despised. Mother either refused to answer Barbara's questions about him (making her feel guilty), or implied that there was a horrible secret about his life which could never be revealed. Mother's behavior increased Barbara's curiosity about her "real" father. While Barbara failed in all of her attempts to locate the father, she never abandoned her psychological quest to know him. Indeed, she over-idealized him and became self-absorbed in daydreams about him. Once she even "believed" that she saw him on television (in what appeared to be a combination wish-fulfillment and delusion). She pictured her father as an omnipotent, loving man who would eventually rescue her from mother. At another juncture, Barbara reported a hypnogogic reverie in which she "saw" and "spoke to" her father.

During childhood Barbara had identified as a tomboy, a behavioral pattern which was reinforced by the stepfather. She did, however, have girlfriends and played girls' games (recalling that she wanted to be near her girlfriends because of the intense sexual feelings she had for them). She also described feeling uneasy around girls because of her wish to be a boy. Barbara could also easily integrate into boys' play and took pride in her prowess, courage, and athletic ability. She enjoyed physical activity and other typically "male" patterns of play. During her girlhood Barbara also developed an intense interest in art and a goal to become a commercial artist.

Barbara's crossdressing, which began around age 5, was done secretively. When she wore men's clothes she felt relaxed, comfortable, and protected. Around the age of 8 Barbara entertained the idea that she really had been a male as a fetus, but that when she turned over to be born, her penis inverted and formed a vagina. When she shared this fantasy with mother she received support for her wish/delusion: mother broke down and cried, admitting that she had desperately wanted a son, and wondered if perhaps Barbara was right and she had been born a boy!

In spite of mother's covert support of Barbara's "maleness" she found her daughter's actual masculine role orientation repugnant (perhaps because of the implied incestual threat, which was expressed as a homophobia). Indeed, mother would beat Barbara whenever she caught her wearing male clothes and playing boys' games. However, while mother bought her frilly, feminine dresses she never encouraged Barbara to wear them. During her ninth year the maternal grandfather died – a death which must have stressed Barbara considerably as she reported that her sexual feelings for girls (including a crush on a female teacher), and her intense gender envy for boys were experienced as "beyond my control." Her chaotic sexuality and violent rages during girlhood set the stage for her chaotic adolescent development.

When Barbara was 12 she had her first homosexual experience. During preadolescence, however, she had engaged in extensive petting and masturbation with both boys and girls. Her sexual drive was experienced as uncontrollable, completely dominating her life, involving her in compulsive daily masturbation accompanied by rituals and intrusive sexual fantasies. These practices and fantasies interfered with her ability to concentrate at school. Indeed, from the fourth grade on her school work had deteriorated. By the ninth grade she could no longer sit at a desk, and quit school. Her increased gender anxiety coincided with two events: Frances's return to the family and her first period. With the onset of menses Barbara felt crushed. There was no turning back; she had to accept an inevitable, but harsh, reality – she was a girl!

Barbara was horrified by her breast development. In an attempt to stave off her emerging femaleness, Barbara bound her breasts with an Ace bandage and began wearing a shirt and tie. In a blind rage she was fighting her biology, a battle which she could never win. The final blow came when the school authorities forced her to wear a skirt or dress to school. Feeling totally defeated she succumbed to her inner male feeling and withdrew from school, stuffing herself with food until she gained almost seventy-five pounds and appeared massive and bloated. She experienced what is known as a masked or smiling depression, marked by psychogenic arthritis and the employment of massive denial.

Having dropped out of school Barbara, now 14 years old, stayed at home masturbating compulsively and engaging in impulsive homosexual activity (entertaining an unending stream of girls in her bedroom). Mother's reaction was to become violent, humiliating and harassing Barbara about her homosexuality. By threatening to abandon Barbara, she controlled her daughter, coercing her into a submissive-masochistic, clinging-dependent relationship with mother. No matter how valiantly Barbara attempted to thwart her homosexual desires, she was unsuccessful. The choice was clear: either Barbara continued to identify as a homosexual and was abandoned by her mother, or she abandoned her homosexual orientation and received her mother's love. Again she was forced to do battle with her biological strivings. Desperately yearning for mother's love, and driven by her homosexual orientation, Barbara arrived at a "solution," a solution which permitted her to avow openly her secret male wishes. She hoped that if mother was convinced that she was a male then mother would view her daughter's sexual feelings for women as heterosexual. In a desperate effort she began to consolidate her male role and identity; picturing herself as a male trapped inside a female's body, she hoped to allay mother's anxiety that she was homosexual. This rationalization, a product of a subtle disorder in her thinking, while helping Barbara to crystallize her male identity, did not placate mother's irrational homophobia.

During her fourteenth year Barbara became increasingly self-absorbed by her male daydreams (in which she pictured herself as a male hero rescuing women in distress). Because she had withdrawn from school, her male daydreams were reinforced, as her stepfather related to her as a "pal." Barbara recalled that "we talked heart to heart, went fishing, built two tractors, took a Chevy engine apart, wore work clothes together," and eventually worked side by side in a factory. She said, "You see one of us you see the other; he always gave me pointers on how to raise a family." The two of them frequented bars together and engaged in brawls and fist fights with other men. Often they had to fight their way out of the blue-collar neighborhood bars. Barbara became known as a tough fighter, a "king of the hill," someone to watch out for and not have angry at you. By age 15 the stepfather was introducing her as "my son Brian."

Whenever Barbara dated a woman, her mother became enraged and violent, openly berating her daughter, cursing her, and shouting obscenities at her. In order to placate mother, Barbara occasionally dated men (with whom she also had sex). She rationalized her sexual involvement with these men as necessary to satisfy her enormous sexual drive and to keep mother off her back. However, as a consequence of a rape, Barbara (15 years old) became pregnant and delivered a boy baby. At the mother's urgings, Barbara married the man who had raped her – a marriage which lasted two weeks and resulted in her beating up the "husband," throwing him out of the house (literally down the stairs), and taking up her lesbian relationships full steam (in mother's house).

The pregnancy was quite traumatic, involving massive denial and dissociation from her body. Barbara felt disgusted by her enlarged female genitalia and breasts. The child, a healthy boy, was named Richard after her "husband." His birth aroused intense jealousy and competitiveness. The boy had a penis, an organ for which Barbara yearned. However, the fact that she could make a baby boy both excited and overwhelmed her. Immediately after the birth Barbara, fighting off an intense postpartum depression, abandoned her newborn son Richard to her mother's care. While Barbara occasionally visited Richard, she did not return for him until he was 4 years old. During those four years Barbara engaged in a series of frenetic, tandem gay relationships. She was profoundly alcoholic – going on binges and suffering from delirium tremens — and while identifying as a lesbian, wore male clothes and alternately played a male/female role.

Barbara returned for Richard when she began living in a stable lesbian relationship. Her lover, Donna, was an impulsive, violent woman who hated men and viciously abused Richard (physically and psychologically). The relationship lasted almost eight years (though Barbara had innumerable lesbian affairs throughout the "marriage"), and terminated with the death of Barbara's stepfather. Fighting off an intense depression, Barbara subsequently developed a psychogenic arthritic condition and could not work. She then entered psychotherapy where she was seen once a week for five months by a colleague who did not recall any mention of transsexualism. The focus of the therapy was on Barbara's symptoms as a depressive equivalent, her need to mourn her stepfather's death, and the need to view her psychogenic symptoms as a depressive equivalent related to her emotional turmoil. Barbara also discussed her chaotic sexuality and confusing gender identity; she used the therapy to extricate herself from the relationship with Donna only to begin immediately a new symbiotic relationship with another woman like her own mother.

Barbara's new lover, Arlene, was a well-known stripper who tantalized and excited men, but would never yield to them. She was plagued by chronic physical disease — stomach ulcers, blindness in one eye, and a heart ailment that required open heart surgery. Arlene yearned for a child, yet a recently diagnosed condition of chronic endometriosis precluded her becoming pregnant. The physicians wanted to perform a hysterectomy but feared she would become psychotic and requested psychological counseling pre-surgery.

Arlene had already miscarried one baby, after being severely beaten in the abdomen by her husband. Yearning for a child, she eagerly attached herself to Richard, then a preadolescent, with whom she maintained an immature, voracious, clinging-dependent, sadomasochistic, symbiotic relationship. She was extremely seductive with Richard and tried to coax him into a sexual relationship — and would have succeeded had Richard not developed severe migraine headaches in her presence and eventually a full-blown psychosis.

Arlene's appearance was telltale; she dressed sloppily and seemed disheveled; her cognitive behaviour was characteristically scattered and confused. Yet she was an extremely verbal individual who latched on to people and engaged in "heady" psychological outpourings which, while reflecting a loss of control over her verbalizations, could easily be mistaken for warmth, empathy and openness. In order to assuage Arlene's need for a child, Barbara agreed to become pregnant to allow Arlene to raise the child. What was remarkable was that Barbara was willing to allow herself to be penetrated, to enact the role of a woman and have sex with a man, leading to a pregnancy which was bound to be tumultuous.

Eventually, Barbara found a man willing to impregnate her (but refused to reveal his identity, thereby recreating for her daughter the same mystery that surrounded Barbara's own birth). At the time of the delivery, Barbara told the nurses about her situation and they arranged for Arlene to take her place in bed and be wheeled out of the hospital with little Arlene (the child was named after her). Barbara, now impersonating a man, walked beside her and handed out cigars! All of this was confirmed by the hospital authorities and testified to how a bizarre life style may be given social support and approval by well-meaning individuals (who understand little about the dynamics of female transsexualism).

With the new baby, Barbara and Arlene settled into a brief but happy period together. However, once in a drunken stupor Barbara's mother confided to Arlene the unusual circumstances surrounding Richard's birth. She admitted that she had arranged for Barbara to be raped so that her daughter, having tasted the fruits of male love, would give up being a lesbian! When Barbara heard the story she could not admit the facts into consciousness. The story, corroborated by Susan, highlights the tragic sense of the family's sadism. After a two-year period of "marriage," Arlene ran off with Barbara's rival Gwen, another female-to-male transsexual.

The situation was bizarre, incestuous, and ludicrous. Barbara, having changed her name to Brian — taking the same name as Richard's father, that is, the man who "raped" her — exchanged lovers with her rival Gwen, and began living with Gwen's ex-lover Alice!

Alice, an attractive, feminine woman, had a serious thought disorder, was agitated, manic, and had an affective illness (manic-depressive disease was ruled out). At this time Barbara's son Richard became acutely disorganized and violent and asked to be hospitalized. One of his psychotic delusions was the fear that he was turning into a woman. Richard was eventually institutionalized for diagnosed paranoid schizophrenia and spent three years in a state hospital, after which he was discharged to his mother, who had undergone SRS and was now his "father." Barbara eventually married Alice and began living in a make-believe "doll's house"-type marriage, attending church, involving herself in civic affairs, and presenting herself as an earnest, responsible, lower middle-class family man. Her facade, which was accepted as genuine by neighbors and employers, was transparent only to the mental health profession and the courts, who knew the real facts about this unusual couple. Indeed, it was this couple, Brian and Alice, that sat outside my office. Two years later Barbara and Alice were to request artificial insemination in order to have a third child.

Formulation of the case

The formulation of Barbara's diagnosis of transsexualism was gleaned from several sources: transcripts from her long-term individual, group, and family therapy; intensive psychological testing; interviews with family members, children, lovers, and friends; and post-operative follow-up data up to four years post-surgery.

In contrast to Tina's family, Barbara's family revealed considerable evidence of emotional pathology. Both women, however, successfully impersonated men and presented a "stable" facade. For Barbara, however, once her family history was acknowledged it was difficult to view her as a "stable" female transsexual. Yet she was reliable. She kept all of her appointments; had a 100 per cent attendance rate for her therapies; paid all her bills; was never obnoxiously demanding or impulsive to hospital staff; and was viewed as a likeable individual who had a stable instability. She split off her impulsivity and chaotic life experiences from the clinic and was never viewed by the staff as unstable apart from what she told us about her personal life. In other words, there was a huge discrepancy between her clinical self-presentation and her reported social history and life style outside the therapy hour (typical of patients with borderline personality disorders). While one might try to explain Barbara/Brian's conflicts as related to her low social class, such an explanation is too simplistic.

Barbara's case history was typical of a large subgroup of self-labeled female transsexuals. Typically, these women appear to have two distinct lives. In therapy they are viewed as compliant, cooperative, good-natured and "stable." Their lives outside of therapy, however, are usually quite chaotic and disorganized, with bizarre family histories and behavior which is generally viewed as psychopathic, impulsive, and alcoholic.

There are several possible explanations for understanding the basis for Barbara's transsexualism. On the one hand, her personality conflicts can be attributed to her transsexualism; one may argue that once Barbara obtains hormone therapy and SRS all her physical symptoms and emotional anguish will be resolved. On the other hand, her transsexualism may be an epiphenomenon of her intergenerational family pathology and enmeshed family dynamics (that is, her symbiotic relationship with her mother) which supported her gender identity conflicts.

It is compelling to view the intergenerational family dynamics as playing a crucial role in the formation of Barbara's gender identity conflicts. Indeed, it was within the family context of two generations of child abuse, chaotic sexuality, and gender identity pathology, that Barbara failed to develop a female core gender identity. From birth, Barbara experienced a continual assault upon her gender identity and role development. Her mother wished for a boy, hated girl children, and communicated to Barbara that only as a boy would mother love and accept her. Moreover, mother surrounded herself with men who crushed Barbara's female gender development and encouraged her to develop as a boy, the stepfather even going so far as to give her a male name and introduce her as "my son." Barbara was not provided the proper milieu in which to form an appropriate female core gender identity. Indeed, there seemed to be a family conspiracy to masculinize Barbara. The result was that she had a disposition for gender diffusion and gender dysphoria which was exacerbated by stressors throughout her life cycle.

Barbara's early developmental history was replete with losses, separations, abandonments, and deaths. These events seemed to mobilize her intense separation anxiety and dread of abandonment, leaving Barbara vulnerable to profound depressive crises (which were acted out through self-destructive behaviors). Mother's oscillation between intense affective bonding and a clinging-dependent relationship to Barbara was followed by threats of abandonment and object withdrawal which heightened Barbara's separation conflicts and made it impossible for her to separate from mother and individuate apart from mother, except by a complete reversal of her gender. Living under the constant threat of abandonment, which Barbara was unable to allay, her only salvation was in dis-identifying mother.

To become a woman through identifying with her mother meant that Barbara had to identify both with mother's destructive aggression, which could annihilate her, and Barbara's self-perception of badness, in which she experienced herself as capable of destroying others. Moreover, mother's seductiveness towards her daughter threatened Barbara with the possibility of destructive incestuous engulfment. Either way Barbara turned, mother held out no means of salvation.

Barbara internalized mother's view that women were helpless, and vulnerable, unable to protect themselves from the onslaughts of male aggression or female seductiveness. Only if she identified as a male and became a male was survival possible. However, while rejecting mother's "femaleness," Barbara identified with mother's counterphobic defenses — that is, mother's role as a "mean," "tough" person. She also established a dependent symbiotic relationship with mother, which provided her with an alternative way of remaining attached to mother without either killing her or being killed by her. By abandoning her female identifications, and rejecting her internalized image of her mother, Barbara rescued herself from a possible suicidal depression, or a psychotic decompensation. There is the suggestion that some aspects of femaleness were, however, facilitated; perhaps as a result of her relationship with mother's sister, for whom she was named, and who had the role of caretaker in the family. Indeed, as a child she was called on to help raise Susan and care for her mother and stepfather. These experiences with a mothering role may have helped to arouse her current interest in childrearing. Even on the Rorschach there was strong evidence of Barbara's "femaleness" — albeit ambivalent femaleness — as seen in her continued pregnancy wishes and her maternal wishes to rear children. One woman in our clinic pointed to Barbara's emotional lability and proneness to cry, her nurturant attitude towards her children, and her use of the telephone as evidence of her feminine characteristics.

By employing primitive defense mechanisms such as denial, splitting, projection, projective identification, omnipotence, Barbara split off the bad mother image and was thereby able to continue her relationship to mother. However, her conduct *vis-à-vis* mother was one of complete helplessness and masochistic submission: always explaining away, or denying, mother's bad behavior and justifying mother's aggression towards her. Barbara's internal self-representation was also split into two elements, reflecting a good and a bad self. The bad self was equated with her femaleness and needed to be denied, split off, and projected outwards. The good self, that is, her male element, developed independently, shielding Barbara from the destructive potential of her female self (which threatened to engulf and destroy her).

By employing primitive and rigid defense mechanisms Barbara could appear confident, headstrong, cocky, and self-assured. Indeed, her girlfriends responded to these aspects of Barbara's personality as if she were a strong masculine figure. While these defenses had an adaptive function, they also severely impaired her ability to reality test (especially when she was under stress). Indeed, Barbara had difficulty organizing and synthesizing percepts (for which she substituted a rigid, dogmatic adherence to a false belief which, conveyed with conviction, could easily disarm her adversary into believing that she was correct).

Barbara's ultimate defense against her inner anxiety was either to employ splitting or to use projection and externalize her inner conflicts. It was her use of projective identification, and its integration into her character structure, which made it all but impossible for Barbara to make effective use of psychotherapy leading to personality changes.

Barbara's good object, that is, her father image, was overidealized and invested with a kind of magical quality, protecting Barbara from being engulfed by her abandonment depression and feared homosexual involvement with mother. Maleness was associated with elation, euphoria, mania (a denial of inner reality), and optimism (a will to stay alive). Barbara enjoyed the kinesthetic sense of maleness, that is, feeling alive through the exercise of her muscles. Maleness became associated with control, power, hope, and life; femaleness was equated with hopelessness, powerlessness, and vulnerability to harm.

Barbara's exposure to chaotic, often overwhelming sexual and aggressive stimuli disorganized her perceptions and left her vulnerable to severe ego impairment and a subtle, but pervasive, thought disorder. Barbara was especially deficient in those ego functions related to judgment. While she was always making snap decisions (with an air of authority and confidence), her judgment was usually poor. She vacillated between making rigid moral judgments which seemed like categorical imperatives, and an apparent lack of any moral consideration, in which every possible behavior was acceptable. Indeed, her decision-making processes were markedly impaired and her superego poorly developed. Barbara was not able to internalize moral norms and standards because of the instability of her object world. She viewed all behaviors as equally viable and judged things in terms of the pleasure they afforded her. Her integrative skills were also impaired. Further, there was evidence of serious ego defects concerning stimulus barrier, frustration tolerance, delay of gratification, and impulse control. Barbara externalized all of her conflicts and experienced little anxiety about her life style. Because of her defensive use of projection and externalization, she rarely experienced anxiety about her life situation. However, when she was stressed through a separation, death, or abandonment, her anxiety emerged full-force. At those times she became panicky, agitated, confused, disorganized, clinging, frightened, whiny, and symptomatic.

Typically, Barbara had great difficulty setting limits, and in organizing her life into a routine. Her chaotic early childhood history had left her without a mechanism to modulate and regulate her affects and impulses. Consequently, she responded to stimuli impulsively and reflexively, with no awareness of the impact she had on other people. She was constantly subject to being over-stimulated, impulse-ridden, and disorganized. The emotional cost of her early childhood history included precocious ego development in some spheres but generally retarded ego development, with manifest ego impairments and non-specific ego weaknesses.

It would appear that while Barbara's stepfather was alive his presence made her gender identity conflicts tolerable and shielded her from a severe depressive crisis. When he died, Barbara's depression over his death was expressed by her wish to fuse with him and become a man — thereby keeping him "alive." His death must have concretely symbolized her annihilation: that is, the death of her "good" or "male" self.

About the time the stepfather died Barbara's son Richard was entering his adolescence. Barbara experienced Richard's puberty traumatically, as signaling her ultimate defeat. She was profoundly jealous of Richard's developing masculinity and the growth of his penis. In an apparent effort to emasculate him, Barbara dressed him as a girl for a Halloween party. Richard's reaction was predictable. He became panicky and delusional, believing that he was uncontrollably turning into a woman — in this case the Bionic Woman. By driving her son crazy with her intention of becoming a man, and depriving Richard of his birthright, Barbara may have externalized her gender conflict for good, thereby sealing off her conflicts from psychotherapeutic intervention.

The relationship between stressful life events and Barbara's transsexualism was clear-cut. Throughout her life she had reacted to losses, changes, separations, abandonments, and deaths with wishes for sex change. For example, Frances's removal from the home, the death of the grandfather, Richard's entry into adolescence, and the death of the stepfather all led in varying degree to Barbara's experiencing intense gender dysphoria, the belief that she was male, and her wish for SRS.

The childhood belief that she had a penis inside her vagina, while common fantasy among girls, was given a special reality by Barbara. The fantasized penis seemed to protect her against profound castration threats and abandonment fears (which she associated with being female). Moreover, the "penis" probably symbolized the stepfather. In trying to obtain a penis, Barbara was acting out a fantasy that the penis = maleness (a crude version of an early childhood cognitive formulation that sexual differentiations are made on the superficial basis of clothes and hair). Mother reinforced Barbara's fantasy by making her believe that something mysterious was associated with her birth and her father. Moreover, mother had wanted a male child. When Barbara received SRS she nurtured her new penis in a tender way, cradling it, as if it were a new-born child. Indeed, her reaction suggested that the penis symbolized her childbearing capabilities and represented a tender part of her self which could only emerge after SRS, in a distorted, caricatured, masculine way.

For Barbara, growing up as a female was dangerous, entailing separations, losses, abandonments, and possible annihilation. Barbara was unable to repress her wishes for a penis for several reasons: her parents actively supported that wish; and it was not simply related to oedipal issues or a neurosis, but was profoundly tied to her sense of self-identity and her very existence. Indeed, one may speculate that Barbara's inability to develop a female core gender identity was inextricably related to her early ego impairments and developmental defects. Each successive life cycle challenge further stressed her already overburdened self-system in terms of increased gender dysphoria.

Barbara's history revealed that her wish to become a man was multi-determined: supported by intrapsychic mechanisms, family dynamics and interpersonal processes. Her gender identity pathology could be traced back two generations (in which all the women in the family had evidenced serious gender identity or role pathology). In the context of a disorganized and sexually chaotic family, Barbara failed to develop a core female gender identity. Her experience of a continual assault upon her normal female gender development led to profound gender diffusion and dysphoria throughout her life cycle.

Barbara was diagnosed on psychological tests as having a borderline personality disorder with impulsive and psychopathic features. Her male identifications were typically shallow and caricatured (similar to those held by latency-aged girls who engage in role-acting maleness). Each new life cycle epoch led to an increasing desire to obliterate her femaleness and consolidate her "maleness," sociologically characterized by role changes from transvestism, homosexuality, to transsexualism. Psychological testing supported the clinical interview diagnosis and highlighted Barbara's bright normal to superior intelligence which she used to enhance her male role impersonation.

From a clinical standpoint, Barbara lacked a cohesive self-system, had an impaired body image and had a severe narcissistic personality and behavior disorder. At times her self-system was fragmented and enfeebled. While she was preoccupied with grandiose, omnipotent, rescue fantasies she was unable to establish reasonable goals for her life. Each life failure increased her susceptibility to further narcissistic injury and personality fragmentation, and led to the emergence of incapacitating hypochondriacal symptoms. This was not a woman beset with penis envy, masculinity complex, or castration anxiety, but one with a severe developmental disorder and a primary narcissistic personality and behavioral disorder.

The picaresque saint: Randi/Randy

The role of the family in the dynamics of female transsexualism is often obscured by the fact that either the parents are unavailable or they refuse to cooperate in their daughter's transsexual evaluation. This was not the case with Randi, an adolescent female transsexual whom I came to know as the "picaresque saint."

Randi first came to my attention through a letter addressed to me from her older brother. It was a deeply moving letter, one that evoked a long and empathic response. The brother, who was visiting family in the US, was anguished by his sister's transsexualism. At the root of his concern was his struggle between his religious orthodoxy, his love for his sister, and the fear that he would be forced to reject her formally for violating God's law. Because of the nature of the letter, I have decided to publish it in its entirety (the only omissions being changes in names and locations in order to preserve the anonymity of the patient and family).

110

Dear Dr. Lothstein,

I've been doing research on gender dysphoria and came across articles you've written concerning group therapy. Of all the many books and articles I've read, I was most impressed by the questions you raise and you're approach. I am therefore writing you for advice on this subject which is new and disturbing to me. Seven months ago my father was tragically killed while riding his bicycle. My sister who was then 18 fell into depression and when she visited me a month after the funeral disclosed to me that she was a lesbian. She told me that our mother knew about it − but that it was being kept secret from me for fear of my disapproval. During the visit my wife (who has a B.S. in psychology and is doing graduate work) further questioned her and my sister said that she's "been a lesbian since she's 12 years old and would have had the sex change operation if it wasn't for her *weak heart*." My sister doesn't have a weak heart − and my wife assumed that this was my sister's form of reducing cognitive dissonance and subconsciously avoiding an operation. Also, the coupling of lesbianism with transsexualism seems to us unwarranted and atypical of true transsexuals. My parents moved to the U.S. three years ago from Europe and my sister was unwillingly uprooted from her social circle and school. Within a 2 year period she's also seen our parents divorce, our father killed, all of her personal belongings were stolen along with our familys lift, 4 of her friends were killed in accidents this year, and she's had 2 serious knee operations. She *was* a striking, precocious, coquetish and willful girl, and now she is unrecognizable. Our father was a holocaust victim who's tortured life greatly affected our childhood and her experience seems to fit the classical literature. But − up till my fathers death she was "in the closet" and I believe that his death awoke in her motives to *become* our father. She has always been compared to our father, physically, personality wise and behavior wise. Our family dynamics even before the divorce were such that my father favored me (excessively) and my mother favored my sister to compensate for this. Prior to my father's death my sister and father had many disagreements and it seems to me that her desire to change her sex is due to (1) Her subconscious wish to be posthumously accepted (as a boy) by my father (2) The death of many of her friends and pets has convinced her that she's cursed (and she killed them) and that with a sex change she will be reborn

111

and cleansed (3) My father had a self destructive drive (why did I survive the camps?) and my sister seems to have these same self destructive traits. This may be a clue to her problem as I don't think this is typical of most cases.

Her adolescent years were of great trauma to my parents — she ran away from home for six weeks when she was 13 and my father liked to blame her for the divorce. So you see, she has suffered great feelings of guilt and she verbally admits that she wants to be reborn. Objective facts which are also important are that she has had heterosexual affairs and was badly disappointed by a boyfriend who married her best friend 2 years after promising to wait for my sister. A year ago at my wedding she dated my best friend for 2 weeks and he said that she cooperated with him sexually until his overtures became too serious (threatening?) — which agrees with the statement that many transsexuals choose this sexual orientation as a retreat from sex.

My sister is very secretive of the treatment she is receiving — and I suspect that she's being treated illegally and seeing a psychologist (M.S.) who is used by the transsexual community for attaining documents saying they are transsexuals getting operations. She coerces people with threats and money to get her own way, and this makes it very difficult to get her into an alliance with a respectable and objective psychologist. She has only started cross dressing in the past 3 weeks and started androgen therapy very intensively since August and has secondary male characteristics. She lives with 2 male to female transsexuals who supply her with hormones and all the "right" answers and information about her case. I would like your advice on how to deal with her — should I encourage her to travel to a gender clinic such as Case Western's — is there a clinic in her area which would help her? Our family is willing to accept her claim of being gay, but we can't believe she's truly transsexual. What do you advise us to do? We can't force her to enter therapy, she doesn't even agree to enter family oriented therapy, which we feel due to our traumatic life experience as children of a survivor is the only correct way to deal with this.

I appreciate any advice you can give me as a clinician and human being who must come in contact with many cases such as this.

Thank you very much,
Mr. S. France

P.S. My sister wants to have the new sex change operation in March — she believes she will be capable even of reproduction so this is of immediate concern to us.

In my response to Mr. France's letter I reviewed his suggestions and offered several alternatives for obtaining a thorough evaluation of his sister's so-called transsexualism. Eventually he decided on meeting with me in the US prior to his return to Europe.

When I first met with Mr. France (Samuel) he was accompanied by his wife Rachel. (He had adopted France as his family name.) They were a striking couple — tall, attractive, dark-haired, severe, and earnest. Both had their heads covered, typical of members of Orthodox Jewish sects. I had the impression that they were on the last leg of a long journey. We got right down to business. Rachel explained that she loved her sister-in-law, but that Orthodox Jewish law would forbid them from "recognizing" her (that is, having any relationship with her) if she underwent a sex change operation. They both agreed that since father's death Randi's personality had changed, with her requests for sex change coming on the heels of father's death. Both viewed sexual reassignment as a horrifying alternative, at best mutilative.

The Frances could accept Randi's homosexuality; indeed, they viewed her homosexual preference as her best level of adaptation. They acknowledged that while Orthodox Judaism viewed homosexuality as sinful (involving possible excommunication), they could compromise on this point. It was apparent that members of their Orthodox community knew of Randi's true female sexual status (she had visited their community), and that the Frances would be forced by the community to make a choice between her or them. It was a painful dilemma. They loved Randi — but they could only love her as a female.

As the Frances talked about Randi, it was apparent that they were a very intelligent and psychologically minded couple. They not only discussed Randi's personality problems, but they also offered interpretations of her behavior. They were desperate. It was as if they were trying to save a part of themselves. Indeed, when they first heard of Randi's SRS wishes they conspired with mother to kidnap Randi. A wild story was concocted; Randi would have to travel to Europe to secure a family heirloom; once there she would be whisked away and deprogrammed. While the plan was eventually abandoned, it reflected the agonizing efforts of the entire family to rid themselves of Randi's transsexualism (which had now become the family's core problem).

The France's described Randi as an immature, attention-seeking adolescent who was strong-willed, stubborn, and rebellious. They described her as a typical impulsive runaway youth, involved in drugs and sex. Moreover, they viewed her as a chronic liar; someone who often exaggerated reality, but also one who told wild stories to "con" people. When she did not get her way, she either threatened suicide or complained about her life-threatening heart condition (a complete fabrication). She used threats and intimidation to coerce and manipulate people to get what she wanted.

Once, on a transatlantic flight, Randi feigned a heart attack and had the stewardesses hovering over her, providing oxygen and a private sleeping space. At other times she became frankly paranoid, blaming others for her problems but also convincing people around her that she was being deprived of some aspect of her rights, or that her life was endangered. She told these stories with such confidence and aplomb that she made them seem credible. She was able to draw money at will from the father's estate by lying to the trustee (an attorney) that her brother in Europe needed it and saying that she was his liaison. While I listened to the Frances' account of Randi's personality — with some degree of scepticism — I was to discover later that their impressions were not only accurate but only touched the surface of Randi's exploits.

By the time I met Randi I felt that I already knew her. Our first interview was arranged as a home visit with her mother present. Randi was a boyish-looking female, dressed in asexual clothing, with her short hair styled in a masculine fashion. She had been self-administering male hormones for several months and revealed some male hair pattern growth, a slightly lowered voice, and, reportedly, an increase in her sexual drive. She looked like a mannish female.

While her affect was generally bland she had a Madonna-like smile. She spoke to me in a monotonic voice, calmly and rationally describing her wishes for sexual transformation. There was no irritation, no strain in her voice. She was putting on a great performance and knew it. Had this been an ordinary clinical interview, I would have been impressed by the apparent lack of pathology. It was only when her mother entered the picture and we had a joint interview that she appeared visibly shaken and upset, her logic becoming questionable and her fragmentation apparent.

It was clear that the mother and daughter were locked in a hostile-dependent symbiotic relationship in which the roles were reversed. The mother dissolved under Randi's threats, looking at me in a pleading, helpless way, begging for advice and direction. Randi was smug; she dominated mother and coerced and controlled her behavior. I was struck by Randi's omnipotence, her inability to separate from mother (and vice versa), and wondered how her need for control related to her transsexual wishes. It was easy to understand how she had already been diagnosed as a true transsexual at a local gender clinic.

Randi proudly displayed her transsexual imprimatur — a letter guaranteeing her transsexual status and acknowledging that she was a candidate for surgery. Whatever my "second opinion" might be, she had already been provided a certificate of approval; from my reading of it I concurred with her brother's appraisal that she had probably gone to a clinic that was more interested in certifying transsexuals than in treating them. In spite of her trump card, Randi had to be ambivalent about surgery since she allowed me to continue to meet with her to explore her gender conflicts. Indeed, my offices, being a thousand miles from her home, certainly offered an obstacle to obtaining a second opinion. None the less, Randi continued to see me, accepted a referral for treatment near her home, and now, several years later, still threatens to have SRS but has never followed through on her threats. It seemed that as long as her mother remained in treatment Randi backed off from her threats of surgery. When mother was strong-willed and refused to participate in Randi's decision regarding surgery, Randi no longer had the need to act out her transsexual wishes for SRS.

Randi's case history has been culled from several sources over a long period of time. These sources included extensive interviews with the patient, her mother (who also provided me with a written document on the early childhood history of her daughter), the mother's boyfriend, the brother, and daughter-in-law. Additional information was obtained from physicians who treated Randi, the family attorney, and the staff of the hospital where Randi was psychiatrically hospitalized for a transsexual evaluation. Moreover, extensive psychological testing on the patient and her mother was obtained.

Randi was born in Cairo, Egypt. Mother reported that "the pregnancy after three months started spotting and I was given medication to prevent a miscarriage and all activity was restricted." During the pregnancy the family made several unexplained moves within the city. Randi's birth, the second live birth of Mrs. Delours, involved a five-hour labor (which was induced). "I had some medication strapped to my wrist which I inhaled and it worked as an anaesthetic." The father, who had some medical training, participated in the birth.

The home situation was quite chaotic, complicated by father's wild rages and extravagant personality and, more recently, by all the unexplained moves. Father was also away from the house a great deal and led a private existence which he did not share with his wife. The older son, Samuel (age 6 and named after father), was prepared for his sister's birth and reacted to her homecoming by spraying her with insecticide, for which father beat him so severely that he required stitches in his leg. Although Randi was breast-fed for two months, mother was not committed to the breast-feeding. While she found breast-feeding to be repugnant, she was also entranced by her large bosom. As a young woman she had been mercilessly teased for being flatchested; she enjoyed being buxom. However, mother was quite conflicted over her nurturant role and she easily gave up breast-feeding. Additionally, both parents had difficulty with touch, and mother reported that "neither of us cuddled nor handled the children." Not long after her birth, mother turned Randi's care over to one of several nursemaids who, in effect, raised Randi.

When Randi was six weeks old the family fled the Middle East and moved to the United States (mother's birthplace). During Randi's first year the family moved five times within and between states, finally moving back to France, the father's homeland. While Mrs. Delours viewed her husband's behavior as irrational, marked by impulsive, manicky behavior, she dutifully obeyed his wishes and helped with the moves.

As soon as the family moved to France, Randi, 11 months old, was separated from mother and hospitalized for a tonsillectomy. After Randi was discharged from the hospital, her mother also had surgery and was hospitalized for over two weeks. Randi was without her mother for almost a month, being cared for by a strange nurse (father was also unavailable, being away on business) during a critical phase of attachment. When Randi was aged $1\frac{1}{2}$ father was hospitalized for an appendectomy and when she was 2 the mother was hospitalized again for one week and "Randi was left with a different maid who was very young, became attached to Randi and would spend her salary on presents for Randi. Randi also cared for her." However, after eight months of employment, mother said, "we had to fire the maid," as she was caught having an affair with the father. It was clear that this was a trauma for all the family.

In spite of all the moves, separations, losses, abandonments, and general family disorganization and stress, Mrs. Delours reported that Randi exhibited no developmental difficulties; standing at 6–7 months, walking at 13 months, talking at 15 months, and being toilet trained at $2\frac{1}{2}$ years. Randi had no serious childhood illnesses, and revealed no unusual behaviors (including no enuresis or encopresis).

Randi reportedly spoke French by age 3, and by age 5 knew some English and Danish. Over the course of her childhood (through age 12) the family moved at least thirty times in six different countries. Because of the moves neither Randi nor the family were able to make any enduring friendships. Mother's response was to surround herself with pets as substitutes for friends.

In kindergarten Randi often got into fights; in one instance she had her hair pulled out by the roots, leaving a bald spot, facial scratches, and a permanent scar. One of Randi's earliest memories (she was then 5 years old) was of a car accident in which she and the mother suffered head injuries. Mother reported that Randi also had a series of minor head injuries (secondary to falls and accidents), some of which may have been the result of child abuse.

When Randi was 6 the family quarreling became so intense that the parents considered divorce. In a fit of rage mother took Randi to live in America with her parents. Samuel, then 12, remained in Europe with his father "to take care of him." After a brief separation the father returned to the US and, reconciling with his wife, returned with his family to France. The hectic pace of the family did not diminish. If father was not "permanently" uprooting his family from one country to another he would "temporarily" uproot them by abruptly announcing that they were going on a long trip. With little notice, the family bags would be packed and off they went. In addition, Randi was separated from her parents during the summers, when they sent her to summer camp, where she would remain for two months.

Randi frequently described childhood memories of having been hurt or beaten. One incident involved a sailing accident in which Randi caught her foot beneath the planks. Mother recalled that "her father finally tugged her foot free causing her great pain." Two other memories which focused on her feet involved an incident around 8 years of age when her big toe was "completely frozen" while she was skiing; and later on when a horse stepped on that same toe. Whenever Randi recalled her childhood these memories immediately surfaced. She also remembered father hitting her head against a radiator and another time in which he "attacked" her because she was "impudent." Randi agreed that, however badly father beat her, it was nothing compared to his beatings of Samuel.

Throughout childhood and into adulthood, Randi had a variety of pets, including exotic birds, cats, dogs, and horses. Almost all of her small pets, however, "mysteriously" died; even a favorite family cat "accidentally" wandered into the clothes washer. Although Randi denied any wrongdoing, her mother and brother insisted that she was sadistic towards animals and killed them — often after they had been with the family for a number of years.

During her girlhood Randi had had few playmates. She was uneasy around her peers (was excessively demanding and clinging), and was frightened that her homoerotic interests would become transparent, thereby further stigmatizing her. While not schizoid, she did have difficulty relating to both boys and girls. Her overt behavior could not be explained as entirely tomboyish. Indeed, she had dolls, wore dresses, and seemed, on the surface, to be evolving a normal female role identity. However, she was intensely jealous of her brother's relationship to father; her envy of father's special treatment of Samuel led Randi to develop a wish to become a boy, and be loved and special — just like her brother.

As Randi's homoerotic fantasies increased, she became increasingly aware of her intense sexual feelings for women. However, these feelings were not limited to girls and older women. Indeed, her heightened sexual feelings could lead in almost any direction. Two sources of trauma, however, seemed to have organized her homosexuality. Once when she had a vaginal infection mother had to apply some medicine internally (to douche her). Randi was horrified and ashamed, and traced her hatred of her female genitals to that incident. Second, when a friend of mother's made sexual advances to Randi she became panicky that her homoerotic feelings were so transparent that she would be sexually vulnerable to all women.

Although Randi was less than enthusiastic about her menarche, she did not rebel against it; nor was she terribly upset about her breast development. It was only later in adolescence, when her transsexual wishes crystallized, that she developed an abhorrent reaction to her breasts and genitals. During early adolescence Randi became involved with a number of men and women in sexual relationships. After a series of confusing sexual incidents — seduction by a friend of her mother; evolving a gay identity by age 12 — Randi eventually had a confrontation with her parents over her relationship with an older man, twenty-two years her senior.

At age 13 Randi ran away from home, hiding out for six weeks in another country. During this period Randi became involved in the gay community and began to formally consolidate her transsexual identity. She was involved in a number of sordid relationships, exposed to a wide variety of underworld practices, and introduced to street drugs. Randi was reluctantly returned home by the police (after spending three days in jail). The family reacted by uprooting themselves and moving to another country.

By mid-adolescence Randi began a heterosexual relationship which ended abruptly when her best girlfriend married her lover. A short while later, after Randi graduated from the equivalent of an American high school, the family moved to the United States. Randi was devastated; she had lost her lover and now had to give up her friends, language, and country. As if things were not bad enough, just after their arrival in the US all the family's personal property and possessions, including all family pictures and mementoes, were stolen. Now they had little, if anything, to serve as a thread for their identityless past. The parents' shaky marriage soon fell apart, as father moved out and began dating girls his daughter's age.

As Randi became more protective towards mother (serving as a surrogate father and husband), she also became more involved in the gay and transsexual community. It was, however, with the death of her father — he was struck down and killed by a car — that she formally came "out of the closet" and announced her wishes to have sexual surgery and become a man. Within a short period of time she was immersed in the gay and transsexual culture, doing a male impersonator act and dating other women in the guise of a man; and living with two male-to-female transsexuals who befriended her and facilitated her role transformation to male (eventually Randi paid for their surgeries with money obtained through father's death benefits).

When mother began living with her new male friend, Mario, Randi became insanely resentful and jealous. She reacted by threatening to abandon mother unless she accepted her as male. Taking advantage of mother's helplessness and guilt, Randi moved into her mother's house with a girlfriend, flaunting her transsexual relationship. While mother objected to the relationship, she felt powerless to do anything, ambivalently resigning herself to her daughter's increasing masculinization (and hoping eventually to get help for her). When Randi learned that her threat to obtain sexual surgery frightened mother (who feared losing her symbiotic bond with Randi), Randi increased her threats and demanded that mother accept her as a transsexual. Randi was testing mother. It was a test that neither person could win because of the unconscious determinants involved.

Two years after father's tragic death, Randi inherited a large sum of money which she promptly spent. Actually, father had disinherited her because of her extravagances, but her brother Samuel, who inherited everything, gave her half. Randi's spending sprees caused the family concern for several reasons — not least of which was their implicit message that she was out of control, perhaps manic. Indeed, her impulsive behavior appeared to be escalating, perhaps to self-destructive levels. The issue of whether she had a manic-depressive illness was raised (but later ruled out).

It seemed as if the father had played a central role in Randi's transsexual wishes. But who was he? How can we explain his behavior? The father, Samuel (for whom his son was named), was described as a violent, pressured, manicky individual who — when not hated — was idolized by the family. A reckless, daring man, he was constantly involved in intrigue and international exploits. He was adventurous and worldly, an international executive by trade, owner of a factory that manufactured clothing, and purported to be a secret agent.

Randi was preoccupied with father's daring, prowess, and physical appearance. She wrote of him:

He escaped three concentration camps [his family being wiped out by the Germans] . . . his physical appearance was that of a boxer, his height was 5′ 7″, his weight about 165 pounds, his skin was very tough and tight since his muscles hardly left place for any fatty tissues. His eyes were brown, his nose was not straight anymore since it had been broken in one of his numerous fights, and black was the color of his hair which there was not too much of.

Mother reported that her husband Samuel had been an only child. The paternal grandfather (for whom father was named) was the second of three children (the youngest being a girl). The paternal grandfather was described as a Catholic nobleman who was disowned by his family when he married a Jewish woman, the paternal grandmother. Their only child, the patient's father, was recklessly spoiled and indulged. Samuel was described, however, as idolizing his mother and hating his father. While he was raised without any religion, the Germans treated the family as Jews and exterminated his parents in a concentration camp. Samuel was described as having been interned in, and having escaped from, three concentration camps. After the war he first settled in the Middle East and then returned to France: the first of a series of moves that resembled flights across most of the Middle East and Europe.

Mother believed that father had survived most of his concentration camp experiences by impersonating various people, especially doctors, and being assigned to special work details in various medical stations and hospitals. After the war he apparently acquired a medical degree in Persia but he never practiced medicine formally, although he did work as a detail man for an international medical supply house located in Europe. Father was described as a loud, boisterous, "con" artist, who had a terrible temper, and often lied, telling fantastic tales to get himself out of trouble. Once when he volunteered as a spy, he was apparently turned down because of his inability to keep secrets.

In the late 1940s father immigrated to the US, married briefly, and had a child, Richard. During his wife's pregnancy he became involved with a 16-year-old woman whom he later married – Randi's mother. Abandoning his first child, Richard, Mr. Delours remarried and moved back to Europe and then to the Middle East. Mrs. Delours had unsuccessfully attempted to explain the large number of family moves. While she believed that her husband might have been involved in espionage, it was clear that she had a rich imagination and at times had difficulty distinguishing fantasy from reality. In effect, there is no way of determining the accuracy of Mrs. Delours's perceptions that many of the family's moves were precipitated by her husband's exploits.

Mr. Delours was described as quite promiscuous and unfaithful. He took pride in his sexual conquests (which he often publicized), and insisted on his sexual rights. He boasted of his sexual adventures, paraded nude around the house (as did his wife), and made no attempt to hide his sexual liaisons from his daughter.

Apparently quite successful in his career, Mr. Delours amassed a small fortune which was turned over to his family after his death. Once back in the US (Randi was 16 years old), he separated from his wife, dated girls his daughter's age, and underwent a series of operations to make him younger looking (he had several face lifts and a hair transplant). Randi proudly described him as having "no fear of operations." With his body rejuvenated, the father lived out the fantasy of being a gigolo. The mother said that at his funeral a large number of young women materialized to pay their last respects (all having been invited by Randi).

Father was a risk taker, a man around whom something exciting and dangerous was always happening. He stirred up lots of excitement and felt terribly guilty for having survived the concentration camp while his parents had been murdered. Randi stated that he said, "I survived because I was no good." While he identified as a Zionist, it was only when Samuel was 12 (and Randi 6) that he "confessed" his Jewishness (his first son by a prior marriage only learned of his "Jewish" origins at his father's funeral). Eventually, Samuel, needing an identity, latched on to his Jewishness and "converted," moving into an orthodox Jewish community.

Father's death was ironic; he had survived some of the most cruel environments of the twentieth century, only to be run down on a relatively traffic-free thoroughfare. In the last analysis, the mother believed that his death may not have been accidental. His burial in the Middle East marked the end of a psychological nightmare for himself and his family.

Mother came from an entirely different family background. Her family, firmly rooted in a small, traditional northeastern city, had originally emigrated from Finland. Her parents were tall with typically Aryan features, being blond-haired and blue-eyed. They were soft-spoken but stern, intrusive, controlling, and domineering, autocratically ruling over their daughter Randi (for whom the patient was named). The maternal grandmother's four sisters lived nearby. All were professional women; none had married. Now in their eighties and nineties, they represented a stern bulwark against feelings, spontaneity, and self-expression.

Mother admired her father and described him as "a great man." She was terribly disappointed when "mother turned him against me" for marrying Mr. Delours. In her youth, mother had been confused and overly dependent. A shy, but attractive woman, she believed that the only way she could move out of her house was by marrying. When she met her husband-to-be she was 16 and he was 30. He was the first man she dated. Three years later she married him. Within a year she was briefly hospitalized for out-of-control behavior, disorganized thinking, and gender identity confusion. One of the precipitants for her hospitalization had been her wish to kill her husband.

Mother was described by her son as being "overgratifying." She was terrified of being rejected or unloved and gave in to the children's smallest demands. She was easily manipulated and often coerced by her children, especially Randi. The situation was compounded by her husband's behavior. He was away most of the time, his absences leaving her without support. Moreover, because the family had been forced to move so often, mother had no friends to serve as a support system. Under stress, mother became agitated and histrionic, developing somatic symptoms and needing to be rescued from her disorganized state by the strength of her husband. Profoundly dependent, she exhibited little common sense, and needed to be reassured about almost everything.

Formulation of the case

The most striking characteristic of the Delours family was their collective identity crisis; no one in the family knew who they were. Father had changed the family's name so many times that it was even difficult for family members to know what to call themselves. The brother, in an attempt to provide himself with some identity, had even assumed as his last name his father's country of origin. By keeping their Jewish origins hidden, father had also cut them off from a strong tradition and support system, one which could have provided the family with the basis for an identity. Moreover, their continual flights from one country to another prevented the family from putting down any roots and so developing a cohesive family system.

Mother's identity crisis left her feeling empty and incomplete. She lacked a cohesive self and only felt whole in the presence of a strong man or her husband. Her ego boundaries were quite fluid and permeable, and she tended to merge and identify with strong personalities (having, like her daughter, an "as if" basis for her personality). The children were identityless. They had no friends, no primary language, and no country of origin. They were spiritually and psychologically bankrupt. In an attempt to achieve some semblance of wholeness, Samuel had turned to Orthodox Judaism and Randi to transsexualism, using ritual, ideology, and doctrine as buttresses for their weak egos and impaired self-systems.

However, to reduce Randi's transsexualism to her identity crisis does not explain why she chose that solution rather than another. Why had she not become a homosexual, a drug addict, a prostitute, a hippie, a member of a religious cult? Clearly, there were many pathways Randi could have chosen to resolve her identity confusion. However, she focused her identity diffusion and confusion specifically around her gender role and identity. What were the reasons for this? Why did she arrive at the conclusion that she was a man trapped in a woman's body? Could anyone with an identity conflict resolve his or her problems by resorting to gender transmutation, or must one already have a disposition for gender identity pathology? For example, must there be something in a person's biology or family structure which predisposes him or her to focus identity conflicts specifically around gender role and identity? It seems that any satisfactory explanation of Randi's transsexualism must address these issues.

An analysis of Randi's case history contraindicates a unitary explanation for her transsexualism. Her gender role and identity conflicts seemed multiply determined. Why she arrived at a transsexual resolution as the final common pathway of her inner conflicts needs to be explained. Whether we can actually determine which of the pathways was crucial for the evolution of her gender disorder also remains to be seen.

While it seems logical to begin our inquiry with Randi's childhood — for it was in the context of her early maternal care that her ego mechanisms were developed and her personality and self-system evolved — there was evidence that her transsexual conflicts might have predated her birth. Mrs. Delours's admission that she was given medication to prevent a miscarriage suggested that one must begin the inquiry with the pregnancy itself. While she did not recall the name of the drug, there was evidence that she was probably given some form of progestin, a drug which, when administered prenatally, has been shown to masculinize a female fetus.

The introduction of certain hormones during critical periods of fetal development has been shown to have a specific organizing effect on a child's subsequent gender behavior. For example, in some cases where mothers received progestins to prevent miscarriages, their female fetuses were masculinized *in utero*. In some of these cases a syndrome called progestin-induced hermaphroditism (PIH) may occur (see Chapter 5). This syndrome, involving the masculinization of the female fetus, is usually restricted "to enlargement of the clitoris plus or minus a certain amount of labial fusion . . . [and] in rare instances masculinization [becomes] complete, producing a penis and empty scrotum" (Money and Ehrhardt, 1972). While Randi's physical exam did not uncover this syndrome in its extreme, Randi's neonatal and early childhood gender behaviors were similar to those reported for girls with PIH syndrome: e.g. tomboyism, a high level of energy expenditure and physical aggression, and a preference for utilitarian clothing and boys' toys. In actuality the research on women with PIH syndrome suggests that while these women are late developers, they are generally heterosexually oriented and fully female in their self-concept and body image. Clearly, this was not the case with Randi. What we cannot know is whether there had been a subtle, but pervasive influence on all aspects of her brain development by her hormonally organized "masculine" brain.

While a biological explanation of Randi's disorder would have been especially welcomed by the patient, there was no way to perform a crucial test of the hypothesis that her fetal brain had been masculinized *in utero* by progestins. On the other hand, such a hypothesis could not be ruled out. While it would be extravagant to attribute all of Randi's masculinity to an unproven hypothesis, one cannot dismiss the possibility that the medication her mother took during the pregnancy may have had an organizing role in Randi's "masculinity complex."

Until we know more about the micro-molecular organization of the fetal brain by specific hormones (no less about micro-structures of femininity), we will be at a loss to explain the real effects of prenatal hormones on brain functioning. Future investigators in brain behavior research in pediatric endocrinology should be encouraged to test their speculations — no matter how exotic — regarding the effect of prenatal hormones on behavior.

However, there was strong evidence to suggest that several interacting factors, including, but not limited to, family dynamics, intra-psychic, and interpersonal processes, played important roles in the etiology of Randi's transsexualism. Moreover, there was evidence of intergenerational gender identity conflicts on both sides of the family. If we look at Randi's early childhood it is clear that her life was one of cumulative trauma, characterized by chronic losses and separations. These events weakened her sense of object constancy, led to severe developmental defects in her personality, and mobilized intense separation and abandonment anxiety. In addition to their physical moves, mother (who had not sufficiently separated from her parental core) was incapable of providing a safe environment for Randi. Indeed, Randi felt exposed, vulnerable, and unprotected; mother failed to provide an adequate maternal shield for Randi against her paranoid and depressive anxieties.

Additionally, an analysis of Randi's early childhood revealed a personality pattern that was typical of those individuals who, as adults, are diagnosed as having severe character pathology and identity diffusion. These individuals are usually diagnosed as having secondary self pathology (a narcissistic behavior disorder), or a severe borderline personality disturbance. Individuals with these disorders have seriously impaired ego functioning and are unable to adaptively organize or synthesize their percepts, concepts, or judgments. While not overtly psychotic, they have a subtle but pervasive thought disorder, disturbances in concentration and attention, impaired reality sense (but generally good reality testing), fluid ego boundaries, impaired social judgment, and are impulse-ridden. Lacking solid ego boundaries and a cohesive self-system, women with these disorders are unable to form a cohesive identity, with some women being unable to form a core female gender identity. The latter group manifests serious gender diffusion and confusion, characterized by bisexuality and atypical gender role adaptations. While one may argue that Randi's narcissistic disorder subserved her gender identity conflicts, it does not fully explain why the focus of her disorder was on her gender identity and role. To answer this question we have to understand the mother's dynamics, since mother was the primary model for Randi's evolving a female core gender identity. While mother was clearly ambivalent about her female status, her conflicts did not arise solely *ab intra* but had their roots deeply embedded within her own family system.

Mrs. Delours's mother was a stern, domineering woman who outwardly admired and idolized her husband but inwardly resented and feared him, being jealous and envious of his power and authority. As a child she had stood in awe of her father and denigrated her mother (whom she perceived as weak and helpless). She felt controlled by her family, lacked a sense of autonomy, and believed that the only way she could resolve her separation conflicts was by getting married (a primitive attempt at separation–individuation which was undercut by her encompassing rage at her husband and her acute psychiatric hospitalization within the first year of marriage).

Mrs. Delours's sisters shared in her feelings and seemed to have serious interpersonal problems and gender conflicts. None of them had married or separated from the home. They distrusted men and never fully separated from their nuclear family system. In an attempt to protect themselves from the authority and power of males, all of the women linked themselves together, forming a bulwark against father's imagined omnipotence.

Mrs. Delours's mother instructed her daughter in self-hatred; taught her to despise her femaleness; and taught her to equate femaleness with states of helplessness, powerlessness, and vulnerability. Mother believed that only a strong, powerful man could protect her against the ravages and caprices of a hostile world. As she entered her teens, Mrs. Delours naturally found herself attracted to older men who could protect her and provide for her. Like her mother, her admiration or adoration of these men cloaked her intense envy and awe of their imagined power, and reflected her own inner emptiness as a female. Mrs. Delours believed that she could only survive if she married a strong man. Indeed she married a "survivor," an able combatant who had endured some of the harshest realities of the twentieth century and "survived." He became the glue for her fragmented self-system.

There was considerable evidence that Mrs. Delours transmitted her disorder to her child. Indeed, Mrs. Delours had severe developmental deficits and lacked a cohesive self-esteem. Mrs. Delours' ego boundaries were quite fluid and at times it was difficult for her to distinguish self from others. Results of psychological testing during her brief hospital admission (at age 19) suggested that her main problems were in the area of boundary formation and sexual differentiation. On the draw-a-picture test male and female figures were interpreted as having fluid boundaries and merging with one another. Indeed, these tests, taken twenty-eight years prior to her daughter's announced transsexualism, revealed a striking finding: Mrs. Delours, then 19 years old, verbalized to her drawing of a male figure: "guess you make him like a woman only stronger — I'll make my husband — this looks like a child or kid — the only thing different he doesn't have breasts — otherwise he just looks like a woman." The evidence was compelling. Mrs. Delours had revealed a serious gender identity disturbance at the same age as her daughter; was it merely a coincidence?

In an intriguing paper Litin et al. (1956) suggested that unusual sexual behavior in children is almost always the result of an unconscious seduction by the parents, who also condone the behavior in their child. They stated:

> Unusual sexual behavior evolves by adaptation of the ego to subtle attitudes within the family, a process that distorts the instinctual life of the child. Perverse sexual acting out and many unusual heterosexual patterns result from unconscious permission and subtle coercion by adults. The parental influences operate reciprocally with the need of the child, so that eventually each participant stimulates the other (Litin et al., 1956, p. 37).

One hypothesis to explain Randi's transsexualism would be that mother, through projective identification, grafted her gender identity conflicts onto her daughter (who was receptive to containing these conflicts because of her reciprocal need system and cross-gender wishes), who then acted them out for the mother.

Indeed, once father died, mother may have unconsciously communicated to Randi just how vulnerable she felt without father to protect her. In this sense Randi may have seized the opportunity to adopt a male identity in order to replace father and rescue mother from her inner anxieties and fears of her femaleness. One can also speculate that Randi may have been fearful of father's incestuous longings towards her; her wish to be a male being a defense against her feared incestuous engulfment by father. Indeed, prior to his death father was dating women Randi's age, behavior which might have aroused Randi's incestuous wishes and fears.

Randi perceived mother's helplessness and need to be rescued as evidence of women's endangered and vulnerable state. Viewing women as weak and helpless, Randi believed that only men could protect themselves from being annihilated. Randi's conceptualization of this process, though grossly oversimplified, provided her with a plan for protecting herself. It was a simple, concrete solution: became a man.

Randi's plan to undergo SRS as a "solution" to her gender identity conflicts was indirectly supported by father, who encouraged Randi to emulate and identify with him. Whenever Randi acted like father he praised her and seemed proud; he reinforced her high activity level, athletic prowess, and masculine pursuits; he dreaded being dependent and passive and discouraged these traits in Randi. For Randi, father was more than a role model; he provided her, as he did her mother, with the glue for self-cohesion.

In an attempt to enhance his masculine appearance, father underwent several cosmetic operations. Within a short period of time Randi repeatedly "injured" her knees such that she had to undergo a series of operations which left her, scarred. She was proud of her scars, which she saw as further identifying her with father. Indeed, Randi seemed to feel that father was subtly giving her permission to undergo her own cosmetic surgery, to turn her into a male. At these times Randi's thinking appeared magical, concrete, autistic. There was considerable evidence that, whereas early childhood influences had laid the foundation for Randi's transsexualism, it was the series of sudden losses, deaths, and knee surgeries, culminating in the death of her father, that were the precipitants for Randi's transsexual wishes. With father's death, the way was now clear for Randi to assume a male identity. As long as father was alive he acted as an external control against Randi's regressive wishes to be a male; his death left Randi unprotected and vulnerable.

Moreover, her brother's conversion to Orthodox Judaism now meant that Randi was free to replace him as the "man of the family." Indeed, the parents viewed Samuel's adoption of an Orthodox Jewish role ambivalently. While father had kept his Jewish background a secret, he was also a fervent Zionist; a secular Jew who offered to be a spy but who distrusted organized religion. His son's conversion meant that he was betraying father's legacy and adopting, not only a whole new life style, but also a new family. Furthermore, father feared that having identified as a Jew, his son would become a target for anti-semitism. He was also ashamed that Samuel had become a religious zealot — a commitment which contrasted with father's anti-clericalism and irreligiosity. By moving out of the country Samuel left a void which Randi tried to fill. However, while father encouraged Randi towards masculine pursuits, he rejected her attempts actually to impersonate a man. In the end, Randi's behavior was wild and erratic, causing father to disown her. Rather than being a prodigal son, Randi was viewed as the black sheep of the family, rejected, and disinherited from father's estate.

While Randi's adoption of a male role and identity had multiple explanations and roots in her development, her wishes for SRS were always couched more in the terms of threats to undergo SRS than in purposeful strivings towards masculinity. Randi's threats of SRS increased whenever she feared abandonment, and her separation-individuation conflicts intensified. Mother reacted to Randi's threats of SRS by becoming powerless, helpless, panicky, and terrified, behaviors which increased Randi's manipulations, coercions, and omnipotence. At those times there was always a real possibility that Randi would act self-destructively and undergo SRS (she always had a number of surgeons who would operate at a moment's notice). Randi's threats reached a peak when mother contemplated making a commitment to live with her new lover, perhaps to leave the country. In effect, whenever she was threatened by narcissistic injury and a lowering of her self-esteem, Randi planned to obtain SRS. Her plans provided her with a feeling of aliveness (or what Kohut (1977) has called "pseudovitality"), and functioned as a goal for her life, giving meaning to her existence. However, her plans were doomed to failure because they substituted fictions for reality and did not address the profound psychological problems which were the basis for her gender pathology.

Randi's demands that mother accept her as a transsexual locked mother and Randi in an ongoing battle. Since she stirred up enormous fear and excitement in mother (relieving her depressive feelings), Randi always had the upper hand. As long as mother kept the issue alive by considering whether or not to accept Randi as a man and give permission for Randi to have SRS, Randi kept the separation–individuation issue alive and avoided the pain of separation and the fears associated with psychological maturation.

With counseling, however, mother was able to strengthen her defensive functioning and take a strong stand against involvement in Randi's decision for surgery. With her mother's refusal to give permission for SRS and so become involved in Randi's conflicts, Randi had no other choice but to give up her demands for surgery. Because of Randi's convincing personality style, her threats always seemed urgent and it always appeared that something drastic would happen unless one supported her. During this period mother showed considerable courage in facing up to her daughter's demands and in following therapeutic instructions. The result was that Randi always backed off from her threats for SRS and, while frequently scheduling herself for surgery, never followed through on her plans.

Randi's case history demonstrated that her female transsexualism was a complex phenomenon which was multiply determined; no one explanation could account for her gender pathology. The wealth of her family input provided additional evidence that intergenerational gender conflicts played an important role in focusing her self pathology around gender-related issues. Indeed, it appeared that Randi's gender had become the target and the focus of the family's pathology. She was not only a scapegoat for a major family problem, but a willing participant who enjoyed being the focus of the family's attention. From an early age Randi's behavior suggested a diffuse gender role and identity. Indeed, while she revealed the typical erotic fantasy life of a pre-homosexual girl (with crushes on girls and teachers beginning in the fourth grade), she also revealed an attraction to males. Indeed, her bisexuality developed *pari passu* with a wish to be transformed into a man. Unlike many female transsexuals, her wish was not fully formed during early childhood. It was not until she was a teenager that her transsexual identity began to form. There is strong evidence that not until age 12, when she ran away from home, did she even seriously consider adopting a transsexual identity. The turning point came when she linked up with a deviant subcultural community in Europe. It was then that she was exposed to a transsexual life style — a solution to her bisexuality — and encouraged by other transsexuals to develop along those lines. One may surmise that she was attracted to a transsexual life style because it provided her with an explanation for her confused inner feelings, and the basis for an identity. While the whole area of the initiation of young teenagers into transsexualism by deviant sexual subgroups has been virtually ignored, every gender clinician knows how powerful a force that is in the consolidation and crystallization of a transsexual identity.

Lacking a cohesive self-system, Randi was constantly searching for an explanation and resolution of her inner confusion. Her concrete view of maleness (as a source of protection) provided her with an inner feeling of strength and wholeness, synthesizing the fragmented elements of her self-system and allowing her to "survive" her imagined inner fears, which she projected onto the world (but which then were interpreted as real, hostile forces in the world). Randi magically believed that in the guise of a male she was invulnerable to those threats from "reality."

Randi's concept of maleness was filtered through the eyes of a child with the mentality of an 8-year-old. She saw herself as a male because of her short hair, her male clothing, and her gestures. While male hormones had facilitated her "maleness" by toughening her skin, distributing her hair in a male pattern, lowering her voice, and heightening her sex drive, they had not provided her with the rich inner sense of maleness which evolves out of a lifelong developmental, biological–familial–individual and social process. She was, in effect, a sheep in wolf's clothing. Her "maleness" was, however, corroborated by her deviant subgroup (which facilitated her role change and gave her support to change sex), and by the medical–psychological establishment which provided her with an imprimatur of "maleness" (a written document stating she was indeed a true transsexual, conferred on her after evaluation at a gender clinic). But this was not enough. Randi desperately needed her mother's permission to change sex. She needed that approval because, fundamentally, she knew she was a female and needed someone of importance to her to corroborate that fact by refusing to participate in her distorted reality sense. In effect, Randi sensed that her real conflict was one of separation–individuation; she held the magical belief that only as a male could she separate from mother (a belief that had a pervasive influence on her entire self-system).

In her everyday life Randi was viewed by her peers as a saint. She distributed her family wealth among her peers; housed wayward girls at her own expense; and paid for two transsexuals' operations. Maintaining a Madonna-like smile, Randi defended all transsexuals with an ideological fervor. She became a transsexual advocate, a spokesperson, threatening lawsuits against those who begrudged her right to impersonate a man, and vigorously defending her friends from imagined or real enemies. She was a martyr, a seemingly self-sacrificing young woman who played the role of victim to the hilt; her friends viewed her as a saint.

In actuality, she was a frightened, clinging, dependent teenager who had erected seemingly impenetrable defenses to protect her from annihilation. Indeed, to counteract her feelings of vulnerability and helplessness as a female she maintained a staunch counterphobic and counterdefensive attitude, appearing tough, independent, and competent. Like father she was adventuresome, risk-taking, expansive, manicky; a roguish woman who was alternately playful and mischievous, cunning and daring. Above all she was a young woman whose life was a series of exciting escapades, which, while no match for father's reputation as a hero, resembled a *roman à clef* in which Randi played the fictional role of an adventuresome man, a modern-day Huckleberry Finn. In effect, Randi viewed herself as a picaresque saint — a role that encompassed all aspects of her character but still left her basically unfulfilled and without hope.

The crazy kid next door: Patricia/Pat

Prior to enrolling in the CWRU gender clinic, Patricia had been hospitalized at a local state psychiatric facility. In fact she had had three admissions during that past year. Her acute hospitalizations were prompted by her suicidal and homocidal threats, and her profoundly depressed affect. Prior to her admissions she was reportedly doing "violent, stupid things — running people off the road, getting panicky, wanting to shoot someone." Patricia volunteered that her disorganized state followed the breakup of a two-year relationship with an older woman, Katy, who abandoned Patricia. "Katy was the first girl I ever loved. I always had a big stone wall inside of me. With her I loved her and believed she loved me." With the breakup of the relationship Patricia made a serious suicide attempt. She secluded herself in a metropolitan park and overdosed on the Seconal that Katy, a nurse, had given her. At the last possible moment she was rescued by a passerby who happened to notice her limp body.

During all three hospitalizations Patricia revealed her wishes to become a man and insisted on being referred for sex reassignment surgery. During her first two hospitalizations Patricia's depression and disorganized thoughts were treated with high dosages of Elavil and Mellaril. The chart notes revealed that on the ward she "continued to hurt herself by cutting herself with pop cans or burning herself with cigarettes." A physical exam revealed a basically healthy biological female with a normal EEG.

After each discharge Patricia had recontacted Katy. With each rebuff she became more disorganized, agitated, and depressed. By the third hospitalization the staff decided to try a course of ECT (six treatments in all). Although some improvement in her depressed condition was noted (Patricia simply stated that "it worked"), she still insisted she was transsexual and wanted SRS. Patricia was discharged from the hospital with a diagnosis of schizoaffective schizophrenia, depressed type. Psychological testing highlighted her destructive tendencies and underscored Patricia's need to "perceive men as over-powering, active and fearsome, while women were seen as necessarily guarded, defensive, and dependently inferior." Her ego boundaries were noted to be quite fluid and she was seen as having a tendency to overidentify and merge with other individuals, losing her self-identity by fusing her ego boundaries with objects.

During all three hospitalizations Patricia was treated by a female psychiatrist in supportive psychotherapy. The therapy progressed well but she developed an intense erotic-symbiotic transference towards her therapist (which had not been resolved by discharge). Unfortunately, the psychiatrist could not follow her as an outpatient. When Patricia was evaluated by our gender clinic she seemed still to be genuinely depressed over the loss of her relationship to Dr. S and had an unresolved transference reaction. She expressed a wish to continue therapy with a female therapist.

Patricia was a thin, boyish-looking female who dressed in unisex clothing, walked with a swagger, and affected a male pose. Now 24 years old, Patricia worked for a car parts distributor, dressed in jeans, a denim work shirt, and boots, and proudly displayed her hands and arms which were stained with motor oil. Patricia described herself as a "man with a puny body"; a person who had tried all kinds of diets and exercises to increase her body build and strength, but to no avail. She believed her real self to be a male; a man trapped in a woman's body, albeit a puny man. Patricia believed that her problems might have been caused "possibly [by] a spirit clash in reincarnation" or a chemical problem, or "it might be caused by emotional trauma from various occurrences in a person's life." The idea that surgery might be the cure for her condition was stimulated by an article on transsexualism which she had read in a pornographic magazine.

When Patricia was 17 years old she threw out all her female wardrobe. However, her impersonation of a male role did not resolve her confusion. Indeed, Patricia confided that she felt an "inability to cope with myself as a female. I crossdress for the most degree but feel alienated from both genders." Moreover, her two marriages to men, her sexual preference for women, and her bisexual gender schema, suggested a confused, chaotic self and gender identity. While she hated her female body and was disgusted by it, she was also sexually attracted to other women, viewing the female body as erotic and beautiful. Assuming the guise of a male and wearing male clothing had not resolved her gender identity conflicts. Indeed, her conflicts seemed heightened and more urgent. Every time she undressed and viewed her naked body she reacted with disgust and shame, realizing that her crossdressing was a mere charade.

Patricia's first memory of wanting to be a male dated back to age 4, "ever since I saw my brother [Stuart] standing up going to the bathroom." She recalled that even at 4 years of age "I prayed to God and used to think that I'd wake up one morning and be a boy." When she voiced these concerns to mother, mother replied, "you'll always be my little girl." These words infuriated Patricia and literally drove her wild; they caused her to lose control, to break and throw things, and also to try to mutilate her body – burning herself with cigarettes or slashing her entire body with knives. Indeed, Patricia's life was punctuated by bouts of wild, out-of-control, destructive, impulsive behavior which sometimes frightened even her.

Patricia was the second of five siblings (an older brother, two younger sisters, and the youngest child, a brother). Patricia's older brother, Stuart, was 4 years old when she was born. Mother reported that her pregnancy with Patricia was normal; there were no birth complications and Patricia weighed over eight pounds, but was long and skinny. As a baby she was quite active, "crawling all over the place and getting into everything." Patricia's earliest memory was "being on a porch dressed in a little dress, 'cause that's what Mom used to do to me. Had a fence around the porch. I remember trying to get off the porch and thinking I was way off the ground."

During Patricia's early childhood the family made many moves. When Susan, who was mild to moderately retarded, was born they celebrated her birth by moving to a new house (Patricia was then $2\frac{1}{2}$ years old). While pregnant with Susan mother was very sick, often disappearing from the house for long periods of time. The situation was complicated by Susan's chronic kidney disease and mental retardation, which forced mother to spend all of her time with her. As a result of drinking contaminated milk, mother and several of the children had terrible bouts with undulant fever. Indeed, family members were often whisked away in the night to the hospital, leaving Patricia feeling empty and frightened. These losses, illnesses, separations, and abandonments left Patricia quite anxious, and rageful at her sister. When Patricia was 5 her second sister Mary-Beth was born, and at age 13 her last sibling, Robert, was born.

Patricia was closest to her oldest brother, Stuart: "I idolized him when [I was] young." However, now they are constantly at odds with each other and she barely speaks to him. Patricia's relationship with Stuart was highly ambivalent, varying from "great to terrible." Patricia claimed that Stuart was mother's favorite child; she also idolized him. Intensely jealous of Stuart, Patricia prayed every night "that I would wake up and be a boy like Stuart."

Vacillating between overidealizing Stuart and hating him, Patricia's fights with Stuart were violent. One argument over who would wear the only pair of Lone Ranger pajamas ended with Stuart "smashing my face on a counter" and Patricia retaliating by "stabbing him with a letter opener." On another occasion, Stuart sadistically threw Patricia down from a tree house. But Patricia always got her revenge. By the time Patricia was in the third grade (she was age 8), her relationship with Stuart became overtly sexual.

Patricia blandly reported how Stuart, a preadolescent, "and four of his friends, raped me sexually." The first sexual assault came when the parents left all of their children alone in the house while they took a weekend trip. Patricia recalled that Stuart threatened that, if she "told on him," he would see that she was punished.

Throughout her girlhood Patricia was repeatedly sexually abused by her brother and his friends. She was also asked to enlist other girls to perform sex acts for her brother. Almost all of the assaults were connected with Susan's kidney problems, as Stuart waited until the parents were at the hospital to rape his sister.

Patricia first ran away from home when she was 13 (when Robert was born). She said that she wanted to get as far away from Stuart as possible. She felt terribly guilty about her incestuous relationship and was unable to share her "secret" with anyone. While she admitted that her sexual involvement with Stuart "really screwed me up," she had become emotionally close to Stuart and felt depleted, empty, and alone when he left her. During her entire girlhood Patricia was avoided by other girls who knew of her sexual exploits and "bad" reputation. She was shunned at school and in her neighborhood, failing to make any friends. She recalled that all of her play was with her brother and his friends: playing with trains, building forts, playing football, and making gunpowder. She also learned to hunt and trap animals. Her parents, frightened by her developing maleness, gave her dolls and dresses, and used physical and verbal force to coerce her into becoming more feminine. Patricia defiantly rebelled against her parents, feeling exploited and abused. At the same time her parents actively supported Stuart's independence.

Patricia's destructiveness and her revenge motives occasionally erupted full-force. Indeed, during childhood Patricia "killed all her pets because they hurt me." She described, in a paranoid fashion, how her pet chickens and rabbits "purposefully scratched me" and how she got revenge by methodically killing them (cutting them open and pulling out their insides). She also took pleasure in drowning, or savagely beating cats. While she seemed to interpret any friendly play by her pets as sadistic, aggressive assaults, she was also fascinated by fire and once burned down the home of a girlfriend whom she felt had spurned her.

Patricia related her aggressiveness and her need to destroy animals to her ancestry; she was one-tenth Algonquin Indian, and interpreted that ancestry to mean that she was a savage, a primitive creature with wild, aggressive tendencies. On a sentence completion test she responded to the stems "I'm sorry that I . . ." and "I dream . . ." with the respective answers "I'm not an Indian brave," "a lot about being Indian." While she attributed the wild, out-of-control part of herself to her one-tenth Indian heritage, she took pride in her aggression and usually did not see it as a problem.

Although she hated small animals, Patricia was symbiotically attached to horses and developed a clinging, dependent relationship with some of the horses on her farm. One incident Patricia recalled from her childhood related to the death of her favorite horse. One day she found her horse just barely alive, having been run over by a tractor. She recalled "holding her head, which was all bloody" and crying, fearful that it would die. Eventually the horse was dragged away from her and towed off by a tractor. She watched helplessly as a hose was put into the animal's throat and a chemical poured down it which killed her. "Dad wanted to call the glue factory. I called him a rotten bastard." Eventually the parents agreed to allow the horse to be buried on their farm. Patricia recalled the event with fiery affect, suggesting that it was still a live issue for her.

Patricia's father a man in his early fifties, was a barber by profession but also managed real estate. Patricia stated that, "We had no real understanding of each other — he had a violent temper." Father was described as a "nasty bastard" who was intrusive, alcoholic, and bisexual and often away from home for long periods. He savagely beat his wife and children, roaming around his farm like a wild animal stalking its prey. During his rages he focused his physical violence particularly on Patricia, who stoically accepted her punishment. Patricia recalled how father would whip her so badly that "sometimes I couldn't go to school 'cause I was black and blue." Whenever father lost control he was unable to curb his fury until he either exhausted himself, or someone stopped him.

Patricia recalled that she often had to protect her younger siblings from father's violence, taking the beatings herself rather than letting them face father's rages. Patricia recalled being told that her father was severely abused by his parents; and that once his paternal grandmother broke his arm for no reason. "Tempers on mother's side are also rough. When her father got mad he used to chop up furniture." Clearly, there was an intergenerational message: men are violent, destructive, out-of-control individuals who are to be feared.

Mother, in her mid-forties, was described as a passive-dependent housewife who spent little time at home and devoted herself to playing the church organ. She had a masochistic relationship with her husband and watched passively as he brutalized the children (whom she seemed to resent). Indeed, her only reason for having children had been her staunch Catholicism which forbade birth control. Mother hated her femaleness, felt unprotected and weak, and placed all her hopes in her two sons. Patricia noted that mother confused her. She could not comprehend why mother really "doesn't understand me and is hurt" by Patricia's wishes to become a man. When Patricia entered adolescence mother became fearful of her daughter's homosexual tendencies and threw out all of her slacks, insisting that she wear skirts and blouses. A combination of factors, including the birth of her brother Robert, led Patricia to run away from home. While she did not overtly reject her mother, Patricia was angry and resentful at her for either abandoning her or leaving her unprotected in the face of father's wrath.

Patricia recalled getting her first period "however old you are when you get your hunting license." She reacted to her menses with rage and confusion, similar emotions to those she had experienced when her horse was killed. Patricia was ashamed of her female body and disgusted with her new bodily changes. Fortunately, she was quite flatchested, which spared her from some of the intense personal anguish over bust development that many female transsexuals exhibited. Typically, mother withdrew from Patricia and was unempathic of her daughter's anguish during this critical phase.

As a teenager Patricia was constantly "horny" and engaged in kinky, bisexual experiences with just about anyone. However, her sexual encounters offered little emotional release or satisfaction. With her partners she maintained a bland, detached, almost dissociated relationship. In the neighbourhood she was known as a "bad girl"; parents urged their daughters not to associate with her. "When I was young I wasn't allowed to go to parties . . . when I started getting into trouble the parents kept their kids from me." "Trouble" included being arrested for breaking and entering, and robbery, and, later, for stabbing a high school teacher by whom she had felt spurned.

When she was 8 years old Patricia developed intense crushes on girls and older women (especially teachers). In school she was constantly aroused sexually and found it difficult to concentrate and attend to her school work. "I was constantly falling in love — even in Church." It wasn't until the ninth grade that she had her first real girlfriend. Understandably she chose a girl whom everyone else avoided, an obese girl whom she nicknamed "Chink." In her sexual relationship with "Chink" Patricia played the masculine role, going down on her, but not allowing "Chink" to have sex with her because she, Patricia, lacked a penis. The relationship ended when "Chink" fell in love with a man and got married. Patricia reacted to the loss by having sex with a man. She stated, "it was strange because I enjoyed it."

From age 14 on Patricia masturbated, an activity that caused her considerable anguish. As a Catholic she believed masturbation to be sinful, rationalizing her homosexual impulses as more acceptable since another person was involved in the act. Patricia masturbated twice a day, but always felt empty, alone, and unfulfilled. Usually she fantasized that she was a man with a penis making love to a woman. During her adolescence Patricia stimulated herself by reading erotographic literature, masturbating to fantasies of bondage, and crossdressing. Occasionally she became frightened when she found she compulsively "super identified with what was happening" in the stories, and often could not distinguish fantasy from reality.

In order to placate her parents, and to try to put an end to her conflictual male feelings, Patricia, then 17 years old, initiated a heterosexual relationship and planned to get married. However, she could not tolerate being heterosexual and eventually ran away from home, ending up in Greenwich Village, panhandling and prostituting. Urged by father to return home, she meekly complied, becoming more withdrawn and self-destructive, beating herself, tearing her flesh, and taking street drugs. Eventually her family had her psychiatrically hospitalized.

Patricia spent four months at a state psychiatric facility which she described as a "dungeon." She did not cooperate with the hospitalization and, believing that she had been tricked by her parents, she "lied like hell to the staff" until she was discharged. After discharge Patricia claimed that she had seduced one of her nurses and engaged in a sexual relationship with her. While Patricia might have been lying about her encounter, the act had symbolic significance. Indeed, several of Patricia's lovers had been nurses. Patricia seemed to entertain a fantasy about being loved and cared for by a nurse, a fantasy which involved being rescued and saved by a caring woman.

After her discharge Patricia went back to work as a groom at a local race track. She spent the next two years wandering around the country working at race tracks and leading a desperate existence. Prior to her twentieth birthday, Patricia was married briefly to another horse trainer ("who looked like me"), but separated from him after he sadistically beat her. After he was imprisoned for grand larceny, Patricia moved to the Sun Belt where she began a series of lesbian relationships and fell in love with another nurse. Eventually she was hospitalized for what appeared to be an acute schizophrenic reaction. Her break with reality had occurred while she was training race horses at a track that was surrounded by large palm trees. "They [the trees] became giant people. I would talk to them and forget what I was doing. One day I took a butcher knife and cut across my stomach." Patricia's lover, a nurse, recommended that she be psychiatrically hospitalized. After a one-month hospitalization she returned to live with her parents and then became involved in an intense sexual relationship with Katy.

At the same time that she became involved with Katy, Patricia also became involved with Ken (and eventually had a *ménage à trois* with them). Pressured by his family and fearful of losing him, she married Ken. In less than six months she moved back in with Katy. In retrospect, it appeared that Ken was probably gay. He continued to see Patricia and supported her relationship with Katy, the relationship which broke down Patricia's pretenses and led to her three successive psychiatric hospitalizations and eventually to our gender clinic, where she formally applied for sex change surgery.

In the course of treatment Patricia's stated goals were to have her sex changed and to become a father. She was obsessed with the idea of having a penis. In order to consolidate her male identity Patricia assumed a new male name, which was randomly obtained by thumbing through the phone book. Patricia stated that she would like to adopt a boy and live a conventional married life with an understanding woman. She was, however, ambivalent about SRS and the possibility of scarring from the surgery, an attitude which, given her own extensive self-mutilation, was curious.

Patricia's ultimate goal was to masculinize herself so that she looked just like her second husband, Ken. Once SRS was accomplished she wanted to become a park ranger (Ken's primary occupation), or continue in her present work as truck driver for an auto parts company. Delusional about what SRS could accomplish, Patricia asked if we could make her 6' 2" and 185 pounds (she was now 5' 4" and weighed about 100 pounds).

Formulation of the case

How are we to understand Patricia's wishes to be a male? Can her gender dysphoria be explained by her schizophrenia? While *DSM* III states that a diagnosis of schizophrenia rules out a diagnosis of transsexualism, it was clear that Patricia's chronic gender dysphoria was distinct from, and could not be entirely explained by, her diagnosed schizophrenia. She never evidenced genital hallucinosis, and delusions of sexual transformation.

While some schizophrenics may exhibit a focal psychosis around their gender role and identity, Patricia knew that she was a biological female; she was not delusional about her gender role and identity. She knew that she did not have a penis, nor did she hallucinate a penis. She wished to become a man, and she wished for a penis. Her reality testing around her sex and gender identity was intact. She did, however, manifest a subtle thought disturbance, impaired judgment and reality sense, and a disturbed body schema and image, and engaged in magical thinking. All of her problems associated with impaired ego functioning played a role in her cross-gender wishes. In addition, family and environmental factors influenced her gender identity conflicts.

While one could dismiss Patricia's stories of sexual abuse as mere delusions, or the fantasy elaborations of a schizophrenic, clinical interviewing and psychological testing supported the idea that her reported sexual abuse probably occurred. In addition, records of previous hospitalizations provided some support for her story. While there is increasing evidence that even the most preposterous schizophrenic delusions may have some basis in reality (as witnessed by recent investigations into the Schreber case), the point is that her psyche behaved as if the events had occurred. The "reality" of her beliefs influenced her behavior. While it would be satisfying to have proof of the sexual assaults, such an empirical basis would not seriously alter our hypotheses.

Rather than focus on Patricia's diagnosed schizophrenia (as explanatory of her transsexualism), it seemed more fruitful to examine Patricia's early developmental history, the analysis of which could provide important clues to the etiology of her gender dysphoria. One was immediately struck by the chaotic family structure: the intergenerational conflicts over aggression, the bisexual status of the father, the incestuous assaults, mother's hatred of her femininity, the intense sibling jealousy and envy (verging on paranoia), and the large number of losses, separations, abandonments, and moves. As a result of the interplay of these factors, Patricia's young ego had been overstimulated, overwhelmed, confused, and disorganized, and had failed to develop along normal developmental lines. Patricia's family milieu was characterized by a lack of organization and structure, impulsivity, sadism, unbounded aggression, a lack of sublimations, inadequate frustration tolerance, an inability to bear anxiety, and evidence of gender identity conflicts. There was strong evidence of intergenerational conflicts of gender identity pathology on both sides of the family. In such a family system Patricia failed to evolve stable ego mechanisms to cope with her affects, aggression, and anxiety. Indeed, her ego mechanisms associated with perception, judgment, attention, concentration, and reality sense seemed to be markedly impaired.

Within the matrix of a disturbed family milieu Patricia's ego development and self-system were impaired and her gender role and identity malformed. One hypothesis might be that the strength of the family's assaults on Patricia's gender identity could account for her focusing and emphasizing this aspect of her impaired self-system (to the exclusion of other foci). Why she, and not another sibling, became the focus of the family's conflicts cannot be answered until the whole family becomes the subject of our inquiry.

While Patricia's parents, being Catholic, felt duty-bound to have children, they were both severely disturbed and incapable of providing their children with an empathic relationship. Their disturbed parenting left Patricia feeling unprotected and exposed, especially to threats of annihilation. By failing to provide an adequate "holding environment" and a protective shield for the children, the parents made it appear to Patricia that it was only the superficial aspects of a male gender identity which could protect one against the dangers of the external world. In Patricia's eyes father's rages made him immune to destruction. Indeed, Patricia viewed father's rages as self-protective; as he intimidated and scared away potential enemies.

Father, symbolizing the cloak of maleness, had free reign to terrorize anyone in the house. His rages controlled the environment and became, for Patricia, the epitome of self-protection. Patricia believed that if she could become a male, like father, she could survive anything, and perhaps even become a whole person. While her reasoning seemed somewhat autistic and magical, it exerted a profound influence on Patricia's cognitive system and her gender identity conflicts. On the most superficial level, her male identifications represented an identification with the aggressor; an attempt to overcome her perceived dependency and what she saw as the passivity of the female role.

Patricia had come to view females as vulnerable, powerless, helpless, and dependent. On the Rorschach she equated femaleness with a fungus growth: a disgusting, ugly structure which symbolized her view of her female genitals and female self-system, revealing her profound underlying depression regarding her femaleness. Patricia viewed women as castrated, lacking the vitality of maleness, living a joyless, detached, isolated, withdrawn existence, and dependent for their survival on male protection. Weakness, which was identified with femaleness, was not only despised, but also dangerous. An admission of dependency, therefore, was not only embarrassing but also dangerous since it resulted in vulnerability and openness to attack and destruction. On the other hand, men were viewed as able to gratify their dependency needs, since they could protect themselves from states of vulnerability by their male prowess and aggressive energies. Patricia seemed to fear that the imagined vulnerability and weakness of the female role would not allow her to be loved without also being destroyed.

Her wishes to be a man also reflected her magical solution to having her dependency needs met; allowing herself, in the role of a man, to be gentle and cared for by a female without opening herself up to attack and annihilation. When she viewed herself as a man, she fantasized herself as strong and safe enough to enter into a loving and caring relationship. Her tough masculine facade can be interpreted as a rigid defense against her vulnerable inner female self.

Patricia's history of erotic involvement with nurses suggested that nurses symbolized for her a caring, maternal source which she sought out in order to repair the damage wrought by her inadequate mothering. She believed that a nurse could empathically relate to her inner, damaged self-system and repair her self-defects. Being nursed as a woman was too endangering to her ego (perhaps too laden with homosexual fears of engulfment). Only in the guise of a man could she allow herself to submit to her passive yearnings and profound dependency needs, which had been inadequately met in childhood. There was also a concrete aspect to her thinking (and symbolism) which cannot be overlooked: one can only be nursed by a nurse.

An important part of Patricia's vulnerable inner self was her capacity for over-identifying with others, losing ego boundaries, and fusing and merging with another personality. Patricia experienced her ego as structureless and helpless; unable to defend her against the regressive pulls of fusing with another person's ego. In this sense she feared that she had no real self apart from the adopted, caricatured male poses; taking on the identity of others; and adopting an "as if" personality, thus merging with strong personalities with whom she identified. Lacking a cohesive inner self-system, Patricia's self-identity was in effect akin to a *person manqué*, an impostor whose outer gender facade served as a protective barrier against her core, structureless self. In an attempt to organize some foundation for her self-system, Patricia affirmed her Indian identity (which also afforded a source of explanation or rationalization for her wild, destructive component-self system). Viewing herself as an American Indian provided a limited but necessary structure for her impoverished self.

The pivotal trauma which had consolidated the idea that femaleness was dangerous was Patricia's sexual violation and penetration by her brother. Subsequently, she believed that having a penis (which represented a magical totem) would protect her against being penetrated and destroyed. Indeed, when Patricia fantasized having a penis, she associated having a penis with dominating a woman (always being on top), and engaging in some form of bondage. These fantasies appeared to be attempts to master her childhood anxiety associated with her brother's sexual assaults. The effect of Patricia's cumulative sexual trauma and the unremitting beatings she received from father led her to evolve a negative self-identity of "badness." Viewing herslef as "bad," however, at least allowed her something substantial to associate with her self-system; the alternative, that she was nothing, was too horrible to bear. To be "bad" implied some form of wholeness: a personality state for which Patricia seemed to yearn. That her "badness" became the *sine qua non* of her self-identity (the proud badge of her self-system), was seen in her pride that her "bad" reputation gave her the status of someone special; someone whom the other girls may have avoided, but also someone they admired.

However, the cost was enormous. Being excluded from normal social networks, Patricia, labeled a deviant, began to develop marginal relationships with other people who were also disenfranchised from society. While she now had a group of people with whom to experiment with her new male gender role and identity, she also failed to develop adequate relationships which could have helped her evolve good social judgment and accurate social perceptions. Consequently, Patricia had no mechanism for obtaining consensual validation of her perceptions and judgments of her new gender role.

Throughout her life cycle Patricia had experienced gender confusion and diffusion. Having failed to establish a social identity (in terms of sexual preference), Patricia struggled to define herself in turn as heterosexual, homosexual, bisexual, or transsexual. Her two marriages seemed to have been defensive attempts to establish some form of social identity and to gain social acceptance, proving that she was not "all bad." However, none of her choices seemed to resolve her gender confusion and diffusion.

Patricia's intense envy of Stuart was a major factor in reinforcing her wish to become a man. The irony is that to identify with him meant that she had to reconcile herself to a life of masculine domination and aggression (or those aspects of maleness which society has called into question). It was not maleness that Patricia cherished and yearned for, but a fantasy of maleness in which arrogance, sadism, forceful aggression, ruthlessness, terror, and hatred were predominant elements. All of these factors, associated in Patricia's mind with maleness, were split off from what we know as maleness, and represented a protective barrier and force against self-annihilation. When she turned 13 and her younger brother Robert was born, Patricia was probably thrown into a panic. Robert's birth coincided with Patricia's first menstrual period and crushed her hopes of making use of adolescence as a time to resolve her gender identity conflicts. Robert symbolized her major self-defect, reminding her that she was a deficient woman. Moreover, he concretely represented another possible torturer in the family: another man who could rape her and destroy her. By running away from home Patricia was placing herself at a safe distance from her perceived source of threat to her survival.

Patricia's chaotic sexuality and gender diffusion may be viewed as the result of her lack of cohesive self-system. Experiencing faulty parenting, early developmental defects, and impairments in ego functioning, Patricia suffered from severe self pathology. She was, consequently, unable to organize and synthesize a stable gender role and identity. Her permeable ego boundaries also led her to develop an "as if" personality structure in which she could move in and out of bisexual relationships in a chameleon-like fashion (assuming various male identities), but never be fulfilled.

Patricia's early developmental history and family system predisposed her to gender dysphoria. Some of the pertinent elements which enhanced this gender dysphoria included: pathological gender envy towards her brother; identification with the aggressor-father; an impulse-ridden personality; the inheritance of an intergenerational history of violent rage reactions; the cumulative trauma of chronic incest and sexual abuse; a hatred of her female body; an identification with the victim; and an unconscious collusion by the parents to kill Patricia. Patricia's gender dysphoria was influenced by her schizophrenia but could not be reduced to it alone.

The misfit: Donna/Douglas

Donna, a black female, was 26 when she first contacted our gender clinic. She had learned of our services through the Cleveland Sex Hotline and was referred by another black female transsexual in our program.

Several years ago she had enrolled in another gender clinic's program but dropped out because "they were too expensive." Donna stated that at age 11 she had a dream that she had been changed into a man and that she had a penis growing out of her navel. This dream became indistinguishable from reality and served as the focus for Donna's developing gender identity pathology.

At the time of the evaluation Donna was unemployed, living with her parents and her 12-year-old sister. Donna was very masculine in appearance. For the past two years she had been taking male hormones (prescribed by a local physician on a fee-for-service basis). As a result of the hormones her voice deepened, her sex drive increased, and her body and facial hair grew. Her appearance was convincingly male. Indeed, she dressed in rather conservative male clothing, bound her breasts, and had learned to mimic male non-verbal gestures.

Donna was known on the streets as "Frenchy," a nickname which identified her special talents for oral sex. A short, muscular individual with a goatee, Donna not only enjoyed her male impersonation, but when she was unable to dress and live as a male she felt empty, depressed, and suicidal. In addition, the effect of the male hormones was to make her feel more alive, by increasing her sex drive and thereby elevating her mood. At the time of the evaluation it was unthinkable to Donna that she would ever be asked to give up her male role and identity and stop taking male hormones.

Donna's family history revealed little evidence of emotional pathology (except for an aunt who had incestuously violated her). Donna's father was the eleventh of twelve siblings in a family which included five brothers and six sisters. A silent, soft-spoken man, father was poorly educated, compassionate, and dedicated to his family. He was unaware of any gender identity problems in his family. Both of his parents were dead, the mother at age 47 from cancer, and the father at age 65 from a stroke. The mother was the fourth of eight siblings (including four sisters and three brothers). Both her parents were alive but, because of geographical distance, played a less important role in their grandchildren's upbringing. There was no history of gender identity pathology on her side of the family. The parents were very concerned about Donna's wishes for SRS. They would be willing to accept her as a homosexual and expressed the hope that Donna would adjust to a male gender role without having to undergo surgery.

Donna was the oldest of four siblings (Melissa, 24; Kirk, 21; and

Leshauna, 12). At the time of Donna's birth mother was 18 and father 24 (this had been mother's first pregnancy). Mother described the pregnancy as "a good one." They had looked forward to Donna's birth and were pleased that the baby was a girl. Mother had no complications during her pregnancy, received no medication, and neither smoked nor drank (to this day mother is anti-drinking and smoking). Mother described her family situation, that is, the extended family, as quite supportive and nurturant.

Although they lived in the black ghetto they did not suffer any unnecessary financial hardships or burdens. Mother was highly educated (college degree) and worked as a school teacher. The father, now 51, had worked all of his life as a drywall contractor and was a good provider for the family. While father did not have the same educational training as his wife, he related well to her and seemed happily married. The couple had been married twenty-seven years. The father had strong paternal needs and had looked forward to have a family. Indeed, he remained actively involved in all aspects of his children's lives.

Mother carried Donna's pregnancy to full term and her labor and delivery were normal (having a five hour labor, general anesthesia, and delivering a 6 lb. 7 oz. normal girl baby). Donna was breast-fed for six weeks, mother stopping because "I didn't like that." During infancy Donna was described as "fretting a lot," "screaming," and "gasping for breath." For some reason Donna developed respiratory distress whenever she slept on her back. During her first year there had been, however, no major illnesses, accidents, or traumas. The family was intact; mother stayed home with Donna and cared for the household. Donna walked at 11 months and, by the middle of her second year, spoke a few words. While mother reported that Donna was toilet trained at 16 months of age, she actually continued to wet her bed until she was 12 years old (a behavior which ceased when she began to menstruate). There was no evidence of developmental difficulties or defects. As Donna entered her second year her respiratory problems decreased. While she was viewed as "fretful" she was also deeply loved by the family.

By the beginning of her second year Donna was weaned from the bottle, which coincided with the birth of her sister Melissa. In response to Melissa's birth Donna's bed wetting increased. Donna was extremely jealous of Melissa and also wanted to be bottle fed, constantly demanding that mother feed her too. Donna's jealousy and fighting, which began in infancy, persists today. Indeed, when the parents brought Mellisa home from the hospital Donna blurted out: "No, that's not my sister." Mother did not know how to respond to Donna's jealous rage. Her attempts to treat them as equals failed miserably. Mother reported that, "I would always buy them the same things but Donna always thought that Melissa's was prettier" and that her gifts were better. Inevitably, Donna would insist that Melissa exchange gifts with her. After inspecting Melissa's gift she would then proceed to argue with Melissa until she got her original gift back. Melissa always gave in to Donna's demands. Donna seemed to feel continually cheated *vis-à-vis* her sister.

When Donna was 5 her brother Kirk was born. Mother reported that Donna then began to "block things out of her mind." She described Donna as seeming self-absorbed, daydreaming, withdrawing from reality and entering a state of reverie (at times exhibiting akinetic-like seizures). No matter how they approached Donna they could not get her to talk about her anxiety and her inner experiences. Her school teachers were concerned about her social withdrawal and viewed her as lazy and preoccupied. Indeed, Donna had considerable difficulty with her school work. However, mother did not recall that Donna had had any difficulties separating from her and going to school. Donna looked forward to entering kindergarten and enjoyed school. However, with Kirk's birth, she became more introverted and preoccupied. From the parents' descriptions, it seems that Donna may not have been merely preoccupied but actively hallucinating. Unfortunately, Donna was not psychologically evaluated at that time.

During latency Donna played with girls her own age, had a strong girl peer group, played girls' games, and had dolls. However, when the parents gave Donna a doll she would be disappointed by it and try to trade dolls with Melissa. She did not object to playing with dolls but insisted that somehow her dolls just did not measure up. While mother remembered Donna as being a pretty girl (for whom father bought dresses), father really adored Melissa and treated her as his favorite. Father recalled Donna as having a pretty face but being stockier in build and not as pretty as Melissa. When mother showed me a high school graduation picture of Donna it was evident that she was an attractive, feminine woman. It was difficult for me to relate the photograph of Donna to the patient Douglas who sported a beard, had a deep voice, and was quite masculine.

The parents were very involved with their children, almost to the point of being intrusive. Their involvement, however, provided them with a sharpened sense of Donna's childhood. Mother was a perfectionist and had high goals and expectations for all her children. It appeared as if all the children were expected to be perfect and to excel.

Both parents denied that Donna ever crossdressed during her childhood. They viewed her gender activities as normal for any girl her age (denying that Donna was ever a tomboy). The mother, a mildly intrusive, over-protective woman, was in command at home and knew everything she needed to about her children. In order to protect them from developing a "ghetto mentality" she provided them with an enriched environment, forbidding them to associate with most of their neighbors, and never allowing her children to sleep over at a friend's house (in order to protect them from the "bad values" that she had experienced while growing up in the ghetto). Mother saw her mission as providing a unique type of environment for her children which would foster their intellectual and creative development and achievement without losing sight of their black roots. Indeed, mother viewed her home, in which the family had lived for the past twenty-two years, as an oasis in the black community. It was not so much that mother was smug, self-righteous, and aloof, but rather that she understood the harsh realities of her community. With her husband she wished to provide the children with a protective shield against developing a street mentality.

Around age 12 Donna had an appendectomy and her first period. She seemed relatively unconflicted about her menses and came to mother for advice (but seemed, according to mother, to know how to care for herself). The parents viewed Donna's reaction to her menses as normal and without apparent strife. However, when her breast development began she seemed conflicted. While appearing to accept her bodily changes in a matter-of-fact fashion, and not resisting wearing a bra, she really experienced considerable anguish and felt crushed that she did not grow a penis and become a man. Mother seemed ignorant of Donna's conflicts and had no way of understanding them.

During late adolescence, as Donna developed a pretty figure, she became enraged and furious. Whenever someone flirted with her she reacted angrily by telling her father, with reference to her female figure, "I wish I didn't have it." She showed little interest in dating but did go out with some boys. One man she dated turned out to be gay. The parents remembered this experience as "heartbreaking" for Donna (and often attributed her wish to be a male to this "broken romance").

However, Donna claimed that she dated the man so as not to arouse suspicion about her own lesbian orientation.

The parents described Donna as being active in church activities, while being uninvolved at school. The church seemed to offer a safe, protective environment for Donna. The parents believed that Donna was fearful of aggression and competition. They saw her as sitting back, refusing to compete, and eventually withdrawing from relationships in which any confrontations were involved. This behavior was in marked contrast to her continued strife with Melissa, strife which intensified as Melissa excelled in school and teachers began to berate Donna for not being as studious and bright as her younger sister.

Donna eventually became more estranged and dropped out of school. Her sister, however, went on to graduate from a major university with a straight A average, and to employment as an executive now earning a very high salary. Her brother was also completing his college education and was considered one of the best amateur athletes in the United States, having been written up in national sports journals while still in high school. In comparison with her siblings, Donna viewed herself as a failure. Her only sense of accomplishment was in her portrayal of a male role.

The mother described Donna as being quite different from the other siblings. A failure in school, Donna was viewed as immature, egocentric, odd, and peculiar. She was withdrawn, preoccupied, and had considerable difficulty relating to her peers. Moreover, she was impulsive and completely lacking in responsibility. The mother described how she was often unable to follow Donna's stream of thought: "She brings up things that don't relate to the conversation, she doesn't think logically." The mother's descriptions of Donna's thought processes suggested gaps in Donna's logic in which *non-sequiturs* were often substituted for rational, coherent responses in conversation. While Donna did not reveal a thought disorder on clinical interview, the psychological testing did corroborate mother's impressions of Donna's disorganized thinking.

Mother noted that whenever she and her husband confronted Donna about her thought confusions, Donna seemed genuinely perplexed, since she felt that she adequately communicated her thoughts, ideas, and feelings. The parents were also quite disturbed at Donna's wishes to be a man, but they also wanted to do what was best for their daughter. They were particularly upset by Donna's relationship with Michael

151

(another black female-to-male transsexual), whom they viewed as a severely disturbed individual and a bad influence on Donna.

The parents felt that Donna had impaired judgment and they worried about whether she would ever be able to care for herself. While Donna had made one attempt to live on her own, she was unable to keep a job for more than a few weeks and had to be financially and psychologically supported by her parents. Indeed, mother recalled having to bring over cooked meals because Donna seemed incapable of learning how to operate the oven, no less of knowing how to mix ingredients. The parents also paid her rent.

At one point the parents helped to support Donna's training as a key punch operator, but she was unable to maintain enough concentration to learn how to do the work. Her concentration and attention span had been so poor that over the past two years she had been fired from, or had quit every job. She could not come to work on time and appeared genuinely confused about how to set up a schedule or routine. The parents viewed Donna as a defective individual with few assets, someone who needed to be sheltered. They were concerned because, superficially, Donna could present herself as a confident, cocky, carefree, independent spirit who did not need help. As a result of this self-presentation she had alienated several agencies which could have provided support. The mother was especially concerned about what would happen when she died and Donna was left on her own.

At the time of her evaluation Donna was living at home, sharing a bedroom with her sister Leshauna (who was 12 years old). Leshauna, who was named after the father and was his favorite daughter, was quite confused about her older sister's gender problems. She complained to mother that Donna wore men's jockey shorts, had a beard, and acted like a man. When Donna undressed, Leshauna became nervous and frightened (especially if Donna asked her to help bind her breasts). Mother was concerned that Donna's behavior would confuse Leshauna as she went through puberty, causing Leshauna herself to develop a gender identity disorder. While Leshauna was now achieving good grades in school mother feared that these would begin to deteriorate as her sister's had done. The parents were quite eager to receive counseling on how to handle this situation at home, especially on how to answer Leshauna's questions about her sister.

Recently Kirk had moved back home in order to save money on room and board (having transferred to a college closer to home). He was intolerant of Donna's wishes for SRS and thought that Donna's judgment had deteriorated since she began taking hormones. He was a star athlete who commanded father's interest and attention, someone of whom Donna was extremely jealous.

Donna described her relationship with her father as "not exactly a father/son one." She regretted the fact that "he won't take me to work with him but he will take my brother." While she yearned for a close relationship with father, it was never clear to father what she wanted from him. In what appeared to be a compensatory gesture Donna developed a very close, almost symbiotic relationship with mother. She described her mother as "always being there," involved with the kids, a traditional housewife and mother.

Donna perceived her mother as treating all the children as equals, expressing warmth and affection for all her children. However, she also felt that her parents compared her to Melissa and that mother wished that Donna could be more like Melissa. Donna felt that mother exacerbated her conflicts with Melissa by placing unreasonable expectations and demands on Donna which she could not satisfy. She recalled that she experienced so much internal pressure as a result of Melissa's accomplishments, that even by age 5 she sensed that she could never measure up to her sister. She began to fantasize about becoming a boy, in the hope that she would no longer be in competition with her sister.

Donna's first sexual experience had been an incestuous one. At age 8 an aunt on the father's side made sexual advances and kissed and fondled her. She was aroused by the experience and recalled having subsequently developed intense erotic feelings towards girls her age (and older women). She also recalled sexual play with her brother and sister, behaviors which ceased when father discovered them and put an end to their "play." Donna described her parents as being extremely modest and never undressing in front of the children. She viewed her parents as strict disciplinarians but also as very loving. She saw herself, however, as being completely unlike her siblings and identified as the "black sheep" of the family. Most of her anxiety focused on her recognition that she was homosexual. She was acutely aware of how society could stigmatize her for being homosexual and began to fantasize that if she were a male, then her erotic feelings towards women would not be viewed as homosexual. She recalled that even at age 8 she felt crushed by her gay feelings, knowing that something was irrevocably wrong with her.

Throughout her childhood Donna yearned for a big brother; someone from whom she could draw strength and with whom she could identify. During her late teens she attached herself to another black female transsexual (Michael) whom she affectionately referred to as "my big brother." This was the same individual whom the parents perceived as a "terrible person," and whom they viewed as exerting a bad influence on Donna. Indeed, her "big brother" had recently been shot in the head and was leading a chaotic sexual life while raising her 8-year-old son, whom social services threatened to remove from the home (a child whom Michael envied and with whom she hoped to identify).

Donna had had several sexual relationships with men, always feeling inferior "with the man being on top and inside." She stated that she felt like a "sissy" when she had sex with a man: "I always wanted to feel myself inside a female." Since her clitoris had enlarged (secondary to male hormones) she had been able to penetrate some of her female partners, a sexual behavior which calmed her anxiety. Although Donna was phobic about her breasts and wanted to have them surgically removed, unlike other female transsexuals she was able to undress completely with her sexual partners. She declared that "when I'm with a female I do everything. I'm like a man." However, she had avoided becoming sexually involved with a really active woman as she needed to control what happened during sex. She described one instance in which her ambivalence was expressed when a female partner asked, "want me to suck your titties?" — to which Donna at first responded angrily, and then succumbed by allowing her partner to suck her breasts. She was also able to have an orgasm with her female partners (but needed to be physically on top), and enjoyed bringing her partners to multiple orgasms.

During intercourse Donna fantasized that she was the man penetrating the woman. Although she wanted SRS she was worried that her penis would not be long enough to satisfy a woman. In fact, she wanted to have a penis just like her brother's (which she had frequently seen). Moreover, the last time she had had sex with a woman and used a dildo, the woman complained that it was too cold and rubbery. Donna felt narcissistically injured and reacted by pouting and withdrawing from her partner. With each new sexual encounter Donna became anxious that she would not be able to satisfy the partner. She had a distorted conception of what phalloplasty could accomplish and had difficulty listening when the therapist tried to inform her of what to expect from the surgery. More recently, her fantasy had led her to imagine herself as a rock star with thousands of women swooning over her.

According to the parents, Donna's most pressing problems were more psychological than sexual. They were particularly concerned about a number of recent events which suggested that Donna wished to hurt herself. Donna had been cited for three traffic violations, including driving without a license and driving while drunk. When she failed to attend her court appearances and expressed the omnipotent delusion that she was immune from the courts, the parents became concerned that her pattern of driving offenses, impulsivity, omnipotence, and poor judgment in front of the law suggested a self-destructive pattern which might signal an emerging suicidal potential.

Formulation of the case

Donna's initial self-presentation suggested a rather intact individual with severe gender identity pathology. Interviews with the parents, psychological testing, and prolonged contact with Donna, however, suggested an entirely different picture. Under stress Donna's thinking became confused, illogical, and derailed, marked by tangentiality, symbolic meanings, and autistic logic. Over time her clinical picture changed and was remarkably consistent with her psychological test results. For example, Donna initially evidenced adequate reality testing, as measured by her Rorschach $F + \% = 83\%$. However, as she provided more responses her reality testing was impaired (as measured by her extended $F + \% = 60\%$). This Rorschach finding paralleled her clinical self-presentation in which her initially good reality testing deteriorated over time. Her discrepant behavior was consistent with the general finding that most female transsexuals, who appeared "healthier" on the initial clinical interview, might have severe character pathology. If these women were not intensively evaluated or given projective psychological testing, they would probably be misdiagnosed, and perhaps be referred for surgery (as was often the case for those gender clinics which evaluated a patient in one day and did not provide projective testing).

Donna's clinical interview diagnosis was that of a borderline personality disturbance. In addition, the possibility of a neuropsychological disorder was raised. Her psychometric diagnosis was that of a psychotic character. The evidence suggested that Donna was a severely disturbed young woman with a functional and, possibly, organic disturbance. Although a neurological examination ruled out gross pathology (her neurological exam and EEG were within normal limits), her early childhood school difficulties, lack of effective ego functioning, and generally poor cognitive behavior suggested that she might have an underlying organic disturbance which was incapable of diagnosis by current standards.

Clearly, Donna had a major thought disturbance. Her thinking was confused, illogical, tangential, and marked by *non-sequiturs*. She held magical beliefs about her "maleness" and at times was described as probably delusional (though Donna never directly admitted to any overt delusional content). Her early history of self-absorbtion, pre-occupation, daydreaming, and withdrawal suggested that she might have been hallucinating. Her TAT themes of violence, envy, separation, and gender confusion suggested some of the possible content of her hallucinations.

Donna's interpersonal relationships were organized along sado-masochistic lines, with incest themes being common. Donna was particularly conflicted about her aggression. Her TAT stories and Rorschach percepts suggested that whenever she became preoccupied with aggressive themes her thoughts became disorganized. Indeed, her aggressive content was primitive and ego alien. Donna seemed unable to control her intrusive, aggressive imagery.

In sum, her psychological test material corroborated the history provided by the parents: suggesting severe ego defects, poorly controlled impulses, poor judgment, and a tendency toward regression and psychotic modes of thinking. Experiencing severe impairments in her concentration and attention, Donna was unable to sustain effectively her involvement in productive work. Social relationships also confused her, as she experienced chronic anxiety, lack of impulse control, and chaotic sexuality, attempting to prevent a full-blown personality decompensation by acting out, and thereby reducing, her anxiety. While not overtly schizophrenic, Donna's developmental defects (with a possible neurological involvement), thought disorder, and personality disturbance were quite profound, leading to severe self pathology and gender identity confusion.

From a purely psychodynamic standpoint there were several possible explanations of Donna's transsexualism. Donna's early respiratory illness may have contributed to her gender identity pathology in bringing her into close contact with her mother, who experienced considerable ambivalence towards Donna (rejecting Donna's femaleness). Mother was a perfectionist who demanded that her children be nothing less than perfect. Because of Donna's early illnesses and apparent deficits, she was unable to meet mother's expectations, thereby being rejected by mother who perceived her as defective.

When Melissa was born Donna became enraged, perceiving her defects more intensely *vis-à-vis* her sister (who was now the enthralling child). From the moment of Melissa's birth Donna had felt cheated, believing that she was missing something important. When Kirk was born Donna's anxiety escalated to unmanageable proportions. Kirk's birth also coincided with Donna's starting school, events which traumatized her by increasing her separation anxiety and fear of annihilation. From age 5 on she withdrew her interest in the real world and became engaged in a fantasy world of "maleness" in which she imagined that all of her defects were repaired.

In her "male" fantasies and daydreams Donna felt protected, strong, and intact. As a "male" she felt whole and unified, triumphing over Melissa and being invulnerable to intrusions or penetrations from the outside world. Her male fantasies were consolidated during her girlhood by three factors: father's adoration of Melissa; her aunt's sexual abuse; and her increasing erotic feelings for girls, in the light of her stigmatized homosexual feelings. The fact that Donna had not been a tomboy was consistent with her need to conceal her conflicts from the outside world. Donna interpreted her father's lack of interest in her, her aunt's sexual interest in her, but her sexual interest in girls to mean that she was not a girl but a boy, thereby confirming her early childhood fantasies in a dream-fantasy that she had a penis growing out of her navel, a fantasy which represented her wish for completeness.

Donna felt that as a girl she was simply inadequate. She believed that if she were a boy she could fulfill mother's expectations and be perfect. Her childhood wish for a "big brother" probably represented her wish to extricate herself from mother's pressure for her to excel. Donna's ambivalence about her body may also have been overdetermined by several factors: father perceived her as stocky and masculine (unlike Melissa who was soft and feminine); her bed wetting, which was uncontrollable, left her feeling that she had a defective female genito-urinary system (and also reinforced her sense of personal failure; the aunt's incestuous violation of her made her feel that had she had a penis, she would have been protected against such violations. By age 16 her narcissism was so endangered that Donna had needed to disown her body. In a paranoid way she fended off compliments about her "female figure" and actively tried to put a stop to her body's female development — by binding her breasts and later by taking male hormones.

Since early childhood Donna had been precociously involved in sexual activity with her siblings and peers. In retrospect much of her involvement was probably self-initiated and overwhelmed her already impaired ego. Her wish for a penis like her brother's suggested that from the moment she saw his genital organ she had concretized her self-defect along genital lines, believing that only the possession of a penis would make her complete and intact. Ultimately Donna's decision to undergo SRS and obtain a penis was the product of her thought disorder. As she grew older, Donna believed that a penis would protect her from succumbing to her over-stimulated sexual self, and protect her from aggression. She viewed women as inferior, weak, vulnerable, and damaged (reflecting her use of splitting as a defense mechanism). Moreover, she associated her incipient depressed feelings with her femaleness and passivity. Once she began taking male hormones her feelings of deadness and her empty depression gave way to elation and euphoria (probably associated with an increased sex drive). These new feelings made her feel alive and joyous, in contrast to her deadened feelings as a female. There was now no turning back. Donna believed that she had finally discovered a nostrum for her inner feelings of deadness and emptiness.

Donna's case illustrates the multidetermined nature of female transsexualism. Although she had not disowned dolls, had many girlfriends, and had not been a tomboy, her feelings of maleness were no less prominent than those for girls whose gender pathology was acted out in their "masculinity conflict." In addition to possible psychodynamic etiology, we have also speculated on the possible organic factors in this case. While Donna, unlike Tina (see Chapter 3), had a clear-cut thought disorder, both patients had initial self-presentations which could be described as "normal-appearing" or "healthy." Only on prolonged investigation and intensive psychological testing did the pathological elements emerge in a way that helped us to understand the nature of these women's gender identity and role pathology. Without such a course of investigation Donna might have been diagnosed as transsexual and provided with SRS. Clearly, her gender identity pathology was related to her marked thought disorder and, according to *DSM* III terminology, she should not be diagnosed as a transsexual. In an attempt to maintain some form of a cohesive self-system Donna identified as a male. Her wishes for sex change represented a primitive attempt to rehabilitate functionally her self-system, which was markedly impaired (functionally and perhaps organically).

Methods of investigation

In this chapter I presented two methods of investigation of female transsexualism: the first involved a presentation of the group data on the fifty-three female transsexuals who applied to the CWRU gender clinic; the second presented detailed case histories of four women who were intensively evaluated and treated over the course of several years. These two methods of investigation could theoretically yield very different pictures of the phenomenon of female transsexualism. Most of what we know about female transsexualism from the literature is based on studies which employ either of the above methodologies. In this section I will explore the ways in which our choice of methodology profoundly affects what we learn about female transsexualism.

The group data approach

In this approach all the data for a given sample of female transsexuals are grouped together. The results, usually presented in a weak statistical form, for example, as percentages, are generally reported in such a way that they seem "true" for all female transsexuals. In most of the studies reviewed in Chapters 2 and 3 it was shown, however, that such important issues as the effect of moderating variables — for example, sampling bias, regional and cultural differences, race, education, and socioeconomic status — on the results have been ignored. Indeed, very few studies have ever used a control group. But the most serious problems in this type of clinical research usually arise from other sources. Rarely are we privy to such factors as: what were the actual questions; who asked them; what was the relationship between the questioner and the patient; what were the conditions under which the questions were asked; what use did the patient believe the examiner was going to make of her answers. For example, could they be used as part of the determination of surgery? It is well known in transsexual research that the majority of patients tend to be less than honest about their personal histories. Some patients are so determined to obtain surgery that they coach each other on how to answer interview-type questions so that they will be labeled as "a good surgical case." In this sense, a major source of methodological error (the conditions under which the patient is asked to fill out so-called objective tests have often been ignored) may be a determining factor in the results. Another source of error may be found in the mystique of statistics. For example, one of my preliminary studies of the white female transsexual patients presented in this study suggested that, for thirty-four of them, their mean MMPI group profile was:

$$456 - 897302 / 1 : F- KL/$$

While this profile described a certain personality type, it would actually be true for only about 30 per cent of the sample. Indeed, a given female transsexual's MMPI profile might be totally different from the mean score. However, while it is common practice to use such a mean profile to describe a clinical reference group (and it has a certain validity and usefulness), it may be misleading for a given female transsexual who may be much more seriously disturbed than the mean profile would suggest. The point is that while aggregate data tell us something about the group, they do not explain individual differences. The importance of the group data approach, however, is that it provides us with a large sample of responses for female transsexuals so that we can try to determine whether there are any patterns which would help in refining our evaluation and treatment of a specific transsexual woman. However, when we are dealing with single case studies, we never know in advance if our conclusions can be generalized beyond a specific case.

In my study of fifty-three female transsexuals a certain pattern of female transsexualism did emerge. The reader, however, should interpret the pattern within the context of the preceding methodological critique. One point of my study does need to be clarified. An "etiologic pattern" (Green, 1974) derived from the aggregate data on our fifty-three female transsexual applicants suggested that a majority of the women had disorganized, chaotic families, characterized by incestuous and violent experiences. For most of the women their childhoods were depicted as a time of unrest, involving losses, abandonments, deaths, moves, and unpredictable changes. As a group, they were depressed, suicidal, and symptomatic. At least 40 per cent had profound psychiatric disturbances. In almost every case there was a major stressor which preceded their requests for sex reassignment surgery.

However, one must be cautious in concluding that because there appeared to be a group of patients for whom the above "etiologic pattern" did not entirely hold, that group was "normal" or "healthy." While such a conclusion may be legitimately assumed in the context of a methodological criticism, it would be clinically gratuitous. Indeed, while there was considerable overlap for a given patient on such variables as incest, family violence, psychological disturbance, and suicidal behavior some women only showed — that is, allowed the interviewer to see — one pattern. One cannot conclude on the basis of omission (that is, the lack of a positive finding) that a given woman is therefore "normal." Many proponents of sexual surgery have been guilty of misconstruing "objective" research in order to demonstrate the "normality" of their patients, hence facilitating the recommendation for surgery. No one among that group of investigators seems to question why a "normal" person would want to have his/her genitals amputated.

In our study most of the answers to the patients' questions evolved out of a long-term psychotherapeutic relationship in which the patient had little to gain by completely falsifying her social history. On the other hand, it is the very nature of any therapy relationship that the patient withholds, distorts, and changes his/her past through the process of therapy.

One must recognize that any research design has its limitations. "Statistical significance" and "objective measurement" are concepts often employed in lieu of intensive investigation of a given subject. While they are often misleading, in that they suggest a higher order of truthfulness, they are also concepts that have been sorely neglected in most transsexual research designs. Future studies of female transsexualism may be able to surmount some of the methodological difficulties I have outlined. Moreover, we may look forward to the day when a research design may be employed in which objective responses can be reasonably obtained and interacting variables be studied discretely. We may only hope that new research methodologies will provide us with a more informed data base for female transsexualism.

The single case approach

The value of the single case approach is that it provides us with an intensive understanding of the complex forces at work in determining a given woman's female transsexualism. This approach typifies biological research in the sense that a phenomenon need only be shown to exist once in order to prove its existence. While multiple proofs are confirmatory of a phenomenon's existence, hence necessary for "final proof," they are not sufficient for that proof. The fact that one cannot show that something exists does not preclude its discovery at a later date. The clinical data from a specific case cannot — and should not — be dismissed as trivial; rather, they should become the focus for generating new questions about the more general aspects of the phenomenon.

One of the criticisms of this approach is that it is logically question-able whether one can legitimately generalize from a single occurrence to a universal phenomenon. While intensive, long-term, psychoana-lytically oriented psychotherapy may provide an in depth look at a particular woman's transsexualism, critics argue that it does not tell us anything about female transsexualism in general.

While the above criticism is true, it is clinically meaningless. There is no substitute for the richness of material which is gleaned from a trusting relationship over a period of time. This is especially true when we are dealing with patients suffering from severe character pathology and serious psychiatric disturbances — where the issue of trust is crucial. In the context of an intense, long-term relationship the patient's statements take on a different meaning.

Unfortunately, previous investigators have not made full use of the methodological power of the case history approach. Instead of dissecting the phenomenon and placing it under the clinical microscope for study, they have seemed more interested in either proving a theory or demon-strating that a given woman was, or was not, a good surgical candidate.

In effect, the single case approach has not been fully explored. While a number of autobiographies have been published, they have not filled the vacuum because of the self-serving needs of the authors. What is needed are presentations of case histories of individuals treated over a long period from various theoretical perspectives, in which the therapist is not too intrusive but certainly available as an active participant. Studies like Bogden's *Being Different: The Autobiography of Jane Fry* (1974), which gives an in depth account of a male transsexual, need to go beyond the person's autobiographical material and challenge that individual to move to a higher level of self-awareness. There is no good substitute for the psychotherapeutic enterprise. A competent therapist can lead a person to a deeper level, hence to a richer understanding of his/her life. Hopefully, as more in depth accounts of the lives of female transsexuals become available, including pertinent material relating to their physiological conditions and family systems, we will be in a better position critically to understand the phenomenon.

Because female transsexualism is not a unitary disorder it is unlikely that a single methodological approach can address all the questions concerning its etiology and pathogenesis.There is a need for future investigators to explore the phenomenon from many different perspectives and using a variety of methodological stand points. Rather than abandon the single case approach, it should become a model for research, an approach by means of which new methodological paradigms may evolve. It is my belief that inquiry has been stifled because clinicians are asking the wrong questions (for example, what are the best predictors for referring a patient for sex reassignment surgery?). Once the clinical focus is shifted to the phenomenon itself, we will then be in a position to ask the right questions, — questions which will lead us to a better understanding of female transsexualism as a phenomenon, not merely as a disorder.

In the following sections I will make use of both methodological approaches employed in this study in order to outline a provisional theory of female transsexualism. I say provisional because it would be a conceptual injustice to foreclose inquiry at this juncture. While there will always be a need for more clinical data on female transsexualism, there is also a point at which an investigator must take stock of his/her data and generate some hypotheses which may become leading ideas for future researchers. It is in this spirit that, after reviewing some of the theories about the biological foundations of female transsexualism, I will present a new psychological theory of the possible etiology of female transsexualism.

Chapter 5
Psychobiological issues in female transsexualism

Background

For more than two decades a select group of researchers has pursued the idea that a biological disorder may be the cause of female transsexualism (Blumer, 1969; Money and Ehrhardt, 1972; Jones, 1974). While this approach might seem too reductionistic, the clinical case material in transsexual research has always had a compelling biological aspect. Moreover, there was considerable evidence from intersexual, hermaphroditic, endocrine, and genetic studies to suggest more than a casual relationship between a biological disorder and a gender identity or role disorder (Money and Ehrhardt, 1972). Perhaps female transsexualism could be explained along the lines of one of the above biological disorders. Indeed, the transsexual literature was replete with cases in which an elegant psychodynamic explanation of a specific transsexual case yielded to eventual laboratory findings in which cerebral pathology (Hoenig and Kenna, 1979), a cytogenetic disorder (Baker and Stoller, 1968), enzyme defect (Stoller, 1979), or a neurohormonal disorder (Money and Ehrhardt, 1972) was eventually reported to be the real "culprit."

The idea that a gender identity or role disorder might have a biological underpinning was not new. Boswell (1980) noted that Caelius Aurelianus, a fifth-century Roman physician, "grouped passivity and opposite gender identification together as a mental disorder" (with no apparent impairment of the individual's mental faculties), and "presented two theories on etiology: it was either the result of a birth defect (improper mingling of sperm and egg) or an inherited disease." In 1961, Sendrail and Gleizes, studying female transsexualism, concluded that the disorder could not be explained by an appeal to psychological processes, but that one also had to take account of possible hormonal conditions.

In some cases of female transsexualism a concurrent organic condition has been demonstrated (although no causal relationship was necessarily implied). These findings suggested that a specific organic condition may have either an organizing or facilitating effect on the patient's trans-sexualism.

The biological explanation of female transsexualism has great appeal in that it provides the clinician, and the patient, with a guiltless explanation of the condition. Moreover, it can be used to justify an aggressive medical approach to the disorder, (i.e. hormonal or surgical therapy). On the other hand, it may turn out to be true.

In this section I will review the literature on female transsexualism in which organic hypotheses (or a mediating role of organic factors) for explaining the disorder were pursued. I will also critically explore the basis for accepting these hypotheses. I will begin with those organic conditions which only make their appearance, usually fortuitously, after the fact, sometimes after many years of psychotherapy have reportedly failed to provide relief for the patient.

Female transsexuals with undiagnosed biological conditions

In an intriguing paper Baker and Stoller (1968) described six individuals "who were raised as members of their assigned sex but who felt that they belonged to the opposite sex . . . [and] at puberty all developed some sort of cross-sex change, in effect confirming their earliest gender wishes." When examined these patients revealed a variety of hidden conditions which contributed to their gender aberrations, including a "girl" who had a clitoris the size of a penis. None of these patients had a "visible anatomical flaw at birth or until puberty." Baker and Stoller concluded that the effects of parental rearing in gender identity disorders may be "overturned" by a biological force. However, in a separate article Stoller (1975) concluded that to date (1975), "there is no convincing evidence yet that transsexualism is caused by a hormonal defect."

In 1979 Stoller described another in his endless series of fascinating cases of gender dysphoric patients. In this instance, he presented the case of a female transsexual patient whom he had seen over a twenty-year period. The report also contained verbatim material from an audiotaped session with the mother. The patient had an incessant drive towards masculinity which was treated solely as a psychological disorder until

Stoller, after reading about a case similar to the patient's, had her tested for a rare hormone enzyme defect (17b hydroxy-steroid dehydrogenase deficiency) which the patient turned out to have. It seemed as if this rare sexual hormone enzyme defect which caused her anatomic hermaphroditism, and which had gone undetected for most of her life, was now viewed as the driving force behind her cross-gender wishes to become a man. It was suggested that the patient's brain could have been prenatally organized as a male, an event which had shaped her underlying male gender identity. Here was an individual who had been misassigned at birth as a female and raised as a female — though she knew all along that she was a male! Cases such as these remind us of the consequences of failing to grasp the importance of biological underpinnings of human behavior.

Sheelah et al. (1972) presented the case of a 21-year-old woman who had had a lifelong gender identity disturbance. An adopted child, she began crossdressing around age 8 and openly declared her wishes to be a boy. During adolescence she "began to feel protective towards girls." She also read avidly the lay literature on transsexualism and sex reassignment. She stated that she had a "male mind in a female body." Laboratory studies revealed a woman with a chromosomal abnormality — XO/XX mosaicism. The patient had a normal female sexual anatomy and was free of psychosis. These findings did not support Money's report (1963) that girls with XO or XO/XX karyotype "have entirely feminine self-concepts and tend to be heterosexual even when there was amenorrhoea and absence of secondary sex characteristics."

Videla and Prigoshin (1976) reported on the case of a 30-year-old woman with a tomboyish history who, with the onset of puberty (menarche age 12), developed a wish to become a male. The patient began crossdressing at age 16 and had been on male hormones for four years. Chromosome analysis revealed a mosaic condition in which 80 per cent of the cells were normal 46XX, and 20 per cent of the cells revealed an abnormality: "4% 47XX +m, 6% 45XO, and 10% XO +m." The authors concluded that, "These data prompted us to put forward a possible causal link between the chromosomal abnormalities and the reversal of the psychological sex found in our patient." What these studies suggested was that a possible genetic factor might be involved in the unfolding of transsexual pathology, but they did not explain why only certain people with the same chromosomal abnormalities were affected.

In all the above cases a woman with a lifelong history of transsexualism turned out to have some biological basis for her gender identity disorder. These findings suggested that clinicians should examine their transsexual patients' physical status prior to making any definite treatment recommendations. However, one must also confront the sobering reality that the transsexual researcher was heavily dependent on new discoveries in medicine to diagnose subtle physiological disorders. Since it is not our purpose to investigate the relationship between intersexual conditions and gender identity disturbances, the reader is referred to the writings of John Money and Anke Ehrhardt (1972). In this section we will focus on the major research areas into the biological basis for female transsexualism in which cerebral pathology increased androgen levels, psychohormonal disturbances, and H–Y antigen factor have all been implicated.

Cerebral pathology

The most obvious place for researchers to look for organic deficit in transsexualism is the brain. Kluver and Bucy (1939) had already demonstrated a variety of behaviors, including bizarre and hyper-sexuality, in monkeys who had bilateral temporal lobectomies. Subsequent research into human analogues suggested that individuals with a variety of sexual psychopathology (including transvestism and fetishism) had either abnormal EEGs (Epstein, 1961) or temporal lobe disorders (Davies and Morgenstern, 1960). Because of the inexact use of the term transvestism (especially in the European literature), some of the findings were more applicable to transsexuals than to transvestites. Indeed, researchers soon focused their analyses on the transsexual group. Here was a group of patients of whom some eventually turned out to have underlying organic pathology, but who were regarded as non-psychotic; having no chromosomal or cytogenetic defect; usually having normal secondary sex characteristics; and who complained about being trapped in the wrong body. Researchers tried to ascertain whether there was evidence for cerebral pathology in this group of patients. It was only natural for investigators to focus first on the most crude measure – the EEG.

EEG measures

In 1969 Blumer summarized the literature on transvestism and temporal lobe dysfunction and reported on the findings of fifteen transsexual patients whose EEGs were recorded. Of these patients, five, including two women, revealed abnormal EEGs. However, Blumer concluded "that definite EEG abnormalities are not a common occurrence in transsexuals." He also reported on three cases of male transsexualism in which epilepsy was involved, and noted that there had been no reports of female transsexuals who were also diagnosed as epileptic. He concluded that: "A review of our present knowledge of temporal lobe dysfunction and sexual aberrations provides good evidence for an occasional close relationship between sexual aberrations (transvestism in particular) and paroxysmal temporal lobe disorders." While the term "occasional close relationship" begs scientific understanding, Blumer's study has often been cited as providing evidence for a direct relationship between transsexualism and temporal lobe disorder. Ultimately, Blumer suggested that "a lobectomy . . . would undoubtedly be preferable in such cases to sex-reassignment surgery."

Späte (1970) investigated the role of the limbic system in the pathogenesis of transvestism (here referring to transsexualism as well). He derived his conclusions from a study of two female transvestites who wished to change sex. Both women had abnormal EEGs with focal paroxysmal sites; one within the temporal lobes and the other deep within the brain stem. While Späte drew his conclusions from a rather narrow data base, he cited numerous studies relating transvestism to disturbances in cerebral functioning to support his argument. However, a careful reading of the two cases (ages 19 and 28) suggested that a psychodynamic explanation might have been more economical.

The first case described a late adolescent girl, an unwanted child whose older brother had died in infancy and was replaced by the patient (seemingly in role and identity). The girl was described as being a runaway, with little direction to her life, but quite enterprising in her male role. While little information was provided on her psychiatric and psychological status, it seemed clear that she had profound psychological problems in addition to her abnormal EEG.

In the second case we are told that the patient, a 28-year-old woman, was born and grew up in a profoundly disturbed family. The father was alcoholic and often beat the mother and six children. The patient was described as "ein Bengel" (a "devil") who was ashamed of her breasts, and is, to my knowledge, the only reported case of a female transsexual who stated that she wished to cut off her breasts. While she desired to live as a man, her relationships with people were shallow and empty. Although Späte did not offer a psychodynamic explanation of the patient, his brief clinical summary suggested that her case was similar to the typical psychodynamic pattern of female transsexuals reported in the literature (Stoller, 1972; Pauly, 1974a, b).

In spite of evidence suggesting a possible psychological etiology of their gender identity disturbances, Späte chose to focus on the women's EEG abnormalities as the cause of their transsexualism. He viewed early developmental cerebral insult as affecting the limbic system adversely, leading to gender pathology, and believed that such insult left the individual susceptible in later life to a sexual aberration which could be documented by an abnormal EEG.

Addressing the question of whether there was evidence for a cerebral dysfunction in transsexualism, Kockett and Nusselt (1976) reported their findings on twenty-one male and seven female transsexuals. They also compared their findings on interview and EEG data with twenty-two normals and thirty mental patients. Of the twenty-eight transsexuals, nine revealed evidence of cerebral insult — though *none* were females ("Alle 9 Transsexuelle mit pathologischen EEG-Befunden waren männlichen Geschlechts"). They did, however, find that, as a group, the male transsexuals had significantly more EEG pathology, and their sex drives were lower. In conclusion, they reported that there was no real basis from which to infer a relationship between cerebral pathology and transsexualism.

In contrast to Kockett's and Nusselt's negative EEG results, Hoenig and Kenna (1979) related EEG abnormalities directly to female transsexualism, thereby supporting Späte's conjectures. In their study, thirty-five transsexual men and eleven transsexual women served as subjects. The relationship between temporal lobe lesions, EEG abnormalities, and the patient's transsexualism was the focus of investigation. EEG abnormalities were found in 48 per cent of the subjects, while borderline abnormalities were reported for another 24 per cent. They reported that "women showed the abnormalities in a significantly higher proportion than the men." The group with EEG abnormalities was generally younger, and they had revealed their transsexualism to their families at a younger age. There was a tendency for EEG abnormalities to occur more frequently in patients with personality disturbances. Patients with EEG abnormalities also had a non-significant tendency to exhibit a lower sex drive. Methodological differences apart, it was unclear how to account for the different findings of the two studies.

169

In summary, the EEG findings seemed contradictory and inconclusive. Moreover, the various methods employed and the lack of systematic use of control groups and normative data made an interpretation of positive EEG results (that is, abnormal findings) problematic. It was clear from several cases that a psychodynamic explanation was just as plausible, if not more economical, as an explanation of the female patient's gender problems. While the role of the limbic system had been implicated in emotional and sexual behavior (McLean, 1955), the results of the trans-sexual studies were only presumptive. This was not to say that a few of the findings, in which transsexual pathology in men was directly related to the onset of cerebral insult, did not warrant serious investigation. Those findings, however, suggested only that a lack of inhibition due to cerebral insult may have acted as a releasing factor, thereby activating already existing areas of gender identity conflict.

The fact that some patients with bizarre sexual psychopathy (including transvestism and fetishism) had given up their wishes for sex change after lobectomy also warranted further investigation. Moreover, the finding of increased EEG abnormalities in female transsexuals needed further clarification and investigation. Given the diagnostic issues in female transsexualism, in which the frequency of personality disorders was greater (versus male transsexualism), might not one expect to find more EEG pathology in such a group? The EEG literature seemed to support the idea that individuals with personality disturbances had a higher frequency of EEG disturbances than individuals with other kinds of non-organic, psychiatric disorders (Hill, 1952). In this sense, the finding of increased EEG pathology among female transsexuals who were known to have personality disturbances, would be interesting but perhaps irrelevant to the etiology of their gender identity disorders.

Increased androgen levels

Given the masculine character of many female transsexuals, it had been speculated that they may have been virilized by their higher base levels of androgen. Since it is quite unlikely that such a complex process as gender identity differentiation should be based on a single biological substratum (no less on such an innocuous factor as increased androgen levels — a hormone readily found in small quantities in all females), the research into this area is highly speculative. Perhaps the single motivating influence for this research was the commonsense idea which suggested that what made those women overly masculine and desirous of changing their roles and identity was an excess of male hormone.

At the Second Interdisciplinary Symposium on Gender Dysphoria Syndrome Jones (1973) tested the hypothesis that female transsexuals had an excess of male hormone. He presented a preliminary paper relating levels of plasma testosterone concentration to the etiology of female transsexualism. The subjects were twelve female transsexuals who were contrasted with twenty-two normally menstruating females and a group of male laboratory workers. Jones measured plasma testosterone, urinary steroid excretion rates, plasma gonadotrophins, sebum ovarian vein plasma testosterone, and karyotyping. All the transsexuals' karyotypes were 46XX (or normal for females). While none of the control subjects showed elevations in plasma testosterone beyond normal expected values for their sexes, two of the transsexuals showed a significant elevation in plasma testosterone (0.06mg/100ml). However, all twelve female transsexuals had been on testosterone therapy prior to the study, but they had stopped all medication 8–12 weeks beforehand. Jones believed, however, that while the primary source of the testosterone was the ovary, he attributed the elevations to the patients' prior history of testosterone therapy. Indeed, both patients had a polycystic ovary. Jones reiterated that "small doses of androgens over a long period of time have been implicated in the development of polycystic ovary." His study did not support the idea that female transsexuals had an increased plasma testosterone level. However, he believed that "additional investigations into polypeptides, intracellular carrier proteins, and even intracellular brain tissue reactivity to various steroid hormones should be carried out."

In a second study into the possible biological underpinning of female transsexualism, Jones and Samimy (1973) investigated the levels of plasma testosterone, 17 ketosterone, urinary 17 ketogenic steroids, and plasma and urine levels during adrenal and ovarian stimulation and suppression. Comparing their results with those for a control group, they found no differences between the groups on all endocrinological results. They concluded that "female transsexualism cannot be simply ascribed to altered levels of testosterone during adulthood."

One of the problems with the research into plasma testosterone levels focused on the unreliability of the measurements involved. For example, many female transsexuals were known to be on illicitly prescribed hormones. However, most of them hid this fact from their physicians for fear that they would be refused sex reassignment surgery.

A case where researchers may have been misled by such a patient may be found in Sendrail and Gleizes's (1961) study. They described a case of a 30-year-old woman who revealed a masculine character and a spontaneous virilization (with some changes in her genitals). The woman, with a lifelong gender identity disturbance, including possible underlying suicidal potential (as seen on psychological testing), had received male hormones from a physician after evidence of spontaneous virilization (and no evidence of hormonal or gynecological pathology). Whereas in 1961 Sendrail and Gleizes accepted the self-reports of the transsexual patient — that is, that she was not previously on male hormones, today there would be much more scepticism regarding such assertions (Lothstein, 1977b). Thus, if a researcher were now presented with a case in which there was spontaneous virilization and increased levels of plasma testosterone in a self-labeled female transsexual with no evidence of physical disease, s/he might conclude that she was indeed self-administering male hormone, but denying it to the doctor.

On the other hand, there are some physical disorders (e.g. Stein-Leventhall syndrome, Cushing's syndrome, metastatic breast cancer treated with testosterone) in which a polycystic ovary, impaired adrenal functioning, or exogenous male hormone (respectively) may lead to hirsuitism and a masculinizing of the female body (all of which may lead to changes in body image and an upsurge of masculine-type feelings). To complicate the matter, some females with a pre-existing gender identity disorder might develop a physical disorder, e.g. Stein-Leventhall disease, which provides them with "confirmation" of their maleness.

Chromosomal-hormonal factors

Hereditary factors (i.e. genetic-chromosomal sex), the neurohormonal system and the psychoendocrine milieu, cytogenetic disorders and chromosomal defects, pre- and postnatal hormones, and the hypothalamic-pituitary-gonadotrophin axis have been hypothesized to play a major role in the evolution of female transsexualism and in other female gender identity disturbances.

The initial studies on female transsexualism focused on the macro variable of chromosomal sex. This was an obvious line of inquiry since female transsexuals were complaining about being trapped in the wrong body. What if they were right? Moreover, a number of puzzling female transsexual cases had already been analysed by researchers in which their apparent "psychological" conflicts later turned out to have an organic basis.

Bleuler and Wiesemann (1956) examined the blood cells of four female transsexuals and found nothing abnormal in their nuclear sex. In a second study, Overzier (1955) also examined the nuclear sex of four female transsexuals and found their genetic sex to be female according to their leucocyte smears. Hoenig and Torr (1964), using a more sophisticated method of chromosome analysis, examined "the condition further by peripheral blood culture and karyotyping." Their group consisted of twenty transsexuals, five of whom were females. The results confirmed previous findings in that for all the patients their physical sex corresponded to their chromosomal sex. All of them had normal karyotypes. Given the prohibitive costs of karyotyping and the unlikelihood of learning anything significant, most gender identity clinics do not routinely test for chromosomal sex. Unfortunately, there are some patients with undiagnosed chromosomal abnormalities who could benefit from karyotyping and other tests for genetic disorders which may underlie their transsexualism.

Money and Ehrhardt (1972) studied a number of self-labeled female transsexuals who had various hormonal disorders. These disorders included: fetally androgenized genetic females (progestin-induced hermaphroditism; female adrenogenital syndrome; some additionally androgenized postnatally); a few patients who also had Turner's syndrome (which was unusual for patients with Turner's syndrome, who typically identify as females). The authors extensively reviewed the behavioral sequelae to these disorders. Some of their findings are presented in this section, since they may bear directly on the etiology and course of female transsexualism. Indeed, these patients form a special kind of control group, since they are women who reportedly wished to become males after their bodies had been masculinized secondary to a chromosomal, genetic, or neurohormonal disorder.

In girls with adrenogenital syndrome (caused by a genetic defect) the adrenal cortices cannot synthesize cortisol, and instead produce a substance which has the same action as androgen. Consequently, these girls are masculinized and must be treated with cortisone therapy. Money and Ehrhardt (ibid.) noted that "there are some who, lacking serious symptoms [which can be as severe as having salt and fluid imbalance and lacking blood pressure regulation], escape recognition and grow up successfully as boys."

Behaviorally these girls, compared with a control group, are described as tomboys ("which did not necessarily include explicit dissatisfaction with being a girl"). They had a high "physical energy expenditure, especially in the vigorous outdoor play, games and sports commonly considered the prerogative of boys"; lacked a tendency for aggressive attack but had a tendency for "dominance assertion"; preferred utilitarian and practical clothing (though they were not averse to wearing dresses on special occasions); exhibited no differences in their childhood sexual play and rehearsal versus the control group; would choose a career over marriage and family; and lacked "a precursor interest in romance and boyfriends from their play and daydreams into adolescent dating." There was no indication that these girls entertained lesbian erotic fantasies. Their sexual orientation was heterosexual but their biological clocks were lagging behind those of their agemates. Money and Ehrhardt wondered about the possible "masculinizing effect on the fetal brain."

In looking at the behavioral sequelae of fetally androgenized genetic females (who were additionally androgenized postnatally — that is, girls who, born prior to 1950, did not receive cortisone therapy), they noted, "These women show the postnatally elevated androgen levels, persisting into adulthood, do not in and of themselves dictate a masculine gender role or identity." They concluded that "postnatal gender-identity differentiation may be capable of overriding prenatal precursors, or at least of modifying them to an extensive degree."

Furthermore, an investigation of girls with Turner's syndrome supported these findings. These girls were shown to have a disorder in which there was an absence of gonadal hormones due to a cytogenetic defect (these individuals usually had only one sex chromosome 45 X/46 or were XX mosaic). Despite all of their handicaps (short stature, infertility, psychosocial immaturity), these girls "reported daydreams and fantasies of being pregnant and wanting to have a baby." Indeed, they all seemed to have differentiated a female gender identity.

Money and Ehrhardt concluded that "in order to differentiate postnatally as feminine, gender identity is not dependent on prenatal gonadal hormones [estrogen and/or androgen] acting presumptively on the brain. Nor is a feminine gender identity dependent on the presence of a second X chromosome." Essentially, the sex of assignment and sex of rearing are the crucial variables in the development and differentiation of gender identity.

An exception to Money and Ehrhardt's social-learning theory hypothesis of gender identity was found in the study by Imperato-McGinley et al. (1979). They reported on thirty-eight cases of Dominican male children who were raised as girls. These children had what is now known as a pseudohermaphroditic condition resulting from a genetically determined deficiency of the enzyme Delta^4 steroid 5 alpha-reductase. This affected their childhood genital appearance such that they appeared more or less female and were usually raised as females. At puberty they developed physically as boys. Of this group, nineteen of whom had unquestionably female upbringings, seventeen changed their gender to male. Sometime between the ages of 7 and 12 (when peer grouping occurred), these children began to feel different and psychologically identified as males, even though they were dressed and raised as females. It was concluded that a combination of prenatal and postpubertal factors, which counterbalanced each other, overrode the effects of sex of rearing. While the methodological weaknesses of the study have been argued by Rubin et al. (1981), and the findings have not been replicated in other cultures with the same enzyme deficiency (Opitz et al., 1971; Walsh et al., 1974), the results of the Imperato-McGinley study point to the need to integrate all approaches when investigating gender identity conflicts.

Seyler et al. (1978) reported a study designed "to determine whether female transsexuals have abnormal hypothalamic-pituitary feedback control." They measured "pituitary LH and FSH secretory responses to synthetic LRH (100 ug iv)." These measurements were taken for "nine female transsexuals with normal menstrual cycles before and after a 7-day course of treatment with diethylstilbestrol − DES; 2 mg/day." A control group of five heterosexual women and seven heterosexual men was included. The finding "that the responses of female transsexuals to DES and LRH were intermediate between the female and male patterns suggests that a biological abnormality accompanies the psychological abnormality in such patients." This finding, while providing some empirical support for a possible neurohormonal explanation of female transsexualism, needed further confirmatory evidence before a final judgment could be made.

Meyer-Bahlburg (1979) reviewed the findings, among others, of the psychoendocrine data on transsexual women. About one-third of the subjects had elevated androgen levels. He reviewed two reports which

175

suggested "abnormalities of the neuroendocrine regulation of luteinizing hormone [LH] secretion in female transsexuals." The development of sexual orientation was found to be independent of the effects of pre-natal or postpubertal hormone levels; he concluded, "but a facilitating neuroendocrine predisposition cannot be ruled out at present."

Ehrhardt and Meyer-Bahlburg (1981), summarizing the findings on the effects of prenatal hormones on gender-related behavior, concluded that, "The evidence accumulated so far suggests that human psychosexual differentiation is influenced by prenatal hormones, albeit to a degree . . . . The development of gender identity seems to depend largely on the sex of rearing."

While it seemed somewhat extravagant to postulate a neurohormonal organizing factor underlying female transsexualism at this point in the research, it was certainly justifiable to assume, with Meyer-Bahlburg, that for some female transsexuals a "facilitating neuroendocrine pre-disposition cannot be ruled out at present." It would appear that there may be some female transsexuals who have a neuroendocrine predis-position to their gender pathology (whatever the underlying mechanism and time of onset).

The current status of neuroendocrine research is still primitive and we cannot dismiss negative findings as unimportant. As new methods and techniques are discovered for investigating the effects of prenatal hormones, and the overall internal hormonal milieu on the female trans-sexual, a biological substratum for certain forms of female transsexualism may be discovered. However, the crucial test of the prenatal hypothesis in humans would involve a serious breach of medical ethics. While it is certainly evident from the animal research that prenatal hormones ad-ministered during the so-called critical phase of fetal development have an organizing effect on sex-related behaviors, there is no way to perform a crucial test of this hypothesis in humans. It is inconceivable that researchers would ever be allowed to experiment with human fetuses by administering various dosages of opposite sex hormones at different levels in fetal development; by following up on those fetuses as they grew into adulthood (by studying their personality development and gender-related behaviors); and then by "sacrificing" some of them in order to perform brain studies. While this is common methodological practice in animal research, it would violate our basic values related to the sanctity of human life. Unless such tests are performed, however, the prenatal hypothesis can never be satisfactorily demonstrated.

H-Y antigen studies

The most recent, and promising research area has focused on a newly discovered H-Y antigen factor. This factor, discovered by Eichwald and Silmser (1955), was "proposed to be the testis-determining substance" by Silvers and Wachtel (1977). Their studies uncovered how the Y chromosome masculinized an individual. The term individual was stressed because the H-Y antigen factor can be found in women as well. Wachtel's investigations of H-Y antigen have also addressed the question of why some women, with no apparent chromosomal defect, and appropriate female secondary sex characteristics, may show varying degrees of virilization, or masculinization.

Wachtel reported that a Y-induced histocompatibility antigen (known as H-Y) was found on the cell surface of all males and, during fetal development, caused the gonads to differentiate as male. It has long been known that the natural state of all human organisms is female (Money and Ehrhardt, 1972), and unless something was added (androgen, or male hormone), the organism — no matter what the chromosomal structure — would differentiate female-appearing external structures. The H-Y antigen factor was initially believed to be the factor by which the male gonad was differentiated. Wachtel concluded that whenever H-Y antigen was found on the cell surface of an individual it "should always be associated with formation of at least rudimentary testes, regardless of phenotypic sex or apparent karyotype."

Eicher et al. (1979) summarized the view by stating that the H-Y antigen should be regarded as "the expression of a group of male determining genes which is suggested to be located on the Y-chromosome." For research purposes Leff (1977) stated that "If a woman's blood tests indicate that she has the Y antigen, she must be presumed to harbor cryptic testicular tissue despite her XX karyotype and normal female genitalia."

In summary, it was initially postulated that normal men are H-Y antigen positive and normal women are H-Y antigen negative. Eicher et al. (1979) stated that "In some females with an anomalous Y chromosome, who test positive for H-Y antigen factor, two possibilities exist: at least a fragment of the missing Y translocated to some other chromosomes . . . [or] the Y may exist as a mosaic present in some but not all of the patient's somatic cells."

In the light of all the confusion regarding transsexualism and its possible biological underpinnings, it was only natural that researchers should have focused their attention on the possible relationship between H-Y antigen and transsexualism. Indeed, Eicher et al. (ibid.) investigated the presence of the histocompatibility of H-Y antigen in seven male-to-female, and seven female-to-male transsexuals. Five of the seven female-to-male transsexuals were H-Y antigen positive (one showed a weak positive reaction, and one was H-Y negative). The results for men were: four H-Y antigen negative, two positive, and one showed a weak positive reaction. They suggested that "the relationship between H-Y antigen and the pathogenesis of transsexuality needs further investigation."

Eicher (1981), expanding on his earlier findings, presented the data from eleven XY male-to-female transsexuals and eleven 46XX female-to-male transsexuals. He reported that eight of the males were H-Y negative and nine of the females were H-Y positive, (with another female being weak positive). Eicher speculated that in those individuals with discordant H-Y antigen there could be "a translocation of interchange of the gene from Y to X chromosome during spermatogenesis in the father." He concluded that there might be two different groups of transsexuals: "genuine transsexuals with H-Y antigen reaction discordant to the primary phenotype and secondary transsexuals with H-Y antigen according to the primary phenotype."

In Hamburg, Pfafflin (1981) seriously called into question the possibility of reproducing Eicher's H-Y findings. Additionally, Guze (1980) questioned Eicher's results and wondered "whether or not these patients received estrogens or androgens and whether such hormones affect the H-Y antigen." It was his belief that the H-Y antigen effect in transsexuals might be related to the administration of opposite sex hormones or "that the abnormal H-Y antigen in some cases may reflect some subtle developmental defect in sexual maturation."

In March 1981 *Science* devoted an entire issue to the question of "sexual dimorphism," with two of the articles discussing the role of H-Y antigen in human sexuality. Gordon and Ruddle (1981) outlined the difficulties faced in H-Y antigen research and suggested that the situation was not as clear-cut as it first appeared. For example, there were several reports of H-Y negativity "in the presence of a normal Y chromosome"; H-Y antigen had not been proved to be the testis-determining gene product; "the H-Y antigen assay has not resolved the apparent contradiction that both arms of the Y chromosome have been associated with testis differentiation."

Haseltine and Sumo (1981) argued that the "regulatory genes for the expression of H-Y antigen are probably on the X as well as the Y chromosome." Moreover, they reported that in one study they found the three patients with 46,XY karyotype, who had both testicular tissue and were H-Y antigen negative. They suggested that in these individuals H-Y antigen may have "lost its antigenic properties while retaining its testicular organizing properties." They concluded, however, that H-Y antigen "has met some of the criteria for a gonadal organizer" whose action can be blocked; and that without its action "cells will undergo early ovarian masculinization." Clearly, there were too many exceptions to the original rule that normal males are H-Y positive and normal females were H-Y negative, thereby challenging the notion that one could use this as a simple litmus test for transsexualism.

While there are serious questions concerning the applicability of the new H-Y antigen research to transsexualism, there is no doubt that the efforts of the basic science research into transsexualism will continue, at least for a time, to focus on the possible H-Y antigen factor in transsexualism. Whether the H-Y antigen factor will turn out to be what Stoller (1979) has called the possible "biological force" in transsexualism remains to be seen.

Overview

In this section I reviewed some of the major research developments which have attempted to uncover the possible biological origins of female transsexualism. The research is quite varied and has focused on diverse biological hypotheses, including the roles of genes, chromosomes, enzymes, neurotransmitters, neurohormones, prenatal hormones, and H-Y antigen in the etiology of female transsexualism. While there is some evidence that any one of the above factors, or combination of factors, may play a facilitating role in the establishment of female transsexualism, there is no hard evidence suggesting that the causes of female transsexualism are purely biological. Moreover, I have suggested that the crucial hypothesis for either proving or disproving a direct causal relationship between a biological force and female transsexualism is neither forthcoming nor feasible.

However, as new insights are gained into the micro-molecular structure and functioning of the endocrine system, we will probably have to change some of our assumptions about how gender identity is formed. Also, with advances in EEG techniques and measurements, researchers might be able to determine more precisely how the brain reacts to and influences gender identity disturbances. We will, however, have to satisfy ourselves with correlational studies and levels of statistical significance versus strict causality. The next few decades will not be without excitement as new lines of inquiry are opened up into how the human bio-system organizes and facilitates the establishment of gender role behaviors; and how imaginal processes related to fantasy and cognition help to establish gender identity and, perhaps, female transsexualism. While there is a subgroup of female transsexuals whose gender pathology can be related to their intersex condition or hermaphroditism, the overwhelming majority of female transsexuals suffer primarily from a psychological disturbance. Even Ehrhardt and Meyer-Bhalburg (1979), who have written extensively on the psychobiology of transsexualism, agree that the most economical hypothesis is that "the development of gender identity seems to depend largely on the sex of rearing."

The idea that transsexualism is primarily a psychological disorder is not a new one. Indeed, it has been more than twenty years since Stoller and Money's pioneering investigations into gender identity were first published, suggesting that gender identity was formed during early childhood, and influenced primarily by the sex of assignment at birth, and parental rearing. While these insights into gender identity were rooted in Freud's psychology (see Chapter 6), Stoller and Money have provided us with a micro- and macroscopic view of the development of gender identity throughout the life cycle which underscores the significance of psychological factors in the etiology of transsexualism.

In the following chapter I will present evidence which clearly suggests that female transsexualism is primarily a psychological disorder, a disorder which has its roots in early childhood development. I will also trace the possible etiological pathways by which a female childhood gender disorder effloresces into adult female transsexualism. The evidence for my arguments comes mainly from the literature on early child development and recent inquiries into the etiology and phenomenology of severe character disturbances (e.g. the borderline and narcissistic disorders) which have been related to transsexual pathology. Finally, I will offer a psychological theory to explain the non-biological aspects of female transsexualism.

180

Chapter 6
Psychological issues and theories of female transsexualism

Female core gender identity

Female sex-gender development: Freud's classic statement

For almost half a century Freud's theories of female sexuality and femininity have dominated clinical thinking (1925, 1931, 1933). While his pioneering studies (which provided rich clinical material and new speculations concerning femininity and female sexuality) have undergone transformations and revisions, they are still viewed as the point of departure for any serious investigations of female sexuality.

Essentially, Freud viewed the little girl as establishing her femininity on a masculine base and having to overcome "biologically and socially based masculinity." He viewed the primary state of all girls as "male"; with their development up until the phallic period (about age 3) viewed as parallel to that of boys. Freud equated the girl's clitoris with a penis and argued that according to her anatomy and genital aims "the little girl is in all respects a little man." That is, because a girl did not appear to have a mental representation of her vagina, Freud (1933) believed that she did not "have" a biologically based female organ to provide her childhood experience with "the center for a feminine gender identity." However, during adolescence a girl's vagina was mentally represented and became the center of her gender and sexual identity, and a focus for the development of her femininity.

According to Freud, the first blow to a girl's self-esteem occurred when she became aware of the anatomical distinction between the sexes (that she realized that she was not a boy). This knowledge literally drove her "away from masculinity and masculine masturbation on to new lines which lead to the development of femininity" (ibid.). While Freud believed that the reason a girl abandoned clitoral masturbation was that she associated it with masculinity (of which she believed she had to rid herself (see Fast, 1979)), he never adequately addressed the question of why she was motivated to do so. It was, however, the girl's awareness of her penisless state (and her heightened castration anxiety) that Freud viewed as inaugurating a girl's femininity. In effect, Freud would have us believe that a little girl's femininity and gender identity develop *only* as a defense against her castration anxiety and are rooted in penis envy, feelings of genital inferiority, masochism, and passivity.

Freud believed that it was more difficult for a girl to achieve her femininity than for a boy to achieve his masculinity. Unlike the boy, the girl had to pass from a masculine to a feminine phase; to change her erotogenic zone from the clitoris (that is, a quasi-penis) to the vagina; to transfer her love object from her mother to her father (that is, from a homosexual to a heterosexual position); and to shift from a negative oedipal relationship with her father to a positive one (her oedipal relationship being initiated with the discovery of castration; whereas for the boy it was terminated with that discovery).

Freud also viewed a girl's unconscious wish for a baby from father as a compromise (an outgrowth of her awareness of her "inferior" anatomical status), one in a series of endless compromises that she would make over her lifetime. Moreover, Freud believed that the girl's preoedipal attachment to her mother predisposed her to homosexuality and the development of such character traits as passivity and dependency.

While Freud hinted at the possibility that the preoedipal period might have an important influence in shaping femininity and female sexuality, he seemed to ignore his own insights and failed to follow through on his ideas. Freud viewed every girl as blaming her mother for her genital inferiority and her castrated state, and as turning to her father to provide her a penis substitute, that is, a baby. Indeed "the turning away from the mother was accompanied by hostility; the attachment to the mother ending in hate." The little girl was seen as holding her mother directly responsible for her defective, penisless state. Clearly, the pathway to femininity was a circuitous one, characterized by rough terrain and numerous roadblocks. According to Freud's theory, a girl's femininity was not guaranteed. Indeed, many girls failed to achieve a female identity, developing either a sexual inhibition and neurosis or a masculinity complex. Clearly, the cards were stacked against a girl's establishing a typical female gender identity. The fact that the majority of girls survived this process of feminization and developed a typical female gender identity was a mystery. Given the masculine origins of her femininity it is difficult to comprehend what such a femininity even means for a girl.

Freudian theory viewed a girl's wish for a penis as neither surprising nor absurd; rather it was the expected state of affairs. Penis envy was a girl's/woman's fate, the bedrock on which her femininity developed. In effect, a girl's penis envy was the rule, a complex which exerted a ruthless grasp on her life — and one which she had little hope of ever resolving. Freud noted that for some women the conflict over penis envy, which was largely unconscious, completely overshadowed their lives. He noted that

> Here, what has been named the masculinity complex of women branches off. It may put great difficulties in the way of their regular development towards femininity, if it cannot be got over soon enough. The hope of one day obtaining a penis in spite of everything and so of becoming like a man may persist to an incredibly late age and may become a motive for strange and otherwise unaccountable actions. Or again, a process may set in which I should like to call 'disavowal', a process which in the mental life of children seems neither uncommon nor very dangerous but which in an adult would mean the beginning of a psychosis. *Thus a girl may refuse to accept the fact of being castrated, may harden herself in the conviction that she does possess a penis, and may subsequently be compelled to behave as though she were a man* (Freud, 1925, p. 253, my emphasis).

Because of Freud's patriarchal value system (see Breger, 1981), or what Schafer (1976) has called his "patriarchal complacency," he seemed to ignore "his tremendous discoveries concerning . . . prephallic factors" (Schafer, 1976, p. 473) in the psychology of women, and centered his theory of female sexuality and femininity on the phallic phase and oedipus complex, leading to the idea that penis envy was the bedrock of a woman's femininity. While Freud did not discuss the issue of transsexualism, his ideas on penis envy and the masculinity complex could be used to explain some manifestations of female transsexualism and, further, to explain some "strange and otherwise unaccountable actions" which may lead a woman to wish to undergo SRS and become a man. Such a process has been documented in at least one outcome study using the methods of psychoanalysis. In that case Grossman and Stewart (1976) described one woman's rather bizarre response to her analysis (which was certainly not a natural outcome of psychoanalysis). The woman experienced her penis envy as such a central issue that she "seriously considered going to Denmark for a transsexual operation in which she expected the transplant of a penis could be accomplished." From the perspective of Freudian theory, her response to her psycho-analysis, though judged bizarre, may be seen as a caricature of so-called successful female analyses in which one goal was to have a woman acknowledge her genital inferiority, her wish for a penis, and her homo-sexual tendencies, weak superego, passivity, and masochism. The fact that this woman responded to her penis envy by requesting SRS may also, however, represent an inherent flaw in Freudian theory, in that the theory of penis envy may be concretized and taken too literally, with penis envy being viewed not as a metaphor and a symbolic concept for narcissistic injury, but as a literal fact. Consequently, an important question posed by Freud's theory of femininity may be, not why do some women become transsexuals, but why do not all women (in the light of some interpretations of penis envy) become transsexuals?

From the very outset, Freud's theories of femininity were attacked by feminist analysts. Indeed, his paper on "Some psychical consequences of the anatomical distinction between the sexes" (1925) seemed to be a direct reply to some of Karen Horney's (1924) criticisms of his theories. Moreover, during the 1920s and 1930s a number of analysts, including Abraham (1927), Horney (1967), Deutsch (1944), Lampl-de Groot (1965), and Jones (1927), critically evaluated and questioned Freud's views of femininity. Fliegel (1973), quoting from Jones's summary (1927) of the main arguments against Freud's view, stated: "In short, I do not see a woman . . . as an 'homme manqué', as a permanently disappointed creature struggling to console herself with secondary substitutes alien to her nature. The ultimate question is whether a woman is born or made." Fliegel (1973, p. 396) noted, somewhat charitably, that Fenichel referred to Freud's critics as engaging in a "lively discussion in which different and sometimes contradictory views have been expressed." Although Freud initially viewed his theories of femininity and female sexuality as tentative, "in urgent need of confirmation," and not providing "necessary proof," he often presented his ideas as if they were fundamental truths and not hypotheses. While addressing his critics, Freud either trivialized their findings or associated their insights with his own thinking and thereby diluted their objections. Breger (1981) explained Freud's intransigence in terms of his personal confrontation between two opposing world views: in which his thinking on female sexuality was seen as not grounded in hard science and objectivity, but molded by his value system, which was based on a male-dominated, patriarchal, and phallocentric view of the world. Moreover, Schafer, while acknowledging Freud's "rich clinical and theoretical discoveries," saw him as philosophically immature and enmeshed in a tradition that represented a "fusion of mechanistic and evolutionary modes of thought" (1976, p. 483), and rooted in "patriarchal complacency." Schafer viewed the basic difficulties with Freud's views of femininity and female sexuality as due to "certain questionable presuppositions, logical errors and inconsistencies, suspensions of intensive inquiry, underemphasis on certain developmental variables, and confusions between observations, definitions, and value preferences" (ibid.). According to Fliegel (1973) some of Freud's conceptual problems may have resulted from his urgency to publish and defend his theory of femininity before possessing the facts. Fliegel related Freud's sense of urgency to several personal crises including, but not limited to, the discovery of his cancer, the death of his grandson, and the internal dissensions which threatened the survival of the psychoanalytic movement.

While Freud's ideas have been subjected to severe criticism, his views have profoundly influenced generations of clinicians in both their understanding and treatment of women. More recently, as new findings derived from child development studies have been published, Freud's critics, rather than throwing out the baby with the bath water, have broadened and revised his speculations.

The critique of Freud: summary of empirical studies

During the early 1970s feminists renewed their attacks on Freud's theory of female sexuality (Miller, 1973). While I will not attempt to review the polemical arguments against Freud, the subject is both a sensitive and important one, and deserves special treatment. Recently, Stoller (1976) elaborated on these criticisms of Freud's theory of femininity, viewing it as "a strange definition of femininity," and one not supported by observational and empirical evidence on child development during the first three years of life. Indeed, what we know about the origins of a girl's sense of herself as female suggests that even during the first two years girls exhibit what have been viewed as stereotypical "female" behaviors; behaviors which eventually consolidate into their female core gender identity. Either Freud's theory of femininity was addressing an entirely different issue in female sexual-gender development, or it was false. Indeed, Freud had cautioned his readers to regard his views on female sexuality as mere speculations in need of confirmation.

The critiques of Freud's theory that I will discuss were not based on metapsychological speculations but on empirical evidence derived from observational and experimental studies of neonates, infants, and toddlers (during the preoedipal stage of development). Each of the findings reported below has been drawn from empirical research, which has enabled clinicians to revise Freud's pioneering views of femininity and female sexuality. It will become clear to the reader that while Freud's views have been broadened and reinterpreted, every researcher is indebted to him for his penetrating insights and his struggle to make sense out of confusing, often chaotic, clinical material. While Schafer argued that "Freud's generalizations concerning girls and women do injustice to both his psychoanalytic method and his clinical findings" (1976, pp. 483–4), there is little doubt but that his formulations of femininity and female sexuality have provided leading ideas for several generations of clinicians and researchers. However, some of the new empirical findings which need to be incorporated into a comprehensive theory of femininity and female sexuality include the following:

1 The clitoris is no longer viewed as an anatomically male organ (Stoller, 1975; Fast, 1978).
2 Neonatal hormones were implicated in postnatal behavior patterns for boys and girls (Money and Ehrhardt, 1972).
3 An *early genital phase* was postulated in which awareness of the vagina by the toddler was recognized (Roiphe and Galenson, 1981).
4 A stage of *primary femininity* was postulated (Stoller, 1976).
5 Women born without vaginas or with an overabundance of male hormone who were raised as girls were found to have achieved a female gender identity (Money and Ehrhardt, 1972).
6 A sense of femaleness was shown to exist in women irrespective of sexual preference (Fast, 1979).
7 A girl's relationship to her mother did not necessarily predispose her to homosexuality (ibid.).

8   A child's sense of sex and gender potential was no longer viewed
     as limited to his/her biological or genetic sex (ibid.).

9   A girl's awareness that she lacked a penis did not necessarily lead
     to catastrophic feelings of inferiority but could lead to the
     realization that "not all sex and gender possibilities [were] open
     to her" (ibid.).

10   There was reason to believe that males and females might have
     different "hormonally primed brains" (Money and Ehrhardt,1972).

11   Femininity was no longer seen as initiating at the "phallic" stage
     (Stoller, 1976).

12   The precursors of gender identity in the girl were viewed as co-
     alescing during the second year into a core gender identity, which
     was seen as firmly established by age 3 (Stoller, 1972).

13   Cognitive factors were viewed as playing an important role in
     gender identity formation (Kohlberg, 1971).

14   Core gender identity was related to the ego's capacity to dif-
     ferentiate (Fast, 1979).

15   Social learning and imitation mechanisms were viewed as playing
     prominent roles in a girl's core gender identity (Mischel, 1966).

16   The parents' "coalition in conveying appropriate gender role
     meaning to the child [was seen as] important" in shaping the
     child's gender identity (Kleeman, 1971b).

17   Mechanisms such as imprinting, conditioning, and learning were
     also viewed as playing an important role in the acquisition of
     gender identity (Money, Hampson, and Hampson, 1957).

18   Healthy interpersonal relationships were a prerequisite for a child's
     developing a core gender identity (Volkan, 1979).

19   A girl's ability to differentiate her gender identity was linked to
     the formation of object relationships and the separation-
     individuation process (Fast, 1979).

As yet none of these findings has been integrated into a comprehensive
theory of femininity and female gender identity.

Normal female gender identity: developmental pathways

My understanding of how female gender identity is formed was arrived
at by synthesizing the above findings in the light of Freud's theories, and

drawing on the clinical and extra-clinical findings from such diverse disciplines as genetics, neuroendocrinology, neurobiology, psychology, anthropology, psychoanalysis, sociology, literature, art, medicine, ethology, and education. It was immediately clear that Freud's views on femininity and female gender identity have, in most cases, been broadened, revised, and at times superseded by a wealth of empirical studies and observations of girls from birth through age 5.

Female gender identity: the empirical evidence

Over the last decade, empirical and observational research in child development has shown that a girl develops her femininity not through a series of defensive adaptations to her recognized inferiority to males (occurring during the phallic period) but through a series of positive and, at times, conflictual exchanges with her parents and caretakers during the preoedipal period. While the girl's first meaningful relationship with her mother provides the basis for her "female" feelings, her female identity and the achievement of an "average expectable feminine gender identity" is the result of the collective effects of her parenting. To the extent that her parents empathically relate to her emerging female gender identity and role in a positive way, resonating with, and supporting her budding femininity and female behaviors, she will evolve a cohesive and stable female gender-self representation and eventually a core female gender identity.

If all goes well, a girl's femininity effloresces prior to the phallic period during a phase of development now labeled as one of *primary femininity*. While this early phase of gender identity involves a complex interactional process of innate behaviors, learned responses, and constitutional issues, all an observer may see is the final product; that is, a feminine-appearing girl even by age 18 months. It is only later in her development (between ages 3 to 5) that a girl's female identity undergoes a shift due to her reaction to her phallic-oedipal stage of development. This phase is now referred to as one of *secondary femininity*. In other words, it appears as if Freud's views of femininity and female sexuality were really related to this second stage of female gender identity and were more descriptive of women with severe neurotic disorders. His major conceptual error was in not following through on his initial hunch that a girl's preoedipal period exerted a prepotent effect on the evolution of her femininity and female sexuality.

Money et al. (1957) identified "imprinting" and "conditioning" as the two major learning mechanisms which shaped a girl's primary femininity. Money also noted that strikingly feminine behavior (that is, caricatured female behaviors) appeared even before the girl's first birthday, with a critical period for female gender behaviors reached about the age of 18 months. His findings suggested that even by age 2 the major precursors of gender identity had already been laid down and were resistent to change. Indeed, by age 2½ a girl's core gender identity and role were already well established. Consequently, Money urged pediatric surgeons not to try to alter the sex of infants with intersexual or hermaphroditic disorders after 18 months of age.

In 1968 Stoller introduced the term *core gender identity* as "the sense we have of our sex . . . [it] develops first and is the central nexus around which masculinity and femininity gradually accrete." Stoller viewed core gender identity (the child's recognition that s/he is a girl or a boy) as consolidating around age 2½. He viewed the process as being the result of a number of interrelated developmental events including: a biological force which organized the fetal brain; the sex assigned to the child at birth; the unending impingements of the parents' attitudes towards the infant's sex; early postnatal effects, including conditioning, imprinting, and other forms of learning; and the developing body ego. Stoller's definition of female gender identity is best described by Gershman's characterization of gender identity as "not unlike a symphonic orchestration which is composed of many motifs intertwined into one integrated theme [that is,] the unresolve[d] passionate relationship to the mother" (1970, p. 65).

Stoller's views were elaborated by Hampson (1971), who argued that the sensitive or critical period for gender identity formation began "no later than 1½ to 2 years"; while "the most basic and persistent elements of gender role [were] acquired between 4–5 years." Eventually, Kleeman (1971a) summarized the child development research and argued that core gender identity was "more or less unalterably established between 3–4 years of age." Two crucial phases of gender development were noted. The first occurred during the early preoedipal phase and the second occurred during the phallic-oedipal phase of development. Accordingly, Freud's theories of female development seemed more related to the second phase of gender identity formation. Although there was some disagreement as to the chronological age when all this occurred (that is, somewhere between 18 months to 48 months of age), it was evident that feminization and the establishment of female core gender identity occurred earlier than Freud had realized.

Indeed, Roiphe and Galenson (1981) argued that Freud "vastly underestimated the role of preoedipal psychosexuality" on the formation of female development. Kleeman (1971b) summed up the contemporary view by stating that by age 3 a "girl is very much a girl and knows it." But how does this process come about?

We know that the precursors of a girl's gender identity are formed well before her birth. Indeed, parental motivations and wishes regarding their child's gender begin to operate even before the child is born. Recently, the procedure of amniocentesis has afforded us rare opportunity to study parental bonding towards their child's sex and gender even prior to birth. A combination of factors, including parental wishes for a certain sexed child, the child's capacity to evoke certain behaviors and responses, and the combined parental dynamics (also influenced by social, environmental, and peer input) help to organize the child's later feelings, attitudes, ideas and expectations about her gender. At the moment of delivery, parental hopes and expectations about their child's sex and gender are awakened. In intersexual and hermaphroditic cases, where there is confusion about the child's sex, it is the sex assigned and the sex of rearing, and not the child's chromosomal sex, that has the most important organizing effect on the child's gender identity. In effect, parents play the crucial role in their child's gender identity development. Indeed, some parents who may have a gender identity or role disorder may "graft" those conflicts onto their newborn (the so-called self-fulfilling prophecy). This process takes place through the parents' communications of the meanings and attitudes they have about the child's sex and gender. Utilizing the defense mechanism of projective identification, some parents may project their gender conflicts onto their child, identifying with the gender conflict which their child now both contains and acts out. The question of whether girls are born or made has, for the most part, been answered: girls (and boys too) are, for the most part, made.

The overriding effects of parental rearing on a child's gender identity have been well documented by Kleeman (1971a, b). Through observational evidence and empirical studies of neonates and infants, Kleeman (1971b) has shown that parental meanings and communications about their child's gender and "identification processes contribute to the establishment of significant beginnings of gender identity before the phallic period and before penis envy, castration anxiety, and the oedipal complex contribute their main influences." Ultimately the parents' approval and liking of their daughter's femaleness (and her genitals) allow her to evolve a typical female gender identity and establish good interpersonal relationships in her female role.

While a girl's awareness that "I am a girl" occurs by age 2–3 (and is an item on the Stanford-Binet intelligence test for 4-year-olds), it does not signify a consolidation of her female gender identity. Rather it provides evidence that a girl is forming a core belief about her female self around which her later female gender identity will evolve. Roiphe and Galenson have pointed out that "these early boy/girl labels, like other early words, are quite unstable during the second year and therefore their use hardly constituted evidence that the child has developed a firm conviction that there are two sexes . . . [or that it] testified to the child's sense of his [or her] own sexual identity" (1981, p. 93). Kohlberg (1961) has argued that gender identity is ultimately related to the maturation of the child's cognitive development. Indeed, Kleeman believed that cognitive issues, which he saw as related to the broader developmental issues of separation-individuation and the differentiation process (see Fast, 1979), played a more important role in female gender identity formation than did castration anxiety, penis envy, and such learning mechanisms as modeling, associative learning, conditioning, imprinting, and imitation.

As the child enters the second half of her second year, she evidences considerable cognitive growth. She is now able to go beyond sensorimotor and presymbolic "meanings" of her gender and to grasp gender concepts on more than a rudimentary level (viewing herself as related to a class of individuals known as girls, whom she identifies sexually by the fact that girls have long hair, wear skirts, and have vaginas). In effect she now evidences semi-symbolic reasoning. However, it is not until she develops the formal logical operations of thought (around age 11) and abstract reasoning (in adolescence) that her female gender identity and character are consolidated into a firm sense of a female self. Moreover, while her cognitive view of female gender identity may attain a high level of maturation and stability, her "sense" of her female gender identity and role is never something completed but always in the process of change and redefinition over her lifetime. In this sense, a girl's *core gender identity* is the bedrock on which her cohesive adult female gender identity is established. Her female gender identity (which changes over her life cycle) is, however, anchored in her core female gender identity.

Roiphe and Galenson's research provided support for the existence of an *early genital phase* in girls (between 15–24 months) which formed the basis for a girl's *primary femininity*. They contended that the girl's experience of an early genital phase helps to organize her self-representation and gender identity. That is, the girl's self-representation was viewed as molded by her early genital and bodily sensations (which were different for boys and girls); her exposure to anatomical sexual differences; and her experience of a *preoedipal castration reaction*. Their observations of neonates and toddlers in a controlled nursery environment led them to conclude that

> penis envy and the feminine castration complex exert crucial influence upon feminine development. However, these occur earlier than he [Freud] had anticipated. They are closely intertwined with fears of object and anal loss, and they shape an already developing although vague sense of femininity stemming from early body and affective experiences with both parents (1981, p. 285).

Roiphe and Galenson viewed their discovery of an early genital phase (between ages 15 to 24 months) and preoedipal castration reaction as, not "merely several of many variables that influence the growing sense of identity . . . [but] they are unique, exemplary, and of equal importance to the oral and anal aspects of psychosexual development which have preceded them." Whether the early genital phase turns out to have equal importance to the other libidinal stages remains to be seen. However, Roiphe and Galenson have demonstrated the important organizing effect of this early genital phase on the girl's ego functions, cognition, and affective experience. Their study suggested that archaic modes of ego functioning were inextricably linked to different subphases of genitality (with special reference to the loss of reality testing that can accompany a girl's denial of the anatomical differences between the sexes). From this standpoint alone, their findings have significant implications for atypical or deviant female gender development, female transsexualism, and the emergence of psychopathology around gender identity formation.

Kleeman (1971b) believed that "optimal gender identity formation required that during early childhood parents worked together to convey meanings and that each assumed his or her respective gender-linked role. Each and every influence varied with the child's age, developmental phase, and specific strength and vulnerability at that time." The basic organizer of a girl's gender identity, however, was the mother-child relationship, specifically the mother's empathy and mirroring of her daughter's evolving femaleness.

Given the above findings, one may conclude that if the mother was uncertain about her own identity (and she manifested considerable gender envy of males and a profound hatred of her femaleness, her female body, and a dread of femininity), her daughter would not be able to evolve a unified and healthy sense of her femaleness (that is, her gender identity would be impaired). Moreover, unless the mother allowed her daughter to separate and individuate from her, her daughter might never be able to develop a separate sense of self. It is, therefore, not surprising that mothers who are symbiotic, have poor self-object differentiation and poor ego boundaries, and are diagnosed as having a borderline personality organization and developmental arrests, also have daughters with impaired ego functions, who are in turn unable to differentiate self from objects, have poor ego boundaries and a disturbed gender identity.

Because of the unusually prolonged preoedipal attachments which most daughters have with their mothers, they are very prone to merge or fuse with their mental representation of mother. Consequently, girls may have more difficulty than boys in developing a separate self from their mothers (fearing being fused with the mother and/or losing their sense of self). From this perspective, the girl's special relationship with her mother, by jeopardizing her sense of separateness, may also lead to feelings of intense hostility and hatred of her mother. Once aroused, these hostile feelings may endanger the girl's need for a close relationship with her mother. Because the conflict is unconscious it may exert a powerful force on the relationship. In many cases the conflict may become concretized in a girl's awareness of her lack of a penis and the irrational belief that her mother consciously deprived her of this important birthright. It is not so much that these girls are angry with mother for depriving them of a penis, but they fear that mother may deprive them of a separate identity. That is, these girls fear merging their self-representation with mother and losing their separate identities. Consequently, a woman's special vulnerability is not that she lacks a penis (or might be a latent homosexual), but that she might lack a separate self from mother (that is, she might never be able to differentiate from her mother and become an independent self). In effect, the penis comes to symbolize a girl's need to separate from mother. In some cases, girls with intense separation conflicts may believe that the only way they can evolve a separate self is by identifying as a female transsexual and thereby disidentifying from mother.

Mahler and Gosliner (1955) pointed out that a typical girl's reaction to a threat of fusion with mother was to use the father (from the third year on) to help her separate from mother. Around this time fathers have been identified as the primary enabler of their children's gender roles and identities (Tyson, 1982). It may be that one of the father's social-evolutionary roles in child development is to help their daughters to separate from their mothers and to establish a separate sense of self (which is necessary for their later independent and autonomous existence from the nuclear family). Some fathers of female transsexuals may also have deliberately kindled their daughters' fusion fantasies with mother in order to "rescue" them.

It appears as if the second half of a girl's second year is a crucial period for child development. At the beginning stages of toilet training she is experimenting with early issues of autonomy, control, and separateness. She is also beginning to develop semi-symbolic forms of reasoning; undergoing an early genital phase; becoming aware of the anatomical distinction between the sexes; revealing a primary femininity; having a preoedipal castration reaction; beginning progressively to differentiate her body image and schema; revealing "an upsurge in object-loss anxiety, negativism and an increased hostile dependence on the mother" from whom she needs to separate (see Mahler's (1967) discussion of the child's rapprochement crisis); is developing a nuclear self-system (see Kohut, 1977); and is establishing her core gender identity as female.

In the course of childrearing it is often difficult to keep in mind all the challenges and conflicts facing the 18- to 36-month-old child. In addition, all these processes are influenced by the unique environmental variables of each child; that is, the girl's overall physical attractiveness; her physical health, or the presence of chronic disease; her intelligence level and overall ego functioning; the birth of a new sibling and her sibling status; abandonments, separations, losses, changes, and deaths in her family; the effects of caretakers and peers; and, finally, all of the non-predictable or random environmental impingements which may significantly affect her life.

In the process of forming the rudiments of her developing self-system every girl during this period refines her ego's capacity to differentiate self/object representations and separates her self-representation from mother. Moreover, while she is beginning to establish firmly the ego mechanisms governing self and object constancy, she is also experiencing herself for the first time as a unity and not as a discontinuous bundle of actions, sensations, and perceptions. While the psychological literature has virtually ignored the developmental emergence of the stability of her gender-self representation, every girl is busily at work trying to unify her gender-self representations into a meaningful whole, expressed as a unique self (a female self) having control over her reality and participating in her interpersonal world in a new, non-dependent way.

Not only does a girl experience a mental representation of her gender-self, but she strives to form and maintain the unity of her gender-self representation over time (as it undergoes transformations secondary to developmental issues). The establishment and maintenance of her gender-self representation, and the coalescing of her gender-self representation into a unity I shall refer to as *gender-self constancy* (an analogue to *object constancy* which is regulated by the same mechanism).

The concept of *self constancy*, though alluded to by Jacobson (1964), Frances and Dunn (1975), Stolorow and Lachmann (1980), and defined by Frances, Sacks, and Aronoff (1977), has been virtually ignored by theoreticians. This is not only surprising but unfortunate, since one would expect that theories which posit the necessity of self and object differentiation would also posit an underlying mechanism by means of which both self and object representations were guaranteed in consciousness.

Frances, Sacks and Aronoff viewed self constancy as an ego function

> involved in establishing a relative cohesiveness and stability over time of the full constellation of self representations. This creates an average expectable self which is both cognitively perceived and affectively felt to be "me" . . . the ego maintains a tonic relationship with an "average expectable self" consisting of such various components as the body-self, the thinking-self, the affect-self, the action-self, the gender-self, the object-relating self etc. (1977, p. 326).

It is my contention that the establishing of a regulatory ego mechanism governing object constancy does not necessarily insure the reciprocal development of self constancy (especially around one's gender-self representation). The establishment of a firm gender-self representation and eventually gender-self constancy is, however, crucial to the development of core gender identity and the formation of a nuclear self; and for some, its failure to evolve contributes to the adoption of an atypical gender-self (which may lead to the adult development of female transsexualism). From this perspective, the second half of the second year of the child's life is a crucial period during which the foundations for female trans-sexualism are established. The developmental period between 18 to 36 months (when a child's major developmental task is that of separation-individuation and the formation of the beginnings of a cohesive self-concept) is thus seen as pivotal for the etiology of child and then adult gender identity and role disorders.

The second half of the second year of life is a generative era: representing the period of the birth of the self and the establishment of the ego mechanism governing *gender-self constancy* (involving the consolidation and stability of the child's gender-self representation); and the experience of the inner continuity and unity of the gender-self representation, which involves both cognitive and affective elements and "a 'tonic relationship' between the executive monitoring functions of the ego with the individual as well as the sum total of the self representations" (Francis et al., 1977, p. 326). The establishment of gender-self constancy also implies the existence of self-object differentiation, the reciprocal achievement of object constancy, and the establishment of a mechanism to unify gender-self representations into a total self-concept. In the midst of conflict, turmoil, and change the girl's female self emerges from her perceived unity of her gender-self representations and radically influences both her own and her parents' reality. She is not only being dressed as a little girl but is beginning to think and "feel" like a little girl.

By age 3 the little girl knows she is a girl and acts like a girl (gender role). Out of her early genital phase and the vicissitudes of cognitive and affective development and maturation, she evolves a female core gender identity which is not static but dynamic, influenced by a multitude of family, personal, and environmental factors. The early recognition of gender ascriptions — for example, "I am a girl" — or core gender identity, is a shorthand notation for the manifestations of what we today call a rudimentary gender-self system. The research suggests that one's core gender identity may be the first manifestation of the self-system. With the girl's recognition of sexual differences she also seems to undergo a crisis similar to that discussed by Freud (only the crisis appears earlier and does not form the core of her femininity). As a result of the recognition of sexual differences, girls seem to heighten their separation conflicts (that is, their need to separate from mother); to consolidate their gender-self representations, and to develop gender-self constancy. In most instances all of this takes place smoothly, preparing the stage for what psychologists have reverently called "the terrible twos."

Sometime during the phallic stage a secondary defensive adaptation (to a newly discovered castration anxiety) takes place which may lead the girl's primary femininity off its tracts and, so to speak, derail her female core gender identity. However, for girls with a nascent, structuralized self-system, one would expect deviant gender development to lead only to impaired sexuality, a masculinity complex, or a neurosis — not to female transsexualism. Over the life cycle one's sense of gender identity also undergoes significant shifts. Depending on how well the child's early milieu provided her with a solid foundation for developing adequate ego functions and healthy object relationships, each of these changes in her self-identity will either be welcomed as a new challenge to her evolving self, or defended against because it threatens her femininity or female sexuality (that is, her female gender-self representation and her gender-self constancy).

To the observer, the girl's gender identity may appear to have been achieved as if by sleight of hand. Actually, it is the end product of a complex process which is achieved with much difficulty and effort. If there is any "magic" it is in those spontaneously occurring feminine behaviors which arise even in girls raised in familes which have discouraged stereotypical feminine behaviors. Some researchers have attributed these behaviors to such innate factors as a "female brain" or the result of endogenous female hormone influences on the fetal brain.

There are other theoreticians who argue that feminine behavior is not innate but entirely learned, a byproduct of a sexist society which manipulates, controls, and exploits those sex roles. While those arguments are salient in terms of socioeconomic parity for women with men, they cannot explain why some women become transsexuals.

Abnormal female development: the roots of female transsexualism

Any theory of femininity and female sexuality must take into account the atypical ways in which girls may develop their gender roles and identity. The most logical place to begin our investigation is at that point during the life cycle when female transsexuals (that is, women who exhibit the most atypical gender identity and role adaptations) report that they first became aware of a wish to become a boy.

Typically, female transsexuals report that around age 5 they became obsessed with a wish to be transformed into a boy. This was probably a screen memory of a much earlier wish (perhaps representing what Khan (1974) described as the result of cumulative trauma). Eventually their cross-gender wishes crystallized into a fixed idea of wanting to become a boy. Most of these women recalled being preoccupied by a compulsive, obsessional, cross-gender wish which they kept secret. While it was impossible to corroborate their self-reports, there are a number of clinical studies which suggest that some children, between 1–2 years of age, demonstrate rigid and stereotyped opposite-sexed behaviors and gestures (Galenson et al., 1974). Some of these children were able to verbalize their hatred of their genitals, and their cross-gender envy and wishes (Bloch, 1975).

In the previous section I demonstrated that what we ordinarily assume to be a smoothly occurring, non-conflictual process (that is, the establishment of a girl's gender identity) is really a complex one involving a number of divergent inputs from a multitude of personal, family, hereditary, and environmental variables that form a final common pathway: the child's conviction that "I am a girl!" Deviations in gender identity can occur anywhere along the continuum of child development during the first three years of life. Depending on where, and to what degree, the girl's problems first appeared, the clinician will have a good idea of how symptomatic and pathologically organized will be the girl's interpersonal relationships and overall functioning.

Table 6.1 schematically depicts the usual and unusual psychosexual pathways of gender-sex development. Whereas the usual course of development leads to the establishment of a core gender identity (in the 2 to 3-year-old) there are a number of girl children who, even at this young age, manifest intense gender confusion. They do not exhibit an identity crisis characterized by confusion as to *who* they are but rather as to *what* they are. That is, they do not know whether they are a boy or a girl. Their gender identity confusion cannot be explained simply by their failure to develop normal cognitive structures (though these girls typically reveal problems with ego boundaries, self-object differentiation, and evidence of developmental arrests).

Figure 6.1 presents a flow chart of some of the typical ways in which the parent-child matrix may lead to the establishment of a pathological gender identity and/or role. During the first two years the mother plays the dominant role in parenting. A mother's defective object relationships, her lack of a cohesive self, her sense of emptiness and rage, her heightened feelings of fragmentation, her wishes for an opposite-sexed child, and her opposite-gender envy and jealousy may all be communicated to her child. Most important is the mother's unique role as a prime target of identification for her daughter. Serving the joint roles of love object and source of identification, mother has the capacity to arouse considerable separation anxiety in her daughter (especially around gender issues). A girl's potential for merging and fusing with her mother may also predispose her to develop a focal gender symbiosis, leading, in adult life, to a dread of her femininity, which she may associate with a loss of self. During the first two years the father's role in "causing" his daughter's gender conflicts is indirect, as he consciously or unconsciously encourages his wife (or partner) to defeminize their daughter. In the course of her development, the father eventually plays the final decisive role in facilitating and encouraging his daughter to masculinize herself and so separate from mother. It is the father's support of her masculinity which seals her fate.

Children raised by transsexual-prone parents report that their parents were either indifferent to, or encouraged their cross-gender roles and identifications. Our clinical findings suggest that these girls were usually raised in atypical homes, characterized by a range of serious emotional pathology (not all families focused on the same problems). Some families exhibited chaotic sexuality and impulsivity; others exhibited patterns of child abuse, abandonments, and generalized violence. Some families demonstrated all of these patterns of conflict, while others emphasized one prominent mode. At the very least the parents or grandparents (who may have been the primary caretakers) either overtly or covertly, jointly or separately, supported their daughters' or granddaughters' cross-gender identifications. Because of the nature of a female transsexual's anxiety, one may speculate that her conflicts probably had their origin in her early genital phase, in which a seductive, intrusive parent may have overstimulated her, heightening her castration anxiety (with her fears focused on penetration) and annihilation anxiety (fearing fusion with her mother and thereby losing her self-identity). The girl's fears may also have led to compensatory fantasizing about how she could protect herself from annihilation anxiety by assuming a male role. Moreover, her state of being overstimulated precluded her developing ego mechanisms for regulating her ego functioning, especially her impulse control balance.

Many transsexuals-to-be may have also reacted to being overstimulated during the early genital phase by engaging in compulsive masturbation

Table 6.1 *Gender-sex development*

Stages in the gender-sex life cycle	Ages	Usual sex-gender development
	0	Congenital psychosexual bisexuality
Early childhood		*Core gender identity*: an infant's developing sense of self as a boy or girl in the second year 'I am a boy/girl'
	5	*Oedipal period*: 'I am a boy/girl'
Childhood		*Latency*: 'I am a boy/girl'
	10	
		Attaining of intimate relationships with opposite sex-gender partners
Adolescence		'I am a boy/girl'
	15	
		Living out of life in original sex-gender pattern of rearing
Adulthood	20	and assignment 'I am a boy/girl'

in order to allay their anxiety. However, masturbation (which was usually accompanied by heightened feelings of object loss or dissolution) may have reinforced their feelings of loss (through heightened castration anxiety). Indeed, most of the female transsexuals in our study evidenced considerable psychopathology, including evidence of developmental arrests, impaired ego mechanisms, poor impulse control and low frus-

Atypical sex-gender development	Atypical sex-gender behaviors
Gender confusion: 'What am I?'	Secret thoughts about one's dual gender Emergence of crossdressing
Gender diffusion: 'Am I both a boy and a girl?'	Severe childhood gender identity disorders
Gender flight: 'I am scared by my gender confusions. I'll be a —'	Emergence of homoeroticism
Gender identity? Adoption of a new gender role inverse to sex 'I am a boy/girl'	Emergence of transsexual wishes and behavior (resolution of experienced gender dissonance)

tration tolerance, and an impaired sense of reality (their reality testing, while generally intact, did show considerable variability). Moreover, their ego functioning was generally impoverished and they manifested problems with ego boundary formation.

It would seem that the severity of a girl's gender identity disorder was directly related to the hypothetical age at which her developmental

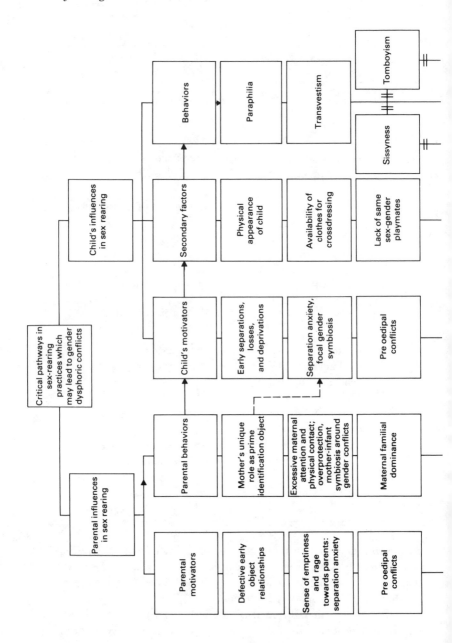

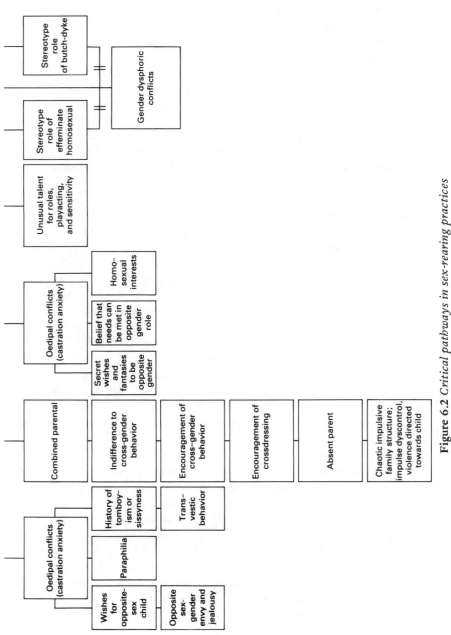

Figure 6.2 *Critical pathways in sex-rearing practices*

arrest occurred. The earlier the age when her mother (or maternal surrogate) interfered with the establishment of her female gender-self representation and gender-self constancy (impairing her core female gender identity) the more severe the girl's gender disorder. Table 6.1 suggests that the question "what am I?" becomes the female transsexual's fundamental question, around which all gender-related (and self-related) issues coalesce. As the girl develops through her life cycle, the question "what am I?" takes on new significance. Lacking a structuralized, cohesive self, and experiencing gender confusion and diffusion, the question may focus, during latency, around her early recognition that she enjoys being with boys and playing with them, while having to adjust to her exclusion from typical girls' groups. Some girls, however, although labeled tomboys, may find themselves drawn to girls' groups because they are sexually excited in the presence of other girls; or they may develop crushes on their teachers or older women (seeking out close, intimate relationships with those women).

It must be noted that the girls we are referring to represent a special group of girls who have predominantly borderline and self pathology and are pre-transsexual. In the course of their development their "tomboy" behavior and "erotic interest in girls and older women" have an entirely different meaning than they would for the average girl. Indeed, the majority of girls labeled tomboys outgrow their interest in mimicking a boy's gender role. During their childhood they may have been attracted to the boy's role for several reasons, all of which reflect a normal pattern of "girlish" behavior. That is, some of these girls may have associated with boys in order to gratify their normal needs for physical exercise and their enjoyment of heightened kinesthetic sensations and motor movements. Some of them are gifted athletes. It is also normal for girls to have occasional crushes on female teachers and girl peers. However, if those crushes on girls and older women become the dominant mode of a girl's erotic imagery (during her preadolescence), they are predictive of homosexuality, but not of transsexualism. The group of girls whom I am here labeling tomboys are really pre-transsexual girls. Typically they have a pathological jealousy and envy of boys and a hatred of their femaleness and female genitals. While they are erotically attracted to other girls, they see themselves as "boys" and wish to become a "boy" in every sense — including having a penis. It is this group of girls for whom the designation "tomboy" and a strong sexual attraction to other girls have an ominous meaning in terms of their possible assumption of a transsexual identity. Unfortunately, the label "tomboy" is often used in contradictory and confusing ways.

With the maturation of her cognitive abilities and her awareness of social prohibitions against homosexuality, the pre-transsexual girl may identify her problem as related to her homoeroticism. She may either view her sexual drives as out of control or believe that she is condemned, evil, or just a bad person; or that she has the wrong body and is defective. She may also engage in a struggle with authorities around wearing dresses, finding girls' clothing repugnant. Because society has fewer restrictions on clothing for girls and women, the gender-disturbed girl can mask her problems by wearing unisex clothing and thereby escape the profound criticism, social rejection, and stigmatization of her male counterpart. Her problems, which may go largely unnoticed, are, however, just as severe as the boy's. However, while the boy is socially ostracized and forced to bear the full brunt of society's homophobia and anxieties over masculinity, most girls may be either admired or ignored for their masculine pretenses. Society's reaction to the gender-disordered child influences the course of the gender disorder, with female transsexuals seeming to exhibit less apparent pathology than male transsexuals. Their anguish, however, cannot be judged as less profound than that of their male counterparts.

Throughout her childhood, the girl's basic gender confusion may exert a profound and pervasive influence over her developing object relationships. Every one of her social encounters may be characterized by her inability to address fully the question "what am I?" In effect, these girls project a false self-image as a female, which if accepted by society will increase the girl's sense of her unreality. A girl's early childhood gender confusion may also consolidate into a global feeling of gender diffusion, experienced as a low-grade chronic anxiety underlying her perception of having a fragmented self-system. The core aspects of her interpersonal relationships will inevitably be viewed as based on a lie. And her self-system may come to be experienced as either bad, defective, dangerous, deficient, empty, or lacking in something fundamental. The girl may ask herself: "What am I? Am I a girl or a boy? Am I both a boy and a girl? Am I an it?"

While the roots of female transsexualism are found in the preoedipal period, the real battles of the gender-disordered girl are not fought out until adolescence. At that time, in spite of all her hopes and wishes to become masculinized, her body feminizes. In response to her bodily changes, she has two options: she can either stubbornly resist the feminization of her body (binding her breasts, dressing in male clothing, denying the existence of her female genitals) and assume a male identity and role (increasing her sense of unreality); or she can succumb to her physiology and drive her gender conflicts underground (in most instances developing hypochondriacal symptoms, inhibited sexuality, or intense psychological conflict).

With the awakening of sexual feelings towards other girls (and her awareness of society's repugnance towards homosexuality), she may resort to primitive magical thinking, reasoning, "I must be a boy trapped in a girl's body." This statement, an example of magical thinking, may become the core of her self-system, allaying her anxiety and focusing her attention away from her hated female body. As she crystallizes her thinking around this statement, the girl buttresses her defenses and may develop an *idée fixe*, or paranoid thinking; the rationalization that she is a boy trapped in a female body becoming the focus of her denial of her female body and female gender-self system.

The issue of why some girls develop into homosexuals or transvestites, while others develop into transsexuals can be explained by an understanding of the fundamental structural ego weaknesses, deficits, and developmental arrests of female transsexuals. That is, while female transsexuals always evidence developmental arrests and ego defects or weaknesses, this is not necessarily true for female homosexuals or transvestites. In this sense I take issue with those clinicians who necessarily equate female transsexualism with homosexuality.

To date there is no hard evidence that homosexuality *per se* involves a disordered self-system. While a subgroup of homosexuals may evidence gender identity disordered behavior (e.g. the butch of "diesel dyke"), the female homosexual is not usually confused by the question "what am I?" She knows she is a woman, has no reason to disparage her sex or gender, and does not wish to change into a man. She may enjoy impersonating the male role, but she does not wish to have a penis.

In the past clinicians have been misled by the apparently "stable" clinical presentation of female transsexuals. This view is based on the superficial clinical presentation and descriptive symptomology of female transsexualism. Consequently, many clinicians have come to believe that, unlike male transsexualism, female transsexualism reflects a more integrated personality development. Such a perspective loses sight of the underlying structural defects, developmental arrests, and self-pathology which are at the heart of the differential diagnostic issues.

While I agree with Stoller (1972) that female transsexualism needs to be understood differently from male transsexualism, I believe this for different reasons. What others see as major differences between the two disorders I see as superficial differences related to sex differences (which are either socially learned, culturally primed, or constitutionally given). Indeed, from the larger social perspective all aspects of female sexuality manifest themselves differently, both behaviorally and dynamically, from male sexuality. These differences are predominantly based on sex differences and need to be recognized as such. It is not surprising that female transsexuals appear more "stable" than their male counterparts. Indeed, female lesbians appear more stable than male homosexuals; and female heterosexuals manifest significantly less sexual psychopathology and acting out than do male heterosexuals. The chief variable among these groups is sex differences. Because of their unique hormonal milieu and radically different socialization, female behavior disorders always seem less severe than their male counterparts.

While there are certain behavioral similarities among the three conditions of transvestism, homosexuality, and transsexualism, the latter is a qualitatively distinct disorder. In effect, female transsexualism is a disorder based on intergenerational family pathology which has been focused on gender-related issues: the female transsexual having a structural disorder of the self, and the transsexual symptomology being a product of developmental arrest with specific vulnerabilities in the woman's gender-self representation and ego mechanism governing gender-self constancy. Because each culture provides its own social nexus for a transsexual life style, the social issues of transsexualism may be manifested quite differently.

Although I use the concept "transsexualism," the term "transsexualisms" is more accurate since there are many different variants of female gender dysphoria conflicts which eventuate in a request for SRS. Moreover, on the basis of a girl's gender-disordered behavior one cannot predict what are her specific dynamic and structural conflicts. Each woman who is diagnosed as transsexual needs to be evaluated separately. Additionally, gender conflicts do not necessarily manifest themselves in a linear fashion. Even when a gender disorder is identified during childhood there is no way to predict what the outcome will be, since the gateways from one developmental stage to another may be closed. Of course, one may make gross predictive statements, but, to be meaningful, they must involve a structural analysis of the child's self and ego.

One research team (Rekers et al., 1975) has distinguished two types of childhood gender disorders which predispose a child to an adult gender identity disorder (transsexualism) or role disorder (transvestism). Whether there is any connection between the postdictive reports of adult female transsexuals and the predictive reports of the child studies remains to be seen. The fact that profound cross-gender role behavior can be demonstrated before age 2 is, however, suggestive of the fact that there may be a link between child and adult gender identity disorders. While it is known that tomboyism may undergo a radical transformation during a girl's adolescence, it is often difficult to determine which gender role pathways a specific girl will take (that is, hetero-, homo- or trans-sexuality). The clinician who wishes to make predictions (as opposed to assessing the girl's problems) would fare better if s/he focused not on the behavior but on such variables as the girl's erotic imagery, transsexual fantasy content, sexual preference, gender role meanings communicated by the parents, and underlying structural issues governing the girl's ego functioning (including her reality testing and impulse-defense balance). Whenever a clinician is evaluating a transsexual s/he should always think in terms of serious self pathology, developmental arrests, profound impairments in ego functions, a disordered gender-self representation, and an impaired ego function governing gender self-constancy.

In the next section I will review the major contributions of diverse theoretical schools to the understanding of female transsexualism and will develop my own theory of female transsexualism. Finally, I will offer a provisional typology of female transsexualism which clinicians can use for diagnostic, treatment, and prognostic purposes.

Theoretical approaches

Some traditional psychoanalytical views

Psychoanalytical theories of transsexualism have mainly focused on the male's problems. They view transsexualism as a perversion: a profound psychological disturbance related to a number of preoedipal issues. These issues range from bonding and a rupture in the mother-child relationship during the separation-individuation period, to oedipal conflicts and castration anxiety. Most analysts have also viewed trans-sexualism as a defense against underlying bisexual and homosexual conflicts. One analyst, Kubie (1974), postulated a fundamental drive to become both sexes, suggesting a latent, and universal, quasi-transsexual drive.

Stoller (1968, 1975), the most prolific of the psychoanalytical investigators, was also one of the first to offer a theory of female transsexualism (1972). His theory was derived from a long-term clinical study involving thirteen female transsexuals, of whom he supervised the evaluation and treatment of seven in psychotherapy, and described information on an additional ten cases with which he was familiar. Stoller (1972) labeled his theory of female transsexualism as "a first approximation" in which he identified some possible "etiological factors." He made no pretense that his ideas formed a coherent explanation for all variants of female transsexualism. Rather, he viewed his ideas as hypotheses to be investigated by future researchers. Stoller noted that for female transsexuals,

> the mother is almost always psychologically removed from the family, usually by depression, early in the girl's development. The father, while a substantial person in most regards, does not support his wife in her suffering but instead sends a substitute into the breach. This surrogate husband is the transsexual-to-be, also chosen perhaps because she strikes her parents as unfeminine in appearance from birth on. Since the family needs the child to function thus, any behavior construed as masculine is encouraged, and feminine behavior discouraged, until the islands of masculine qualities coalesce into a cohesive identity. Evidence for this theory comes not only from parents but from the subjects' fantasies, which are of rescuing endangered, motherly women. That these girls' masculinity seems to originate in part from traumatic disruption of mothering suggests that the condition may be allied to some forms of female homosexuality (1972, p. 47).

In 1968, Stoller described true male transsexualism as a disorder of a small group of male patients requesting SRS which evolved out of a "nonconflictual, learning process on the order of imprinting, conditioning, shaping, and identification." Female transsexualism, however, was viewed as a "defense against trauma and the erection of identity structures to prevent identity destruction by recurrence of trauma — which especially allies female transsexualism to the homosexualities" (Stoller, 1976, p. 62). Stoller also believed that the etiology of transsexualism was rooted in family dynamics and intergenerational family conflicts.

Another psychoanalytical investigator, Socarides (1969, 1970) argued that transsexualism was a perversion. He related it to a fixation occurring during the preoedipal period (between 1½–3 years of age). Socarides viewed the transsexual's nuclear conflicts as related to his/her inability "to pass successfully through the symbiotic and separation-individuation phases of early childhood." The "pivotal nuclear complex" of the transsexual was viewed as an "urge to regress to a pre-oedipal fixation in which there was a desire for, and a dread of, merging with the mother in order to reinstate the primitive mother-child unity." In effect, Socarides believed that transsexualism was primarily a defense against homosexuality.

While Socarides (1969) mainly addressed the issues of male transsexualism, his theories were equally applicable to female transsexualism. Socarides viewed transsexualism as neither a wish nor a diagnosis. It was "entirely a psychological disorder" rooted in conflict and trauma during the first three years of childhood development. In those homosexuals who wished to change their sex, he saw the mechanism of denial as being prominent. For girls, Socarides noted that "parents who accept, respect, and love the little girl as a girl and a father who accepts her femininity are vitally important" (1969, p. 1423). Like Stoller, Socarides believed that it was a harmful family environment which created the fertile soil for the growth of transsexualism. "As a result the individual cannot pass through the separation-individuation phase from one-and-a-half to three years of age, in which his [or her] gender identification [was] solidified."

While Limentani (1979), a British psychoanalyst, disagreed somewhat with Stoller's and Socarides's position, he also viewed transsexualism as a serious psychological disturbance arising during the preoedipal period. Limentani concluded that some of the prominent factors in the etiology of transsexualism involved the following: the father played a prepotent role "in the development of persistent transsexual fantasies or serious disorders in gender identity" (1979, p. 146); there was a lack of introjection of the good breast "which [was] central to the psychopathology of transsexualism"; the transsexual, while not overtly psychotic, had a disturbance in symbol formation and his/her thinking had an "unquestionable psychotic flavour"; "beneath the castration anxiety [lay] the most profound disturbances in object relations and it was separation anxiety [often equaled to a fear of annihilation] which would finally mobilize our attention"; and transsexuals utilized "violent projective identificatory mechanisms" (ibid., p. 147).

Limentani believed that the female transsexual, in contrast to the male transsexual, had the more serious psychological disturbance, related to her inability to separate fully from mother and "to be able to experience a body of [her] own." According to Limentani, the female transsexual's wish to become a man enabled her to resolve "the conflict over the desired and yet dreaded engulfment by mother." He dismissed the idea that "the masculinity of the female transsexual [was] rooted in an identification with a father who prefer[red] her to be a boy." He did not, however, explain how the female transsexual's male identifications evolved; why she came to believe that she was a boy; or what effect her cross-gender wishes had on her overall psychological functioning.

While psychoanalytically oriented clinicians have offered diverse hypotheses about the etiology of male transsexualism, few of them have offered a comprehensive theory of female transsexualism. Indeed, psychoanalysts have exhibited considerable disagreement as to the etiology of the disorder. Certain ideas do, however, stand out. All psycho-analytical investigators view female transsexualism as primarily a psychological disorder which has its roots in the preoedipal, mother-daughter relationship. As a consequence of their being raised in disturbed families, female transsexuals are viewed as having impaired ego mechanisms and underlying structural ego defects. Their transsexual pathology is a result of conflict defense, ambivalence, and trauma. However, psychoanalysts vary considerably in their views as to the effect and role of mothering on the etiology of the disorder. Clearly, the mother plays a crucial role in the etiology of female transsexualism. How this comes about is unknown. There is also some disagreement concerning the role of the father in the etiology of female transsexualism. It would appear that future analytical investigations on female transsexualism might benefit by focusing on the specific ways in which gender meanings are communicated within the family. In addition, the transsexual woman's disturbances in symbol formation need to be understood.

Above all, psychoanalysis has provided one of the best methods for investigating the phenomenon of female transsexualism, which includes investigating the underlying fantasy content and unconscious motivation of the transsexual's wish for sex reassignment surgery. However, the exclusive focus on genitality (and the concepts of drive, instinct, derivative instincts, part and whole objects), have led psychoanalysts to over-emphasize drive theory interpretations of female transsexualism. By focusing on the drive aspects of transsexualism (and the defensive aspects of the female transsexual's behavior), it is never clear how the trans-sexual's disorder is to be understood in terms of the self or person. Moreover, given the empirical findings that transsexualism does not seem to be a unitary disorder — and that a diversity of clinical variants present with female transsexual pathology — it seems gratuitous for some analysts to explain all manifestations of female transsexualism as a defense against homosexuality.

Behaviorism and social learning theory

The main premise of behaviorists (Barlow et al., 1973) and social learning theorists (Mischel, 1966) is that all gender-related behavior is learned. Unfortunately, most of the clinical studies have focused on young boys who were labeled "sissies." The clinical emphasis on studying "sissyness" may have stemmed from the fact that, as a result of social stigmatization, once boys were labeled as sissies they demonstrated more behavioral problems. However, there is no reason to suspect that the principles of learning would be different for males and females.

Behaviorists and social learning theorists have suggested that a few main principles (involving imitation, modeling, and the rules governing associative learning) are involved in how a girl learns her gender role. For the most part these theorists avoided using the concept of "gender identity" except as it could be used descriptively to label the totality of a girl's gender role behaviors. These learning principles were subject to a complex social reinforcement system in which the girl's parents, siblings, peers, and culture helped to shape her gender role behaviors.

Essentially, social learning theory viewed a girl as modeling her mother's behaviors; imitating her mother and other females; and associating a particular gender behavior with a social reward or punishment. Gender role behaviors which were rewarded were reinforced and became part of the girl's behavioral repertoire. With the girl's progressive cognitive maturation, she was able to generalize what she had learned and evolved new gender behaviors and roles. Within her family structure she learned to imitate and model her mother's behaviors (because of their higher reinforcement value). Her gender appropriate behaviors were then shaped by her peers and culture.

Brierley (1979) suggested that a conditioning paradigm (in which behaviors which had a reinforcing value were retained while behaviors which did not have a reinforcing value were discarded) could be used to explain how a girl learned to identify with her father and adopt a trans-sexual role. Brierley argued that "there [was] no reason why gender learning should not be simple associative learning which involve[d] both reinforcement of gender identity and role taking congruent with sex and some elements of punishment of incongruent behavior" (p. 55). He did not feel compelled to introduce such "mysterious" notions as imprinting to explain female identifications.

For the behaviorist, a girl's gender appropriate behaviors could be easily identified and labeled. Consequently, it was not a difficult task to identify inappropriate behaviors which needed to be changed. For example, in treating a girl who had learned an inappropriate sex-gender role, the behaviorist and social learning theorist would first begin by identifying her "male" gender behaviors and then try to change her "male" behaviors to "female" behaviors. This would include: assessing the intensity of a girl's wishes to wear boys'/men's clothing; observing her mannerisms and gestures to see whether, or how well, she tries to pass in the male role; listening to her voice to see if she tries to emulate a masculine voice inflection and employs predominantly "masculine" speech mannerisms; assessing her sexual preferences for girls versus boys; observing her social relationships and seeing if she shows a preference for boy playmates; taking note of the extent to which she avoids anything labeled as a feminine activity; finding out from her how she views her behavior, that is, whether she sees herself as a tomboy or whether she hates her female genitals and/or female self; and finally, whether she reveals a strong desire, or preference, to be a boy. Once these issues were clarified, the therapist could determine whether a psychological intervention was necessary.

While the behaviorist would deny that such factors as motivation, cognition, imagery, fantasy, wishes, and desires, and dreams played important roles in a woman's cross-gender behavior, such a theoretical position (naive realism) seems too simplistic and untenable. However, for the strict behaviorist only observable behavior is considered worthy of investigation. Behavioral explanations of female transsexualism have wide appeal because of their focus on commonsense explanations of human behavior. Behavior theory and therapy are not, however, value free. Indeed, the assumptions that certain behaviors should be labeled as masculine and feminine (and seen as desirable) are important values implicit in the theory. These values were derived from cultural and social norms which placed an emphasis on preserving the status quo at the expense of novelty. There was no assumption of human bisexuality or a questioning of the motivation or correctness of sex-gender roles. These were issues which behaviorists unfortunately reserved for ethicists or philosophers.

Many behavior therapists have instructed the parents of tomboys to reinforce unequivocally their daughters' feminine behaviors. Implicit in these instructions is the value that girls ought to exhibit stereotypical female behaviors. These behavior therapists do not seem to recognize that for some girls tomboyism is a normal variant of feminine behavior. There are also, however, some girls for whom tomboyism may reflect an underlying wish to transform their sex and to actually become a boy. In fact, those girls have serious ego defects and structural ego deficits, and the behavioral therapists' exhortations to give up their tomboyism and their wishes to become a boy are too simplistic an approach to the complexity of their emotional problems.

Rekers et al. (1974) have suggested that abnormal sex-role development in childhood should always be treated in order to prevent adult transsexualism, or another adult sex-role deviation. However, since the majority of girls labeled as tomboys eventually evolve a typical female gender role and identity during adolescence, their recommendation that all tomboys receive treatment is at least questionable, if not ethically suspect. The focus on behavior alone tends to oversimplify the issues, ignoring the powerful ways in which a person's behaviors may be related to fantasy content, unconscious motivation, or intergenerational family dynamics.

Clearly, behaviorism and social learning theory can help us to understand how certain aspects of sex-role identity and gender role are learned. The learning mechanisms of modeling, imitation, and associative learning are, however, by themselves inadequate to explain the phenomenon of female transsexualism, no less normal female gender development.

Additionally, behaviorists have not satisfactorily explained how, or why, associative links are established; that is, why girls are motivated to establish such links. For example, what are the internal mechanisms that allowed imitation and modeling to play such a profound role in the child's gender role and identity development? There was no attempt to explain how and by what mechanism, one's gender identity was formed (no less, what motivated the child). Clearly, gender role and identity are products of learning. But the explanations of the mechanisms underlying this learning process have been inadequate.

Cognitive developmental theory

Kohlberg (1966) was critical of both the psychoanalytic and the social learning theory approaches to gender identity formation. He believed that "the process of forming a constant gender identity [was] not a unique process determined by instinctual wishes and identifications, but a part of the general process of conceptual growth" (p. 98). He viewed the child's progressive cognitive differentiation of the self and the object world (along a Piagetian cognitive developmental framework) as being responsible for the child's gender identity and later sex-role concepts and attitudes (Piaget, 1949). Indeed, Kohlberg stated that "sexual identifications with parents are primary derivatives of the child's basic sexual identity and his [or her] self-maintaining motives — not the reverse, which is what psychoanalysis and social-learning theories have held" (1966, p. 88).

Kohlberg viewed the child's categorization of self as "boy" or "girl" as "the critical and basic organizer of sex-role attitudes." The child's statement "I am a girl" was the result "of a cognitive development which [was] quite independent of variations in social sex-role training." While the child was seen as knowing her sex by age 3 (with this information about gender identity serving as a "stable organizer of the child's psychosexual attitudes"), the stabilization of gender-identity concepts was directly related to the broader cognitive developmental issues of judgments related to other physical constancies. That is, the child's gender-identity constancy was related to such issues as body constancy, size constancy, object constancy, and his/her progressive cognitive maturity.

Kohlberg concluded that if there were specific parental influences on the child's gender identity they were negative, not positive. That is, Kohlberg stated that "certain parent attitudes may create specific anxieties and conflicts inhibiting the development of appropriate sex-role attitudes." Essentially, a child's unfolding of gender identity was dependent on two main sources. The primary source was determined by the child's cognitive maturity: "the result of the child's cognitive-developmental organization of a social world." The secondary source was viewed

215

as the child's motivational need "to preserve a stable and positive self-image."

Kohlberg's view that there was a natural tendency "to ascribe worth to the self [as] . . . an innate process" suggested to Lewis (1979), that he had capitulated to a view of primary narcissism akin to Freud's. Moreover, Kohlberg's view that "gender identity was perhaps the most stable of all social identities" suggested that its stability may have had more to do with an innate process (a motivational state) than with cognitive-developmental issues.

In spite of the above criticisms, Kohlberg's views on cognitive maturity and gender identity can neither be treated lightly nor discarded. Indeed, his cognitive theory has clarified some of Kleeman's (1971a, b), Fast's (1979), and Mahler's (1967) ideas on the issue of differentiation phenomena as they are related to the issue of gender identity. The importance of Kohlberg's contributions was twofold. First, he established an important link between gender identity and cognitive maturity, recognizing that gender identity was related to the cognitive issue of the child's capacity to stabilize her judgments (both spatially and temporally) of the physical world. Second, his notion of a connection between gender identity ("as the most stable of all social identities") and sex-role attitudes (which were the social, cultural enactments of cognitive-developmental trends) has had a profound influence on research.

Kohlberg's theory could explain certain aspects of female transsexualism. For example, he might explain a woman's confused gender identity as related to her "negative parental influences." Alternatively, her failure to stabilize her gender-identity concepts (secondary to a failure in cognitive developmental growth) might have led to her confused gender identity. His theory could not, however, explain why a woman might have an impaired motivational basis for ascribing worth to her self and "preserv[ing] a stable and positive self-image." It would appear that one would either have to explain psychologically why a woman was not motivated to become feminine, or show how a structural ego defect might have interfered with her sex-role cognitions. Kohlberg's ideas do not seem to go far enough in appreciating the specific intra-psychic issues of a particular woman; the varied intergenerational communication patterns within a given family; and the unique psychodynamics within a family matrix that provide the fertile soil for the development of female transsexualism.

216

Family dynamics and female transsexualism

Stoller suggested that the possible etiology of female transsexualism was that "too much father and too little mother masculinizes girls" (1968, p. 205). This rather cryptic statement paved the way for his hypothesis that family factors had an overriding influence on the etiology of female transsexualism, and provided an important working hypothesis for investigating the family dynamics theory of female transsexualism.

Pauly (1974a, b), following up on Stoller's ideas, painted a dim picture of the female transsexual's family. He reported that "the mothers of female transsexuals are perceived by their masculine daughters to be in need of protection from father, to have preferred a boy instead of a girl, to be emotionally disturbed" (Pauly, 1974a, p. 469). Moreover, the fathers were perceived to be assaultive, physically abusive, large, and masculine. Pauly noted that female transsexuals

> clearly identified with their fathers rather than their mothers, despite the fact that their view of their fathers was generally negative, if not frightening. The mother was seen as weak, sick, emotionally disturbed, or unavailable and in need of protection from tyrannical, abusive, and often alcoholic fathers. The relationship between these parents was quite often unhealthy (1974a, p. 498).

Pauly concluded: "I can think of *few worse fates* [my emphasis] than to be the life-long victim of the kind of family discord or ignorance which breeds gender identity problems" (Pauly, 1974b, p. 522). The fact that parents can have a profound influence on their child's sexual and gender development was not a novel hypothesis. The mechanisms by means of which this influence takes place were, however, not entirely known. One research team studying parental influences in unusual sexual behavior in children suggested that

> unusual sexual behavior evolves by adaptation of the ego to subtle attitudes within the family, a process that distorts the instinctual life of the child. Perverse sexual acting out and many unusual heterosexual patterns result from unconscious permission and subtle coercion by adults. The parental influences operate reciprocally with the needs of the child, so that eventually each participant stimulates the other (Litin, Giffin and Johnson, 1956, p. 37).

They maintained that the acting out of the unusual sexual behavior "results from a permitted defect of superego and ego." The genesis of the child's and adult's antisocial acting out stemmed from what Johnson and Szurek (1952) labeled as superego lacunae: a defective superego related to a covert parental process whose aim is to have the targeted child act out the parents' focal unconscious conflicts.

While some family studies have focused on the mother's unique role in shaping her daughter's transsexualism (Stoller, 1966; Brown and Sadoughi, 1979), a few have focused on families in which more than one child was transsexual (Liakos, 1967; Stoller and Baker, 1973), and on the family dynamics of transsexualism (Weitzman et al., 1970, 1971). Unfortunately, the literature on the family dynamics of female transsexualism is scarce. Indeed, the only lengthy study is a master's thesis researched at the CWRU gender clinic, entitled "Familial Factors Influencing Female Transsexualism" (Buck, 1977).

In that study, Buck argued that "in order to assess the critical role played by family dynamics . . . it is most useful to have working data on three generations." Her study, based on thirteen patients (who were part of my study group of 53 female transsexuals) suggested that Stoller's etiological factors applied to only half of the CWRU cases. Buck concluded that "there [was] not enough commonality, or perhaps not enough family information to identify any one model." Her study indicated that gender pathology was found to exist across family generations; that serious character pathology of the designated patient was the rule; and that the female transsexual had resolved her inner conflicts "not as her mother had in adjusting her expectations, but by denying the biologic reality." Buck's study suggested that the female transsexual's family revealed a tendency towards increased pathology through successive generations, which usually effloresced in the female transsexual's gender pathology. Indeed, the female transsexual may have been the first family member to become symptomatic, although the rudiments of gender pathology could be traced across many family lines.

Research into family factors, influences, and dynamics of female transsexualism seems to yield the most significant evidence of how critical gender meanings are communicated from parents to daughters. The piece of behavior that we eventually label as transsexual (the observable cross-gender role) turns out to be a complex behavioral pattern occasioned by a particular family dynamic, with the female transsexual's gender conflicts being the final common pathway for acting out the intergenerational family gender conflicts. In some families, more than one child may become the target of the family pathology.

It may be that the concepts of imprinting and conditioning (discussed elsewhere) simply designate the process by means of which gender meanings are communicated within a family. Indeed, Lichtenstein (1961) had argued that the infant's search for an identity may be a result of imprinting with the mother (with the term imprinting meaning variously: an innate releaser mechanism, the somatic responsiveness of the infant, a mirroring experience, a reciprocal identification, a symbiotic *Umwelt*, a stimulus cast of the mother's unconscious, an innate identity, sensory responsiveness, or an identity theme). Lichtenstein argued that "the mother does not convey a sense of identity to the infant but an identity . . . this 'released' identity will be irreversible, and thus it will compel the child to find ways and means to realize this specific identity which the mother has imprinted upon it" (1961, p. 78). While more innovative work needs to be done, Lichtenstein's ideas suggest how a transsexual identity theme may be "imprinted" by a mother on her child. Because of the importance family dynamics have in the etiology of female transsexualism, future investigators ought to involve the female transsexual's extended family in their research protocols. At the very least, two generations of family members ought to be interviewed and psychologically evaluated.

Object relations (interpersonal) theory

While there is little disagreement about whether object relations theory is an extension of psychoanalytic thinking, there is disagreement as to whether it is a separate theory of personality. Fairbairn (1952), a prominent exponent of object relations theory, epitomizes its basic departure from psychoanalysis by viewing "libido [as] not primarily pleasure-seeking, but object seeking." On the whole, object relations theorists generally view the establishment of social relationships as a primary human drive.

Guntrip (1964), who has provided an excellent review and history of object relations theory, considered it as "the gradual emergence of the forefront of the personal as against the impersonal, or natural science, element in Freud's thought." While object relations theory has been associated in England with such names as Klein (1975), Fairbairn (1952),

Guntrip (1964), and Winnicott (1965), in the United States it has been primarily associated with Jacobson (1964), Mahler (1967), Modell (1968), Giovacchini (1972), and Kernberg (1975). Only three object relations theorists, Person and Ovesey (1974a, b) and Volkan (1976a, 1979), have related object relations theory to transsexualism.

Unfortunately, Person and Ovesey chose to focus entirely on male transsexualism, which they viewed as having its origins in the preoedipal period, and related it to "unresolved separation anxiety during the separation-individuation phase of development" (1974a, p. 4), in which the male transsexual attempts "to counter separation anxiety . . . [by] a reparative fantasy of symbiotic fusion with the mother" (ibid., p. 5). They believed that this reparative fantasy was "laid down before the child was three years old." In summary, they viewed the male transsexual as

> schizoid-obsessive, socially withdrawn, asexual, unassertive and out of touch with anger . . . [having] a typical borderline syndrome characterized by separation anxiety, empty depression, sense of void, oral dependency, defective self identity, and impaired object relations, with an absence of trust and a fear of intimacy (ibid., p. 19).

Person and Ovesey's characterization of the male transsexual can, for the most part, be applied directly to the female transsexual. However, rather than wishing to fuse with the mother, female transsexuals are seen as dreading being engulfed by mother and so losing their self-identity.

While Volkan's theories have also focused exclusively on the male transsexual, they can be extended to the female transsexual as well. He believed that the male transsexual was searching for perfection of his body, "a search to be uncontaminated by aggression." Indeed he felt that "what is called 'sex reassignment surgery' might as well be called 'aggression-reassignment surgery.'" Viewed from the perspective of internalized object relations (the transsexual's internal mental representations of the object or interpersonal world), Volkan believed that the transsexual used primitive splitting as a basic defense in order to maintain the split between his/her male/female self.

Volkan hypothesized that during a critical period of child development the pre-transsexual child was unable to internalize good object relations because of a combination of factors subsumed under the headings of defective mothering and developmental arrests.

Whereas the male transsexual needed to rid himself of aggression, the female transsexual needed to become aggressive (in this sense SRS for the female transsexual could be viewed, by Volkan's example, as "aggression assignment surgery"). Feeling vulnerable and unprotected, she may fear that, as a female, she could only be penetrated and annihilated. Only by splitting off her female parts (which were viewed as dangerous and "all bad") could she survive. Her primitive anxiety was associated, not with too much aggression which threatened to destroy the "all good" parts, but with not being aggressive enough. From an object relations perspective, the female transsexual would be seen as having a bad female self and a good male self. In an effort to perceive herself as good and to protect her true self (see Winnicott, 1965) from being annihilated by aggression, she split off her bad female self (along with the contradictory and frightening images associated with that female self). In a concrete way she associated aggression with being male and hoped that by becoming a male (that is, by erecting a false self-defense) she would become aggressive (and thereby survive). For the female transsexual, the phallus became a kind of totem, a magical charm associated with survival and symbolizing her "all good" male parts.

Ultimately, the real dangers to the female transsexual came from within; that is, from her passivity, tendency towards emotional surrender, and vulnerability associated with her femininity. She feared that the joining together of opposing elements in her personality would leave her vulnerable to destruction by her feminine parts. Indeed, she mentally represented her feminine parts as attacking internal objects. While she yearned for "wholeness," she associated it with a regression to a symbiotic union with mother (which would threaten her separateness as a person). Indeed, both the introjected mother and the real mother were viewed as threats to her very survival. But it was the internal representation of the mother (the female transsexual's powerful negative and "all bad" female introject) that she needed to disown. It was only by expelling that toxic female introject that she believed her psychic survival was possible.

Volkan's view of the transsexual as exhibiting a predominantly borderline personality organization was consistent with my view (Lothstein, 1979b). In an unpublished paper, Volkan concluded that psychotherapy was usually avoided with transsexuals because it was difficult and painful: "To get well means to mend their representational splitting, and since the mending [involves] the bringing together of aggressively contaminated self- and object representations with the libidinally contaminated, [it] is accompanied by the need to face intense and painful emotions and to tolerate emotional flooding" (1976b, p. 12).

Volkan's ideas on the pathologically internalized object relations of narcissistic individuals have been applied by Kernberg (1975) to individuals with predominantly borderline pathology. And, while Kernberg never directly addressed the issue of transsexualism, his ideas on the borderline personality organization seem to describe adequately the pathologically internalized object relations of the female transsexual.

Kernberg saw the borderline individual as failing to evolve the capacity to unify opposing and contradictory primitive affective states. Indeed, during her childhood, the borderline individual was seen as engaging in primitive splitting (a defense mechanism to keep opposing and contradictory good and bad self- and object-representations apart) in order to preserve her "all good" self-image. Ultimately, borderline personality organization was viewed as representing a stable character pathology which was formed during the first three years of life. This type of personality organization was characterized by rigid and primitive character defenses; good reality testing but a poor reality sense; and specific and non-specific ego weaknesses (low frustration tolerance, inadequate impulse control, lack of sublimatory channels, low anxiety tolerance). On clinical interview the person with a diagnosed borderline personality appeared stable or intact. Indeed, this was a main feature of borderline pathology. These borderline features were also identified as important elements in the transsexual's personality organization (Person and Ovesey, 1974a; Lothstein, 1977b; Meyenburg and Sieguesch, 1977). The recognition that transsexual patients had predominantly borderline personality organization helped to explain their ambiguous clinical presentation.

Masterson (1976) pointed out that in normal development, by the end of the second half of the second year (stage 4 of Kernberg's four stages of normal internalization of object relations), the "'good' and 'bad' self-images should ordinarily coalesce into an integrated self-concept." In other words, he believed that "self-images established coherence and continuity under the impact of polar opposite emotional-interpersonal experiences" (p. 21). This stage of development was viewed as a critical period for the internalization of object relationships. Indeed, all children had to learn to maintain relationships in spite of ambivalent feelings.

They had to establish intimate relationships in which disagreement was possible and to experience anger without resorting to destructive rage towards the ambivalently perceived object. Individuals who resorted to splitting mechanisms tended to see everything as either all black or all white. One minute they were idolizing a person, and the next minute they devalued that person. It was hypothesized that the female transsexuals never reached Kernberg's stage 4. They relied predominantly on the employment of the defense mechanism of pathological splitting (which distorted their interpersonal relationships and forced them to view potential helpers as persecutors). These women "split" off their female-self component, which they experienced as "all bad." Consequently, the female transsexuals could not synthesize opposing affective states (which they concretely associated as either male or female) and were unable to establish good object relationships. In this sense, their fundamental drive towards objects (which according to object relations theory was a primary one) was impaired. The result was severe psychopathology.

Object relations theory allows us to see how parental gender meanings are internalized and function as primary organizers of the self. The theory labels the ego mechanisms underlying such processes as identification, introjection, and incorporation (processes which are crucial for forming internal mental representations for the development of interpersonal relationships). By focusing on the primacy of the social world, object relations theory views social relationships as the core of the female transsexual's problems. The theory also helps us to understand the aging female transsexual's belief that by becoming a male she may be able to achieve good object relationships and a sense of immortality.

It is not ironic that the very splitting mechanism which underlies the female transsexual's construction of object relations is normally consolidated during the second half of the child's second year. Throughout this section we have seen how critical this period is in the girl's life. It would appear that this is not only a crucial period for female sexual and cognitive development, but also for gender-self and self development. A girl's failure to exhibit normal developmental progress during this period of her life cycle will have serious consequences for her later development. Specifically, she will reveal a profound developmental arrest, impairment in her ego functions, and a possible thought disorder. Moreover, she will probably be diagnosed as having a borderline personality organization, specific and non-specific ego defects and weaknesses, a primitively organized defense system, impaired object relations, a profound disturbance in her core gender identity, and a severe impairment in self development. It is to this problem that we now turn.

Self psychology

While the concept of the self has a long history in psychology (Wylie, 1961; Fingarette, 1963), and was certainly implicit in Freud's theory, it was not until Kohut's (1971, 1977) investigations of narcissistic disorders that the construct of the self attained an importance equal to that of other major psychological constructs such as the ego, id, and superego. The current appeal of Kohut's self psychology is that it attempts to provide a unified theory of the self which stresses the positive and healthy developmental progression of narcissism, leading to the fulfillment of important life goals. As opposed to mechanistic theories which seemingly reduce the person to his/her component parts (e.g. libido, drives, instincts, habits, conditioned responses, stimuli, cathexis, rewards and punishments, etc.), self psychology posits a more humanistic language of the self, viewing it as a totality. While there is always the danger that theories which employ a more "humanistic-appearing language" are really contentless and substitute linguistic appeal for real theoretical issues, that is not the case with Kohut's theory of the self. Indeed, while Kohut's self psychology has refocused Freud's ideas it is also a theory which is deeply enmeshed in psychoanalytical theory, employing a developmental framework and utilizing the transference. Self psychology diverges from psychoanalysis in its reinterpretation of narcissism (relating it to healthy and normal human drives leading to self-esteem, self-assertiveness, ambitions, achievements, ideals, and goals). Self psychology also lays reduced emphasis on pure interpretation and posits the treatment of selfobject transferences and the real relationship of the therapist with the patient as the curative factors. In addition, the goals of therapy are shifted from a total reconstruction of the personality to repair of the damaged self-system. The goal of therapy is the achievement of a cohesive self.

Kohut arrived at his theory of self psychology while treating narcissistically disturbed patients, for whom appeals "within the framework of classical drive-and-defense psychology" could not explain these patients' disorders or transferences. Kohut reasoned that the nature of the transferences differed because these narcissistically disturbed patients exhibited selfobject transferences which could not be explained by classical libido theory. These findings led Kohut to reconsider the whole issue of narcissism. Whereas Freud generally, but not always, viewed narcissism as pathological, involving a primitive human state which represented the first stage of a person's investment of energy and interest in the self (involving a focus of energy on the self versus the interpersonal or object world), Kohut viewed narcissism positively (as a healthy and normal process underlying self-esteem). For Freud, narcissism was generally a pejorative term which was associated with selfishness, self-interest, autoeroticism, and an inability to relate to people (a first stage of ego libido prior to object libido). For Kohut, narcissism was the basis for the development of our most creative and important relationship to the world: that is, our self-assertiveness, ambitions, achievements, goals, and ideals. While narcissism could be pathological, Kohut came to see the positive and universal aspects of narcissism involved in all human experience. While I am taking liberties with both Freud's and Kohut's theoretical views of narcissism (reifying them for purposes of analysis), I also believe that a careful reading of Freud in the original German would place his thinking in less stark contrast to that of Kohut.

Kohut (1977) argued that the self-system formed from primitive self nuclei into an archaic infantile self (characterized by grandiosity and exhibitionism). He viewed the archaic infantile self of the child as providing the rudiments of healthy self-esteem. If the child was provided a sufficiently good environment, the infantile self would eventually develop into a cohesive self-system in which positive life goals were attainable. In this sense, a child's grandiosity and exhibitionism formed the bedrock for his/her healthy narcissism. But certain developmental phases had to be successfully negotiated if the transformation from an infantile archaic self to a cohesive self were to be accomplished (that is, a transformation from grandiosity and exhibitionism into healthy assertiveness, ambitions, achievements, goals, and ideals). The basis for this transformation was located by Kohut within the mother-child relationship.

While I am focusing on parental roles in this discussion, I shall use the terms "mother" and "father" in a functional sense; that is, to mean any mothering or fathering source. In this sense, the girl's father/mother, or any surrogate male/female, might also be the child's "mothering" or "fathering" source. Accordingly, in a two-parent family the couple may share the "mothering" and "fathering" roles, and their effects on a girl's gender conflicts.

225

For Kohut, the extent to which a mother was capable of attuning to her child's needs determined whether his/her narcissism would remain developmentally arrested (at an archaic infantile level) or would progress to a cohesive self-system. In order to allow for the development of a cohesive self, the mother had to convey to her child a genuine empathy for his/her grandiose and exhibitionistic needs, while partially frustrating her child's needs for omnipotence. If all went well, and the mother appropriately mirrored her child's grandiose and exhibitionistic needs, the child could then develop a cohesive archaic self and, eventually, a cohesive self-system (via a process labeled transmuting internalization). That is, the child could then grow into his/her adulthood with a positive narcissistic basis for attaining social goals; having good self-esteem; and being assertive, successful, and ambitious (without fearing that aggression would destroy his/her ability to attain life goals). Once these needs were experienced as parts of the child's self-system, they could be used by the self for the development of assertiveness, ambitions, and achievements. This process described one pole of the child's developing self-system. Kohut postulated that in the course of child development the mother's mirroring function would become internalized as part of the child's rudimentary self-esteem. The internalization of the mother's function as a mirroring selfobject eventually became a critical aspect of child development, especially as it related to the child's need to differentiate and separate from the mother-child unity. For some children, a mother's defective mirroring of her child's exhibitionistic and grandiose needs left them developmentally arrested and lacking in vitality. Unable to differentiate fully from mother, these children evidenced severe self pathology; and an infantile archaic self characterized by primitive identifications and selfobject transferences which distorted their interpersonal relationships (and emerged in their therapies as unique transferences which needed to be resolved in order that they could become "whole" people and develop good object relationships).

Kohut and Wolf defined selfobjects as "objects which we experience as parts of the self; the expected control over them is, therefore, closer to the concept of control which a grown-up expects to have over his [or her] own body and mind than to the concept of control which he [or she] expects to have over others" (1978, p. 414). They defined two types of selfobjects; one, a mirroring selfobject, related to the mother's mirroring function of the child "and confirm[ed] the child's innate sense of vigour, greatness, and perfection" (ibid.).

As the child developed from an infantile archaic self to a more co-hesive archaic self, s/he entered a second stage of early self development in which idealization and idealizing needs were formed and transformed. Consequently, a second type of selfobject evolved, which was labeled an idealized omnipotent selfobject. Kohut viewed the tendency towards idealization and the establishment of an idealized omnipotent selfobject as crucial to the consolidation and cohesion of the archaic self. Unless this occurred the self's narcissism could not develop along healthy lines. For Kohut, idealization formed the basis for the second pole of the self, leading the self to develop admiration for others, and its own goals and ideals.

Kohut associated the child's idealization with the second parent, the father. He saw the child as overvaluing the father, viewing him as an omnipotent idealized parent image who became a target for the child's merger. By merging with this idealized parent image (a new selfobject), the child's internal self structures were hypothesized to undergo impor-tant transformations so that s/he could maintain an idealized, omnipotent selfobject. In effect, this second selfobject was an internal object to "which the child can look up and with whom he [or she] can merge as an image of calmness, infallibility, and omnipotence." Unless the self went through certain developmental progressions and transformations of its narcissism and self-system, the individual would remain develop-mentally arrested. This meant that the individual would be unable to develop healthy object relationships and would maintain archaic self-object transferences which colored his/her interpersonal relationships.

For Kohut and Wolf the goals of the self were to develop from an archaic infantile self to

a firm self, resulting from the optimal interactions between the child and his [or her] selfobjects [which] is made up of three major con-stituents: (1) one pole from which emanates the basic striving for power and success; (2) another pole that harbors the basic idealized goals; and (3) an intermediate area of basic talents and skills that are activated by the tension arc that establishes itself between am-bitions and ideals (1978, p. 414).

Kohut postulated that if the child's parents were not capable of facilitating the healthy development of their child's narcissism, the child's evolving self-system would be impaired. In order to facilitate their child's development of a cohesive self the parents had to establish an empathic link with his/her needs and optimally gratify and frustrate their child's wishes. Kohut argued that unless these minimum conditions were met, the child would develop a disturbance of the self-system in which his/her narcissism was pathologically organized.

If the child's structures and mechanisms for internalization were impaired or damaged, then she would also be unable to evolve a coherent, cohesive, integrated self. Such children would evidence various degrees of self pathology, including pathological shame (not self-assertiveness, ambitions, and achievements), and envy (not admiration for others and goals and ideals) as major components of their enfeebled, fragmented self-systems. The recognition of a new set of emotional disorders (i.e. self pathologies) suggested that as a consequence of a profound developmental arrest (involving an inability to internalize necessary structures for developing a cohesive self) these individuals were prone to develop disorders involving their self-system as a whole. Their major anxiety was based on a fear of the fragmentation, disintegration, enfeeblement, or dissolution of their self-systems. These metaphorical expressions suggested that their experienced anxiety was more akin to annihilation anxiety than to castration anxiety. Individuals with self pathology were viewed as having a disturbance in their narcissistic balance and the regulatory function of their selfobjects. Kohut distinguished between primary and secondary self pathology. His distinction focused on the approximate developmental age at which parental disturbances in empathy severely affected the child's development (that is, led to a developmental arrest in the natural progression of selfobject differentiation). Kohut viewed primary self pathology as focused on such disorders as psychoses, borderline states, narcissistic behavior disorders, and narcissistic personality disorders — the major disorders of female transsexuals. The critical period for the development of primary self pathology occurred sometime during the second year of the child's life. It was then that the nuclear self emerged. Kohut conceptualized the nuclear self as "a bipolar structure" in which archaic nuclear ambitions formed one pole and archaic nuclear ideals formed the other.

Self psychology and female transsexualism

Although Kohut never addressed the issue of female transsexualism, his speculations on the origins and development of the self-system, healthy narcissism, and self-esteem can be employed to help us understand some of the focal conflicts of the female transsexual.

All of the following speculations on the etiology of female transsexualism are my own constructions based on Kohut's self psychology. It is my belief that at the same time that a female transsexual's rudimentary gender-self structures were being formed (in terms of gender-self representations, gender-self constancy and core gender identity), her infantile archaic self was also developing into a more structured and cohesive archaic self (in which her grandiose, exhibitionistic, omnipotent, and idealized needs were being formed and transformed). During that period of development the mothers of female transsexuals were unable to link empathetically with and support their daughters' developing femininity. Consequently, these women were vulnerable to feelings of deadness, inferiority, and imperfection of their female bodily self. Indeed, the mother's hatred of, or rejection of, her daughter's emerging femininity may have led to an impairment in her daughter's self-esteem around her emerging gender-self system (especially as it related to her gender-self representation, gender-self constancy, and core gender identity). Consequently, the female transsexual's grandiose, exhibitionistic, and omnipotent needs may have been ignored, or inadequately responded to; leaving her rudimentary gender-self system depleted, empty, enfeebled, and fragmented around these issues. In essence, these women could be viewed as having developed a poorly structuralized gender-self representation secondary to an impaired ego mechanism governing their gender-self constancy.

In one context Kohut and Wolf stated that

> when the baby is born, the encounter with the child's actual structural and functional biological equipment will, of course, influence the imagery about its future personality that had been formed by the parents. But the parental expectations will, from birth onward, exert a considerable influence on the baby's developing self. The self arises thus as the result of the interplay between the new-born's innate equipment and the selective responses of the selfobjects through which certain potentialities are encouraged in their development while others remain unencouraged or are even actively discouraged (1978, p. 416).

229

The theory of self psychology would predict that as a result of the female transsexual's disturbed selfobjects she could not evolve a healthy narcissism around her female self. Hence her gender-self lacked cohesion and became disordered, fragmented, and enfeebled. Kohut's views supported the idea that a mother's inability to mirror her daughter's gender-self representation could leave her vulnerable to developing a severe gender identity disorder. In effect, her gender-self structure was left empty and deplete. By failing to have her gender-self representation confirmed and mirrored by her mother, the female transsexual could then develop a pathological narcissism. Indeed, the only way her grandiose, omnipotent, and exhibitionistic needs could then be met was through a complete distortion of their aims. Consequently, the female transsexual might believe that the only ways to change her defective body image was through male gender impersonation and SRS.

The archaic nature of the female transsexual's selfobjects would be seen as distorting her self-esteem and leading to profound self pathology. Consequently, she would evidence an eternal quest to repair her underlying self defect, a defect which she concretized as an overinvestment in merger with the idealized, omnipotent selfobject of the father (that is, her male element). In this sense, the female transsexual's quest for perfection (through merger with the idealized, omnipotent male image) could be viewed as a desperate attempt to repair her underlying structural narcissistic defect (primarily an impaired mirroring selfobject) through a defensive maneuver to merge with the idealized omnipotent selfobject. In addition, merging with the father could provide an escape route from a possible symbiotic fusion with, or engulfment by, mother. Of course, the structural defect could not be repaired by surgery but only through a modified form of reconstructive psychotherapy. While sexual surgery might be viewed as a compensatory procedure to gain time for the female transsexual's troubled self, it could never provide the necessary internal structure (that is, the sense of cohesiveness of the self that resulted from a "cohesive parental self that was in tune with the changing needs of the child").

Kohut's theory could also explain the apparent stability or "normality" of some female transsexuals. It could be that the fathers of some female transsexuals perform a secondary mirroring function (while also serving as idealized selfobjects). That is, some fathers may mirror their daughters' exhibitionistic and grandiose needs. By empathizing with their daughters' perceived male wishes (that is, serving as a surrogate mirroring selfobject), they distorted a piece of their daughters' reality, but also supplied some of the internal structure necessary for the development of their daughters' gender-self systems. These fathers may also have provided their daughters with a motive for the libidinal cathexis of their bodies, albeit a fantasized male body image. In this sense, some female transsexuals may be rescued from a total hatred of their bodies which would lead to total self-alienation and self-destruction (that is, a schizophrenigenic solution to their lack of self-cohesion). By positing a male body as a goal, these women would be able to limit and control their vindictiveness and sadomasochism directed against their female bodies (through fantasized sex reassignment surgery), thereby preserving one aspect of their body ego and self (which provided them with a certain inner sense of hope and vitality). For the most part, these girls would be viewed as having grown up associating their self-assertiveness, ambitions, and achievements only with maleness. Indeed, they would be profoundly ashamed of anything female and, as adults, would seek out feminine women to confirm and admire their "maleness." In effect, these women are "mirror-hungry personalities," individuals with a profound thirst for selfobjects to "nourish their famished self."

The fathers of these girls would also be seen as having severe psychological problems which were acted out through their exploitation of and control over their daughters. However, in some cases a father's close relationship with his transsexual daughter may also have gone unanalysed because it was envied or admired, thereby closing it off to analysis. In effect, those fathers engaged in what Masterson viewed as "depersonification" of their children. That is, they "project upon [their daughters] the image of one of [their] own parents or of a sibling . . . or use [their daughters] to defend [themselves] against [their] own feelings of abandonment" (Masterson, 1976, p. 38).

From a clinical perspective, female transsexuals report feeling complete and whole only when they act out their inner feelings of maleness. Wearing male clothes, seducing women, and confirming their maleness seem to perform a self-soothing function for the female transsexual. Kohut's theory suggests that individuals with self pathology may experience intense annihilation anxiety (associated with feelings of disintegration of their gender-self representation), feelings of fragmentation, and a sense of enfeeblement of their gender-self system. The female transsexual is hypothesized to defend against this anxiety by engaging in defensive and compensatory male behaviors (including crossdressing and the development of perversions). The goals of self psychology for the female transsexual would be the repair, not the reorganization, of her gender-self representation and the mechanism governing her gender-self constancy. While these goals might seem insignificant (from the point of view of total personality reconstruction), they are experienced by the female transsexual as life-saving. The constructs of self psychology could explain female transsexualism as a disorder of the self-system; that is, as a lack of a cohesive self-system. For these women, the transsexual wish for SRS can be seen as a restitutive attempt to prevent the disintegration of the self.

Recently, Brod (1981) has also developed this idea. Utilizing a Kohutian framework, Brod relates "gender dysphoria" to "poor 'self' development" and views the transsexual drive as "a reparative effort at completion." He interprets the transsexuals' gender dysphoria or unhappiness as a "form of erotic despair" in which they are unable to establish "linking" relationships with objects. During masturbation (an experience in which one develops pleasurable feelings of the body/sexual-self) the transsexual cannot use fantasy to overcome her/his profound feelings of loss and alienation. Instead, s/he turns away from her/his genitals because of the dangers associated with the expectation of eternal object loss. Brod defines eroticism broadly, viewing it in terms of daydreaming and fantasy imagery and seeing eroticism as providing "a manifest feeling for discovering the potential of the self." Consequently, masturbation is seen as a primary experience by means of which individuals develop feelings of their genital self-system. Brod also believes that masturbation is never a solitary act, because most individuals (other than the transsexual) can always use mental imagery to conjure up a "partner" and thereby overcome their feelings of isolation and aloneness. For the transsexual, who is object starved, masturbation is only a reminder of her/his objectless state. In an attempt to link up to, and reincorporate, objects, the transsexual attempts to internalize the sexual signalling system of the opposite gender and thereby to attract objects. In essence, transsexuals hope that by undergoing SRS they will resolve their basic self-deficiency.

Ultimately, it is only through psychotherapy that the female transsexual's selfobjects can be transformed and her exhibitionism, grandiosity, and idealization be successfully internalized so that the goals of the self can be rerouted away from sex reassignment surgery. Indeed, Volkan's notion (1967a) that the transsexual attempts to achieve perfection through SRS and polysurgery is supported by my research. However, it is psychotherapy, not surgery, which is the treatment of choice. Transsexuals' perfectionistic ideals and goals need to be associated with their self-defects, and their views of the father as an idealized, omnipotent selfobject realistically interpreted so that SRS can be avoided.

Kohut's notion of a cohesive self, while involving some conceptual difficulty (see Levine, 1979; Gediman, 1980), offers a sound basis for providing a provisional conceptualization of some aspects of the female transsexual's pathology and stated quest for wholeness. Kohut's theory also provides a possible explanation of empathy as the way in which parents convey important communications to their children, as their children develop a gender-self representation, gender-self constancy, and core gender identity. Kohut's theory provides an important link in our effort to understand the complex ways in which parenting affects the establishment of core gender identity and may lead to a transsexual adaptation. While Kohut's theory of self psychology was never intended to explain female transsexualism, it has provided us with the necessary conceptual tools to understand how a developmental arrest may have occurred and what the consequences of defective parenting on a child's developing self-system have been.

A proposed theoretical framework for female transsexualism

Throughout this book I have presented historical material and clinical evidence which suggested that female transsexualism was not a normal variant of sexuality or an alternative life style, but a profound psychological disorder. Moreover, an analysis of my clinical sample suggested that female transsexualism has its roots in the preoedipal period. It is a disorder which is "caused" by family dynamics, in which parents communicate and transmit distorted gender meanings to their daughters. Consequently, by the second half of the second year of life some girls are unable to establish a core female gender identity and a nuclear self-system. Moreover, all female transsexuals were shown to have borderline pathology, developmental arrests, and a primary disorder of their self-systems. In this section I will expand on these notions and present a theoretical model of female transsexualism which will facilitate the diagnosis and treatment of this phenomenon.

While I view female transsexuals as a diverse group of clinical variants, each of whom has her own unique personality structure, developmental history, and clinical course, my theory stresses that, while it is their male impersonation, male fantasies, and requests for SRS which are the specific leitmotifs of their transsexualism, it is their specific structural ego and self defects which predispose them to elaborate their profound gender identity pathology.

While the following theory of female transsexualism is one that best fits the clinical facts, it is also a provisional theory which can be put to a further clinical test. It is a theory rooted in psychoanalytical psychopathology and in recent developments in ego psychology, object relations theory, and self psychology. It is predominantly a theory highlighting the importance of parenting, intergenerational family dynamics, and the communication of gender meanings within a family.

I regard female transsexualism as primarily a psychological disorder of the self which has its origins during the first two years of life. From an early age, women who identify as transsexuals have been targeted by their parents to develop a profound gender disorder. Their parents constantly assault their daughters' femininity and female sexuality. Consequently, those girls were unable to develop a core female gender identity. Instead, they identified as transsexuals. It is hypothesized that all female transsexuals have a primary structural ego defect which impairs their gender-self representation.

Female transsexuals manifest what Stolorow and Lachmann (1980) called an "insufficiently consolidated and structuralized self representation," a failure in structuralization which I see as focused on their gender-self representation. Individuals with defective self-representations have been shown by Giovacchini (1975) to experience a constant state of void, always trying to fill that void "by incorporating significant external objects." Such individuals are forever "hungry," trying to fill in their structureless selves with external supplies. Along these lines, I see the transsexual woman as needing to incorporate male images (i.e. male gender-self representations). She does this in order to "fill up" her inner state of void (which is how she experiences the effects of her poorly structuralized gender-self representation). The void was created when her parents "deprived" her of the necessary inner psychic structure on which she could have developed a female gender-self representation and, thereby, a core of female gender identity. Because of individual differences, however, not all female transsexuals experience the same impairment of their gender-self representation and ego mechanism(s) governing gender-self constancy. This would account for the diverse clinical variants found among female transsexuals.

At the furthest end of the female transsexual spectrum are those women whose ego mechanism governing gender-self constancy is profoundly impaired. These women are usually unable to maintain even a partial female gender-self representation. They experience a fluidity, and oscillation, of partial gender-self representations (consisting of fused male and female gender images). These women are alternatively convinced that they are either "males" or "females" (depending on which gender image is prepotent at a given point in time). They also have poorly consolidated defenses and impaired ego functioning in non-gender areas of their personality. Additionally, they evidence minimal self-object differentiation. The majority of female transsexuals in this group are overtly psychotic. Some of these women may be diagnosed as schizophrenic.

At a higher level of development are those women with predominantly borderline personality organization who exhibit a variety of low-level character pathology (schizoid and paranoid disorders), and various stages of narcissistic behavior and personality disorders. The overwhelming majority of women who identify as female transsexuals are found in this latter group. These women are viewed as having severe borderline personality disorders. They also represent a wide range of clinical variants. As a group they have diverse symptomology, different precursors to their disorder, and a variety of borderline personality disorders.

What differentiates female transsexuals from other borderlines is their *pan gender dysphoria*. Our clinical data suggest that their gender dysphoria is traceable to their specific family dynamics and pathology. However, why these girls were targeted by their families to become transsexuals could only be understood by investigating the child's/woman's unconscious fantasies and wishes which organized her transsexualism. In all of the transsexual families we investigated we noted that most, if not all, of the patients' siblings also manifested serious emotional pathology (see the case of Donna/Douglas for the exception). In some families more than one child was gender dysphoric. In those families where only one child manifested transsexual pathology, the clinician had to answer several questions. Why was this child chosen as the target of the family's gender pathology? Was there a specific family crisis around the mother's pregnancy? Was there a sense of disappointment over the sex of the child? What were the effects of birth order, sibling position, and parallel roles (similar to the parents' own family constellations) which might have "caused" the girl's transsexualism? Were there specific gender stresses among parents — that is, was one, or both, parent(s) a transvestite? What was the status of the mother's relationship with her own mother? How did the mother's bisexual conflicts affect her daughter? Why did this girl respond positively to her parents' cross-gender messages and communications? Was there something about the girl's personality which caused her parents to respond to her as a boy? Did she exhibit "male" physical attributes (e.g. a larger, more muscular body type)? Did she have only boy agemates to play with? Did she have a unique ability to play a male role? Did she experience an inner need for physical aggression, rough-and-tumble play, and enjoyment in the kinesthetic feelings of strong athletic movement? Was there another major caretaker who "masculinized" her? All of these questions need to be addressed for each girl or woman presenting with a gender problem.

It is imperative, however, that the clinician address these issues with the understanding that for the non-gender-dysphoric girl none of these patterns of behavior is necessarily atypical or abnormal. Indeed, the overwhelming majority of girls with male physical attributes, who have a muscular body type, and who enjoy physical aggression and athletics, do not have a gender problem and do not become transsexual. There is no reason to believe that these girls have an impaired gender identity. Their athleticism and "masculine" features are a normal part of their female gender role and identity and should not be confused with similar "male" behaviors and physical attributes in girls with predominantly borderline personality disorders who have *pan gender dysphoria*. It is only for girls in this latter group (that is, pre-transsexual girls) that we are urging the clinician to address carefully each of their gender-related problems so that a thorough evaluation of their gender status can be made.

The case histories of our patients demonstrated how each of the girl children targeted for transsexualism evidenced a poorly structuralized female gender-self representation, a lack of gender-self constancy, and a failure to develop a female core gender identity. These structural problems of the girls' ego and self-system organized their transsexual pathology. However, since each female transsexual elaborated her own unconscious transsexual fantasy, they were not a homogeneous group. In the psychotherapy of these girls and women it is the task of the therapist to help them understand the process and content of their transsexual fantasy, and the ways in which their male behaviors represent a primitive attempt to restructuralize their impaired gender-self representation. While female transsexuals may have different personalities, they all experience a constant threat of gender-self fragmentation. Consequently, a good portion of their behavior is defensive, aimed at "shoring up precarious representational structures" around their gender-self representation. They are, to use Kohut's phrase, "mirror-hungry personalities." I view the female transsexual's wish for sex reassignment surgery as a reparative wish to restore her crumbling female gender-self representation, to prevent a fragmentation of her self-system, and to insure her psychic survival.

As part of the female transsexuals' attempt to consolidate their gender-self representation and to develop gender-self constancy, they employ primitive and rigid defense mechanisms, including denial, projection, projective identification, splitting, omnipotence, and devaluation. These defenses are part of their predominantly borderline personality organization. They are adaptive defenses in so far as they insure the survival of the female transsexual's gender-self system. As a consequence of their rigid defense systems, the majority of these women appear psychologically intact, stable, or normal. However, their "intactness" is illusory; it is merely a superficial manifestation on the effect of the way in which they control their anxiety by employing primitive, rigid, and pathological defenses.

It has been commonly assumed that the absence of anxiety among some female transsexuals is evidence of their "stability." Meissner (1980), however, has pointed out that in individuals with predominantly narcissistic pathology "anxiety may be less likely to appear." Indeed, the female transsexuals' lack of anxiety might relate to several factors, including the spectrum of their psychiatric symptomology, and their variety of character structures and personalities. Typically, these women rid themselves of their toxic anxiety by employing primitive psychological defenses. While these women may appear to be "intact" because they are devoid of anxiety, they are actually quite disturbed. Indeed, their transsexualism is maintained at considerable cost to their personality development, typically involving emotional impoverishment and shallowness, compliancy, and a passive-dependent personality.

My investigation into female transsexualism suggested that the words "stable," "intact," or "normal" were always code words for an inadequate clinical investigation (a failure to employ intensive psychological testing, or a lack of familiarity with psychoanalytical psychopathology and object relations or interpersonal theory). Whenever clinicians have made comparisons between female and male transsexuals, they have chosen the wrong level of analysis. For example, the fact that females with gender pathology did not appear to experience the profound social alienation of their male counterparts was a cultural artifact of sex differences. This finding has consistently been mistaken for a logical explanation of the female transsexual's supposedly higher developmental level of functioning (versus the male transsexual). However, there is a simpler explanation. Because society tolerates tomboyism (and handles sex-role learning differently for girls and boys), a girl with a childhood gender disturbance is not as stigmatized as a boy. Consequently, she is able to attend school without serious harassment, and can enter into friendships without fear of immediate rejection. In effect, the female transsexual can usually keep her conflict better hidden than can her male counterpart. However, as she reaches adolescence the female transsexual's conflicts are acted out, and the forces of social stigma begin to play a greater role in shaping her identity as a transsexual.

If we acknowledge the impact of child development on the etiology and course of female transsexualism, the evidence is clear-cut. During the second half of the second year of life, the female transsexual-to-be is targeted by her parents to change her gender to male. As a result of her evolving borderline personality organization, she fails to consolidate an ego mechanism to regulate self-constancy and thereby fails to consolidate the stable gender-self representation necessary for the formation of a female core gender identity and nuclear self-system. These failures are not the result of biological causes, but are the direct result of the untoward influence of the female transsexual's parents on her developing self-system. As a consequence of her mother's defective mothering and impaired empathy, the transsexual woman is developmentally arrested and evidences problems in separation and individuation. Her parents pushed her away from femininity because of its destructive and threatening potential. Consequently, she experienced a constant state of gender confusion and diffusion (involving an oscillation between male and female gender-self representations). As an adult, such a woman also has serious cognitive problems, including defects in symbol formation and subtle thought disturbances. All of these defects influence the girl's/woman's transsexual "male" beliefs. While in most non-gender areas of development the transsexual-to-be may have exhibited adequate separation-individuation (which ruled out psychosis), she is never able fully to separate her gender-self representation from her mother and be successful in work and love. Consequently, all female transsexuals are vulnerable to regressive fusions with their mothers. Moreover, they all experience profound anxiety over their awareness of a lack of self-cohesion. By identifying as males, these women appear to be primitively solving their separation-individuation conflicts. As a consequence of their pathological narcissism, all these women have distorted goals, ambitions, and ideals (with the focus of their life goals being on sex change).

Throughout her life cycle the female transsexual is engaged in three tasks: first, she attempts to provide stability and cohesion for her precarious gender-self representation; second, she tries to repair her ego mechanism governing gender-self constancy; third, she also tries to structuralize and consolidate her female core gender identity. Because of her persistent fear of loss of self, her hatred of her female body, her needs for perfection, and her pathologically organized narcissism, she is always in a state of near panic. At times, her magical belief that SRS will make everything perfect serves to calm her anxiety and reassure her that she will not go "crazy." Behaviorism misses the point because it is not her behavior which is primarily disordered but her underlying gender-self representations and the structural aspects of the self-system. Given these facts a woman's transsexual behavior can be viewed, on one level, as her best possible level of adaptation to her emotional pathology.

Stolorow and Lachmann have shown how "both sexual fantasy and perverse activity can serve to repair or maintain insufficiently structured [developmentally arrested] self and object images" (1980, p. 169). If we apply these ideas to the female transsexual, it could be hypothesized that crossdressing as a male, and the experience of acute and transient wishes for sex reassignment surgery, may serve to "repair or maintain [the] insufficiently structured" gender-self representation. That is, the female transsexual's behaviors and wishes could be viewed as primarily defensive to ward off feelings of self-fragmentation of the perceived enfeeblement of her self-system. In this sense, the function of the female transsexual's crossdressing and wishes for SRS is not to defend against castration anxiety but to soothe her annihilation anxiety. The female transsexual's solution — to become a male — can then be viewed as a primitive attempt to provide self-cohesion through maintaining gender-self constancy and unifying her gender-self representation.

My research suggested that all female transsexuals have experienced a less than "average expectable environment" and, therefore, a less than "average expectable self." Their mothers are viewed as defective and lacking empathy for their daughters (Kohut, 1977). They are unable to attune their mothering responses to their child's needs and resonate with their daughter's developing female self-system. These mothers depersonify their daughters and employ projective identificatory mechanisms to externalize their gender conflicts onto their daughters. The result is always a girl with a chaotic gender structure, a disordered narcissism, and a defect in her exhibitionism and grandiosity (two issues central to the female transsexual). Why a specific female child is chosen as the target for the mother's pathological projections can only be answered after intensive psychotherapy in which the underlying transsexual fantasy content is elicited.

While the actual clinical presentation of female transsexualism is quite diverse (especially as related to its course over the life cycle), the underlying structural conflicts are always the same. The female transsexual's request for sex reassignment surgery should always be viewed in the light of her attempt to provide a temporary solution to both the perceived threat of the dissolution of the gender-self representation and her fear of going "crazy." In retrospect, the female transsexual's memory of wanting to be a boy since age 5 should be viewed as a verbalization of her damaged gender-self system which was already evident even before she was 3 years old. What makes her self pathology unique, and often seemingly irreparable, is her rigid, stereotypical portrayal of a masculine role. This portrayal is the result of many years of adapting to a unique life style in which her wishes to be male were not only imaginatively developed but also acted out. Moreover, her masculine portrayal is often given support from many sectors of her community. In effect, large segments of society have served a mirroring function for the female transsexual. By promising SRS or supporting her life style as a male they have shored up her impaired gender-self representation and provided her with a promise of gender-self constancy and cohesion. The female transsexual's exhibitionistic and grandiose needs have also been gratified by segments of her society. The result has been to close the door to further personality growth and a richer inner life. In effect, the surgeon and members of the gender clinic may function for the female transsexual as surrogate idealized selfobjects. The more extensive and cohesive the female transsexual's social support systems, the more likely that SRS will "predict" a successful outcome. However, as these support systems tend to be quite plastic (changing over time) one cannot predict what the long-term effects of SRS will be, even for those women who initially appear to be "good candidates." That is, while SRS might appear to "shore" up a woman's defective gender-self representation, it does not radically change her internal structures. Indeed, her disposition towards gender confusion and diffusion (leading to a transsexual adaptation) might flare up again at any time.

I see the notion of a true self/false self system as described by Winnicott (1958), Laing (1966), and Khan (1974) as also providing important explanatory concepts for female transsexualism. Indeed, many female transsexual patients use the metaphor of a *true* versus *false* self in describing the core clinical features of their transsexualism (a metaphor which probably describes the effects of an impaired gender-self representation and the effects of defensive splitting on their personalities). These women see their true self (the opposite gender) as residing inside, hidden from view, and secreted from the world. The transsexual's social self or gender role is a *person manqué*, a false self, which she has defensively adopted to ward off disintegration anxiety. Her anxiety results from several factors related to her ego and self pathology including: a lack of gender-self cohesion, a fear of dissolution of the gender-self representation, fears of annihilation stemming from fantasies of fusion with the mother, and a need to disidentify as a female in order to fend off murderous impulses directed at her by her mother.

In order to protect her gender-self representation from complete annihilation, and allow conflict-free spheres of her ego to develop, the female transsexual needs to integrate her bipolar gender-self representations (that is the "all good" male self and the "all bad" female self). Rather than integrate these representations, she externalizes her "all bad," toxic, female self-images and ejects them outside the self. While maintaining the existence of a secret male identity initially helps some female transsexuals establish their separateness and independence from mother, it does not fully prevent a total loss of self via fusion with mother. To the extent that the true self (the male self for the female transsexual) is hidden from public view, the woman will be able to achieve some degree of success in love and work. To the extent that the true self is acted out, the woman's capacity for sublimation (leading to the fulfillment of goals) will be severely compromised, leading to a self whose goals are all directed towards transsexual impersonation. It is this impersonating role, however, which provides an illusion of gender-self cohesion (one which is buttressed by the social support the female transsexual may receive from various segments of society). The importance of secrecy and secrets for boundary formation (Margolis, 1966), ego development (Gross, 1951), and self-identity and impersonation (Finkelstein, 1974) has been well established.

The need for some female transsexuals to maintain a false gender-self system is viewed as originating in their mother-child relationship. The secret male self, however, is not entirely a secret since it is confirmed and supported by the family dynamics (often involving intergenerational family support). The maintenance of a false social identity through role impersonation, though dangerous, is adaptive in that it allows the person to establish minimum object relationships and to maintain contact with social reality while providing an illusion of self-cohesion.

Some mothers of female transsexuals are also viewed as experiencing their daughters' prolonged and continued female identifications as a threat to their own very survival. These mothers hate their daughters as females and tend to harbor intense murderous impulses towards them, impulses which are managed by pushing their daughters away from feminine identifications. In effect, these mothers communicate the following message to their daughters: "I can only love you as my son." For all intents and purposes, the daughter becomes the pathological container of her mother's bisexual conflicts, her gender confusion, aggression, and hatred of her femaleness. As a young child, the girl cannot refuse to contain her mother's contents (that is, her conflicts) since this would threaten her very object tie to mother – her very existence. However, once the transsexual child identifies with her mother's pathological view of femaleness, the mother can then act as if the problems resided wholly within her daughter. The mother is then able to tolerate her aggressive drives and control her inner conflicts by managing her daughter. The daughter, however, typically experiences that process as leading to a possible fusion with mother and, therefore, to a loss of self-cohesion. As long as their daughters adopt a male role, these mothers are able to deflect their aggression and destructiveness away from their children. In this way the transsexual's mother insures her daughter's survival. The mothers of these children also allow their daughters to develop in all areas unrelated to gender. Moreover, by driving their daughters to identify as male, these mothers may also be attempting to respond adaptively – protecting their daughters from their own murderous rage. By disidentifying from mother and trying to change sexes, these girls insure their very survival. However, they substitute a pathological omnipotence for a false independence and never really separate from mother.

Another subgroup of female transsexuals is identified. Its members have a higher level organization of their object relations (though they are still quite primitive and impoverished). Among this group of women it is not mother's aggression that is feared, but her lack of it. For these women transsexual surgery may be viewed as "aggression assignment surgery."

The women in this group fear that by identifying with their mothers they are identifying with a victim who may be the object of father's murderous rage. Indeed, during clinical interviews their mothers generally appear helpless, vulnerable, confused, and upset with their daughters' gender identity problems. While these mothers usually deny any responsibility for their daughters' transsexualism, many of them "give in" to their daughters' wishes for SRS. Because of the mothers' defensive rigidity (which may emerge as compliance and deference to the interviewer), the clinical material provided by them must be viewed cautiously.

In those cases where a mother may "masculinize" her daughter in order to protect herself from her perceived male partner's wish to annihilate her, the message is clear-cut: femaleness is dangerous and must be disowned from her daughter's self-system. However, unlike the schizophrenic's parents, the female transsexual's parents seem to focus their attacks on the female part of their daughter's self-system, thereby leaving other parts of her self-system free to develop. This may explain why most female transsexuals are not overtly psychotic. The non-gender-related parts of their self-systems, however, are also incompletely developed and poorly consolidated, lacking unity and cohesion.

From one perspective, the female transsexual may be viewed as needing to reinstate what Guntrip has called a "lost core to the personality" (1964). I am hypothesizing that the "lost core" is an inadequately developed gender-self representation and lack of an ego mechanism governing gender-self constancy. Consequently, these women experience a perpetual state of gender diffusion and confusion. This confusion is partially resolved during adolescence when, according to Ovesey and Person (1974a), they learn "of the existence of transsexualism . . . [and they] resolve the ambiguity through a transsexual identity and sex reassignment." It is not surprising that this resolution takes place during adolescence since that is the normal time frame for refocusing and resolving identity issues.

Erikson (1968) noted that there are many adolescents who, having suffered irreparable defects at an early stage of development, could not typically respond to the normative crises of adolescence. These disturbed adolescents were seen as opting for a negative identity in order to achieve some sense of mastery and wholeness. While the female transsexual's identity falls within this framework, it must be clarified that she does not choose such an identity. The consolidation of a female transsexual identity is obligatory and must be viewed as a desperate attempt by those women to provide a sense of wholeness and intactness to their impaired self-systems. The quest for sex reassignment surgery is no more than a fantasied solution of perfection and a desperate attempt to provide self-cohesion.

When the wish for sex reassignment surgery occurs late in the life cycle, it is usually precipitated by a profound loss; that is, the death of the father. Up to that point in the female transsexual's life the father had served as the "glue" for her self-cohesion. In effect, the father's death activates the female transsexual's conflicts, it leaves her feeling empty and depleted, with SRS serving to link her back with father as an eternal, mirroring, and idealized selfobject. A combination of factors underscores the aging woman's compulsive quest for sexual surgery, including a quest for immortality (involving a denial of death and aging, and rebirth fantasies), and a fantasy that good interpersonal relationships will be possible. In the final analysis, sex reassignment surgery cannot succeed in healing the split in the self (it may, however, in many cases abrogate the patient's anxiety). The reparation of the self can only be facilitated through intensive psychotherapy. To accomplish this the therapist must establish an empathic link to the female transsexual's hitherto ignored narcissistic needs and acknowledge that the structural defects of her gender-self system have left her isolated, unable to establish satisfactory interpersonal relationships which could reroute her away from SRS.

Conclusions

While it has been my intent to provide a developmental and comprehensive psychological theory of female transsexualism, there is no pretense that my views on the subject provide the only consistent and coherent explanation of all cases of female transsexualism. Clearly, we are just on the threshold of understanding the etiology of female transsexualism. My theoretical views are offered as hypotheses which need to be tested by future clinical experience. While I have not explained the small number of cases in which a woman's transsexualism may have been caused by a biological factor, the clinician must never lose sight of the need to provide each woman with a thorough medical evaluation in order to rule out a biological basis for her disorder (see Chapter 7). Ultimately, the clinician can only understand a specific woman's transsexualism if s/he understands the specific dynamics and the unconscious fantasy content which guided the transsexual wish for SRS.

Throughout this chapter I have emphasized the importance of employing psychoanalytical psychopathology in order to understand the basis of female transsexualism. While too many critics have disparaged Freud's methods of inquiry because of what they perceived to be his inadequate understanding of femininity and female sexuality, it is time to place his views in their correct perspective and not, as some have done, to discard them wholesale. Clearly, there is no inconsistency in employing the organizing principles and methods of psychoanalysis while also acknowledging the shortcomings of Freud's theory of femininity and female sexuality. While many of Freud's ideas about female psychology were grossly inadequate and, at times, false, his psychoanalytical method and his penetrating analysis of human *psychosexual bisexuality* have provided the groundwork for constructing a sound theory of female psychology.

Recently, Kubie (1974) expanded Freud's notion of bisexuality and postulated a fundamental drive to become both sexes. Indeed, he urged analysts to look beyond the resolution of the oedipal conflict and castration anxiety in their psychoanalyses, and to focus instead on the importance of the preoedipal period, in order to deepen their understanding of the person by acknowledging and integrating those opposite gender qualities of the personality that had previously been ignored but, none the less, exerted a powerful influence on the personality. It is equally important that each clinician expand on the psychoanalytical perspective and incorporate such diverse theoretical models as *systems theory* (von Bertalanffy, 1968), *family dynamics theory* (Weitzman et al., 1971), *object relations theory* (Volkan, 1976), and *self psychology* (Kohut, 1971, 1977) in order to expand understanding of female transsexualism.

Our inquiry has suggested a number of important hypotheses which may help us to understand the nature and etiology of female transsexualism. The major organizing principle is found in the girl's preoedipal relationship with her mother and the effect of the joint parental and family dynamics on the growth and structuring of her ego and self. Throughout this book I have argued that the precursors for development of gender identity disorder are rooted in early childhood. They are not the product of mysterious forces, but rather the effects of specific parental communications of gender meanings to their children, and the reciprocal willingness of the child to accept those interpretations from her parents. For various reasons some girls, who are raised in families which have a predominant borderline personality organization, are also especially prone to fail to consolidate a female gender-self representation. Rather than being able to develop and enrich various aspects of their personalities, these girls remain developmentally arrested, as their parents exploit, manipulate, and control their emerging gender-self systems. Consequently, these girls are unable to evolve typical mechanisms for achieving "femininity" and "femaleness." They have a defective ego mechanism regulating their gender-self constancy, an impaired female gender-self representation, and an impaired core female gender identity. They constantly experience a sense of dread that they will go "crazy," and resort to cross-gender behavior and fantasies of SRS in order to stabilize their perceived fragmenting self. In this sense, a woman's wish for SRS is viewed as a reparative attempt to restore some sense of cohesion to her perceived fragmenting self-system and to ward off either a psychosis or personality decompensation.

A girl's special relationship to her mother (who is bent on destroying her daughter's femaleness) makes her especially fearful that if she fuses with her maternal representation she will either lose her sense of self-cohesion or be in physical danger of being annihilated. Consequently, her flight from femininity to masculinity is, in most cases, adaptive, insuring her very survival. However, her flight towards father provides only an illusion of safety. At first the father is overidealized and perceived as both a rescuer (saving his daughter from mother) or as an ideal model (functioning as a "secondary mirroring selfobject") who restores some cohesion to his daughter's fragmented self-system. While these fathers provide their daughters with some protection against complete withdrawal from reality and a total personality fragmentation, they also distort their daughters' sense of reality (by reinforcing their hatred of their female bodies). These fathers not only seduce their daughters to become males, but they exploit, manipulate, and control them.

All female transsexuals view "femaleness" as a liability, associating it with vulnerability, helplessness, and powerlessness. As a result of their impaired ego functioning and defects in symbol formation, they employ primitive psychological defenses and exhibit quasi-concrete thinking about maleness. Splitting off their bisexual elements into an "all bad" female self and an "all good" male self, these women are unable to integrate their good and bad gender images. This process is facilitated by their lack of an ego mechanism to regulate gender-self constancy and a lack of a structuralized female gender-self representation. In effect, they manifest a borderline personality organization, employing rigid and pathological defenses which may make them appear quite "intact" and "normal." However, their "intactness" and "normality" are fictions, the joint product of their pathological defenses and the result of many years of support for their cross-gender roles by sectors of their community. Many female transsexuals are overly compliant, dependent, and passive, hoping that after SRS they will become more assertive, aggressive, and "male." In this sense, the wish for SRS may be viewed as a desire for "aggression assignment surgery" (see Volkan, 1976).

In the majority of cases the precipitant for a woman's transsexual wishes can be identified. Usually it relates to a death, loss, or abandonment. Short-term counseling and psychotherapy can usually address the woman's anxiety and put an end to her requests for SRS. Our study suggests that, in the future, researchers should focus their efforts on the transsexual family-as-a-whole, with specific clinical emphasis on the evaluation and treatment of children with gender identity and role disturbances.

However, in order to understand the etiology of a specific woman's transsexualism, the clinician will have to inquire into her underlying transsexual fantasy content, the nature and extent of her erotic imagery, the unconscious symbolism of her dream life, and her daydreams and conscious imagery. All of these experiences and processes need to be teased out and understood if we are to grasp the etiology of a specific woman's transsexual wish. In this sense, psychoanalysis offers the best method for investigating the etiology of transsexualism. While self psychology offers a new set of constructs for understanding the transsexual's self deficiencies, it places too little emphasis upon the unconscious wishes and fantasies which form the basis for the transsexual's self pathology.

Prior to taking a leave of absence from my clinical work to write this book, I received a number of calls from mothers who had intentionally tried to "masculinize" their 1-year-old girls (or "feminize" their 1-year-old boys) in order to prepare their children for what they viewed as radically new social roles. To their dismay, their experiments were failing. As their children reached age 4, instead of exhibiting an androgynous sex role, they were evidencing a stereotypical cross-gender role which was frightening to their parents. While these parents seemed to be appropriately concerned with their children's gender development and were attempting to cultivate a full range of human capacities in their children, something was going wrong. Although detailed case histories were not available, it appeared that these were not parents with violent, incestuous, or chaotic backgrounds. However, it did seem that these parents were substituting one set of rigid gender roles for another. The result was a child who was quite confused about her/his gender role. Whether or not these children will eventually turn out to have gender identity disorders is unknown. Clearly, however, their parents were very concerned about their cross-gender role behaviors and were requesting needed counseling.

It would seem that as clinicians and parents we need to be informed about the consequences of certain gender communications to very young children and to educate ourselves about the risks of gender experimentation. While none of the parents who called me were "experimenting" with their children's gender roles in a cold-blooded way, the effect was to undermine their children's gender identity. Although it is important for us as parents and as a culture to allow children to develop androgynous sex roles, it is also clear that small children are especially vulnerable to gender communications and messages from their parents, who are themselves products of their culture. Indeed, unless children have a firm conviction of themselves as female or male and have developed a core gender identity, their parents' attempts to provide them with an appreciation of a wide range of gender possibilities will only be confusing and may lead to a chaotic gender-role adaptation. Once a child has consolidated a core gender identity, however, parents can be effective in helping to free their children from the trammels of stereotypical sex roles.

If Pauly (1974b) was correct in his assessment of female transsexuals (that there are few worse fates than to be raised in such a family), then it is our responsibility to address these issues with clinical acumen and good clinical sense, with the best interests of the child always in mind.

A typology of female gender pathology

A developmental framework for assessing the degree and severity of female gender identity pathology may be constructed which is based on the diagnosis and assessment of the primitiveness of the female transsexual's defenses, and on the severity of the impairment of her ego mechanisms and reality testing. In constructing such a framework the clinician must determine whether the female transsexual's gender pathology is based primarily on structural defects or on a defensive process. That is, did her gender disorder have its roots in early childhood ($1-2\frac{1}{2}$ years) during the period of "primary femininity" and the "early genital phase," in which there was significant interference with the structuralization of the ego, or did her gender difficulties first appear during her later genital-oedipal phase (4–6 years), her "secondary femininity" stage? Clearly, the earlier the developmental defect the more severe will be the woman's gender disorder.

The typology of female gender identity disorders presented is delineated according to the distinction between primary and secondary femininity. It reflects the synthesis and interplay of such diverse variables as family dynamics; the girl's ego mechanisms and defensive impulse system; constitutional system; and effects of her early genital phase on her body ego and rudimentary self-system. While the typology reflects an emphasis on gender-related issues, it relies on Kernberg's (1975) formulation of borderline personality organization and Kohut's (1971, 1977) formulation of self pathology.

Table 6.2 summarizes the three types of gender pathology. Females presenting with Type 1 gender disorders would be diagnosed as having *primary gender pathology*. This group would include women whose gender confusion and disorganization were related to their diagnosed psychoses or schizophrenia. However, their gender disorders could not entirely be explained by their diagnosis. Typically, women with a diagnosis of schizophrenia have little if any defensive structure to cover over their gender defects. They also have profound ego defects and impaired reality testing. Because of the nature of the maternal infant bond (and the importance of gender identity to the formation of a nuclear self), these women may exhibit a spectrum of what appear to be "appropriate" female gender behaviors and roles; that is, they may have developed traits associated with the stage of primary femininity (including girlish traits which were conditioned, imprinted, or learned

Table 6.2 *Typology of gender pathology*

	Type 1 (primary)	*Type 2 (secondary)*	*Type 3 (tertiary)*
Age of onset	0–1 year	1–3 years	3–5 years
Stages of femininity	primary femininity	primary femininity	secondary femininity
Self-object differentiation	not evident or inadequate; merging or fusion with the object; lack of, or poor ego boundaries	partial differentiation; occasional merging and fusion with the object; ego boundaries are generally maintained	complete self-object differentiation; no evidence of merging or fusion with the object; firm ego boundaries
Object constancy	completely impaired	may be partially to wholly impaired	no impairment
Gender-self constancy	completely impaired	partial to complete impairment	no impairment
Gender-self representation	wholly impaired	impaired; oscillation between female and male images	no impairment

Thought process	classical thought disorder	defect in symbol formation; subtle disorder	no thought disorder
Reality testing	poor to impaired	usually intact; if breached can be quickly reconstituted	intact and unimpaired
Early genital phase	overstimulation, further disorganizes ego and self-development; heightened body-ego anxiety	overstimulation, leads to gender chaos and heightened castration anxiety	overstimulation, may impair typical female gender development
Core female gender identity	not achieved	ambiguous; gender diffusion and confusion	achieved
Male gender behaviors	may be evident	may be evident	may be evident (tomboyism)
Gender identity and role disorders	transsexualism (obligatory); related to severe psychopathology	transsexualism (obligatory); related to impaired mechanism regulating gender-self constancy and impaired gender-self representation	male gender envy (role); penis envy; inhibited femininity; masculinity complex; male impersonation; atypical transsexualism

independent of their psychosis or schizophrenia). In this sense, an observer might view their gender as "normal."

In so far as these women focus their delusions and hallucinations on their body and gender identity they are probably viewed as less disturbed than non-gender-disordered, psychotic, or schizophrenic women (whose delusions and hallucinations are not focused totally on their gender-self representation and body ego). The parents of this group of transsexual women appear to focus their sadistic attacks on their daughters' gender-related structures, while allowing other, non-gender-related aspects of the self to materialize.

DSM III's failure to recognize the continuum between certain forms of psychoses, schizophrenia, and gender disorders must be corrected to reflect the actual clinical phenomenon. The sufficient condition for the diagnosis of primary gender pathology is that the condition *not* be transient and acute but reflect a chronic, lifelong gender identity disturbance. The degree of primary gender pathology is measured in terms of the quality of a woman's overall ego functioning, work and object relationships, and gender identity structures and behaviors. Because of the chronicity of this disorder some clinicians may argue that remissions in their gender pathology (and schizophrenia) may occur if some of these women receive sex reassignment surgery (see Fisk, 1978). Recent evidence proves this to be a naive assumption.

Females presenting with Type II gender disorders would be diagnosed as having *secondary gender pathology*. These women would be viewed as having first established their gender pathology after their passage through the phase of primary femininity (sometime during the first three years of life). That is, their gender disturbance would be seen as linked to separation-individuation phenomena; related to the early genital phase (during that period in which core gender identity and the nuclear self were established); and inextricably bound up with impaired narcissism due to a failure of maternal empathy and defective mirroring of the narcissistic and exhibitionistic needs of the self. The majority of women who, as adults, request sex reassignment surgery would fall within this group. Women with secondary gender pathology are viewed as having structural ego defects and weaknesses, defects in symbol formation and subtle but non-intrusive thought disorders, but generally good reality testing. All of these women have a defect in their ego mechanism regulating gender-self constancy and an impaired gender-self representation. Consequently, they experience a constant fluctuation and oscillation between male and female gender-self representations, phenomenologically perceived as gender confusion or diffusion. As a group they manifest primitive psychological defenses including projection, projective identification, denial, omnipotence, devaluation, and splitting. The majority of these women are viewed as having fairly low level character pathology, including borderline personality structures and narcissistic disorders. On clinical interviews they may appear quite intact, presenting a facade of mental health. It is only after intensive psychotherapy, extensive projective psychological testing, or in response to acute stress, that their structural ego defects and weaknesses become manifest. In later life some of these women may decompensate under stress and be viewed as acutely psychotic or schizophrenic. However, their psychotic or schizophrenic episodes are transient and acute (sometimes lasting only a few hours).

Females presenting with Type 3 gender disorders would be diagnosed as having *tertiary gender pathology*. Women in this group would have developed their gender conflicts only after having passed through the secondary femininity stage (sometime after the phallic-oedipal stage). While most of these women would be characterized as having gender conflicts rooted in penis envy, castration anxiety, and feelings of gender inferiority, they would reveal two separate paths of development. One would lead to adult transsexual wishes. The other path would lead to inhibited female sexuality; a masculinity complex; or a female gender identity which is marred by a nagging sense of incompleteness, a pervasive depressive aura, and a masochistic attitude towards parts of the female body ego and gender-self system. Women in the first group would have a stable character neurosis in which subtle, but significant underlying ego weaknesses (related to a partially consolidated gender-self representation) are activated under extreme stress, leading to wishes for sex reassignment surgery. Some women in this second group may also request sex reassignment surgery; however, they are quickly responsive to interventions which redirect them back to their original female gender identities. Most of those women who have been previously labeled as stigmatized homosexuals, request surgery to reduce their cognitive dissonance, fall into this second group.

I would maintain, however, that those women with tertiary gender pathology (that is based primarily on a defensive solution to an established female gender identity) who actively request, and seek out sex reassignment surgery and are unresponsive to psychotherapy, could be shown to have either an undiagnosed organic condition or a misdiagnosed developmental arrest (involving structural ego weaknesses or defects). Under intensive investigation of their childhood (combined with intensive projective testing), these women could be predicted to reveal significant structural ego defects (including a defect in their gender-self representation, a subtle thought disorder, or disturbance in symbol formation) and non-specific ego defects. Even for women with apparent tertiary gender pathology the transsexual solution which is urgently and chronically sought cannot be reduced to a primary defensive or neurotic solution to an inhibited female sexuality or a masculinity complex, but would always involve some organic defects, structural ego weaknesses, or defects in the woman's gender-self representation related to a severe, undiagnosed gender identity disturbance. In this sense tertiary gender pathology would be reserved for those disorders recognized by Freud as derailments of ordinary femininity and female sexuality; that is, inhibited sexuality, a masculinity complex, and other defensive resolutions of and neurotic adaptations to conflict and trauma around female sexuality.

Chapter 7
Psychological and biological treatment of the female transsexual

In this chapter I will review the various strategies and recommendations for the evaluation and treatment of the female transsexual, which involve *psychological* (counseling and psychotherapy) and *biological* (hormones and surgery) approaches.

The psychological evaluation of self-diagnosed female transsexuals

The female patient who presents with transsexual symptomology as defined by *DSM* III criteria should be provided a complete psychiatric and psychological evaluation. Where indicated, an appropriate medical referral should also be made. It is imperative that the clinician rule out any major psychopathology (e.g. schizophrenia, manic-depressive illness, psychosis) or organic pathology (e.g. chromosomal abnormality, cytogenetic defect, enzyme deficiency, hormonal imbalance, intersex condition). In some cases a complete chromosomal, hormonal, and neurological workup may be indicated. Some women may need psychiatric hospitalization or psychotropic medication to treat their severe depression and/or anxiety.

There is increasing evidence that certain life events (e.g. losses, separations, deaths, or changes in relationships) can precipitate SRS wishes in an individual with an underlying gender identity disorder (Person and Ovesey, 1974a; Lothstein, 1979c). In some instances a full-blown regressive episode may occur (see Childs, 1977), a reaction which may involve genital hallucinosis and delusions and/or genital mutilation.

As I pointed out in the previous chapter, female transsexuals have predominantly borderline and narcissistic personality disorders, developmental arrests, and impaired ego functioning. In addition, their object

255

relations are quite impoverished. Consequently, when threatened by object loss they are very prone to ego fragmentation and feelings of loss of self. One recent study has identified the death of the father as being a major precipitant for SRS requests among women (Bernstein et al., 1981). In some cases a deteriorating love relationship may also lead to regressive gender episodes and magical thinking (in which the patient may believe that SRS will provide her with a penis which will protect her from separation and loss). In other cases a transsexual's lover who wishes to end the relationship may urge the patient to get SRS, only to use the SRS as an excuse for abandoning her.

The female transsexual's heightened anxiety may also pressure her to act out in a self-destructive manner. Her anxiety may also be activated either internally, by feelings of self-fragmentation, or externally, by family rejection or societal homophobia. Moreover, impersonating a male causes considerable daily stress, with the woman fearing that her real identity may be uncovered. Consequently, both the intrapsychic and interpersonal aspects of female transsexualism need to be psychologically evaluated. Because of the stresses these women are under, many of them also have serious psychosomatic illnesses which need to be treated concurrently with their gender disorders.

The clinician should assess the availability of the patient's support systems and her use of them; her overall level of adaptation; ego strengths and weaknesses; defensive functioning; and object relations. In many cases it will be necessary to interview the patient's lovers, friends, family, or other relatives. Written permission to interview these individuals should always be obtained from the patient.

The most urgent therapeutic issue is suicide potential. Some patients make overt suicidal threats and gestures in a manipulative way to obtain hormones and surgery. In some cases where a mental health professional has given in to such threats, the patient may refuse to take the hormones. It is always medically unsound to prescribe hormones either on demand or to female transsexuals who threaten suicide. The evaluator must take a firm stance, insisting that if the patient is suicidal she belongs in the hospital. Once in the hospital the patient's demands for hormones and surgery will usually cease. The classic case addressing this issue was described by Hastings (1973), in which a male patient, who had a prison record and who had mutilated his genitals, was denied SRS by a gender identity clinic. The patient then threatened suicide unless SRS was prescribed. Under duress, Hastings brought in six outside judges from

Minneapolis. The judges, hearing the story, urged the clinic to perform surgery. One month post-surgery, the patient insisted on reverting back to living as a man.

Some physicians argue that they are justified in recommending SRS to these desperate individuals since it is an alternative to suicide. However, there are no published statistics, only anecdotal reports, which suggest that transsexuals are at higher risk for suicide, or have a higher suicide rate than any other population group.

It is imperative that the evaluation focus initially on the source of the patient's pressure to obtain hormones and SRS. In one of my cases a 28-year-old woman's insistence on obtaining male hormones was eventually related to her need to strengthen herself against her mother's psychotic intrusions into her family. The woman believed that by taking male hormones she would become strong and powerful enough to confront her mother's destructive impulses. Indeed, the patient's mother often showed up at her daughter's house at any time of the day or night, occasionally insisting on bathing her 12-year-old grandson. Once the patient had to call the police to remove her mother from the home. When the patient's fantasy was elicited and her separation-individuation issues clarified, her cravings for male hormones ceased.

Attempting to *uncover* any aspects of the female transsexual's psyche has inherent risks. These women are extremely sensitive to being penetrated and intruded upon. As females they feel exposed and vulnerable to assault and attack from males. They may perceive their evaluators as intruders or invaders and make every effort to control and manipulate them. They may also lie about their past in an effort to keep the evaluator at a safe distance from their inner lives and secrets. Because these women have the capacity to merge and fuse with idealized figures (putting them on a pedestal and idolizing them as "all good" objects), the evaluator should carefully monitor his/her relationship to the patient. For some female transsexuals, just being in the presence of an idealized person may stir up intense transference feelings which may threaten the woman with overwhelming panic and anxiety — fearing that she may lose her self-identity. The evaluator must be aware of this capacity for ego dissolution and self-fragmentation in the female transsexual. Indeed, s/he should initially make every effort to diffuse the transference issues by becoming a real object for the patient. However, in order to accomplish this the evaluator must know what transference is and how one handles it in a developing psychotherapeutic relationship.

While the evaluator should remain neutral about the patient's cross-dressing, s/he should always be curious about the meaning of that behavior. The evaluator's neutrality enables the patient to remain involved with him/her and interested in motivational issues without endangering the delicate therapeutic balance. In some cases a female's crossdressing may need to be supported in order to lessen her anxiety and facilitate a working therapeutic alliance. Indeed, some female transsexuals have enrolled in our clinic after having been on male hormones and having lived and worked in the opposite gender role for years. To begin a relationship with these women by insisting that they stop taking hormones and cease their male roles would be, at best, counter-therapeutic, undercutting the very fabric of their marginal identities. The psychotherapeutic tactics and techniques for engaging these patients in psychotherapy will be discussed later.

It is imperative to confront those patients who do not successfully pass in the male role about their inability to successfully impersonate a male. Indeed, some women go to considerable lengths to appear male, even stuffing their pants with cotton (cotton wool) to stimulate a penis. Their reality distortions must be confronted to insure that their exposure to ridicule and harassment does not lead to a personality decompensation. The evaluator should always phrase interventions in terms of the patient as a whole and not just in terms of the patient's gender dysphoria. If s/he focuses only on the patient's gender issues, and not on the underlying self pathology, the patient's evaluation will be ineffective and the evaluator's attempt to establish a working alliance with the patient will fail.

In addition to the evaluator's willingness to work with these difficult patients in psychotherapy, his/her theoretical orientation is a crucial variable, especially when one is considering the aims and goals of a treatment program. Unless the evaluator approaches these patients from within the framework of object relations theory and self psychology, it will be impossible for him/her to understand the patient's communications. While some behaviorally oriented clinicians may insist that one does not need to understand the patient's motivations in order to change her behaviors, such an approach oversimplifies the issues. By focusing solely on the observable behaviors, behaviorists neglect both the source of the problem (rooted in an early childhood developmental disturbance), and the important fantasies, wishes, beliefs, attitudes, and cognitions which are at the core of the patient's identity confusions. Moreover, because of the female transsexual's developmental arrests she needs to be in therapy over a long period, a fact which requires that the therapist have the specialized training in treating severely disturbed, character-disordered patients in intensive, long-term therapy. While some short-term interventions may ameliorate the patient's acute gender anxiety (taking the edge off her request for SRS), these methods do not address her chronic gender identity disorder. Consequently, whenever her life stresses (usually a loss, death, or change in a relationship) become un-manageable, her gender anxiety and wishes for SRS resurface.

In some cases the evaluator may conclude that the woman's gender identity and role should be consolidated as a male. Indeed, there is a group of women who can only maintain object relationships when they impersonate males. Many of these women have lived for years imper-sonating the male role, in both their love and work relationships. Usually, a prolonged psychological evaluation will establish the fact that the only way these women can achieve self-cohesion is through their adaptation to the male role. Consequently, it would be therapeutically dangerous for the evaluator to tamper with these women's defensive, and precarious, male adaptations. The evaluator should therefore support those women in their transsexual adaptation as "males." Treatment programs for such women should be directed towards helping them lessen their guilt, anxiety, and depression, while facilitating their masculine goals (which may include recommending and supporting hormones and surgery). However, this is a highly experimental procedure and must be under-taken with great care. Currently there are no *a priori* rules for determining which female transsexuals should be encouraged along these lines. Ultimately, the decision should be a therapeutic one, shared by both the patient and therapist. It is not a decision which can be made in the course of a short-term evaluation, but only after prolonged, intensive psychotherapy. Therapists who advise their patients to undergo medical-surgical procedures for their gender dysphoria share, with the physician, full medical-legal-ethical responsibility for the patient's treatment. All patients who are referred for hormone therapy and SRS continue to need psychological help. It is never a matter of either psychotherapy or surgery.

Because a woman's gender dysphoria is chronic and intense, and deeply embedded in her character structure, it is generally unresponsive to short-term therapy interventions. Whenever the decision for therapy is made, the recommendation should always be understood in terms of intensive, long-term individual and/or group psychotherapy. Indeed, that is the treatment of choice for most female transsexuals. The patient's and society's resistance to accepting such a treatment program will be discussed in the next section.

Typically, many female transsexuals have been initially evaluated by individuals who are the least trained to understand their underlying psychopathology (that is, surgeons and other medical specialists); or by transsexual advocates who, in the guise of counselors, have set up programs to assist the female transsexual in her male identity and role. Because of the profound effect this type of counseling has had on the phenomenon of female transsexualism, it is imperative to distinguish the goals of counseling from those of psychotherapy. Because I am using the term counselor in the generic sense, I am not limiting the term counseling to any professional group.

Psychological approaches

Counseling the female transsexual

As opposed to intensive, long-term psychotherapy (the treatment of choice for female transsexuals), counseling, which involves a less intensive relationship between the counselor and patient and entails less stringent demands and goals, has traditionally been identified as involving an advocate role. Indeed, many transsexual counselors have advertised that they aim to assist the female transsexual in her gender identity and role transformation. These counselors are supportive of the female transsexual's male wishes, providing her with a sympathetic ear and advice as to how she can be successful in her new male role. Rarely is there an attempt to help the female transsexual understand her motivations to become a male, no less to help her consolidate a female gender identity. Some counselors have even set up specialized training programs which cater to the needs of their female transsexual clientele, providing advice on dressing as males, giving lessons in male non-verbal gestures and behaviors, offering body-building programs, and providing access to male paraphernalia such as moustaches and beards. While these counseling programs seem to address directly the female transsexual's request for gender transformation, some of the advice may be ill-conceived, premature, and perhaps unwarranted — preventing the female transsexual from receiving the necessary psychological treatment. Rarely too, does one hear from a female transsexual that she was referred by a counselor to a trained psychotherapist — a professional often viewed by counselors as playing an adversary role to the female transsexual. In a few cases, counselors who support a female transsexual's request for hormones or surgery (without psychological backup) may intensify her psychological distress. Because of the nature of her underlying psychological turmoil, any clinical approach which is directed towards the consolidation of the female transsexual's male role and identity should be carefully considered.

Even when counseling has been directed towards helping the female transsexual ameliorate her depression and anxiety, the ultimate aim has been to help her adjust in her new male gender role. Rarely is the female transsexual's motivation for seeking sex change challenged or explored. Typically, the counselor's support and encouragement of the female transsexual's wishes for SRS will alleviate her acute anxiety and dysphoria, making it appear as if she is now free of emotional turmoil and ready for surgery.

Other counselors, with more ambitious goals, may wish to help the female transsexual become more aware of her social impact: of how her rigid, stereotypical, and compulsive ways of relating to other people compromise her social relationships. These goals, while aimed at making the female transsexual a less rigid person, are still focused on helping her make a satisfactory adjustment in the male role. In summary, the goals and methods of counseling should not be confused with the goals of a reconstructive or anxiety-supportive psychotherapy (which would be more stringent and focused on changing the patient's impoverished object relationships, borderline character structure, developmental difficulties, and self pathology).

Most counseling programs are also time-limited. Typically the results of such short-term counseling programs (which have never aimed at changing the female transsexual's underlying psychopathology) have then been used as evidence that psychotherapy is useless with the transsexual and that SRS was the treatment of choice. The term "useless" has generally referred to the inability of those counseling goals to completely change the woman's gender role back to female. However, since counseling is not psychotherapy, nor are the goals of counseling directed towards reconstructive changes in the personality, it is, at best, misleading to use the findings of counseling to prove that psychotherapy is useless in the treatment of transsexualism.

When counselors claim that what they are doing is psychotherapy (in the general sense), it is reasonable to question those claims. Indeed, one must inquire about the training of those counselors and their theoretical orientation. If a counselor is not trained in clinical methods, s/he will not be able to grasp the underlying psychopathology of the female transsexual. How then will s/he be able to provide an adequate and responsive treatment program for the patient? Since it is common practice for gender clinics to rely on non- and para-professional volunteers and a wide spectrum of mental health professionals, as transsexual counselors, it is crucial to specify what was their clinical training. In many cases individuals with little or no clinical training have had their interventions — advice, exhortations, lectures, support, passing remarks, comments, etc. — labeled as psychotherapy, and the negative results of their "treatment" labeled as "psychotherapy failures." These so-called "psychotherapy failures," which have then been used to justify SRS, are a sham. They reflect more on the counselors' inadequate training and lack of knowledge of the personality disturbances of female transsexuals than on the failure of psychotherapeutic methods.

If counselors wish to label themselves as transsexual advocates (and counsel female transsexuals towards a consolidation of their male roles), they should advise their clients about the limitations and risks of their interventions and the availability of alternative solutions to their transsexualism. However, if a counselor wishes to provide psychotherapy to the female transsexual, s/he should have had specialized supervisory clinical training, including training in psychoanalytic psychopathology, descriptive psychiatry, and medical psychology. In addition, the counselor should have had prior intensive supervision in the evaluation and psychotherapy of patients with severe character pathology, narcissistic disturbances, and primitive mental states. Without such specialized training the counselor who wishes to go beyond the role of advocate will be unable to understand the patient's meanings and will probably intervene prematurely and inappropriately.

Psychotherapy with female transsexuals

Because female transsexualism is primarily the consequence of a profound early childhood disturbance, intensive long-term psychotherapy, not surgery, should be the *initial* treatment of choice. As a disorder of the self-system female transsexualism involves a profound developmental arrest; severe character pathology; impaired ego functions; and the employment of morbid, primitive, and rigid psychological defenses which impair the woman's reality sense and act as a barrier to the engagement in a therapeutic relationship.

Not all psychotherapies, however, are the same. Some, like psycho-analysis or behavior therapy, involve distinct methods and are applicable to specific patient groups with circumscribed emotional problems. However, for some female gender dysphorias either of these methods may be the treatment of choice. All intensive, psychoanalytically oriented psychotherapies, however, utilize a common methodology (relying on transference phenomena, the analysis of transference, and the genetic determinants of adult behavior) and a common aim (understanding, insight, and change of maladaptive personality patterns and a lessening of the untoward effects of anxiety and depression on behavior). In contrast to psychoanalysis the methods are more eclectic and less rigid, allowing the therapist greater latitude in experimenting with various modifications of technique.

I hope to show that the pessimism regarding the outcome of psycho-therapy with female transsexuals is unwarranted. Over the last few decades our understanding of primitive mental states has grown exponentially. As a result new techniques for treating these patients have been discovered and more and more characterologically impaired patients have been successfully treated by therapists who employ modified versions of traditional psychoanalytically oriented psychotherapy. Employing insights from object relations theory, therapists now have a better rationale for making effective interpretations and interventions with the female transsexual. This type of therapy, however, requires that the therapist be extensively trained in clinical methods related to psychoanalytic psychopathology, object relations theory, and self psychology. Once the gender identity and role pathology of the female transsexual patient is reconceptualized in terms of the above theoretical frameworks, the basis for treating her successfully can be established. These issues will be spelled out in detail.

The anti-psychotherapy tradition among transsexual researchers

It was not surprising that most of the early psychotherapy successes were with female transsexuals (Barlow et al., 1973; Rekers et al., 1974). What was surprising was that those women were even referred for psychotherapy. Indeed, the pervasive anti-psychotherapy tradition among transsexual clinicians made it all but impossible for transsexuals to be referred for psychotherapy prior to 1970.

While there was no single psychological reason why female transsexuals were referred for psychotherapy, there was a compelling medical one: surgeons lacked the techniques for constructing an aesthetically appealing and functionally capable penis. While most female patients were referred for psychotherapy for the wrong reasons — because SRS was not available — a number of them received help with their gender pathology. Counseling objectives and psychotherapy goals may have been facilitated because the patients did not have the option of SRS to sabotage their psychotherapies. I do not believe that it was fortuitous that some female transsexuals benefited from psychotherapy. Rather they did so because their psychotherapists intuitively employed the kinds of modified treatment paradigms which focused on the severe developmental disturbances of these patients; recognized the need to use hospitalization when necessary, and conceptualized the treatment in terms of the woman's impaired object relationships rather than of her preoccupation with becoming a man.

While there are a few reports of transsexual "cures" with behavior therapy (Agras, 1973; Davenport and Harrison, 1977), an analysis of those treatment parameters suggested alternative explanations. That is, the methods employed may have been less effective than the quality of the relationship established between the therapist and patient. For example, while Agras (1973) reported on a male who was successfully treated with behavior therapy, it appeared that he had received a lot more than behavior therapy. The patient was seen about three to five days a week for 1½ years. Indeed, the patient was enveloped by therapists and caretakers and involved in an extensive, multimodal therapy. The crucial variables of the treatment seemed to relate more to the intensity, length, and quality of the supportive psychotherapy (which led to the patient's ability to develop object relationships) than to the specific behavioral techniques employed.

Another explanation of why psychotherapy was successful with female transsexuals may relate to the fact that the initial treatment "cures" were with adolescent patients. All of the therapists involved were specialists in adolescence, with the adolescent therapists being accustomed to treating character disorders and employing a more eclectic approach to their interventions. In this sense they were in a better position to treat "intuitively" the characterological difficulties of their transsexual patients. Moreover, since sexual identity conflicts and identity diffusion are common problems in adolescent turmoil, those therapists were less likely to be "taken in" by the transsexual symptom, and would not focus solely on the girl's gender pathology as many "transsexual" experts might have done.

The dictum of Hertz et al. (1961) that "transvestism [what we call transsexualism] resists psychiatric treatment," summarized the prevailing view, and had a profound effect on the course of treatment for transsexual patients (Hastings and Blum, 1967; Pauly, 1968; Laub and Fisk, 1974). This view was given official sanction when the American Psychiatric Association Committee on Human Sexuality published its written report in 1972, which suggested that a combination of hormones and surgery, not psychotherapy, was the treatment of choice for the diagnosed transsexual (AMA, 1972). The rejection of psychotherapy was not, however, based on empirical evidence but on anecdotal reports and impressionistic evidence.

However, a review of the literature provided only one case of a psychotherapy failure, in which the therapist's goals of "converting" the patient back to her "original" gender identity and role seemed unrelated to the patient's therapeutic goals. A few patients, however, reportedly terminated their therapy because they felt misunderstood. Some patients also believed that the therapists' goals for them (complete reversal to their female gender role) were too stringent and divergent from their own expectations (especially given the lack of empathy which their therapists had for their severe inability to relate to others).

The view that "psychotherapy is useless with transsexuals," was uncritically accepted (especially by transsexual advocates) for several reasons: (1) patient pressure for a medical-surgical intervention; (2) the surgeon's interest in performing the surgery; (3) the conflict between psychiatry and medicine regarding the role of psychiatry in medicine; and (4) reports of transsexual "cures" with SRS.

Evidence against psychotherapy?

At the same time that psychotherapy with transsexuals was being attacked, several studies were also published which heralded SRS as the treatment of choice for transsexualism — with reports of 80 per cent cure rates (see Benjamin, 1966; Wålinder and Thuwe, 1974). On the one hand there were those mental health practitioners who were transsexual advocates, serving either as handmaiden or middleman for the surgeon by providing a written document approving surgery; on the other, there were those who came to be regarded as transsexual adversaries, i.e. the psychotherapists. Indeed, the SRS candidate who was referred for psychotherapy often felt betrayed, believing that she was misunderstood and that once the door to SRS was closed all hope would be lost. Consequently, the referral to a psychotherapist implied an obstacle to be overcome (before obtaining hormones and surgery), rather than an opportunity to receive needed psychological help. It was not uncommon for a female transsexual to be told that whether or not she would be referred for hormones or surgery was dependent on the outcome of her psychotherapy. Imagine the bind this placed on the therapy! Naturally, the chances of such a psychotherapy contract ever succeeding were small.

At the same time the female transsexual was attending her "therapy" sessions, she may also have been keeping intermittent appointments with her surgeon (on occasion failing to communicate that fact to her therapist). Consequently, the patient typically developed a bipolar view of her "treatment team," with the surgeon being viewed as an all-powerful, "grandiose regulator," omnipotent and "all good" object, while the psychotherapist was viewed as a "paranoid persecutor," devalued and "all bad" object. This conceptualization was multidetermined, reflecting both a struggle between various professional groups treating the female transsexual and the effects of the patient's primitive defensive functioning on her relationships. Until recently it was a dynamic which was generally unrecognized for its deleterious effect on the psychotherapy relationship.

The real effects of psychotherapy: a sobering view

A review of the treatment literature was quite sobering. Indeed, for the past two decades a number of diverse clinical case studies have been published which support the idea that psychotherapy may not only be useful with transsexuals, but may be the treatment of choice. Indeed, the psychological treatment of transsexual patients has been quite diverse, reflecting the individual needs of the patient and the wide spectrum of therapeutic interventions; for example, intensive psychoanalytic psychotherapy (Sperling, 1964; Greenson, 1966; Stoller, 1970), ego supportive psychotherapies (Green et al., 1972; Roth, 1973), behavioral therapies (Gelder and Marks, 1969; Rekers and Lovaas, 1974; Bates et al., 1975), management psychotherapy (Baker and Green, 1970; Myrick, 1970), and group therapy (Forester and Swiller, 1972; Green and Fuller, 1973; Sadoughi et al., 1973; Lothstein, 1979a; Althof and Keller, 1980). Two recent reports have firmly indicated that psychotherapy plays a significant role in the overall treatment plan for transsexuals. In one study of group therapy with twenty-eight transsexuals (including seven females) 43 per cent of the patients chose non-surgical solutions to their gender conflicts, with the female patients being recognized as benefiting most from the treatment (Keller et al., 1981). In another study, which included some of the patients in the previous study, 70 per cent of fifty self-labeled transsexuals benefited from individual and group psychotherapy and chose non-surgical solutions to their disorder (Lothstein and Levine, 1981).

The above studies suggested that while psychotherapy may be stubbornly resisted by transsexual patients, it may eventually provide them with the most successful form of treatment. The theoretical orientation of the therapist, and the treatment modality employed, seemed to influence the goals of the therapy (which had to be adjusted to the needs of each patient). While many of the therapists would not have designated their theoretical framework as psychoanalytic or object relations oriented, the studies clearly suggested that a variety of sophisticated supportive psychotherapies (which at times included some anxiety-provoking techniques and investigatory work) were employed.

As most trained clinicians know, good supportive psychotherapy is a special skill required for treating chronically disturbed patients. The term "supportive" is misleading since the therapists do not support the patients' defenses and life style, but attempt to engage them in a variety of techniques and manoeuvers to bolster their defenses, support their coping mechanisms, and help them to establish better object relationships. The supportive psychotherapist attempts to accomplish these goals by establishing an empathic relationship with those chronically disturbed patients whose severely impaired object relationships and profound character pathology are difficult obstacles to overcome. The psychotherapy tactics and techniques employed enable the patients to adapt and cope with their lives, developing more beneficial social relationships and support systems.

In the outcome studies with transsexuals, the positive psychotherapy results were the product of therapies involving a variety of goals, ranging from: attempting to help the patient consolidate her new male gender identity (free of debilitating psychiatric symptomology); stabilizing the patient to a pre-surgical adaptation to her cross-gender role; to total reorientation of the patient back to her female gender identity and role.

The female transsexual as psychotherapy patient

There is no question but that the majority of female transsexual patients pose a difficult if not arduous task for the psychotherapist. They are "driven" to find a medical solution to their disorder and have been described as exhibiting little or no motivation for psychotherapy. Moreover, there are various sectors of the medical community which support alloplastic solutions to transsexualism by recommending surgery, and so reinforcing the patients' defenses against entering exploratory psychotherapy. It is not uncommon for a female transsexual to accept passively the referral for psychotherapy, yet to try simultaneously to undermine its effects. Therapists report that female transsexuals are alternately friendly, cooperative, and passive, while also stubborn, guarded, manipulative, and controlling. Above all, they are fearful of being intruded upon by the therapist. The initial sessions may be filled with demands for hormonal or surgical intervention, ramblings about how badly they need breast surgery so that they can be normal, or stories about their current life situation which suggest a complete absence of emotional problems except for their gender identity disturbance.

Typically, the female transsexual may refuse to discuss anything other than hormones, breast surgery, or phalloplasty. While she may openly discuss her gender problems, she may also appear constricted and inhibited around non-transsexual issues. The female transsexual's intransigence against analysing her past has usually been interpreted as reflecting her untreatability. However, it is just this pathologically organized defensive process (that is, her massive use of denial, splitting, projective identification, and her "blank self" defense) that is in need of treatment.

All clinicians who have worked with a female transsexual have, at one time, been taken in by her "pat story," only later to find themselves chagrined by the real facts of the case. Several clinicians have suggested that one cannot accept the transsexual's social history at face value and must seek corroboration through interviews with friends and family members (Pauly, 1965; Money, 1974). Walker (1981) has even presented a study of thirty-five cases of "Factitious Presentations Of 'Transsexualism'" in which male and female transsexuals falsified their diagnostic data (e.g. by forging a psychiatrist's stationery, and hiring people to impersonate family members); feigned transsexualism "to obtain social service benefits and to avoid social interaction and responsibility"; and exhibited an illusion of transsexualism to ward off homosexuality. Some of the patients were diagnosed as having Munchhausen's syndrome.

Most therapists are also unprepared to deal with the pervasive feelings of excitement, confusion, anxiety, frustration, and rage which characterize and impede the treatment process. Moreover, these feelings may spill over beyond the therapy session and affect other staff, who may complain about the patients' behavior, especially if they use the men's room (sometimes comically referred to as "toilet trauma"). During the initial phase of treatment the patients may appear flamboyant, extravagant, grandiose, and narcissistic in their dress, mannerisms, and speech. Many of the female transsexual patients in our study displayed a gender role facade in which counterphobic mechanisms were prominent. One 16-year-old female patient dressed in a cowboy-type outfit, wore an enormous dildo under her pants, and had a challenging, abrasive personality. She was constantly bullying younger males and maintained her bravado in the therapy room. The patient's exhibitionism was often ritualized and grotesque.

During the initial phase of treatment some female transsexuals may exhibit poor judgment and lack of impulse control. While they need the therapist as an auxiliary ego, their own impaired ego mechanisms may make it impossible for them to use the therapist's ego effectively. For others, their bland facade (concealing a fundamental greediness, infantilism, and voraciousness) may lure an unsuspecting clinician into a calm which leaves the patient without effective therapeutic leadership. Some female transsexuals may also place unrealistic demands on the therapist to gratify their narcissism immediately. One female transsexual patient overtly seduced a female therapist (in a highly caricatured way). Her behavior suggested a need for confirmation that she was viewed as a male by the heterosexually oriented female therapist. Some patients

269

may also make direct requests for compliments regarding their personal appearance. These requests suggest an insecure male image and ambivalence about their male roles. If the therapist is unresponsive to the patient's need for flattery and attention the patient may become enraged and quit therapy, as the female transsexual's narcissism is so easily threatened. Because of her impaired object relations, the female transsexual is also unprepared to deal with the therapist as a real object (which is a double bind for the therapist, whose chief role is to function as a real object for those patients). The therapist's attempt to reach out to the patient via a two-way dialogue may also be construed as criticism and rejection, providing a negative cast to the developing therapeutic relationship.

During this phase of treatment the therapist may experience voyeuristic excitement regarding the female transsexual's self-presentation. Many therapists who become preoccupied with the management issues of their patients may be avoiding the deeper therapeutic issues of their voyeuristic and exhibitionistic excitement while omnipotently controlling the patient. Some therapists with primitive superegos and internal prohibitions against "looking" may condemn a patient who appears bizarre and refuse to treat her. Other therapists may experience intense guilt feelings which are not infrequently acted out in terms of punishment and retaliation fantasies against the patient, e.g. by referring the patient for hormones or SRS.

Perceptions of the therapist: grandiose regulator, paranoid persecutor

The female transsexual patient may vacillate between two identifiable communication styles (Lothstein, 1977b). On the one hand she may engage in a confessional outpouring of clinical material (often in a bland or affectedly staged way). On the other, she may manifest a "blank self" (Giovacchini, 1972), characterized by a guarded paranoid stance — withholding all personal material from the therapist. During these episodes the therapist may be perceived as a "paranoid persecutor," a devalued, degraded, "all bad" object. At other times, the therapist may be perceived as a "grandiose regulator," an omnipotent, "all good" object. In effect these patients engage in defensive "splitting" and clinically resemble the borderline patients described by Kernberg (1975).

By understanding the pathologically internalized object relations of the patient (and attending to these issues in therapy), the therapist may preclude the defensive disengagement or emotional discontinuation of treatment which is characteristic of therapists who treat transsexuals and other character-disordered patients. In some instances, the therapist's psychological equilibrium may be threatened. Eber (1980) suggested that the transsexual patient may be avoided in psychotherapy because s/he is perceived as endangering the emotional equilibrium of the therapist by stirring up too much psychic pain in the therapist.

Therapist vulnerability: empathic regression

Kernberg has pointed out that there are many pitfalls in establishing a therapeutic relationship with the borderline patient. These relate to the necessity for the therapist to engage in "empathic regression" in order to understand the patient's important but nonverbalized communications. During a state of "empathic regression" the therapist may experience a transient state of personality decompensation. This state is activated by the very nature of the treatment process. That is, because the borderline patient's rigid psychological defenses often preclude direct therapeutic engagement with the therapist, the therapist must explore other communication channels. Kernberg suggested that often the most salient clinical material is obtained only through an analysis of the counter-transference issues. However, "the very mechanism by which the therapist has access to a deeper understanding of the patient's pathology may be dangerous to the therapist" (Lothstein, 1977a). Kernberg suggested that some of the dangers include micro-paranoid attitudes towards the patient; reactivation of the therapist's neurotic character traits; emotional discontinuation of the treatment; and possible unrealistic total dedication to the patient.

Con-fusional issues: pronoun distress

During psychotherapy the therapist may become disorganized by the con-fusion (that is, a combination of feeling disorganized yet fused with the patient) of the therapeutic process and the patient's self-presentations. This is most pronounced when there is dissonance between the patient's perceived gender role and the therapist's experience of that role. The therapist may become unduly confused about what pronouns to use regarding the patient and find her/himself experiencing perplexity about the true nature of the patient's problems. At times the therapist's con-fusion may be manifested by his/her states of boredom, tiredness, or active hostility directed toward the patient. In addition, although the patient may insist that she is a man, she may reveal innumerable instances in which individuals outside the gender clinic were confused by her gender and labeled her a woman. The following clinical example highlights the Gordian knots of con-fusion that may permeate the clinical picture.

Gloria, an 18-year-old anatomical female, has chosen the name of Ray to designate her chosen gender. She knows that by conventional, anatomical, genetic, and chromosomal criteria she is female; however, she believes herself to be a male in gender and acts accordingly, adopting male mannerisms and gestures which accurately reflect stereotypical male behaviors. Looking at Gloria one would never know that she is a biological female. In all of her peer relationships she passes as Ray and is known as Ray. She asked us to call her Ray and to refer to her by male pronouns; if we don't she gets upset. She is asking us to believe with her that she is male in spite of the fact that we know she is anatomically a female. Since gender is a psychological term describing purely psychological attributes of maleness and femaleness, we are able to rationally assent to "his" wish and call "him" Ray and act as if we also believe with "him" that "his" gender is male. Although we know that Ray is an anatomical female (having a vagina, uterus, and breasts) and Ray also knows these facts, at times we experience confusion as to how to refer to Ray with the correct pronouns. Ray emphatically says that "he" experiences no confusion, but this is really not the case.

At home, mother usually refers to her child as "my daughter", "she", "her". Mother knows that her child relates to peers in the male gender role and she disapproves. However, Ray wants mother to accept "him" as a male, so she agrees to take phone messages for "my son" and to refer to her child as Ray and to use masculine pronouns. But to her friends and peers, mother calls her child Gloria and refers to her as "my daughter" and uses the correct female gender pronouns. Mother is confused by her child's sex and gender. Ray knows that mother does not believe in "his" male gender role but that she agrees to go along with "him" out of her confusion and love for her daughter.

Ray's friends do not know that "he" is anatomically female. "He" lives out "his" masculine role quite successfully. "He" knows that "he" is misleading and deceiving "his" friends by "his" gender role but not about "his" gender identity. In this sense, "he" does not feel deceitful but wishes "he" could tell people about "himself." "He" experiences "his" greatest difficulties when dating. Ray's sexual preferences are for anatomical and gender role females. "He" flirts with the girls and has everyone believing "he" is a male. "He" is a good actor, but "his" sense of being a male is highly exaggerated. While on a date "he" keeps secret the fact that "he" has a vagina and never goes far enough with girls to allow them to find out the truth about "his" gender role. When Ray goes home at night "he" worries that someone might find out about "him"; while secretly longing for self disclosure, "he" is also terrified that it may happen. Ray sees "himself" as having a true self (represented by "his" male gender role and identity) and a false self (represented by "his" sexual anatomy). Although "he" denies being confused about "his" identity, "his" behavior in therapy, "his" psychological test responses, and "his" self as manifested through "his" relationships suggest otherwise.

Ray insists that "he" is not homosexual. As Gloria, this patient would never think of having sex and intercourse with another woman; that would be unacceptable. Gloria does not criticize or judge homosexuality, but reacts with disgust when it is mentioned. Gloria has no sexual interest in men and says "they don't turn me on"; sexual needs and expressions are almost non existent. It could be said that Gloria is asexual. As Ray, the patient finds "himself" aroused by women. "His" arousal seems typical for an adolescent male and is expressed in an exaggerated male fashion by wolf whistles, sexual slang, preoccupation with "getting laid", etc. Ray blushes when "he" sees a woman and immediately becomes sexually aroused. Ray has a girl friend whom "he" referred to anonymously as "Ms. Voluptuous" and later as Virginia. Virginia is in her mid-thirties, married, and has two children, ages ten and thirteen. Ray met Virginia accidentally when phone wires crossed during a telephone conversation. "He" put off meeting her as long as possible but could no longer resist when "he" found "himself" in love with Virginia. "He" then revealed "his" secret identity to Virginia who was excited about the idea that her male telephone lover was really a woman. Virginia rescued Ray from "his" home and took "him" to live with her in her home, but as Gloria not Ray. This deception was maintained so that Virginia could carry on a sexual relationship with Gloria without arousing her husband's suspicions. Virginia appears to be bisexual: while she relates to Gloria as a woman in a lesbian-type relationship she also has had many extra marital affairs with men. Ray loves Virginia and wants to believe that Virginia loves Ray and not Gloria. However, "he" thinks that Virginia may be confused by her relationship with "him." For example at the height of orgasm Virginia will call out "Ray, Ray." Her screams arouse Ray who believes she is responding to "him" as a gratifying male lover (though it seems she is responding to Ray as a woman). However "he" is only a servant for Virginia's sexual pleasure; none of "his" own bodily pleasures are gratified.

In Virginia's house Ray feels estranged and isolated when the children, husband, and sometimes Virginia call "him" Gloria and relate to "him" as a woman. Ray is confused because "he" knows that when Virginia calls "him" Ray she implies a female element Ray, and a male element Ray. In therapy, Ray refers to the female element as the "not me" and the male element as the "real me." Virginia's perception of Ray as a split composite of a male and female element confuses Ray. "He" is not adjusted to the fact that for Virginia the relationship is thoroughly enjoyably lesbian in which she allows her lover the pleasure of transsexualism in name only. She is no believer.

Ray's statement that "he" has no confusion about "his" sexual and gender identity (a claim made by most female transsexuals) contrasts with the known facts in which multiple sexual and gender disturbances are manifested as Ray moves in and out of the interpersonal underworld and is subject not only to "his" personal representations of reality but the confirmation or nonconfirmation of that perception by significant others.

In working with Ray we have found that at those times when Ray is least confused about "his" gender role, the therapist is most confused. The therapist has tried to explain this unusual series of events by concluding that when Ray is not confused "he" projects "his" confusion onto the therapist and identifies with that confusion (an example of projective identification). Additionally, it is difficult and sometimes impossible for the therapist to act as though he believes in Ray when in fact, he is genuinely confused (Lothstein, 1977a, pp. 575–7).

This clinical case material highlights the con-fusional issues that are involved in treating a female transsexual. The therapist is asked to respond (and at times, for therapeutic reasons, should respond) to the patient in her assumed gender role. However, the patient's insistence that everyone respond to her as a male may not always be realized or be the correct therapeutic tactic.

The primitive organization of the patient's defenses

The case of Gloria/Ray demonstrates how the enactment of the patient's primitive psychological defenses (splitting, denial, omnipotence, projection, projective identification) may be employed in the psychotherapeutic situation. Unless the therapist grasps the significance of the patient's gender communications (in the context of the patient's severe character pathology and self pathology), treatment will almost certainly come to a stalemate and hormones and SRS will inevitably be prescribed. The new conceptualizations of the female transsexual patient in terms of self pathology, narcissistic and borderline personality disorders, and severe developmental arrest have given rise to new therapeutic approaches which have facilitated therapeutic engagement. Indeed, the female transsexual's profound defects in symbol formation (Limentani, 1979); problems with her gender-self representation and gender-self constancy; crises around separation-individuation leading to profound separation anxiety for some patients (see Lothstein, 1979b); and profound impairment of object relations (Volkan, 1979) cannot be treated by hormones or surgery.

From theory to therapy: new techniques

The female transsexual's severe characterological disorders necessitate the employment of modified techniques for handling her various developmental impairments. Clinical research suggested that a complete reconstruction of the female transsexual's personality, while unreasonable for most female transsexual patients, failed because the wrong treatment methods and theories were employed. For example, psychoanalysis usually failed because it was not the treatment of choice for all of these patients (failing to take into account the preoedipal issues and object relations problems of the transsexual and focusing instead on oedipal issues and castration anxiety). Behaviorally oriented psychotherapy occasionally succeeded in curbing the patients' behavioral transvestism and exaggerated male mannerisms (which caused them much shame and ridicule), but did not address the main issue of the patients' gender identity as males.

A modified psychoanalytic approach involving long-term therapy, in which the therapist is more flexible, active, and directive, seems to be the primary psychotherapeutic treatment strategy for female transsexuals. The crux of the female transsexual's psychotherapy is the establishment of a therapeutic alliance. The therapist has to become a real object for these patients, establish him/herself as an empathic object, and work through what Kohut (1977) has called their "selfobject" transferences. Through careful and deliberate therapeutic work the patient can begin to repair her self defects and injured narcissism (her mirroring and idealizing transferences) in a modified psychoanalytically oriented psychotherapy. Because of the primitive nature of these patients' pathology the "functional rehabilitation" of the self's defects could take many forms. The goals for each patient have to be specified according to the patient's gender-self pathology.

Therapeutic goals

Whereas the female transsexual's goals reflect her disturbed narcissistic equilibrium (and usually focus on the total change of her self via SRS), the therapist can reintroduce a variety of goals, related to the aims and ambitions of the patient, along a narcissistic continuum; this allows the patient to focus on her self-as-a-whole and to establish goals and ambitions which are independent of her wish for SRS, thus allowing her to make gender-related adaptations without resorting to surgery. For a few select patients, SRS in addition to psychotherapy may, however, be the treatment of choice.

The goals of treatment should not be viewed solely in terms of sexual orientation, sexual preference, and gender-role adjustments (e.g. homosexual, transvestic, or heterosexual adjustments). Rather, they should be viewed in terms of the patient's self-system as a whole. Such a view reflects an appropriate understanding of the female transsexual's severe character pathology, developmental arrest, and gender-self pathology, recognizing her plea for SRS as one for wholeness (or the recognition that her gender-self system is in a state of fragmentation and dissociation and needs to be unified). A woman's desire to become a male should always be understood and interpreted as a rationalization of her perceived fragmented state and her wish to have a cohesive self.

Some therapists have viewed psychotherapy only as an adjunct to surgery: as helping to reduce the female transsexual's sense of isolation; relieving her of a compulsive desire for SRS (which may drain her of all energy for other pursuits); and as ameliorating her guilt, anxiety, panic states, self-reproaching attitudes, and suicidal behavior. However, once the therapist recognizes the primitive character pathology of the patient and the way it shapes and directs her transsexualism, and accepts the fact that psychotherapy can be more than an adjunct to surgery, the newer techniques of psychotherapy can be employed.

In treating female transsexuals I have used a number of therapeutic strategies which have been successful in terms of helping these patients adjust to life without resorting to SRS (see Lothstein, 1977b; Lothstein and Levine, 1981). These strategies included (but were not limited to):

1 setting realistic goals;
2 the therapist's being active, directive, confrontative, supportive, flexible, non-judgmental, and investigative;
3 utilizing the hospital to control the patient's suicidal depressions and self-destructive, impulsive, acting out;
4 interpreting the countertransference material, which may often be central to treatment;
5 engaging the patient in a two-way dialogue and taking leads from the patient as to how she should be approached;
6 being cognizant of the various stages and life cycle issues as they affect the therapy;
7 responding directly to questions and only later attempting to analyze them;
8 realizing that lateness and absences probably result from the patient's defective object relations behaviors, which should be initially accepted as part of the patient's pathology;
9 occasionally providing didactic material about SRS, hormones, etc.,

which lessens the internal pressure of the patient to act out her wishes;

10   not initially challenging the patient's decisions, e.g. to take hormones;

11   never labeling the patient's wish for SRS as psychotic (unless the patient is psychotic or schizophrenic) because that usually closes off the possibility of engaging the patient in therapy;

12   focusing on the patient's defective gender-self representation and impaired ego mechanism governing gender-self constancy;

13   disclosing the patient's defects in symbol formation and tendency towards a subtle thought disorder, enabling the patient to become aware of how she distorts reality without losing her reality testing;

14   making her aware of her impairments in ego functioning and how they relate to her gender disturbances;

15   uncovering the communication patterns in her family which led to her gender disturbances, revealing the intergenerational gender conflicts and the meaning her wishes for SRS have in her family;

16   focusing on her developmental arrest and need to employ primitive psychological defenses (especially splitting, projective identification, and denial) and enabling her to become more aware of how these distort her reality sense and relate to her wishes for SRS;

17   facilitating her awareness of how such precipitants as death, losses, and changes in relationships enhance her gender anxiety and underlie her wishes to become a man, thus freeing her from the compulsive reaction to loss of resorting to intense separation anxiety and reparative male fantasies;

18   focusing on her impoverished object relationships and how object hungry she is, covering over this major defect by a preoccupation with becoming a male;

19   understanding how important it is to establish an empathic relationship with the patient, attuning her real needs for object attachments (not her wishes for SRS);

20   viewing the wishes for SRS as an omnipotent wish for control and autonomy which is misdirected, with the wish for a penis symbolizing a concrete solution to her fears of loss of control and helplessness as a female;

21   focusing on her failure to progressively differentiate her body image and schema and relate that to her naive assumptions about maleness and her overall problems in gender-self differentiation;

22   working through her need to polarize male and female elements
      into "all good" and "all bad" opposites, reflecting her split into a
      true male self and a false female self;

23   appreciating her need for intensive long-term psychotherapy,
      employing Kohut's suggestions on how one treats patients with
      primary and secondary self pathology by working through their
      selfobject transferences;

24   always keeping in mind that the female transsexual has failed to
      develop a core female gender identity and that her ultimate defect
      is a psychological one related to her lack of a nuclear female self
      and a cohesive gender-self system.

The therapist must learn to tolerate many unusual behaviors of female
transsexuals, both in and out of therapy. At times they need to be
treated in a psychiatric hospital; setting limits in an outpatient treatment
situation is often ineffective. All therapeutic interventions must focus
on the patient's gender-self pathology and her impaired object relationships. If the patient's SRS wishes are viewed solely in terms of neurotic
or oedipal conflicts (e.g. penis envy, masculinity complex, identification
with the aggressor), the therapist remains disengaged from the *core*
issues of the female transsexual. Consequently, the therapist will be unable to establish an empathic link with the patient and her core self
pathology. Occasional didactic lectures on some aspects of transsexualism
may also serve to diffuse the transference and facilitate treatment by
providing a protective shield for the patient.

Overview

Using the theoretical frameworks of object relations theory, self pathology, and borderline personality disturbances allows the clinician a
fresh approach for developing psychotherapy treatment strategies for
female transsexualism. The crux of the treatment for the female transsexual is the establishment of a therapeutic alliance in which the patient's
selfobject transference can be identified, clarified, and worked through.
The treatment strategy involves the establishment of an empathic link
by the therapist to the patient's previously unmet narcissistic, exhibitionistic, and voyeuristic needs. Through a focus on the patient's pathologically internalized and defective object relations, the patient comes to

appreciate that her perceived solution to her impoverished object world — that is, to become a male through SRS — is at best inadequate.

Kohut (1977) recognized that it was the internalization of the therapist as a good object (who served as a selfobject for the patient) capable of establishing an empathic link to the patient (and thereby repairing her narcissistic defects and self pathology) and not necessarily interpretations, which led to changes in these patients. Once the patient appreciated the fact that her real conflict related to her developmental arrest, borderline pathology, impaired narcissism, and lack of object relatedness, psychotherapy could be beneficial. Through empathically linking with the patient's core defective gender-self, the therapist forms an alliance with the patient and provides a way out of her transsexual dilemma (by providing an understanding that healthy object relationships are possible without sex change). Thus, by empathically responding to the female transsexual's real problems (her lack of a cohesive gender-self system), the psychotherapist becomes her link to reality and, ultimately, her true advocate.

The transition to maleness

In certain cases the female patient has either already taken irreversible steps in her transition to maleness, or it is recommended that she receive hormonal and surgical sex reassignment. In the following section I will review the latest findings on hormonal and surgical sex reassignment. I wish to make it clear that the following material is a review of the *medical* literature; I am not an M.D. (qualified medical practitioner) and do not recommend any of the following treatments. My intent in this section is to supply the clinician with the most updated information on hormonal and surgical treatment for transsexuals. While it is apparent that I view psychotherapy as the primary intervention for female transsexualism, there are some cases in which hormone therapy or SRS may be recommended.

While there are no variables which allow us to predict with certainty which female transsexuals would benefit from SRS, it is clear that some patients have benefited from surgery. Typically, these women have established chronic histories of living as males and their impersonation offers them their only prospect of establishing satisfying object relationships. There are also a number of female transsexuals whose rigid defensive structure can only be penetrated after SRS; that is, they are amenable to psychotherapy only after a profound intervention (e.g. SRS) has disrupted their rigid defensive structure. For these few patients SRS is a prelude to psychotherapy.

Hormone therapy for female transsexuals

The availability of "street hormones"

Many self-labeled female transsexuals obtain male hormones illicitly or from physicians on a fee-for-service basis. These patients have been described as at high risk for liver problems since they are typically ingesting testosterone (usually 17 a-methyltestosterone) orally. Indeed, in order to achieve any physiological effects with orally administered testosterone, patients need to take massive dosages, which can cause serious liver damage. These oral preparations usually have no therapeutic effect (in terms of masculinizing the patient) because the dosages are too small or the testosterone is excreted before it can be effective. However, some women, after a complete hysterectomy, may show virilizing signs from orally administered androgens.

In some cases patients have ingested substances which have no chemical relationship to testosterone. Some female transsexuals have even ingested home-made capsules filled with so-called male hormone cremes and oils advertised to enhance erectile functioning and grow hair. One can also buy a variety of street drugs which are advertised as male hormones but which bear little resemblance to the real thing.

When patients are prescribed male hormones by physicians who treat drug addicts and transient street people, it has been our experience that they are usually provided oral preparations of testosterone. Normally, they receive little advice about the therapeutic indications for the drug or its dangerous side effects. In most cases these patients present to the physician as having a chronic, unalterable gender identity disorder for which hormonal therapy is desired. Since there are no federal constraints or laws against the prescribing of male hormones (these drugs are not strictly classified as controlled substances), the physician is literally free to prescribe them on the basis of his/her own medical opinion. The situation is complicated by the fact that until 1979 there were no standards of care for the transsexual patient. Even today the interested physician can only be informed about the appropriate hormonal and surgical treatment of transsexualism by word of mouth, reviewing the scant and obscure medical literature, or through the Harry Benjamin International Gender Dysphoria Association's (HBIGDA) mimeographed handout on *Standards of Care* for the transsexual (Walker et al., 1980).

Since most female transsexuals are wary about admitting to taking hormones (because they fear that such actions might appear to contra-indicate acceptance into a gender identity clinic), they rarely report this to their doctors. There are even some female transsexuals who stop taking male hormones prior to registering in a gender clinic. Some of these patients have then claimed that the bodily changes noted on physical exam were the result of spontaneous virilization (hoping there-by to suggest a biological basis for their condition, which they believe will enhance their prospects for referral for SRS). Indeed, some of these cases may account for the reportedly high incidence of Stein-Leventhall syndrome, polycystic ovary, or cases of spontaneous virilization in female transsexuals (Sendrail and Gleizes, 1961).

The female transsexual who wants to obtain male hormone may be driven by complex psychological factors which need to be assessed prior to the decision to prescribe hormones. For example, Billowitz (1981) suggested that hormones may be prescribed "at least in part, to allay anxiety, to reduce suicidal tendencies òr threats, or to prevent patients from obtaining hormone pills on the streets." Moreover, because of the existence of a number of neuroendocrine disorders which may cause virilization in a female (e.g. adrenocortical tumors or congenital adrenocortical hyperplasia) every patient should be provided a complete and thorough physical and endocrinological exam. Consequently, it would appear medically unsound, if not unethical, to prescribe hormones for a self-labeled female transsexual who has not undergone extensive psychological and medical evaluation. The prescription of hormones on demand is always contraindicated.

The decision to prescribe male hormones

The patient's decision to take male hormones (or the referral for male hormones by a physician) is not diagnostic of transsexualism. The decision to prescribe male hormones to a self-diagnosed female transsexual should be made only after an extensive psychological evaluation and comprehensive physical exam (including an endocrinological workup). It should never be made on demand or without peer review of the private practitioner. In most cases the female transsexual hopes that by taking male hormones she will become a complete male. Some patients may even refuse to obtain a job until male hormones are prescribed, in effect trying to bribe the physician. The HBIGDA recommends that the female transsexual requesting hormones be known to the physician for a specified amount of time in a psychotherapeutic relationship (with the patient living and working in the opposite sex role) before the recommendation for hormonal sex reassignment be made. The physician who believes that the patient's mental status will change positively after taking male hormones may be quite disappointed. While the patient may state overtly that she wants male hormones to masculinize her body, she may not be aware of her underlying motivation, so it is imperative for the physician to understand her fantasies and so reveal her covert motivation. Some of the motivations for obtaining male hormone among our patient group included the following:

1   viewing the pill as a small male homunculus which, once taken into her body, would totally masculinize her;
2   providing her with the strength and courage to ward off mother's paranoid onslaughts and physical intrusiveness into her life;
3   protecting her from the feared vulnerability as a woman; to penetrate versus being penetrated;
4   suffocating her passive strivings and fear of surrendering to a male;
5   protecting her from annihilation anxiety;
6   making her feel more alive (overcoming feelings of internal deadness);
7   magically removing her breasts;
8   growing a penis;
9   stopping her menses and thereby calming her anxiety about her femaleness;
10   making her smarter and more competent (i.e. as a man);
11   saving a relationship in which she fears that a lover might abandon her if she does not become more masculinized;
12   increase her sexual libido in order to compete with other men for female lovers;
13   protecting her from a sense of self-fragmentation;
14   warding off depressive affects which threaten to engulf her.

This is by no means an inclusive list, but it is representative of the kinds of motivations for requesting hormones brought out in psychotherapy. Clearly, no pill or nostrum could be therapeutically responsive to such a wide array of psychological ailments.

There are no firm criteria to determine which patients one should refer for hormonal treatments. The decision should be left to the psychotherapist, the consensus of members of a gender clinic, and subject to peer review. Those patients who meet the minimal criteria for a diagnosis of *DSM* III transsexualism and who fall within the prescriptions of the standards of care set by the HBIGDA, meet the necessary, but not the sufficient conditions for hormonal referral. Hormone treatments are still experimental, and the decision to refer a patient must be viewed as experimental. One should not refer a patient for either hormone therapy or psychotherapy; the two treatment modalities are not mutually exclusive.

Recommended dosages of male hormone

Benjamin (1966) recommended that "the immediate method of choice as to therapy would then be a series of androgen injections to the patient and suppressing menstrual periods and keeping them suppressed with the smallest possible dose." He recommended a therapeutic dose to be about 1 cc. Delatestryl (containing 200 mg. testosterone enanthate). He started each patient with about 100–150 mg. weekly until the first menses was missed (he also took a vaginal smear to demonstrate decreasing cornification and lowered estrogenic activity). Benjamin felt that with 500 mg. monthly amenorrhea would occur within one month. He then recommended two injections per month I.M. of between 150–200 mg. Delatestryl. Three years later Benjamin (1969) suggested that increased dosages of between 200–250 mg. were needed to maintain the desired effects. While oral preparations were seen as offering little help (while possibly harming the liver), Benjamin suggested that they could be used after a total hysterectomy and mastectomy. He recommended the use of Buccal Oreton^R Proprionate (testosterone proprionate) rather than methyl-testosterone.

Vogt (1968) recommended 250 mg. testosterone enanthate every two weeks. He felt that injections alone were not enough, since the exogenous male hormone could not entirely suppress the intact female endocrine system. He also recommended X-ray treatments to destroy ovarian tissue, and surgical castration.

Hamburger (1969) argued that injections of testosterone I.M. can be given in two ways: in an aqueous suspension of testosterone isobutyrate crystals, or in an oily solution of long-acting testosterone esters. He also suggested that suppositories with free testosterone (in 50, 100, 200 mg. dosages) may be given overnight.

Whether one prescribes the testosterone orally, intra-muscularly, or rectally, Laub (1973) advises that the "supervision of [an] endocrine . . . program" should be carried out "with a physician skilled in this area."

Goals for hormone therapy

Various clinicians have enumerated several goals for hormonal therapy, both psychological and physiological. The patient's goals may differ from the physician's. Clearly, the female patient who believes that ingesting male hormone will make her totally a male is at best misinformed, perhaps delusional. The major physiological goals of hormone therapy were noted by Hamburger (1969) to be twofold: the suppression of existing sexual features, and the development and maintenance of sexual features belonging to the other sex. Since sex hormones are not, strictly speaking, sex specific (all females have an internal source of male hormone secreted by the adrenal glands), there is still some confusion over the organizational versus activational role of the major hormones in males and females. The introduction of an increased exogenous source of androgen in the female does, however, have the effect of chemically castrating her. Some of the effects of hormone therapy are irreversible, while others are transient and cease when hormone administration is discontinued.

What sexual features in the female are suppressed by her taking male hormone? A literature review suggested that the answer to this question is only partially known. One needs to conceptualize "suppression" in terms of the entire female hormonal milieu; for example, the presence of naturally occurring female hormone in a woman can be seen as having both an excitatory effect and an inhibitory effect. The suppression of female features, therefore, needs to be seen along a continuum of possibilities.

All researchers agree that the administration of male hormones to a female causes only moderate breast atrophy. Indeed, if complete breast agenesis is to occur, male hormone would have to be administered during puberty. Since this rarely occurs (and would be medically unethical to prescribe), there is no experimental evidence to prove that breast agenesis would occur. The data on breast agenesis in non-transsexual women comes from research with adolescent girls with medical problems, in whom estrogen levels are depleted (organic estrogen being either unavailable or incapable of utilization by the cells). There are no reports of pre-teen or early teenage girls treated for transsexualism with hormone therapy.

The research clearly shows that adult women with moderately ptotic (pendulous) breasts reveal no significant change in breast size even with large dosages of male hormone. The female transsexual's wish that her breasts will atrophy when taking exogenous male hormone remains just that — a wish. The female transsexual who believes that by openly or illicitly taking male hormones her breasts will be reduced or eliminated is certainly engaging in wishful thinking, if not being misinformed and misguided. The only "cures" for the female transsexual's hatred of her breasts are either psychotherapeutic (to deal with her distorted body image), or surgical (which I shall discuss in the next section).

The female transsexual who takes male hormone will also fail to develop a male muscular-skeletal system. There are, however, variable changes in the external musculature (with a tendency away from typical female fatty deposit tissue areas into more or less male-appearing distribution of fatty tissue, and a hardening of the skin). However, only a body building program (in conjunction with taking male hormones) can provide the necessary, but not the sufficient condition, for attaining a male-type musculature. Most female transsexuals are short in stature (averaging about 5'6") and well below the height of the average American male (about 5'10"). Some of these women magically believe that by taking male hormones they will grow taller. There is *no* evidence that female transsexuals increase their height when taking male hormones. Women with small bodies, slight frames, poor musculature, small hands, and delicate features will not reveal dramatic changes when taking male hormones; they will appear as small-framed, slight, delicate-appearing males.

Clinical evidence suggests that taking male hormone may lead to a moderate weight gain and water retention (which can be treated with a diuretic). Some women, however, look forward to the weight gain, as it reinforces a psychological feeling of strength and power through increased body size. However, there are attendant risks to obesity, including hypertension, overall bodily stress, and possible shortened life span.

Male hormone: physiological changes

According to endocrinologists, the following physiological changes will occur in those female transsexuals taking male hormones: an increase in clitoris size; a thickening of the vocal cords; an increase in libido; and the development of a male hair pattern (including beard growth and possible baldness). In terms of female anatomy, there is marked atrophy of the uterus, salpinges, and ovaries. Some of these changes are irreversible (see Table 7.1). Large dosages of male hormones will suppress menses but may also make the woman infertile. Some transsexual women taking male hormones, who lower or stop their dosages, resume their periods.

Table 7.1   *Effects of exogenously administered male hormones on females*

Irreversible effects	Reversible effects
Thickening of the vocal cords (deepening of the voice)	Increase in size of clitoris
	Acne
Hypertrichosis (increased growth of hair)	Cessation of menses
	Increase in libido or sexual arousal
Possible liver damage (which may be fatal)	Weight gain and water retention
Possible infertility	Atrophy of salpinges, uterus, and ovaries (usually reversible)
	Hardening of surface quality of skin — appears "tough," like a man's

One of the major side effects of androgen therapy is the development of profound acne, the only treatment for which is the discontinuation of the therapy. Another side effect is an increase in libido (which may threaten to overwhelm some patients, especially the asexual or schizoid patient for whom sexual feelings may be ego alien).

Some women who take male hormone experience acute psychological disorganization secondary to their increased sexual libido. Benjamin

(1966) recommends that by adding progesterone to the testosterone solution the woman's libido will be decreased and her feelings of ego dissolution abate. This type of treatment parallels recent trends toward the use of antiandrogenic medication (medroxyprogesterone acetate) in treating men with paraphilias (Berlin and Meinecke, 1981; Gagné, 1981). Several reports also suggest that the increase in libido may be related to the growth of the clitoris (up to 3" in length), which now may function as a micro-phallus (a quasi-hypospadic penis). The enlarged organ is viewed as an irritant, rubbing against the patient's clothing and causing increased sensitivity through friction, thereby enhancing the woman's pleasure. Some women can use their enlarged clitoris sexually to penetrate their female partners. Indeed, some investigators view the hormonal facilitation of an enlarged clitoris as equivalent to chemical surgery — i.e., as chemical phalloplasty.

Testosterone therapy in females has also been shown to suppress the secretion of freely occurring estradiol and progesterone. For some women infertility can be a serious side effect, especially if they later decide to change their plans to become a man and wish to become pregnant. Likewise, the thickening of the vocal cords (leading to the deepening of the voice and increased facial hair growth) is irreversible. Recently, a female-to-male transsexual sued a gender identity clinic for misdiagnosing her and prescribing male hormones. Although they withdrew the prescription for hormones when the patient abruptly left their clinic (later she obtained surgery elsewhere on a fee-for-service basis), the patient's suit caused the clinic to close (an important "side effect" of the recommendation for hormones!). The patient argued that the treatments had caused irreversible changes in her appearance and voice which in turn caused her anguish and suffering in her "new" female role.

I concur with the authors of *Standards of Care* (Walker et al., 1980) that "psychiatrists and psychologists, in deciding to make the recommendation in favor of hormonal and/or surgical sex-reassignment share the moral responsiblity for that decision with the physician and/or surgeon who accepts that recommendation." In *Emergence* (1977), the only published autobiography of a female-to-male transsexual, Mario Martino warns of the dangers of hormone treatment:

> All transsexuals — female-to-male and male-to-female — must maintain hormone treatment for the rest of their lives. Because recent research indicates that with prolonged use of testosterone on genetic males

for three conditions — eunuchism, scanty sperm, and menopause —
liver tumors may result, the female-to-male is cautioned to have a
liver function test at least once each year (Martino, 1977, p. 265).

Meyer et al., (1981) even suggested that all transsexuals should receive
baseline hormonal measures, including testosterone, LH, FSH, estradiol,
and androstenedione. They also recommend that measurements of
clitoral length and breast size be made in order to obtain standardized
clinical data on these patients (almost all data on these variables now
come from anecdotal reports and the subjective opinions of the patients).
Moreover, they reported abnormal liver enzymes and elevated blood lipids
in female transsexuals and recommended periodic monitoring of the
patient's blood chemistry.

Summary of hormone treatment

Female transsexual patients place enormous pressure on the medical
establishment to provide them with hormones and SRS. Often a patient
will appear at a doctor's office demanding to be prescribed male hormones. Their stories are compelling. Feeling trapped in their female
bodies, they report experiencing considerable anguish and torment,
hoping to be relieved of their suffering by changing sexes. In the past
some physicians have reacted to their demands by prescribing hormones.
Recent evidence suggests that such prescribing on demand is at least ill
advised, perhaps unethical.

While there are no officially sanctioned standards of care for the female transsexual, the Harry Benjamin Association suggests that male hormones and SRS should not be given on demand. The female transsexual
should be under long-term psychological care and the recommendation
for hormones should be initiated by her psychiatrist or psychologist.
Because of the implications of referring a patient for hormones only
specialists trained in differentiating the intersexual, cytogenetic, chromosomal, and psychosexual disorders should be involved in helping to make
the recommendation. The patient should be under strict psychological
supervision for between three months to a year or more before any
recommendation for hormones is made. The recommendation should
only come from the psychotherapist. No adolescent patient should be
referred for hormone treatment. The reason for this is that there are

several cases of women who, after entering a gender treatment program, later abandon their male goals and resume living as women. Since adolescence is a period of the life cycle defined in terms of personality growth, change, and development, it is medically unsound and probably unethical to prescribe and implement a hormonal and surgical treatment program which has irreversible effects on the teenage girl's health and childbearing capacity.

While many of the long-term effects of testosterone therapy on normal women are apparently irreversible, little is known about the possible hazardous effects of long-term androgen therapy in female transsexuals. However, the danger of liver damage which could be fatal is serious enough to warrant extreme caution. Clearly, any female prescribed male hormones should be medically managed by an expert in endocrinology. Experts agree that treatment should include routine follow-up studies, including baseline levels of hormones, blood chemistry levels (with special reference to liver function tests), and objective physical measurements procured on all bodily changes which virilize the female transsexual.

There is increasing evidence that male hormones alone do very little to masculinize the female transsexual. While I am familiar with reports of virilization, I am also aware of several female transsexuals who did not exhibit beard growth and who were quite disappointed with the effects of male hormone. Indeed, the patient's fantasy about what would happen as a result of taking male hormone should be elicited prior to administration. The patient should then discuss her expectations in therapy in order to prepare for a less than perfect outcome.

The female transsexual's craving for male hormones is multi-determined and needs to be investigated. Because of the psychological nature of the disorder, the primary physician should always be a clinically trained behavioral scientist. Whenever male hormones are prescribed all persons involved assume medical-legal-ethical responsibility and should continue to be involved with the patient over her lifetime. At the present time, all hormonal interventions are experimental and pose certain risks for the patient.

Surgical treatment for female transsexuals

Breast surgery

The most urgent surgical request by female transsexuals is for a mastectomy. With the onset of adolescence and the growth of the breasts the adolescent transsexual may become quite agitated and suicidal. One patient, a 17-year-old female, reported that, "when I was small I didn't know that I was a girl. I almost went nuts when I grew breasts and had a period. I did not want to be a woman. All of a sudden it hits you — you're not going to be a man . . . when mom explained my period to me I became frightened. I knew it meant I was a girl — I couldn't pretend anymore." Another teenage girl bound her breasts and wore male clothing to hide her developing body.

Breasts are the most obvious insignia of femaleness. A girl's period is private. She can conceal her menses but not necessarily her breasts. However, the female transsexual can go to ingenious lengths to try to conceal her developing, often large breasts. Typically an Ace bandage is wrapped around the body, and the breasts are pressed tightly against the sternum. This reduces arm mobility and makes it difficult for the patient to move freely. If the bandage is tightly bound the patient's posture may also be affected (as she appears rigid and stiff). Several of our patients reported breathing difficulties due to the stress the bandage placed on their lungs. Other patients have reported that they could not answer the door and respond to personal messages for fear that they might be caught without their "bandages" on. In most cases the female transsexual's partners supported their need for breast surgery (some even helped them bandage their breasts).

The most common complaints were that they could not go swimming, appear in a bathing suit, or work as a man until their breasts were surgically removed. While most of the patients reacted with phobic disgust to their developing breasts, none of them threatened to mutilate their breasts. Indeed, there is only one published report of a patient who threatened to amputate her breasts (Späte, 1970). While surgeons are reluctant to amputate the healthy breast tissue of a female transsexual, they routinely operate on non-transsexual women (including adolescents) who want reductive or augmentative mammoplasty. As long as a woman does not identify as a transsexual, she can have a variety of cosmetic procedures performed on her breasts. I have personally known of two cases of male-to-female transsexuals who had augmentative mammoplasty performed without the surgeons knowing of their true biological status. While I am not an advocate of breast surgery for female transsexuals, I think the medical community has yet to face up to their double standards.

According to the surgical literature, the female transsexual who is referred for breast surgery can expect one of two procedures to be employed depending a great deal on the size of her breasts. The first procedure, making a "keyhole incision," involves the excision of breast tissue through a circumaureolar incision. The breast is literally reduced by scooping out large masses of tissue through a small incision. This procedure is the least radical, involves the least scarring, but is not used on large-breasted women. It is carried out under general anesthetic, and the patient is usually hospitalized for 3–5 days.

The second procedure is more radical, involving the amputation of the entire breast (either a partial or complete mastectomy). Moreover, the nipple is removed and relocated. Sometimes the free nipple graft does not take and the surgeon has to construct a nipple-like structure from labia skin. This procedure involves considerable scarring, taking up to a year for the scars to heal (though the scar line never fades completely). The cosmetic appearance of the scars varies considerably, depending on the keloid potential of the patient (the potential for the patient's skin to develop masses of hyperplastic, fibrous, connective tissue at the site of the scar). The grafting of the nipple is quite tricky and, if the graft does not take, the patient may lose her entire nipple. The new nipple has no sensitivity (a factor which may play an important role in the patient's diminished sexual arousal). This procedure is also performed under general anesthesia and involves up to 5 days in the hospital. Postoperative recovery is also more lengthy.

A few patients have complained about the experience of a phantom breast post-surgery (Lothstein, 1980b). To date, this has been a limited phenomenon not persisting beyond the post-operative period. However, there are no long-term follow-up studies focusing on the phantom breast phenomenon. Most studies suggest that the post-operative recovery is quite smooth, with the patients expressing complete satisfaction with any procedure employed. However, given the extent of scarring and the need to employ the second, more radical procedure (because the binding of the breasts has usually distorted the breast tissue), most patients may find themselves having to explain to friends and lovers why their chests are so scarred. Several patients in our study were particularly fearful that their scarring would be tell-tale of their previous female existence — and that they would be discovered to be females.

While the surgeons play down the risks of breast surgery (by labeling it cosmetic and reductive mammoplasty), the reality is that infection and poor cosmetic results are fairly common. Some patients may also develop keloids and need additional surgery, while others may develop infections which affect their general health. There are also serious risks involved with general anesthesia, and death is always possible.

All surgery involves some changes in the patient's emotional status. The loss of any body part also affects the patient's enduring body schema and image (which has a psychological and physiological component). After the post-surgical period of elation and hypomania, the female transsexual may experience profound depressive feelings. She may also be unable to acknowledge these feelings because of her repressed guilt. It is imperative that psychological follow-up be provided to all patients post-surgery; even if they refuse the recommendation, the referral ought to be made.

In a study of seven of our patients who had breast surgery (all of whom had the second procedure performed), none missed their breasts or regretted the surgery. In spite of some rather poor cosmetic results (Lothstein, 1980b) most of the patients enjoyed being barechested and exposing their bodies to public view (a narcissistic behavior which was avoided pre-surgery). All of the women were, however, concerned about the poor aesthetic appearance, and diminished erotic sensitivity, of their breasts and hoped their partners would like their new bodies.

In summary, the female transsexual ought to be psychologically counseled pre- and post-surgery about the reality and expectations of breast surgery. Surgeons tend to gloss over these issues and to concentrate on the "perfect" outcome rather than on the patient's psychological reactions to her new "male" body. Only a surgeon who is comfortable working with the transsexual patient should be chosen to operate. Some surgeons have strong reactions to transsexual patients and often, if the surgery is done in a teaching hospital, the surgeon turns out to be a resident or staff member who is offended by the procedure. In one case with which I am familiar, the patient's massive scars were probably the result of the surgeon's unconscious sadism and wish to scar the patient for "going against nature." In spite of the "poor cosmetic results" (surgical jargon for a rather grotesque appearance), the patient was pleased with the outcome (a reaction which speaks to the poor reality sense of some female transsexual patients). Once breast surgery is performed, the female patient, unlike her male counterpart, will almost always wait for a prolonged period of time before raising the issue of hysterectomy, oophorectomy, salphingectomy, and phalloplasty.

Sex reassignment surgery (SRS) for female transsexuals

Few psychiatric issues have stirred up as much controversy and emotional turmoil as the prescription of SRS as a treatment modality for transsexualism (Brady and Brodie, 1978). Those clinicians who espouse SRS as a legitimate form of treatment view it as either a palliative or a cure for the transsexual's intense social-emotional anguish. On the other hand, those clinicians who consider SRS as an illegitimate form of medical-surgical treatment usually characterize it as mutilative and anti-therapeutic. They point to the complex psychological, medical, legal, bio-ethical, and political issues which are neglected, bypassed, or rationalized by SRS procedures. They argue that SRS leads to mistreatment and mismanagement of the female transsexual. Indeed, in a study completed in the mid-1960s, Green et al. (1966) reported that a majority of 300 physicians queried about SRS procedures indicated opposition to SRS for transsexuals. Today, however, the same study would probably yield just the opposite results.

As more and more female transsexuals request SRS, the issue of what is appropriate treatment for them becomes critical. Moreover, as techniques for phalloplasty are being refined the demand for that procedure is increasing (Lothstein, 1982). A combination of several factors — the availability of surgery, media exposure of post-operative female transsexuals, the existence of national and international referral centers and information sources for SRS, and the establishment of many gender identity clinics — has made it necessary for clinicians to take a stand for or against SRS.

It is currently estimated that there are about 10,000 transsexuals in the USA (or about 4000 female transsexuals). This is probably a conservative estimate. One researcher, Prince (1976), has suggested that the number of requests for SRS has reached epidemic proportions. A fairly recent estimate suggests that over 1000 transsexual surgeries (about 400 female-to-males) were performed in the USA alone in 1980 (Walker et al., 1980). Most of the SRS is done on a fee-for-service basis with little evaluation, poor SRS results (both cosmetically and functionally), and no post-operative follow-up or care. The situation is rather dismal.

As long as there are no universally accepted standards of care, hospitals can either restrict or prohibit SRS; or allow SRS to be performed as needed, either on an experimental or fee-for-service basis. While all practitioners should be concerned about the unrestricted use of SRS, it appears that, for some patients, SRS may be the treatment of choice. Those clinicians who espouse SRS must determine which self-labeled transsexuals are its best candidates. And those clinicians who object to SRS need to empirically (and not anecdotally) demonstrate that SRS is neither a palliative nor a cure.

Review of the literature on SRS for women

During the early 1930s Abraham (1931) published a number of reports on SRS for male transsexuals. It was not until the publication of the semi-autobiographical book *Man Into Woman* (Hoyer, 1933), that SRS became a popular and, perhaps, practical solution for the transsexual's dilemma. In that book, Neils Hoyer edited the writings of the Dutch painter Einar Wegener (also known under the pseudonym Andreas Sparre) who, in 1931, underwent a sex conversion operation in Dresden. The actual surgical techniques were never revealed, though it appeared that the patient underwent a series of operations (including castration, penectomy, transplant of "ovarian tissue from a healthy young woman of twenty-six," and finally "another operation, the nature of which was not explained, though it had something to do with the insertion of a canula"). The patient died post-operatively (probably of an autoimmunization response due to transplantation of ovarian tissue), an apparent victim of the final experimental surgical procedure which was performed in order to enable the patient to function fully as a woman and to become a mother!

However, it was not until 1961 that the first study on female transsexual surgery was reported. There Hertz et al. (1961) reported on the surgery and post-surgical functioning of three female transvestites. The women were provided defeminizing procedures which included a bilateral mastectomy, hysterectomy, salpingo- and oophorectomy (removal of the breasts, uterus, fallopian tubes, and ovaries respectively). Additionally, the women were given androgen replacement therapy. All were viewed as suffering from serious depressions. Their post-operative periods were 3.5 years, 6 years, and 16 years respectively (suggesting that the last patient was operated on during the mid-1940s). The authors concluded that the patients all had satisfactory outcomes. However, a review of the case histories suggested considerable emotional disturbance in all three patients, including the presence of a thought disorder in one patient, suicidal depressions in the other two patients, marginal social relationships in all patients, an inability to separate from mother in the third patient, and one case of psychiatric hospitalization. Hertz et al. (1961) viewed the patients as requiring SRS in order to legitimize their homosexual relationships and concluded that "the sex changing operation was more encouraging in the three female patients [than in the male patients]."

The Hertz et al. (1961) study has become a model for all subsequent studies on SRS. Their conclusions, which often seemed unrelated to the case presentations, and reflected serious methodological problems, have been used by subsequent researchers to implement and justify SRS for female transsexuals. To date I have located published data on 189 cases of female transsexuals who have received SRS (Lothstein, 1980b). This is a conservative estimate since there are no data on those patients who obtain SRS on a fee-for-service basis. Indeed, in a recent personal communication from one prominent surgeon he writes, "The phalloplasty operation has been performed by me in over 150 patients."

During the 1960s and 1970s a number of follow-up studies on post-operative male and female transsexuals were reported. The early studies focused entirely on gross social-psychological measures of improvement. Benjamin (1966) reported a 95 per cent satisfactory outcome for twenty females who received SRS; and Randell (1969) reported an 83 per cent satisfactory outcome for six females post-SRS. It was generally accepted that traditional psychiatric interventions were useless with transsexuals and that SRS was the treatment of choice.

Throughout the 1970s increased numbers of female transsexuals sought SRS. Spurred on by changing views of societal sex roles, large numbers of women were given external support to change their sex (rather than understand the nature of their psychological distress). Moreover, lacking standards of medical-surgical care, the mental health professions were unprepared to respond adequately to the transsexual's dilemma. In addition, SRS was available to almost any self-labeled transsexual who could pay the fee, and the surgery was often performed secretly, with few patients available for follow-up. There was little a dynamically oriented clinician could do to intervene with psychological

methods. Moreover, Wålinder and Thuwe (1974) published their comprehensive follow-up study on male and female transsexualism and concluded
that "taking men and women together, the outcome was clearly favorable in approximately 80% of the cases" (with 91 per cent of the females
revealing favorable outcomes).

The post-operative studies of the late 1970s and early 1980s, however,
challenged the idea that SRS was a palliative, no less a cure for transsexualism. While there was some support for the finding that SRS led to
better social-economic functioning (for some patients), transsexual
patients were now viewed as having severe psychopathology which was
unaltered by SRS. Sturup (1976), an early proponent of SRS, noted
that "In some of the early cases the reluctance on the part of therapists
to adopt an active therapy [had] been too great." The studies of the
1970s, however, ended on a sour note with the media distortion of the
results of a Johns Hopkins post-SRS follow-up hospital study: that SRS
was of little or no benefit. This conclusion, unsubstantiated by the data
of the Meyer and Reter study (1979) has already become a focus of
much debate.

Most of the female transsexual patients studied post-operatively
were a self-selected group who had voluntarily enroled in a hospital- or
university-based gender identity clinic. However, because of their
defensive structure, it was very difficult to get baseline data concerning
their true psychological state pre-SRS. Moreover, the majority of transsexual patients had obtained SRS illicitly and were not available for any
kind of evaluation. Consequently, it was quite difficult to know what
changes could be attributed to the SRS procedures alone.

While a few studies have provided us with insights into the female
transsexual's post-operative functioning, they are beset with serious
methodological difficulties, which make their conclusions suspect. The
methodological problems of these studies have been well documented
(Lothstein, 1979b). In effect, the conclusions of all SRS studies are
dependent on which parameters were used to investigate the female
transsexuals post-SRS. Using global ratings (which focus on overall
social-emotional functioning) clinicians have reported a positive change
rate for female transsexuals post-SRS of between 70–90 per cent. On the
other hand, those researchers who used more discriminative evaluation
criteria (focusing on discrete psychological variables) not only failed to
replicate the success rates, but occasionally reported negative results in
the social-economic areas of post-SRS functioning. All of these findings

must be viewed in the light of the various methodological weaknesses of the studies reported.

As long as SRS remains a viable treatment modality it is reasonable to ask how one determines which patients will most benefit from it. Currently there are no universally acceptable criteria aside from the "real life test" suggested by Money and Ambinder (1978). This test requires that the patient live and work in the opposite gender role for at least two years. While SRS has definite medical-surgical limitations, there is as yet insufficient evidence to warrant its termination. SRS should only be considered as part of a rehabilitative program for a patient — and not as a "cure." How one identifies which patients may most benefit from SRS is another matter. SRS is still an experimental procedure and should be reserved only for those few cases in which all else has failed. It is my opinion that intensive long-term therapy is the *primary* treatment of choice for all female transsexuals. For those women who receive surgery, psychotherapy should always be prescribed pre- and post-surgery.

Hysterectomy, salpingo-, and oophorectomy

A review of the surgical studies on transsexualism suggested that female transsexual surgery was usually accomplished in several stages. Prior to the use of radical surgical procedures, some female transsexuals received X-ray treatments to ablate their ovarian functioning. For some physicians this procedure constituted SRS surgery (and appeased those surgeons who were reluctant to remove healthy tissue through surgery). In some cases where a partial or complete hysterectomy (including removal of the fallopian tubes and ovaries) had been performed, surgeons depended on the counsel of mental health specialists to document the need for such surgery.

Non-transsexual women who requested elective gynecological surgery to remove their childbearing organs form a natural control group to compare with female transsexuals. Studies on the psychological response of these non-transsexual women to elective gynecological surgery suggested that they are also at high risk for serious depressive episodes up to two years post-surgery (Barker, 1968). Indeed, the surgical procedures are quite radical and take their toll both physically and emotionally. Unfortunately, there are no long-term follow-up studies on female transsexuals post-hysterectomy to determine how they psychologically integrate and experience their surgery. Once a female transsexual has her childbearing organs removed these *cannot* be surgically replaced; the woman is permanently sterile. This can have serious consequences for a female-to-male transsexual who later decides that her decision to change sexes was wrong and she now wants to bear a child.

Since most of the surgical procedures are irreversible, the female transsexual should be provided intensive counseling regarding her decision to undergo elective SRS procedures. For some female transsexual patients the question of informed consent is moot, since a subtle thought disorder may guide their "decision-making" process.

Phalloplasty: the construction of a penis

According to Hoopes (1969), "creation of the male external genitourinary apparatus is not accomplished easily and is fraught with rather serious hazards." In most cases phalloplasty is carried out in conjunction with the removal of the female organs. Phalloplasty (the creation of a penis) involves multiple hospitalizations, extensive surgical procedures, and enormous financial and psychological cost to the patient. The first report of phalloplasty (for males who received injuries to their genitals) appeared during the 1920s. Hoopes, quoting a review of the literature on phalloplasty (Gelb et al., 1959), reported that the first "total reconstruction of the penis was by Bogoras in 1936."

The surgical techniques employed usually involved some sort of abdominal tube pedicle flap. The surgery was done in several stages (in order to guarantee an adequate blood supply to the graft). Usually the patient was brought back to surgery one month after each procedure or when satisfactory healing occurred. During the initial stage (when the pedicle flap was made) the patient received her hysterectomy. The clitoris and the vagina were not surgically removed. All procedures were done under general anesthesia and involved many risks. In spite of various claims for surgical success, few, if any, surgeons can construct a phallus that is aesthetically and functionally acceptable. Some of the post-operative complaints of the patients have included: considerable scarring of their abdominal area; a penis which was too small; an inability to urinate through the new penis; a dysfunctional penis which could only become erect by insertion of a rod; the need for the creation of a scrotum to give a full male appearance. Recently, surgeons have adopted a technique for use with female transsexuals that is also used with impotent men. A reservoir of fluid is implanted in their lower abdomen, and they can make the neo-phallus erect by manipulating fluid into it.

All of the techniques are experimental and fraught with difficulties.

After SRS some patients experienced serious problems, including fistulae, urinary tract infections, and incontinence. In some cases where a surgeon had attempted to connect the urethra to the new penis (to allow the patient to urinate through the new organ), the results were disastrous; some cases included a complete lack of bladder control. In one case I observed a female transsexual's newly constructed penis fall off, causing the patient to become extremely anxious. The new penis had to be totally reconstructed. Another patient had to have part of her penis reconstructed after some of the tissue from a graft did not take. Both patients developed massive castration anxiety.

In order to maintain an erection for sexual intercourse a stiff rod may be placed in the penis. In some of the early surgeries a piece of the patient's rib was used (conjuring up some interesting Biblical images of Eve). The new penile skin (taken from the abdomen) is generally less sensitive than the skin of a male's penis. However, the patient's clitoris is usually left intact, and the pressure of the rod on the clitoris provides the woman with sexual stimulation.

Availability of phalloplasty techniques
While urologists, plastic surgeons, and physicians who practice general surgery may perform phalloplasty, it is a highly specialized surgical technique which is still quite primitive and experimental. Most of the surgeons who perform this surgery claim that only their surgical techniques guarantee an adequate result.

Recently, I received a letter from a well-regarded transsexual surgeon who specializes in female-to-male surgery. He was advertising a new service in which phalloplasty was provided on an outpatient basis with follow-up "hospitalization" at a local hotel, necessitated because of religious-community pressure which had forced his practice out of the hospital. I was reminded of Stoller's comment on the "circus atmosphere" that can surround transsexual surgery.

Psychological follow-up at CWRU: post-SRS
In a study of six females who underwent SRS at our clinic, it was concluded that the results were less than satisfactory (even if the patient insisted on being relieved at having obtained the surgery). Some of the reactions to SRS included: fears that the female transsexual could not satisfy her partner, that the penis would fall off, and that lovers might

react unfavorably to the patient's new penis. Additionally, the patients experienced gender insecurity related to: gross physical scarring; an unaesthetic neo-phallus; the retention of the clitoris (which still organized their orgastic response); short stature; an inability to attain erectile and ejaculatory capability; lack of sensitivity of their nipples (and a poor appearance); and an inability to procreate. While SRS had resolved some issues, the genital surgery had resulted in further gender insecurity and conflict. In some cases SRS had abrogated a patient's rigid defensive structures. This process seemed to facilitate the emergence of psychological material which had previously been withheld, thereby preparing the patients for entering psychotherapy.

In summary, it appeared that while SRS may be the treatment of choice for a small number of female transsexuals, there are no universally acceptable criteria for determining which women should be referred for SRS. Until such criteria are established, each clinician will be dependent on his/her own judgment for recommending a female transsexual for SRS. At the present time SRS is still an experimental procedure. Moreover, the surgical techniques for phalloplasty are still rather primitive, and the patient is at the mercy of the surgeon's skills. It is clear that, whether or not SRS is indicated, the initial treatment of choice for female transsexuals should be intensive, long-term psychotherapy. While it is also clear that psychotherapy and not SRS should be viewed as the primary treatment of choice for the female transsexual, there will always be a small number of female transsexuals who will receive SRS. For those patients who receive SRS, it should never be a matter of either surgery or psychotherapy. Indeed, all surgical patients should not only be advised of the possible emotional risks post-SRS, but they should be routinely referred for some form of psychological intervention or psychotherapy.

Chapter 8
Overview and future prospects

As we have seen, female transsexualism is a universal phenomenon, "un mal ancien" which has historical, cultural, literary, and mythological roots. Over the last century, however, female transsexualism has also been transformed from a purely cultural phenomenon into a medical-surgical entity, as women who reportedly experience a profound psychological disturbance in their gender identities and roles are now being treated surgically rather than culturally or psychologically. However, along with the advances in the surgical technology of sex reassignment surgery (specifically phalloplasty), we have also witnessed an increase in the gap in our understanding of the etiology of female transsexualism. In response to that problem I hoped that, by addressing the dilemmas of the female transsexual from a non-surgical standpoint, through detailed case histories and data from intensive long-term psychotherapy, we could gain a better understanding of the etiology of the disorder.

Our data suggest that the non-biological aspects of female transsexualism evolve within the family matrix and can be explained by an appeal to family dynamics. The female transsexual is born into a family rampant with gender pathology; a family, however, in which the female transsexual may be the first family member to become symptomatic and be designated as a transsexual patient. Typically, the transsexual-prone family's gender pathology is not expressed solely in terms of transsexualism or transvestism (or obvious gender confusion) but in terms of severe, violent, and chaotic acting out behaviors by one or more family members. The designated female family member who becomes transsexual evolves her gender pathology through a complex family communication process in which her parents constantly express their displeasure at her emerging primary femininity, and hatred of anything female. Throughout their daughter's preoedipal period they consistently assault and thwart the development of her *primary femininity* and *core female gender identity*. The parents are also seen as overstimulating their daughter during her *early genital phase*. As a result of being raised in a chaotic family milieu, the female transsexual is also viewed as unable to evolve stable ego mechanisms and functions. In addition to her gender identity pathology, she also evidences profound developmental arrests; abandonment depressions; impaired ego functioning; non-specific ego weaknesses; primitive and pathological defense systems; and typically borderline and narcissistic personality disturbances. While the majority of the women are not overtly psychotic, they all evidence (on psychological testing and intensive interviewing) defects in reality sense and symbol formation and exhibit subtle thought disturbances.

What distinguishes the borderline aspect of their pathology from that of non-transsexual women, is the focus of their pathology on gender identity and role issues. That focus is viewed as the outcome of a consistent, but typically unconscious strategy of their parents to thwart their developing femininity. Consequently, those women are unable to develop an ego mechanism regulating gender-self constancy and evidence a profound impairment in their gender-self representation. Rather than evolving a core female gender identity they evolve gender diffusion and confusion, focusing their feelings of self-hatred on their developing female body image and ego — experiencing intense hatred of their female genitals and disgust at anything related to their femaleness. In order to prevent their gender-self system from dissolution (and to ward off an intense suicidal depression), these women split off their perceived "all bad" female self-image and posit an "all good" male self-image which is highly idealized and omnipotently conceived. Consequently, these women experience an oscillation between their "all good" male images and their "all bad" female images which prevents them from evolving an integrated gender-self system (that is, one in which male and female elements are fused). Employing primitive defenses (denial, splitting, omnipotence, devaluation, and projective identification), these women attempt to integrate their fragmented self-systems and to preserve their existence by rationalizing that they are "males trapped in female bodies" and by postulating an "all good" male self-system which provides them with a goal for hope, self-esteem, and personal survival.

While all female transsexuals experience a need for wholeness and integrity (for which SRS serves as their life goal), each transsexual woman has a different character structure, unique family history, and different psychogenetic precursor of her disorder. What these women share are not similar personalities, but similar underlying structural ego weaknesses and defects. It is the structural, rather than functional, differences in their ego functioning and self-systems that characterize their disorder. These women are also hypothesized to have experienced an adequate environment during the first year-and-a-half of life which "innoculated" them against a severe disorder like schizophrenia. However, at some time during the rapprochement period of separation-individuation (around age 2) it is hypothesized that their mothers were unable to link empathically with their daughters or to provide them with the kind of responsiveness which would have enabled them to develop a separate and cohesive female self-system.

While my understanding of the phenomenon of female transsexualism has undergone a number of revisions (as new clinical data forced me to alter a previously held belief), I believe that my current theory of the structural problems underlying female transsexualism will stand the test of future empirical investigations and, rather than being radically changed, will be enhanced by new clinical findings. The following clinical example is pertinent. Recently a colleague sent me a detailed case history of a 17-year-old white female who expressed a wish to become a male ballet dancer and then to have "homosexual" relationships with other men. This is the first reported case of a female transsexual with distorted, but clearly heterosexual interests who viewed herself as a "male homosexual."

The clinical material suggested that the young woman had had a life-long gender conflict which was exacerbated as she entered adolescence. Indeed, the patient recalled that her first wishes for SRS occurred after she had gotten hold "of some homosexual erotic literature that described sex among males." She recalled that she "got genitally wet and was disgusted with her genital wetness." She reportedly "view[ed] her genitals with derision and [felt] as though they [were] carved out with a knife or saber . . . [that] she [was] gashed or wounded . . . she hate[d] their functions, she hate[d] their odor, she hate[d] the wetness especially in response to sexual excitement." Her solution was to become a man and to be penetrated by other men anally. Her evaluator described her as having empathic powers whereby "a person who . . . is with one person . . . becomes that person and then switches around and identifies with another person." On psychological testing she revealed a severe ego boundary disturbance; evidenced intense sexual preoccupation (and on the Rorschach reported many disembodied percepts of genitalia); viewed people as either damaged or menacing; engaged in magical thinking; revealed a pattern of sexual excitement which served as a kind of pseudo-integration of her fragmented and objectless world; evidenced defective gender-self images; and employed primitive defenses. Like the majority of her female transsexual counterparts, the patient was viewed as having a borderline personality. In other words, although she presented clinically with an entirely new dimension (that is, her perception of herself as a "male homosexual"), the underlying structural issues were still the same as those of other female transsexuals.

As I have argued, the treatment of choice for female transsexualism is intensive, long-term psychotherapy. The female transsexual's underlying structural ego deficits cannot be treated by SRS. Clearly, it will take a long time for this new knowledge to filter down to the average clinician treating female transsexuals. During that time more and more women will probably receive SRS and attempt to integrate themselves into society. Moreover, for a small select group of patients SRS will probably always be provided as the "treatment of choice." However, it is not known *a priori* which female transsexuals can benefit from SRS. As long as some women continue to identify as transsexuals, there will always be a number of them who wish to make the complete transition to maleness (thereby making the transition back to femaleness all but impossible). What this means is that mental health professionals must look beyond the female transsexual's clinical pathology and either support legislation to change the laws governing SRS, or help the transsexual make the appropriate adjustment in society.

In response to the female transsexual's plight in society Waltz summarizes the legal notion that the law should "defer to the medical profession in this area" and "give its support and protection to the transsexual, especially after medicine has helped in the only way that it knows — by giving a sex change operation" (1979, p. 214). While I have argued that SRS is not the *only* way to treat female transsexuals, I share Waltz's concern that as long as our society continues to permit SRS to be performed it should also allow the surgically revised person to assume a normal role in society. Clearly, this is a biosocial issue which needs to be addressed. As long as it is legal for surgeons to perform SRS it ought to be the obligation of the law to provide a mechanism by means of which the transsexual is provided support and protection, in order that the female transsexual can become productive in society and live and work without fear of legal harassment. Clearly, the law must also acknowledge that surgery is not the *only* recognized and effective treatment modality for female transsexualism.

Indeed, SRS has created a number of legal, social, family, community, religious, ethical, and bioethical dilemmas which cannot be addressed and answered solely by the medical surgical community. Even if SRS were outlawed, the female transsexual would still "exist" and pose important bioethical problems for herself and society.

Our clinical data suggest that female transsexualism is primarily a psychological disorder of the self-system which should first be treated by psychological methods. However, as long as insurance companies will pay for SRS but not for psychotherapy; as long as psychotherapists abjure responsibility to the surgeon and back off from learning the new techniques with which to treat transsexuals psychotherapeutically; as long as transsexual self-interest groups are allowed to lobby effectively for surgery (on the basis of their being recognized as a sexually discriminated against minority); as long as society remains mesmerized by the "romantic" aspects of sex change without addressing the important, underlying psychological problems of the transsexual; then the female transsexual issue will remain what it has been in the past, a mere curiosity item to be indulged in for its voyeuristic-exhibitionistic interest and excitement and, while dealt with sensationally in the media, ignored as a legitimate psychological disorder which needs to be treated.

Our clinical data also suggest that when girl children present with gender identity and role pathology the pediatrician or attending physician should not tell the parents in cavalier fashion that their daughter will outgrow it. In effect, they are collaborating with the parents in an unconscious effort to destroy the girl's emerging femininity and core female gender identity. All childhood gender identity disorders should be responded to with a sense of seriousness and urgency and a realization that something important is going wrong with the child's development. As in all fields of mental health, the best prevention is primary prevention. Families at risk for raising daughters with gender pathology should be identified and provided appropriate psychological interventions. No matter how entrenched the child's cross-gender identity and role, every effort should be made to treat the problem psychologically, identifying the current stressors (and removing them) and prescribing long-term intensive psychotherapy. To view female transsexualism as an alternative life style is not only a logical error but has serious clinical consequences for the woman who may be asking for psychological help, only to be supported in her acting out behavior.

At the beginning of this book I addressed the question of the legitimacy of prioritizing female transsexualism as an important field of inquiry for mental health professionals. I hope to have persuaded the reader that rather than being an exotic subspecialty, the study of female transsexualism involves us in all aspects of female psychology, embracing character formation and synthesis, the development of the self and ego, and the evolution of normal and abnormal female core gender identity. In addition, I have addressed the major myths surrounding female transsexualism and have attempted to demythologize the field so that serious research can take place.

Although it is tempting to engage in metapsychological inquiry, we must never lose sight of the person involved. At the outset I reprinted a letter from a patient (Barbara) who had earnestly sought out help for her gender identity problems, only to be treated as a "freak" and avoided both socially and psychologically. Hopefully, this book will enable the clinician and non-clinician alike to relate empathically to the seriousness of the female transsexual's dilemma and to respond to her plight, both by addressing her underlying psychological problems and, when SRS is called for, by assisting in her integration into society. It is also my hope that the historical, clinical, and theoretical presentations in this book will have aided in our understanding of female transsexualism and will generate a renewed interest in studying this phenomenon, thereby furthering our knowledge of how female gender identity and roles are formed and malformed and providing us with a basis for exploring some of the broader issues of self-development in female psychology.

Appendix: prevalence and sex ratio of female transsexualism

If the media announcement of Christine Jorgenson's sex reassignment surgery in Denmark (1953) was not enough, with what Stoller (1968) has called the "carnival like atmosphere" which pervades the aura of such an event, Hamburger (1953) further shocked the world by reporting that he had received 465 letters of inquiry regarding SRS. Of these letters, 108 or 23 per cent were from women who wanted to be transformed into men. These letters provided the first indication that there were large numbers of gender-dysphoric women who desired the costly, and often painful, SRS procedures. Moreover, Lukianowicz's view (1959) that "transsexualism" was solely a male disorder was disproved.

On the basis of Hamburger's findings it appeared that the transsexual male-to-female ratio was 4.3:1. It was, however, his opinion that these letters represented just the tip of an enormous iceberg.

Over the past three decades a number of studies have either focused on transsexualism or provided data concerning the prevalence, incidence, and sex ratio (male:female) of transsexualism. The majority of these studies have come from Sweden, because the Swedish government maintains precise data banks on the social life and health of each patient. In order to make sense out of the prevalence, incidence, and sex ratio data it is necessary to review the findings in chronological order. This will not only provide the reader with a sense of how transsexualism manifests itself socio-culturally, but will also provide a framework for examining some basic assumptions about transsexuals.

Benjamin (1964) reported that the male-to-female ratio of transsexualism was approximately 8:1. By 1966 this figure had not changed at all — in spite of the fact that Benjamin was clinically evaluating and "seeing" at least as many transsexuals as anyone else in America. He reported that he had personally evaluated over 700 patients. One researcher, Wollman (1973), has reported data on his case load of 1000 transsexuals.

Pauly (1969) reported the sex ratio of males to females as varying from Benjamin's reported finding of 8:1, to Randell's report in 1959 of 2:1. In an earlier study Pauly (1963) had reported the ratio to be about 3.7:1. Pauly also noted in his 1969 review of female transsexualism that there was considerable difference of opinion regarding the male:female ratio. He attributed the discrepancies to the fact that almost all the transsexual researchers were male and proposed that they might have been subtly discouraging females from applying to their clinics, not merely as a consequence of the primitiveness of the female-to-male surgery techniques.

During the 1960s some preliminary data on the prevalence of trans-sexualism was published. In Sweden, Wålinder (1967, 1971) reported that for males it was 1/37,000 and for females 1/103,000 (with the sex ratio being 2.8:1). Pauly noted that in the United States the figures were 1/100,000 for males and about 1/400,000 for females. The incidence of male/female transsexualism was also supported by Christodorescu (1971). If we suppose that at that time the US population was about 180 million people (divided about equally between men and women), this would mean that there would have been about 900 male transsexuals and 225 female transsexuals. From what we know about the phenomenon today, these figures are far too conservative.

In the early 1970s Benjamin and Ihlenfeld (1970) reported a change in the sex ratio of male transsexuals to female transsexuals, with the new ratio being 2:1. They estimated that there were at least 10,000 transsexuals in the US. It is interesting to note that four years later Ihlenfeld reported the male to female sex ratio to be 4:1 (1972). In 1973, while Stoller seemed alarmed by the fact that the transsexual phenomenon was rapidly proliferating and that "by now thousands of males have been sexually transformed," he made no mention of a parallel increase in female patients seeking or obtaining SRS. Shave (1976) reported that during the first $2\frac{1}{2}$ years the Johns Hopkins University Gender Clinic received 1500 requests for SRS. He reported that the prevalence of male transsexualism was similar to that found in Sweden: males, 1/34,000, females 1/108,000 (or about 1,000 female transsexuals).

Recent studies comparing the sex ratio and incidence data on trans-sexualism for the populations of Sweden (Wålinder, 1967); England and Wales (Hoenig and Kenna, 1974); and Australia (Ross et al., 1981) suggested that the male to female ratios for those countries were 2.8:1, 3.2:1, and 6.1:1 respectively. The annual sex ratios per 100,000 people over the age of 15 in those countries were reported to be 1:1, 1:1, and 5:1 respectively. In 1981 the first *Standards of Care* were drafted by the Harry Benjamin Gender Dysphoria Association. It was reported that there were between 3000 to 6000 adults who had been hormonally and surgically revised and between 30,000 to 60,000 persons worldwide who wished to have SRS. In a review article on patients who had received SRS (as documented from the literature), I reported that at least 189 women are known to have received some form of surgical revision of their sex (Lothstein, 1982). It is fair to say that this represents a conservative figure, since only those patients who are less impulsive, less anxious, and less urgent about SRS register at the approximately forty clinics that are set up to diagnose and treat transsexualism. Moreover, as surgeons are becoming more skilled in phalloplasty, one can expect increasing numbers of women to apply for sexual transformation procedures. Over the past two years at the CWRU clinic we have noticed a dramatic change in our intake, with women accounting for approximately half of the sex change applicants (a ratio of 1:1). In addition, there have been certain periods when female applicants have outnumbered the male applicants.

How are we to evaluate the incidence, prevalence, and sex ratio data on female transsexualism? Not only do researchers in different countries disagree, but there is also disagreement among researchers working together in the same clinic. Some of the confusion and disagreement may stem from the fact that gender clinics tend to have their own unique identities (often depending for their existence on the availability of a surgeon). For the most part, these clinics receive little, if any, hospital or community support and little, if any, private funding for research. Richard Green et al. (1966) has also documented the fact that transsexuals are viewed negatively by the medical profession, and many female transsexuals may avoid reputable gender programs in hospitals for fear of being stigmatized. Indeed, most transsexuals do not go to a gender identity clinic to obtain surgery. Rather, they go directly to a surgeon, where few questions are asked, a lot of money changes hands, and no statistics are kept. In sum, there are no currently available reliable data concerning the prevalence, incidence, and sex ratio of female transsexualism. Even *DSM* III, which included transsexualism as a disorder, listed it as a rare disorder (with the male:female ratio hypothesized to be between 8:1 and 2:1). The problem with analysing the data by sex ratios is poignantly depicted by non other than a transsexual herself — Nancy Hunt (1978). In her autobiography Ms. Hunt notes that of her graduating class of 1500 at Yale three were transsexuals. Hunt argues that "that's a ratio of 1 in 500, which I shamelessly apply to the national population," and she comes up with the figure of 350,000 males and 80,000 females. While Hunt's reasoning may be taken to task, the irony is that given the methodological problems involved in such research, her formulation is as good as any other available in the field.

No matter how much hair-splitting takes place about the incidence and prevalence of female transsexualism, three conclusions can be drawn: there is widespread social and clinical interest in the phenomenon of female transsexualism; the male-female sex ratios are approaching 1:1; and more and more women are applying to sex clinics for SRS. Whatever the reasons, female transsexualism is a growing phenomenon which needs to be taken more seriously. The equalizing of the sex ratio statistics alerts us to the fact that women are viewing sex change as a viable option.

The medical establishment, willing as it is to support women in their quest for surgery, must also be prepared to support more basic research into the phenomenon itself. In addition, society must begin to seriously examine female gender and sexual problems, and, more specifically, those of female transsexualism. As more and more women change their gender identities and roles, and attempt to integrate into their communities, the very nature of our social-political existence will be affected, for the complex social, ethical, and political implications of female sex change will have a dramatic effect on everyone.

Bibliography

Abraham, F. (1931), "Genitalumwandlung an zwei männlichen Transvestiten," *Zeitschrift für Sexualwissenschaft*, 18, pp. 223–6.

Abraham, K. (1927), "Manifestations of the female castration complex,"
in K. Abraham, *Selected Papers on Psychoanalysis*, Basic Books,
New York.

Agras, S. (1973), "Case study on the behavioral treatment of a transsexual," abstract, *Second Interdisciplinary Symposium on Gender
Dysphoria Syndrome*, Stanford University Press, Palo Alto, Calif.

Althof, S. (1980), "Name change: its significance among patients with
gender dysphoria," *Bulletin of the Menninger Clinic*, 44, pp. 617–27.

Althof, S. and Keller, A. (1980), "Group therapy with gender identity
patients," *International Journal of Group Psychotherapy*, 30,
pp. 481–9.

American Heritage Dictionary (1979), Houghton Mifflin, Boston, Mass.

American Medical Association (1972), *Human Sexuality*, AMA, Chicago,
Ill.

American Psychiatric Association (1952), *Diagnostic And Statistical
Manual Of Mental Disorders (DSM)* I, Washington, D.C.

American Psychiatric Association (1968), *Diagnostic And Statistical
Manual of Mental Disorders (DSM) II*, Washington, D.C.

American Psychiatric Association (1980), *Diagnostic And Statistical
Manual of Mental Disorders (DSM) III*, Washington D.C.

Bak, R. and Stuart, W. (1974), "Fetishism, transvestism, and voyeurism:
A psychoanalytic approach," in S. Arieti and E. Brady (eds), *American
Handbook of Psychiatry*, vol. 2, 2nd edn, Basic Books, New York.

Baker, H. and Green, R. (1970), "Treatment of transsexualism," in J.
Masserman (ed.), *Current Psychiatric Therapies*, vol. 10, Grune &
Stratton, New York, pp. 88–99.

Baker, H. and Stoller, R. (1968), "Can a biological force contribute to
gender identity?," *American Journal of Psychiatry*, 124, pp. 1653–8.

312

Barahal, H. (1953), "Female transvestism and homosexuality," *Psychiatric Quarterly*, 27, pp. 390–438.

Barker, M. (1968), "Psychiatric illness after hysterectomy," *British Medical Journal*, 2, pp. 91–5.

Barlow, D., Reynolds, E., and Agras, S. (1973), "Gender identity change in a transsexual," *Archives of General Psychiatry*, 28, pp. 569–76.

Bates, J., Skilbeck, W., Smith, K., and Bentler, P. (1975), "Interventions with families of gender disturbed boys," *American Journal of Orthopsychiatry*, 45, pp. 150–7.

Bell, A., Weinberg, M., and Hammersmith, S. (1981), *Sexual Preferences*, Indiana University Press, Bloomington.

Benjamin, H. (1964), "Clinical aspects of transsexualism in males and females," *American Journal of Psychotherapy*, 11, pp. 458–69.

Benjamin, H. (1966), *The Transsexual Phenomenon*, Julian Press, New York.

Benjamin, H. (1969), "Appendix for the practicing physician: suggestions and guidelines for the management of transsexuals," in R. Green and J. Money (eds), *Transsexualism and Sex Reassignment*, Johns Hopkins University Press, Baltimore, Md.

Benjamin, H. and Ihlenfeld, C. (1970), "The nature and treatment of transsexualism," *Medical Opinion and Review*, 6, no. 11.

Berlin, F. and Meinecke, C. (1981), "Treatment of sex offenders with antiandrogenic medication: conceptualization, review of treatment modalities, and preliminary findings," *American Journal of Psychiatry*, 138, pp. 601–7.

Bernstein, S., Steiner, B., Glaister, J., and Muir, C. (1981), "Changes in patients with gender-identity problems after parental death," *American Journal of Psychiatry*, 138, pp. 41–5.

Billowitz, A. (1981), "Hormone therapy in gender identity disorders," in I. Pauly (ed.), *Abstracts and Proceedings of the 7th International Gender Dysphoria Association*, Lake Tahoe, Nevada.

Bleuler, M. and Wiesemann, H. (1956), "Chromosomengeschlecht und Psychosexualität," *Archives of Psychiatry*, 195, pp. 14–19.

Bloch, D. (1975), "The threat of infanticide and homosexual identity," *Psychoanalytical Review*, 62, pp. 579–97.

Blumer, D. (1969), "Transsexualism; sexual dysfunction and temporal lobe disorders," in R. Green and J. Money (eds), *Transsexualism And Sex Reassignment*, Johns Hopkins University Press, Baltimore, Md.

Bogden, R. (1974), *Being Different: The Autobiography of Jane Fry*, Wiley-Interscience, New York.

Bogoras, N. (1936), "Über die volle plastische Wiederherstellung eines zum Koitus fähigen Penis (Penisplastica totalis)," *Zentralblatt für Chirurgie*, 63, pp. 1271–6.

Bibliography

Boswell, J. (1980), *Christianity, Social Tolerance and Homosexuality*, University of Chicago Press, Ill.

Brady, J. and Brody, H. (eds), (1978), *Controversy In Psychiatry*, Saunders, Philadelphia, Pa.

Breger, L. (1981), *Freud's Unfinished Journey*, Routledge & Kegan Paul, London.

Brierley, H. (1979), *Transvestism: A Handbook With Case Studies for Psychologists, Psychiatrists, and Counselors*, Pergamon Press, New York.

Brod, T. (1981), "The psychotherapeutic evaluation of 'transsexuals': clinical quandaries posed by recognizing self-deficiencies," in I. Pauly (ed.), *Abstracts and Proceedings of the 7th International Gender Dysphoria Association*, Lake Tahoe, Nevada.

Brown, D. (1964), "Transvestism and sex role inversion," in A. Ellis and A. Arbarbanel (eds), *Encyclopedia Of Sexual Behavior*, Hawthorn, New York.

Brown, M. and Sadoughi, W. (1979), "The degree and intensity of mothering as related to the occurrence of male transsexualism." Unpublished manuscript presented at the International Gender Dysphoria Symposium, Norfolk, Va.

Buck, T. (1977), "Familial factors influencing female transsexualism," master's thesis, Smith College School for Social Work, Northhampton, Mass.

Bullough, V. (1975), "Transsexualism in History," *Archives of Sexual Behavior*, 4, pp. 561-71.

Bullough, V. (1976), *Sexual Variance in Society and History*, University of Chicago Press, Ill.

Cath, S., Gurwitt, A., and Ross, J. M. (eds) (1982), *Father and Child: Developmental and Clinical Perspectives*, Little, Brown, Boston, Mass.

Cauldwell, D. (1949), "Psychopathia transsexualis," *Sexology*, 16, pp. 274-80.

Childs, A. (1977), "Acute symbiotic psychosis in a post-operative transsexual," *Archives of Sexual Behavior*, 6, pp. 37-44.

Christian v. Christian (1973), Docket no. 32964, First Judicial Court, Nevada.

Christodorescu, D. (1971), "Female transsexualism," *Psychiatry Quarterly*, 4, pp. 40-5.

Davenport, C. and Harrison, S. (1977), "Gender identity change in a female adolescent transsexual," *Archives of Sexual Behavior*, 6, pp. 327-40.

Davies, B. and Morgenstern, F. (1960), "A case of cysticercosis, temporal lobe epilepsy and transvestism," *Journal of Neurology, Neurosurgery and Psychiatry*, 23, pp. 247–9.

Derogatis, L., Meyer, J., and Boland, P. (1981), "A psychological profile of the transsexual," *Journal of Nervous and Mental Disease*, 169, pp. 157–68.

De Savitsch, E. (1958), *Homosexuality, Transvestism, and Change of Sex*, Charles C. Thomas, Springfield, Ill.

Deutsch, H. (1944), *The Psychology of Women*, Grune & Stratton, New York.

Dixen J. (1981), "Characteristics of 767 applicants evaluated by the gender dysphoria program, Palo Alto, California," in I. Pauly (ed.), *Abstracts and Proceedings of the 7th International Gender Dysphoria Association*, Lake Tahoe, Nevada.

Eber, M. (1980), "Gender identity conflicts in male transsexualism," *Bulletin of the Menninger Clinic*, 44, pp. 31–8.

Eber, M., (1982), "Primary transsexualism: a critique of a theory," *Bulletin of the Menninger Clinic*, 46, pp. 168–82.

Ehrhardt, A., Grisanti, G., and McCauley, E. (1979), "Female-to-male transsexuals compared to lesbians: behavioral patterns of childhood and adolescent development," *Archives of Sexual Behavior*, 8, pp. 481–90.

Ehrhardt, A. and Meyer-Bahlburg, H. (1981), "Effects of prenatal sex hormones on gender related behavior," *Science*, 211, pp. 1312–17.

Eicher, W. (1981), "Transsexualism and H-Y antigen," in I. Pauly (ed.), *Abstracts and Proceedings of the 7th International Gender Dysphoria Association*, Lake Tahoe, Nevada.

Eicher, W., Spoljar, M., Cleve, H., Murken, J., Richter, K., and Stangel-Rutkowski, S. (1979), "H-Y antigen in trans-sexuality." Letter, *Lancet*, II, no. 8152, 24th Nov., pp. 1137–8.

Eichwald, E. and Silmser, C. (1955), "Skin," *Transplantation Bulletin*, 2, pp. 148–9.

Ellis, H. (1936), "Eonism," in H. Ellis (ed.), *Studies in the Psychology of Sex*, vol. 2, Random House, New York.

Epstein, A. (1961), "Relationship of fetishism and transvestism to brain and particularly temporal lobe dysfunction," *Journal of Nervous and Mental Disease*, 133, pp. 247–53.

Erikson, E. (1968), *Identity: Youth and Crisis*, Norton, New York.

Fairbairn, W. R. (1952), *Psychoanalytic Studies of the Personality*, Routledge & Kegan Paul, London.

Fast, I. (1978), "Developments in gender identity: the original matrix," *International Review of Psycho-Analysis*, 5, pp. 265–73.

Fast, I. (1979), "Developments in gender identity: gender differentiation in girls," *International Journal of Psycho-Analysis*, 60, pp. 443–53.

315

Feinbloom, D. (1976), *Transvestites and Transsexuals: Mixed Views*, Delacorte Press, New York.

Fenichel, O. (1953), *Collected Papers I*, Norton, New York.

Fielding, H. (1960), *Female Husband*, Liverpool University Press, England.

Fingarette, H. (1963), *The Self In Transformation*, Harper Torchbooks, New York.

Finkelstein, M. (1974), "The imposter: aspects of his development," *Psychoanalysis*, 43, pp. 85–114.

Fisk, N. (1973), "Gender dysphoria syndrome," in D. Laub and P. Gandy (eds), *Proceedings of the Second Interdisciplinary Symposium on Gender Dysphoria Syndrome*, Stanford University Press, Palo Alto, Calif.

Fisk, N. (1978), "Five spectacular results," *Archives of Sexual Behavior*, 7, pp. 351–69.

Fleming, M., Jenkins, S., and Bugarin, C. (1980), "Questioning current definitions of gender identity: implications of the Bem sex-role inventory for transsexuals," *Archives of Sexual Behavior*, 9, pp. 13–26.

Fleming, M., Koocher, G., and Nathans, J. (1979), "Draw-a-person test: implications for gender identification," *Archives of Sexual Behavior*, 8, pp. 55–61.

Fleming, M. and Nathans, J. (1979), "The use of art in understanding the central treatment issues in a female to male transsexual," *Art Psychotherapy* (Oxford), 6, pp. 25–35.

Fleming, M. and Ruck, C. (1979), "A mythic search for identity in a female to male transsexual," *Journal of Analytical Psychology*, 24, pp. 298–313.

Fliegel, Z. (1973), "Feminine psychosexual development in Freudian theory: a historical reconstruction," *Psychoanalytical Quarterly*, 42, pp. 385–408.

Forester, B. and Swiller, H. (1972), "Transsexualism: review of syndrome and presentation of possible successful therapeutic approach," *International Journal of Group Psychotherapy*, 22, pp. 343–51.

Frances, A. and Dunn, P. (1975), "The attachment-autonomy conflict in agoraphobia," *International Journal of Psycho-Analysis*, 56, pp. 435–9.

Frances, A., Sacks, M., and Aronoff, M. (1977), "Depersonalization: a self-relations perspective," *International Journal of Psycho-Analysis*, 58, pp. 325–31.

Frances, B. v. Mark, B. (1974), vol. 78, New York Misc. Reports, 2nd series, p. 112; vol. 355, New York Supplement, 2nd series; vol. 712, Supreme Court.

Freud, S. (1911), "Psychoanalytical notes on an autobiographical account of a case of paranoia (dementia paranoides)," *Standard Edition*, vol. 12, pp. 3-82, Hogarth Press, London, 1958.

Freud, S. (1925), "Some psychical consequences of the anatomical distinction between the sexes," *Standard Edition*, vol. 19, pp. 248-58, Hogarth Press, London, 1961.

Freud, S. (1931), "Female sexuality," *Standard Edition*, vol. 21, pp. 233-43, Hogarth Press, London, 1961.

Freud, S. (1933), "Femininity," *Standard Edition*, vol. 22, pp. 112-35, Hogarth Press, London, 1961.

Friedreich, J. (1830), *Versuch Einer Literargeschichte Der Pathologie Und Therapie Der Psychischten Krankheiten*, Würzburg.

Gagné, P. (1981), "Treatment of sex offenders with medroxyprogesterone acetate," *American Journal of Psychiatry*, 138, pp. 644-6.

Galenson, E., Vogel, R., Blau, S., and Roiphe, H. (1973), "Disturbance in sexual identity beginning at eighteen months of age," *Journal of the Philadelphia Association of Psychoanalysis*, February 26.

Garfinkel, H. (1967), *Studies in Ethnomethodology*, Prentice-Hall, New Jersey.

Gediman, H. (1980), "The search for the self. Selected writings of Heinz Kohut." Book review in *The Psychoanalytic Review*, 67, pp. 505-14.

Gelb, J., Malament, M., and LoVerme, S. (1959), "Total reconstruction of the penis," *Plastic and Reconstructive Surgery*, 24, pp. 62-73.

Gelder, M. and Marks, I. (1969), "Aversion treatment in transvestism and trans-sexualism," in R. Green and J. Money (eds), *Transsexualism And Sex Reassignment*, Johns Hopkins University Press, Baltimore, Md.

Gershman, H. (1970), "The role of core gender identity in the genesis of perversions," *American Journal of Psychoanalysis*, 30, pp. 58-67.

Giovacchini, P. (1972), "The blank self," in P. Giovacchini (ed.), *Tactics and Techniques in Psychoanalytic Therapy*, Science House, New York.

Giovacchini, P. (1975), *Psychoanalysis of Character Disorders*, Jason Aronson, New York.

Gittelson, N. and Dawson-Butterworth, K. (1967), "Subjective ideas of sexual change in female schizophrenics," *British Journal of Psychiatry*, 113, pp. 491-4.

Gordon, J. and Ruddle, F. (1981), "Mammalian gonadal determination and gametogenesis," *Science*, 211, pp. 1265-71.

Green, R. (1967), "Sissies and tomboys: a guide to diagnosis and management," in C. Wahl (ed.), *Sexual Problems: Diagnosis and Treatment In Medical Practice*, Free Press, New York.

317

Green, R. (1969), "Mythological, historical, and cross-cultural aspects of transsexualism," in R. Green and J. Money (eds), *Transsexualism and Sex Reassignment,* John Hopkins University Press, Baltimore, Md.

Green, R. (1974), *Sexual Identity Conflicts in Children And Adults,* Basic Books, New York.

Green, R. (1978), "Sexual identity of 37 children raised by homosexual or transsexual parents," *American Journal of Psychiatry,* 135, pp. 692–7.

Green, R. and Fuller, M. (1973), "Group therapy with feminine boys and their parents," *International Journal of Group Psychotherapy,* 23, pp. 54–68.

Green, R. and Money, J. (eds) (1969), *Transsexualism and Sex Reassignment,* Johns Hopkins University Press, Baltimore, Md.

Green, R., Newman, L., and Stoller, R. (1972), "Treatment of boyhood 'transsexualism': an interim report of four years' experience," *Archives of General Psychiatry,* 26, pp. 213–17.

Green, R., Stoller, R., and MacAndrew, C. (1966), "Attitudes towards sex transformation procedures," *Archives of General Psychiatry,* 15, pp. 178–82.

Greenson, R. (1966), "A transvestite boy and a hypothesis," *International Journal of Psycho-Analysis,* 47, pp. 396–403.

Gross, A. (1951), "The secret," *Bulletin of the Menninger Clinic,* 15, pp. 37–47.

Grossman, in re (1974), vol. 127, New Jersey Superior Court, p. 13; Atlantic Reporter, 2nd series, vol. 326, p. 39.

Grossman, W. and Stewart, W. (1976), "Penis envy: from childhood wish to developmental metaphor," *Journal of the American Psychoanalytic Association,* 24, pp. 193–212.

Gunderson, J. and Singer, M. (1975), "Defining borderline patients: an overview," *American Journal of Psychiatry,* 132, pp. 1–10.

Guntrip, H. (1964), *Schizoid Phenomena, Object Relations, and The Self,* International Universities Press, New York.

Guze, S. (1980), "H-Y antigen in transsexuality," *Psychiatric Capsule and Commentary,* 2, p. 5.

Hall, Radclyffe (1929), *The Well of Loneliness,* Covici, Friede, New York.

Hamburger, C. (1953), "Desire for change of sex as shown by personal letters from 465 men and women," *Acta Endocrinologica,* 14, pp. 361–75.

Hamburger, C. (1969), "Endocrine treatment of male and female transsexualism," in R. Green and J. Money (eds), *Transsexualism and Sex Reassignment,* Johns Hopkins University Press, Baltimore, Md.

Hampson, J. (1971), cited in J. Kleeman, "The establishment of core gender identity in normal girls, II. How meanings are conveyed between parent and child in the first 3 years," *Archives of Sexual Behavior*, 1, pp. 117–29.

Haseltine, F. and Sumo, S. (1981), "Mechanisms of gonadal differentiation," *Science*, 211, pp. 1272–8.

Hastings, D. (1973), "Experience at the University of Minnesota with transsexual patients," in D. Lamb and P. Gandy (eds), *Proceedings of the Second Interdisciplinary Symposium on Gender Dysphoria Syndrome*, Stanford University Press, Palo Alto, Calif.

Hastings, D. and Blum, J. (1967), "A transsexual research project at the University of Minnesota Medical School," *Journal Lancet*, 87, pp. 262–4.

Herschkowitz, S. and Dickes, R. (1978), "Suicide attempts in female-to-male transsexuals," *American Journal of Psychiatry*, 135, pp. 368–9.

Hertz, J., Tillinger, K., and Westman, A. (1961), "Transvestism, report on five hormonally and surgically treated cases," *Acta Psychiatrica Scandinavica*, 37, pp. 283–4.

Hill, D. (1952), "EEG in episodic psychotic and psychopathic behavior: classification of data," *Electroencephalography and Clinical Neurophysiology* (Amsterdam), 4, pp. 419–42.

Hill, E. (1980), "A comparison of three psychological testings of a transsexual," *Journal of Personality Assessment*, 44, pp. 52–100.

Hirschfeld, M. (1910), *Die Transvestiten: Eine Untersuchung über den Erotischen Verkleidungstrieb*, Alfred Pulvermacher, Berlin. Also abstracted in *Sexual Anomalies*, Emerson Books, New York, 1956.

Hirschfeld, M. (1922), *Sexual Pathologie. Ein Lehrbuch Für Ärtze und Studierende*, Marcus & Weber, Bonn.

Hoenig, J. and Kenna, J. (1974), "The prevalence of transsexualism in England and Wales," *British Journal of Psychiatry*, 124, pp. 181–90.

Hoenig, J. and Kenna, J. (1979), "EEG abnormalities and trans-sexualism," *British Journal of Psychiatry*, 134, pp. 293–300.

Hoenig, J. and Torr, J. (1964), "Karyotyping of transsexualists," *Journal of Psychosomatic Research*, 8, pp. 157–9.

Hollingshead, A. and Redlich, F. (1958), *Social Class and Mental Illness*, Wiley, New York.

Hoopes, J. (1969), "Operative treatment of the female transsexual," in R. Green and J. Money (eds), *Transsexualism and Sex Reassignment*, Johns Hopkins University Press, Baltimore, Md.

Horney, K. (1924), "On the genesis of the castration complex in women," *International Journal of Psycho-Analysis*, 5, pp. 50–65.

Horney, K. (1967), *Feminine Psychology*, Norton, New York.

Hoyer, N. (1933), *Man Into Woman*, Dutton, New York.

Hunt, N. (1978), *Mirror Image*, Holt, Rinehart & Winston, New York.

Hyde, J. (1981), "How large are cognitive gender differences? A meta analysis using w^2 and d," *American Psychologist*, 36, pp. 892–901.

Ihlenfeld, C. (1972), "When a woman becomes a man," *Sexology*, June.

Imperato-McGinley, J., Peterson, R., Gautier, T., and Sturla, E. (1979), "Androgens and the evaluation of male gender identity among male pseudo hermaphrodites with a 5-alpha-reductase deficiency," *New England Journal of Medicine*, 300, pp. 1233–7.

Jacobson, E. (1964), *The Self and the Object World*, International Universities Press, New York.

Johnson, A. and Szurek, S. (1952), "The genesis of antisocial acting out in children and adults," *Psychoanalytical Quarterly*, 21, pp. 323–43.

Jones, E. (1927), "The early development of female sexuality," *International Journal of Psycho-Analysis*, 8, pp. 459–72.

Jones, J. (1973), "Plasma testosterone concentrations in female transsexuals," in D. Laub and P. Gandy (eds), *Proceedings of the Second Interdisciplinary Symposium on Gender Dysphoria Syndrome*, Stanford University Press, Palo Alto, Calif.

Jones, J. and Samimy, J. (1973), "Plasma testosterone levels and female transsexualism," *Archives of Sexual Behavior*, 2, pp. 251–6.

Keller, A., Althof, S., and Lothstein, L. (1982), "Group therapy with gender identity patients: a four year study," *American Journal of Psychotherapy*, 36, pp. 223–8.

Kernberg, O. (1975), *Borderline Conditions and Pathological Narcissism*, Jason Aronson, New York.

Khan, M. (1974), *The Privacy of the Self*, International Universities Press, New York.

Kinsey, A., Pomeroy, W., and Martin, C. (1948), *Sexual Behavior in the Human Male*, Saunders, Philadelphia, Pa.

Kinsey, A., Pomeroy, W., Martin, C., Gebhard, P. et al., (1953), *Sexual Behavior in the Human Female*, Saunders, Philadelphia, Pa.

Kleeman, J. (1971a), "The establishment of core gender identity in normal girls, I. (a) Introduction; (b) Development of the ego capacity to differentiate," *Archives of Sexual Behavior*, 1, pp. 103–15.

Kleeman, J. (1971b), "The establishment of core gender identity in normal girls, II. How meanings are conveyed between parent and child in the first 3 years," *Archives of Sexual Behavior*, 1, pp. 117–29.

Klein, M. (1975), *The Psychoanalysis of Children*, Delta, New York.

Kluver, H. and Bucy, P. (1939), "Preliminary analysis of the functions of the temporal lobes in monkeys," *Archives of Neurology and Psychiatry*, 42, pp. 979–1000.

Kockett, G. and Nusselt, L. (1976), "Zur Frage der cerebralen Dysfunction bei der Transsexualität," *Der Nervenarzt*, 47, pp. 310–18.

Kohlberg, L. (1966), "A note on the interaction of cognitive set, stimulus artifact, and sex-role attitudes in a projective measure of sex-role identity," Unpublished mimeograph, Center for Advanced Studies in Behavioral Sciences, Palo Alto, Calif.

Kohlberg, L. (1971), "A cognitive developmental analysis of children's sex-role concepts and attitudes," in E. E. Maccoby (ed.), *The Development of Sex Differences*, Stanford University Press, Calif.

Kohut, H. (1971), *The Analysis of the Self*, International Universities Press, New York.

Kohut, H. (1977), *The Restoration of the Self*, International Universities Press, New York.

Kohut, H. and Wolf, E. (1978), "The disorders of the self and their treatment: an outline," *International Journal of Psycho-Analysis*, 59, pp. 413–25.

Krafft-Ebing, R. von (1894), *Psychopathia Sexualis*, trans. F. Klaf, Bell, New York.

Kubie, L. (1974), "The drive to become both sexes," *Psychoanalytical Quarterly*, 43, pp. 349–426.

Kubie, L. and Mackie, J. (1968), "Critical issues raised by operations for gender transmutation," *Journal of Nervous and Mental Disease*, 147, pp. 431–444.

Laing, R. (1966), *The Divided Self*, Penguin, Baltimore, Md.

Lampl-de Groot, J. (1965), "Problems of femininity," in J. Lampl-de Groot (ed.), *The Development Of Mind*, International Universities Press, New York.

Laub, D. (1973), "Total management and responsibility for transsexual patients," in D. Laub and P. Gandy (eds), *Proceedings of the Second Interdisciplinary Symposium on Gender Dysphoria Syndrome*, Stanford University Press, Palo Alto, Calif.

Laub, D. and Fisk, N. (1974), "A rehabilitation program for gender dysphoria syndrome by surgical sex change," *Plastic and Reconstructive Surgery*, 53, pp. 388–403.

Leff, D. (1977), "Genes, gender, and genital reversal," *Medical World News*, April 18, pp. 45–59.

Léger, J., Ranty, Y., Blanchinet, J., and Vallat, J. (1969), "Un Cas de transsexualisme féminin," *Annales Medico Psychologiques* (Paris), 1, pp. 164–72.

Levine, F. (1979), "On the clinical application of Heinz Kohut's psychology of the self," *Journal of the Philadelphia Association for Psychoanalysis*, 6, pp. 1–19.

Levine, S. and Lothstein, L. (1981), "Transsexualism or the gender dysphoria syndromes," *Journal of Sex and Marital Therapy*, 7, pp. 85–114.

Lewis, H. B. (1979), "Gender identity: Primary narcissism or primary process?", *Bulletin of the Menninger Clinic*, 43, pp. 145–60.

Liakos, A. (1967), "Familial transvestism," *British Journal of Psychiatry*, 113, pp. 49–51.

Lichtenstein, H. (1961), "Identity and sexuality," *Journal of the American Psychoanalytical Association*, 9, pp. 179–260.

Limentani, A. (1979), "The significance of transsexualism in relation to some basic psychoanalytic concepts," *International Review of Psycho-Analysis*, 6, pp. 139–53.

Litin, E., Giffin, M., and Johnson, A. (1956), "Parental influence in unusual sexual behavior in children," *Psychoanalytic Quarterly*, 25, pp. 37–55.

Lothstein, L. (1977a), "Countertransference reactions to gender dysphoric patients: implications for psychotherapy," *Psychotherapy: Theory, Research and Practice*, 14, pp. 21–31.

Lothstein, L. (1977b), "Psychotherapy with patients with gender dysphoria syndromes," *Bulletin of the Menninger Clinic*, 41, pp. 563–82.

Lothstein, L. (1979a), "Group therapy with gender-dysphoric patients," *American Journal of Psychotherapy*, 33, pp. 67–81.

Lothstein, L. (1979b), "Psychodynamics and sociodynamics of gender-dysphoric states," *American Journal of Psychotherapy*, 33, pp. 214–38.

Lothstein, L. (1979c), "The aging gender dysphoria (transsexual) patient," *Archives of Sexual Behavior*, 8, pp. 431–44.

Lothstein, L. (1980a), "The adolescent gender dysphoric patient: an approach to treatment and management," *Journal of Pediatric Psychology*, 5, pp. 93–109.

Lothstein, L. (1980b), "The postsurgical transsexual: empirical and theoretical considerations," *Archives of Sexual Behavior*, 9, pp. 547–64.

Lothstein, L. (1982), "Sex reassignment surgery: historical, bioethical, and theoretical issues," *American Journal of Psychiatry*, 139, pp. 417–26.

Lothstein, L. and Levine, S. (1981), "Expressive psychotherapy with gender dysphoric patients," *Archives of General Psychiatry*, 38, pp. 924–9.

Lothstein, L. and Roback, H. (1981), "Black female transsexuals and schizophrenia: a serendipitous finding?", in I. Pauly (ed.), *Abstracts and Proceedings of the 7th International Gender Dysphoria Association*,Lake Tahoe, Nevada.

Lukianowicz, N. (1959), "Survey of various aspects of transvestism in the light of our present knowledge," *Journal of Nervous and Mental Disease*, 128, pp. 36–64.

Machover, K. (1949), *Personality Projection in the Drawing of the Human Figure*, Charles C. Thomas, Springfield, Ill.

Mahler, M. (1967), "On human symbiosis and the vicissitudes of individuation," *Journal of the American Psychoanalytic Association*, 15, pp. 740–63.

Mahler, M. and Gosliner, B. (1955), "On symbiotic child psychosis. Genetic, dynamic, and restitutive aspects," in *The Psychoanalytic Study of the Child*, 10, International Universities Press, New York, pp. 195–212.

Margolis, G. (1966), "Secrecy and identity," *International Journal of Psycho-Analysis*, 47, pp. 517–21.

Martino, M. (1977), *Emergence*, Crown Books, New York.

Masterson, J. (1976), *Psychotherapy of the Borderline Adult*, Brunner Mazel, New York.

McCully, R. (1963), "An interpretation of projective findings in a case of female transsexualism," *Journal of Projective Techniques and Personality Assessment*, 27, pp. 436–47.

McLean, P. (1955), "The limbic system ('visceral brain') and emotional behavior," *Archives of Neurology and Psychiatry*, 73, pp. 130–4.

Meerloo, J. (1967), "Change of sex in collaboration with the psychosis," *American Journal of Psychiatry*, 124, pp. 263–4.

Meissner, W. (1980), "Differential diagnosis of narcissistic personalities from borderline conditions," Paper presented at the University of Miami School of Medicine.

Meyenburg, B. and Sieguesch, V. (1977), "Transsexuals in West Germany: Therapeutic guidelines and legal problems," mimeograph. Paper presented at the Fifth International Gender Dysphoria Symposium, Norfolk, Va.

Meyer, J. (1974), "Clinical variants among applicants for sex reassignment," *Archives of Sexual Behavior*, 3, pp. 527–58.

Meyer, J. and Hoopes, J. (1974), "The gender dysphoria syndromes," *Journal of Plastic and Reconstructive Surgery*, 54, pp. 444–51.

Meyer, J. and Reter, D. (1979), "Sex reassignment," *Archives of General Psychiatry*, 36, pp. 1010–15.

Meyer, W., Finkelstein, J., Stuart, C., Webb, A., and Walker, P. (1981), "Hormonal treatment of 86 male and female transsexuals," in I. Pauly (ed.), *Abstracts and Proceedings of the 7th International Gender Dysphoria Association*, Lake Tahoe, Nevada.

Meyer-Bahlburg, H. (1979), "Sex hormones and female homosexuality: a critical examination," *Archives of Sexual Behavior*, 8, pp. 101–19.

Miller, J. (ed.) (1973), *Psychoanalysis and Women*, Penguin, Baltimore, Md.

Mischel, W. (1966), "A social learning view of sex differences in behavior," in E. E. Maccoby (ed.), *The Development of Sex Differences*, Stanford University Press, Palo Alto, Calif.

Modell, A. (1968), *Object Love and Reality*, International Universities Press, New York.

Money, J. (1963), "Cytogenetics and psychosexual incongruities with a note on space form blindness," *American Journal of Psychiatry*, 119, pp. 800–27.

Money, J. (1973), "Gender role, gender identity, core gender identity: usage and definition of terms," *Journal of the American Academy of Psychoanalysis*, 4, pp. 397–403.

Money, J. (1974), "Intersexual and transsexual behavior and syndromes," in S. Arieti (ed.), *American Handbook of Psychiatry*, Basic Books, New York.

Money, J. and Ambinder, R. (1978), "Two-year, real-life diagnostic test: rehabilitation versus cure," in H. Brady and J. Brody (eds), *Controversy In Psychiatry*, Saunders, Philadelphia, Pa.

Money, J. and Brennan, J. (1968), "Sexual dimorphism in the psychology of female transsexuals," *Journal of Nervous and Mental Disease*, 147, pp. 487–99.

Money, J. and Brennan, J. (1969), "Sexual dimorphism in the psychology of female transsexuals," in R. Green and J. Money (eds), *Transsexualism and Sex Reassignment*, Johns Hopkins University Press, Baltimore, Md.

Money, J. and Ehrhardt, A. (1972), *Man and Woman, Boy and Girl*, Johns Hopkins University Press, Baltimore, Md.

Money, J., Hampson, J., and Hampson, J. (1955), "Hermaphroditism: recommendations concerning assignment of sex, change of sex, and psychologic management," *Bulletin Johns Hopkins Hospital*, 97, pp. 284–300.

Money, J., Hampson, J., and Hampson, J. (1957), "Imprinting and the establishment of gender role," *Archives of Neurology and Psychiatry*, 77, pp. 333–6.

Money, J. and Russo, A. (1979), "Homosexual outcome of discordant gender identity/role in childhood: longitudinal follow-up," *Journal of Pediatric Psychology*, 4, pp. 29–41.

Myrick, R. (1970), "The counselor-consultant and the effeminate boy," *Personnel and Guidance*, 48, pp. 355–61.

Newman, L. and Stoller, R. (1974), "Non-transsexual men who seek sex reassignment," *American Journal of Psychiatry*, 131, pp. 437–41.

Omni (staff) (1981), "Transsexual reincarnation," 4, p. 111.

Opitz, J., Simpson, J., Sario, G., Summitt, M., New, M., and German, J. (1971), "Pseudo vaginal perineoscrotal hypospadias," *Clinical Genetics*, 3, pp. 1–19.

Overzier, C. (1955), "Beitrag zur Kenntnis des männlichen Transvestitismus," *Zum Psychotherapie Medizinischer Psychologie*, 5, pp. 152–71.

Ovesey, L. and Person, E. (1976), "Transvestism: a disorder of the sense of self," *International Journal of Psychoanalytic Psychotherapy*, 5, pp. 219–36.

Pauly, I. (1963), "Female psychosexual inversion: transsexualism," in American Psychiatric Association, *Summaries of the Scientific Papers of the 119th Annual Meeting of the American Psychiatric Association*, Washington, D.C.

Pauly, I. (1965), "Male psychosexual inversion: transsexualism," *Archives of General Psychiatry*, 13, pp. 172–81.

Pauly, I. (1968), "The current status of the change of sex operation," *Journal of Nervous and Mental Disease*, 147, pp. 460–71.

Pauly, I. (1969), "Adult manifestations of female transsexualism," in R. Green and J. Money (eds), *Transsexualism and Sex Reassignment*, Johns Hopkins University Press, Baltimore, Md.

Pauly, I. (1974a), "Female transsexualism: Part I," *Archives of Sexual Behavior*, 3, pp. 487–507.

Pauly, I. (1974b), "Female transsexualism: Part II," *Archives of Sexual Behavior*, 3, pp. 509–25.

Person, E. and Ovesey, L. (1974a), "The transsexual syndrome in males: I. Primary transsexualism," *American Journal of Psychotherapy*, 28, pp. 4–20.

Person, L. and Ovesey, L. (1974b), "The transsexual syndrome in males: II. Secondary transsexualism," *American Journal of Psychotherapy*, 28, pp. 174–93.

Pfafflin, F. (1981), "H-Y antigen in transsexualism," in I. Pauly (ed.), *Abstracts and Proceedings of the 7th International Gender Dysphoria Association*, Lake Tahoe, Nevada.

Philippopoulos, G. (1964), "A case of transvestism in a 17-year-old girl," *Acta Psychotherapeutica*, 12, pp. 29–37.

Piaget, J. (1929), *The Child's Conception of the World*, Harcourt Brace, New York.

Pomeroy, W. (1975), "The diagnosis and treatment of transvestites and transsexuals," *Journal of Sex and Marital Therapy*, 1, pp. 215–28.

Prince, V. (1976), *Understanding Cross-Dressing*, Chevalier Publications, Los Angeles, Calif.

Randell, J. (1969), "Preoperative and postoperative status of male and female transsexuals," in R. Green and J. Money (eds), *Transsexualism and Sex Reassignment*, Johns Hopkins University Press, Baltimore, Md.

Redfearn, J. (1979), "Comment on 'a mythic search for identity in a female to male transsexual,'" *Journal of Analytical Psychology*, 24, pp. 314-17.

Redmount, R. (1953), "A case of a female transvestite with marital and criminal complications," *Journal of Clinical and Experimental Psychopathology*, 14, pp. 95-111.

Rekers, G., Bentler, P., Rosen, A., and Lovaas, I. (1977), "Child gender disturbances: a clinical rationale for intervention," *Psychotherapy: Theory, Research and Practice*, 14, pp. 2-11.

Rekers, G. and Lovaas, I. (1974), "Behavioral treatment of deviant sex-role behaviors in a male child," *Journal of Applied Behavioral Analysis*, 7, pp. 173-90.

Rekers, G., Lovaas, I., and Low, B. (1974), "The behavioral treatment of a 'transsexual' preadolescent boy," *Journal of Abnormal Child Psychology*, 2, pp. 99-116.

Roback, H., McKee, F., Webb, W., Abramowitz, S., and Abramowitz, C. (1976), "Psychopathology in female sex-change applicants and two help seeking controls," *Journal of Abnormal Psychology*, 85, pp. 430-2.

Rochlin, G. (1980), *The Masculine Dilemma*, Little, Brown, Boston, Mass.

Roiphe, H. and Galenson, E. (1981), *Infantile Origins of Sexual Identity*, International Universities Press, New York.

Rosen, A. (1974), "A brief report of MMPI characteristics of sexual deviation," *Psychological Reports*, 35, pp. 73-4.

Ross, M., Wålinder, J., Lundström, B., and Thuwe, I. (1981), "Cross-cultural approaches to transsexualism, a comparison between Sweden and Australia," *Acta Psychiatrica Scandinavica*, 63, pp. 75-82.

Roth, H. (1973), "Three years of ongoing psychotherapy of a trans-sexual patient," in D. Laub and P. Gandy (eds), *Proceedings of the Second Interdisciplinary Symposium on Gender Dysphoria Syndrome*, Stanford University Press, Palo Alto, Calif.

Rubin, R., Reinisch, J., and Haskett, R. (1981), "Postnatal gonadal steroid effects on human behavior," *Science*, 211, pp. 1318-24.

Sadoughi, W., Overman, C., and Bush, I. (1973), "Group therapy as an integral part of surgical experience," in D. Laub and P. Gandy (eds), *Proceedings of the Second Interdisciplinary Symposium on Gender Dysphoria Syndrome*, Stanford University Press, Palo Alto, Calif.

Schafer, R. (1948), *The Clinical Application of Psychological Tests*, International Universities Press, New York.

Schafer, R. (1976), "Problems in Freud's psychology of women," *Journal of the American Psychoanalytical Association*, 24, pp. 459-84.

Segal, M. (1965), "Transvestism as an impulse and a defense," *International Journal of Psycho-Analysis*, 46, pp. 209–17.

Sendrail, M. and Gleizes, L. (1961), "Le Transsexualisme feminin et le problème de ses conditions psychiques ou hormonales," *Revue Française Endocrinologica Clinique*, 2, pp. 35–41.

Seyler, L., Canalis, E., Spare, S., and Reichlin, S. (1978), "Abnormal gonadotrophin secretory responses to LRH in transsexual women after diethylstilbestrol priming," *Journal of Clinical Endocrinology and Metabolism*, 47, pp. 176–83.

Shave, D. (1976), "Transsexualism as a concretized manifestation of orality," *American Journal of Psychoanalysis*, 36, pp. 57–66.

Sheelah, J., Orwin, A., and Davies, D. (1972), "Sex chromosome abnormality in a patient with transsexualism," *British Medical Journal*, 3, p. 29.

Shen, J. and Jones, S. (1981), "Sociological and psychological characteristics of female-to-male transsexuals: a review of four year clinical data on 39 patients," in I. Pauly (ed.), *Abstracts and Proceedings of the 7th International Gender Dysphoria Association*, Lake Tahoe, Nevada.

Shtasel, T. (1979), "Behavioral treatment of transsexualism: a case report," *Journal of Sex and Marital Therapy*, 5, pp. 362–7.

Silvers, W. and Wachtel, S. (1977), "H-Y antigen: behavior and function," *Science*, 195, pp. 956–9.

Simon, R. (1967), "A case of female transsexualism," *American Journal of Psychiatry*, 123, pp. 1598–1601.

Socarides, C. (1969), "The desire for sexual transformation: a psychiatric evaluation of transsexualism," *American Journal of Psychiatry*, 125, pp. 125–31.

Socarides, C. (1970), "A psychoanalytic study of the desire for sexual transformation ('transsexualism'): The Plaster-of-Paris man," *International Journal of Psycho-Analysis*, 51, pp. 341–9.

Sorensen, T. and Hertoft, P. (1980), "Sexmodifying operations in Denmark in the period 1950–1977," *Acta Psychiatrica Scandinavica*, 61, pp. 56–66.

Späte, Z. (1970), "Zum Abteil des limbischen Systems in der Pathogenese des Transvestitismus," *Psychiatrie, Neurologie, und Medizinische Psychologie*, 22, pp. 339–44.

Sperling, M. (1964), "The analysis of a boy with transvestite tendencies: a contribution to the genesis and dynamics of transvestism," *Psychoanalytic Study of the Child*, 19, pp. 470–93.

Stekel, W., (1923), *Der Fetichismus*, Urban & Schwarzenberg, Berlin und Wien.

Stoller, R. (1966), "The mother's contribution to infantile transvestic behavior," *International Journal of Psycho-Analysis*, 47, pp. 384–95.

Stoller, R. (1968), *Sex And Gender*, Science House, New York.

Stoller, R. (1970), "Psychotherapy of extremely feminine boys," *International Journal of Psychiatry*, 9, pp. 278–82.

Stoller, R. (1972), "Etiological factors in female transsexualism," *Archives of Sexual Behavior*, 2, pp. 47–64.

Stoller, R. (1973), "Male transsexualism: uneasiness," *American Journal of Psychiatry*, 130, pp. 536–9.

Stoller, R. (1975), *Sex And Gender, Vol. 2. The Transsexual Experiment*, Jason Aronson, New York.

Stoller, R. (1976), "Primary Femininity," *Journal of the American Psychoanalytic Association*, 24, pp. 59–78.

Stoller, R. (1979), "A contribution to the study of gender identity: follow-up," *International Journal of Psycho-Analysis*, 60, pp.433–41.

Stoller, R. and Baker, H. (1973), "Two male transsexuals in one family," *Archives of Sexual Behavior*, 2, pp. 323–8.

Stolorow, R. and Lachmann, F. (1980), *Psychoanalysis of Developmental Arrests*, International Universities Press, New York.

Strassberg, D., Roback, H., Cunningham, J., McKee, E., and Larson, P. (1979), "Psychopathology in self-identified female-to-male transsexuals, homosexuals, and heterosexuals," *Archives of Sexual Behavior*, 8, pp. 491–6.

Stürup, G. (1976), "Male transsexuals: a long term follow-up after sex reassignment operations," *Acta Psychiatrica Scandinavica*, 53, pp. 51–63.

Tyson, P. (1982), "The role of the father in gender identity, urethral eroticism, and phallic narcissism," in Cath, S., Gurwitt, A., and Ross, J. (eds), *Father and Child: Developmental and Clinical Perspectives*, Little, Brown, Boston, Mass., pp. 175–88.

Uddenberg, N., Wålinder, J., and Hojerback, T. (1979), "Parental contact in male and female transsexuals," *Acta Psychiatrica Scandinavica*, 60, pp. 113–20.

Vague, J. (1956), "Le Désir de changer de sexe," *a Presse Médicale*, 64, pp. 949–51.

Videla, E., and Prigoshin, N. (1976), "Female tran-sexualist with abnormal karyotype," *Lancet*, II, no. 7994 Nov., p. 1081.

Vogt, J. (1968), "Five cases of transsexualism in females," *Acta Psychiatrica Scandinavica*, 44, pp. 62–88.

Volkan, V. (1976a), *Primitive Internalized Object Relations*, International Universities Press, New York.

Volkan, V. (1976b), "Aggression among transsexuals," Unpublished paper presented at the 129th Annual Meeting of the American Psychiatric Association, Miami, Florida.

Volkan, V. (1979), "Transsexualism: as examined from the viewpoint of internalized object relations," in T. Karascu and C. Socarides (eds), *On Sexuality*, International Universities Press, New York.

Von Bertalanffy, L. (1968), *General System Theory*, Braziller, New York.

Voyles, v. Davies Medical Center (1975), vol. 403, Federal Supplement 456, Northern District, Calif.

Wålinder, J. (1967), *Transsexualism: A Study of Forty-Three Cases*, Scandinavian University Books, Göteborg.

Wålinder, J. (1971), "Incidence and sex ratio of transsexualism in Sweden," *British Journal of Psychiatry*, 119, pp. 195–6.

Wålinder, J. and Thuwe, I. (1974), *A Social-Psychiatric Follow-up Study of 24 Sex Reassigned Transsexuals*, Scandinavian University Books, Göteborg.

Walker, P. (1981), "Factitious presentations of 'transsexualism' — 35 cases," in I. Pauly (ed.), *Abstracts and Proceedings of the 7th International Gender Dysphoria Association*, Lake Tahoe, Nevada.

Walker, P., Berger, J., Green, R., Laub, D. et al., (1980), *Standards of Care: The Hormonal and Surgical Sex Reassignment of Gender Dysphoric Persons*, mimeograph. Distributed by the Harry Benjamin International Gender Dysphoria Association, c/o Paul Walker Ph.D., 1952 Union St. San Francisco, Calif. 94123.

Walsh, P., Madden, J., Harrod, J., Goldstein, P., MacDonald, I., and Wilson, J. (1974), "Familial incomplete male pseudohermaphroditism, Type 2," *New England Journal of Medicine*, 291, pp. 944–9.

Waltz, M. (1979), "Transsexuals and the law," *Journal of Contemporary Law*, 5, pp. 181–214.

Warner, G. and Lahn, M. (1970), "A case of female transsexualism," *Psychiatric Quarterly*, 44, pp. 476–87.

Warnes, H. and Hill, G. (1974), "Gender identity and the wish to be a woman," *Psychosomatics*, 1, pp. 25–31.

Weigert-Vowinkel, E. (1938), "The cult and mythology of the Magna Mater," *Psychiatry*, 1, pp. 348–78.

Weitzman, E., Shamoian, C., and Golosow, N. (1970), "Identity diffusion and the transsexual resolution," *Journal of Nervous and Mental Disease*, 151, pp. 295–302.

Weitzman, E., Shamoian, C., and Golosow, N. (1971), "Family dynamics in male transsexualism," *Psychosomatic Medicine*, 33, pp. 289–99.

Westphal, C. (1869), "Die konträre Sexualempfindung," *Archiven für Psychiatrie und Nervenkrankheiten*, 2, pp. 73–108.

329

Bibliography

Winnicott, D. W. (1958), *Collected Papers*, Tavistock, London.
Winnicott, D. W. (1965), *The Maturational Processes and the Facilitating Environment*, International Universities Press, New York.
Wollman, L. (1973), "One thousand transsexuals," Paper presented at the Second Interdisciplinary Symposium on Gender Dysphoria Syndrome, Stanford University Medical Center, Palo Alto, Calif.
Wylie, R. (1961), *The Self Concept*, University of Nebraska Press, Lincoln.

Index

abnormal female development, 197–208
Abraham, K., 184, 294
adolescence, 34, 38, 43, 44, 206, 264
adrenogenital syndrome, 173
aggression, 221, 242, 243
Agras, S., 264
Althof, S., 92, 267
Ambinder, A., 298
American Psychiatric Association, 4, 59, 265
amniocentisis, 190
androgen levels, 170–2
annihilation anxiety, 199, 231, 237
Aronoff, M., 195
art therapy, 41
as-if personality, 73, 144, 146
associative learning, 212
atypical gender identity disorder, 60
average expectable self, 240

Bak, R., 54
Baker, H., 37, 164, 218, 267
Barahal, H., 24, 25
Barbara, letter, 1, 16
Barker, M., 298
Barlow, D., 212, 264
Bates, J., 217
behaviorism, 212–15
Bem Sex Role inventory, 42
Benjamin, H., 4, 22, 27–8, 56, 266, 284, 296, 308; crossdressing typology, 56–7
Berlin, F., 288
Bernstein, S., 256
Billowitz, A., 282
bio-medical ethics, 3

bisexuality, 15, 93, 245
black females, 42, 46–7, 146–59
blank self, 73
Bleuler, M., 173
Bloch, D., 37, 198
Blum, J., 265
Blumer, D., 164, 167
Bogden, R., 55
Bogoras, N., 299
borderline personality, 11, 68, 222, 237, 270
Boswell, J., 14, 19, 164
Brady, J., 294
breast, 286; amputation, 291; surgery, 291–4
Breger, L., 183, 185
Brennan, J., 29–30
Brierley, H., 213
Brod, T., 10, 232
Brodie, H., 294
Brown, D., 56
Brown, M., 218
Buck, T., 218
Bucy, P., 167
Bullough, V., 14, 19, 54

Caelius Aurelianus, 164
Captain Tweed, 22
cases, Anny, 32; Barbara/Brian, 95; Donna/Douglas, 146; Frl. N., 21; Gloria/Ray, 272; Joe, 28; Patricia/Pat, 133; Randi/Randy, 110; Tina/Tim, 63
Case Western Reserve University, 17, 46, 66, 87, 218, 300, 310
castration anxiety, 183, 199
Cauldwell, D., 23, 56

cerebral pathology, 164, 167
children, 37, 208
Childs, A., 255
Christodorescu, D., 34
chromosomal factors, 172–7
chromosomal mosaicism, 166
Cleveland Metropolitan General Hospital, 66, 87
clitoris, 288
cognitive theory, 215–17
cohesive self, 13, 204
conditioning, 189
contrary sexual feelings, 21
contrasexism, 56
Cook, D., 19
core gender identity, 189, 195; defined, 189
Coulter, J., 19
counseling, 260–2
Count Sandor, 51
crossdressing, 93, 231
Cushing's syndrome, 172
cytogenetics, 164

Davenport, C., 38, 264
Davies, B., 167
Dawson-Butterworth, K., 28
depersonification, 231
de Raylan, 20
Derogatis, L., 46
De Savitsch, E., 20
Deuteronomy, 8
Deutsch, H., 184
developmental arrest, 200, 228, 234, 239
Diagnostic and Statistical Manual, 10, 59, 83
Dickes, R., 41
diethystilbestrol, 175
disavowal, 183
disidentifying, 193
Dixen, J., 91
draw-a-person test, 41, 68
Dunn, P., 195

early genital phase, 192, 197
Eber, M., 59, 80, 271
EEG, 167–70
ego functions, 192, 234
ego mechanisms, 194, 223
ego weakness, 206
Ehrhardt, A., 42, 164, 173, 180

Eicher, W., 177–8
Eichwald, E., 177
Ellis, H., 20, 56
empathy, 226, 228
enzyme defect, 164, 166, 175
eonism, 56
epilepsy, 168, 170
Erikson, E., 244
exhibitionism, 225

Fairbairn, W., 219
false self, 205, 241
family dynamics, 217–19, 233, 246
family pathology, 199, 207
Fast, I., 182, 191, 216
father, 199, 230–1; death of, 244, 256
Feinbloom, D., 55
female brain, 197
female gender identity, 181; abnormal, 197–208; average expectable, 188; defined, 181; normal pathway, 187–96
female schizophrenia, 28
femininity, 181, 184, 221; flight from, 246; secondary femininity, 188
feminists, 4, 185
Fenichel, O., 54
fetal androgens, 174
fetishism, 170
Fielding, H., 20
Fingerette, H., 224
Finkelstein, M., 242
Fisk, N., 59, 252, 265
Fleming, M., 41–2, 68
Fliegel, Z., 184, 185
focal gender symbiosis, 199
Forester, B., 267
Frances, A., 195
Freud, S., 53, 181–6
Friedreich, J., 50
Fuller, M., 267

Gagné, P., 288
Galenson, E., 81, 190, 198
Garfinkel, H., 55
Gediman, H., 233
Gelb, J., 299
Gelder, M., 267
gender dysphoria, 47; syndrome, 59
gender identity defined, 60; gender identity formation, 189; precursors, 190; role of the mother, 198–9

gender identity disorder of childhood, 78–80
gender-self constancy, 195, 196, 229, 234
gender-self representation, 195, 204, 230, 234
gender-self system, 195
gender symbiosis, 199
genital hallucinosis, 28
Gershman, H., 54, 189
Giffin, M., 217
Giovacchini, P., 220, 234, 270
Gittleson, N., 28
Gleizes, L., 164, 282
Gordon, J., 178
Gosliner, B., 194
grandiose regulator, 266, 270
Green, R., 30, 37, 40, 78, 267, 294, 310
Greenson, R., 267
Gross, A., 242
Grossman, W., 184
group psychotherapy, 267
Gunderson, J., 68
Guntrip, H., 219, 243
Guze, S., 178

Hall, M., 20
Hall, R., 20
Hamburger, C., 284, 308
Hampson, J., 189
Harrison, S., 38, 264
Harry Benjamin Association, 12, 283, 309
Haseltine, F., 179
Hastings, D., 256, 265
Hedwig, S., 20
hermaphroditism, 166
Hertoft, P., 44
Hertz, J., 61, 265, 295–6
Herschkowitz, S., 41
Hill, D., 170
Hill, E., 76
Hirschfeld, M., 22, 54, 56
Hoenig, J., 164, 169, 309
homocentric, 7
homophobic, 14, 43, 205
homosexuality, 182, 206
Hoopes, J., 299
hormones, 281–4; effects, 287; goals, 285–7; illicit, 281; motivation for, 283; physiologic changes, 287

Horney, K., 184
hospitalization, 256
Hoyer, N., 294
Hunt, N., 310
H-Y antigen, 177–9
hypersexuality, 167
hypnosis, 53
hysterectomy, 298

idealization, 227
identity disorder, 61
Ihlenfeld, C., 34, 309
Imperato-McGinley, J., 175
impersonation, 242
imprinting, 189, 219
incest, 93, 144
Institute of Sexual Science, 22
intersexuality, 164, 167

Jacobson, E., 220
Joan of Arc, 20
Johns Hopkins, 66, 297, 309
Johnson, A., 217–18
Jones, E., 184
Jones, J., 164, 171
Jorgenson, C., 24, 308
Jung, C., 41

karyotyping, 171, 173, 179
Keller, A., 267
Kenna, J., 164, 169, 309
Kernberg, O., 66, 220, 222, 249
Khan, M., 198, 241
Kinsey, A., 27, 56
Kleeman, J., 189–90, 192, 216
Klein, M., 219
Kluver, H., 167
Kockott, G., 169
Kohlberg, L., 215
Kohut, H., 224–5, 229, 240, 245, 249, 276, 280
Krafft-Ebing, R. von, 50–3
Kubie, L., 58, 209, 245

Lachmann, F., 234, 239
Lahn, M., 32
Laing, R., 241
Lampl-de-Groot, J., 184
Laub, D., 59, 265, 285
Leff, D., 177
Léger, J., 31–2
lesbians, 42

Index

letter, Barbara, 1–2
Levine, F., 233
Levine, S., 47, 81, 267, 277
Lewis, H., 217
Liakos, A., 218
Lichtenstein, H., 219
limbic system, 170
Limentani, A., 55, 210, 275
Litin, E., 217
lobectomy, 168
Lothstein, L., 44, 46, 47, 83, 172, 221,
  222, 267, 270, 275, 277, 292, 294,
  296, 297, 310
Lovaas, I., 81, 267
Lucian, 19
Lukianowicz, N., 308

Machover, K., 68
Mackie, J., 58
Mahler, M., 194, 216, 220
male hormones, 282–90
Margolis, G., 242
Marks, I., 267
Martial, 19
Martino, M., 39, 40, 288
masculinity complex, 182
masochism, 182
Masterson, J., 222, 231
masturbation, 200, 232
McCully, R., 25–6, 76
McLean, P., 170
Meerloo, J., 54
Meinecke, C., 288
Meissner, W., 237
metamorphosis sexualis paranoica, 56
methodology, 48, 159
Mexican, 31
Meyenburg, B., 222
Meyer, J., 43, 58, 289, 297
Meyer-Bahlburg, H., 175, 180
Miller, J., 185
Minnesota Multiphasic Personality
  Inventory (MMPI), 32, 35, 66, 160
mirror-hungry personalities, 231
Mischel, W., 212
Modell, A., 226
Money, J., 29–30, 78, 164, 167, 173,
  177, 189, 269, 198
Morgenstern, F., 167
mother, fusion with, 239–40, 242, 246
mothers, transexuals, 36
Munchhausen's syndrome, 269

Muslem, 19
Myrick, R., 267
myths of transsexualism, 5–14

names, 92
narcissism, 224–5
Nathans, J., 41
negative identity, 244
negative oedipal, 182
neurohormonal disorder, 164
Newman, L., 59
nonspecific ego weaknesses, 222
nuclear self, 194, 228
Nusselt, L., 169

object constancy, 195
object loss, 192
object relations, theory, 219–24
oophorectomy, 298
ovarian stimulation, 175
Overzier, C., 173
Ovesey, L., 55, 220

pan gender dysphoria, 235
paranoia transsexualis, 56
paranoid persecutor, 266, 270
paraphilia, 60
Parkhurst, C., 19
passing, 55
patriarchal complacency, 183
Pauly, I., 20, 23, 31, 35, 36, 56, 169,
  217, 248, 265, 309
penis envy, 183
Person, E., 55, 220
perversion, 208
Pfafflin, F., 178
phallic period, 181, 188
phallic woman, 55
phalloplasty, 299
phantom breast, 292
Philippopoulos, G., 26–7
Piaget, J., 215
plasma testosterone, 171
polycystic ovary, 171
Pomeroy, W., 43
Pope John VIII (Pope Joan), 20
prenatal hormones, 176
preoedipal castration rection, 192
preoedipal period, 182, 189
preoedipal psychosexuality, 190
pretranssexual, 205
Prigoshin, N., 166

primary femininity, 188, 192, 249
primary gender pathology, 249
primary transsexualism, 58
primitive psychological defenses, 222
Prince, V., 294
progestin induced hermaphroditism, 173
projective identification, 237
psychoanalysis, 208–12, 247
psychological evaluation, 33, 255–60
psychological tests, 67–8, 95
psychopathia transsexualis, 23, 56
psychosexual disorders, 60
psychosexual inversion, 56
psychotherapy, 262–76; goals, 276–9
pure transsexualism, 56

Randall, J., 296
rape, 103
ratio of male/female transsexualism, 308–11
Redfearn, J., 41
Redmount, R., 23–4
Rekers, G., 78, 80, 208, 214, 264, 267
Reter, D., 297
Roback, H., 38, 46
Rochlin, G., 326
Roiphe, H., 190, 192
Rorschach test, 68, 73, 155
Rosen, A., 38
Rubin, R., 175
Ruck, G., 41
Ruddle, F., 178
Russo, A., 78, 120

Sacks, M., 195
sadomasochism, 55, 231
Sadoughi, W., 267
Samimy, J., 171
Sand, G., 20
Schafer, R., 76, 183, 185
schizophrenia, 28, 37, 93, 249
Schreber, D., 53–4
Science, 178
secondary femininity, 188
secondary gender pathology, 252
secondary transsexualism, 59
Segal, M., 54
self constancy, 194–5
self defect, 230
self-object differentiation, 196
selfobjects, 226; mirroring and idealized

omnipotent, 374; transferences, 225
self pathology, 228
self psychology, 224–8; and female transsexualism, 228–33; fragmentation, 228
self-representation, 192, 234
Semeniak, M., 22
semi-symbolic reasoning, 194
Sendrail, M., 164, 282
separation anxiety, 220
separation-individuation, 193, 210, 252
sex differences, 207
sex orientation scale, 56
sex ratio, 308–11
sex reassignment surgery (SRS), 294–301
sex role inversion, 55
sexual fantasy, 239
sexual identity, 191
sexual inhibition, 182
sexual inversion, 53
Seyler, L., 175
Sheelah, J., 166
Shen, J., 92
Shtasel, T., 42
Sieguesch, V., 222
Silmser, C., 177
Silvers, W., 177
Simon, R., 29
Singer, M., 68
single case approach, 162
sissy, 212
Slater, L., 19
Socarides, C., 58, 210
social learning theory, 212–15
Sorensen, T., 44
South African, 32
Späte, Z., 37, 168, 191
Sperling, M., 54, 267
splitting, 222–3
spontaneous virilization, 172
stable personality, 237
standards of care, 11
Stanford-Binet Test, 191
Stanford University, 35
Stein-Leventhall syndrome, 37, 172
Stekl, W., 22
Stewart, W., 54, 184
stigmatized homosexual, 10, 43
Stoller, R., 15, 34–5, 36, 54, 57, 59, 164, 165, 169, 179, 185, 207,

209, 217, 218, 267, 308, 309
Stolorow, R., 234, 239
Strassberg, D., 43
street hormones, 281
Stürup, G., 297
suicide, 41, 94–5, 256–7
Sumo, S., 179
superego lacunae, 218
supportive psychotherapy, 267
Swiller, H., 167
symbol formation, 210, 247
Szurek, S., 218

temporal lobe dysfunction, 168
Tennessee Self Concept Scale, 43
terrible twos, 197
tertiary gender pathology, 253
testosterone, 284–5
Thematic Apperception Test, 32, 69, 73
thought disorder, 156
Thuwe, I., 266, 297
toilet trauma, 269
tomboyism, 29, 50, 77, 166, 174, 204, 238
Torr, J., 173
transference, 276
transsexualism, defined, 56–7, 61, 207; bioethical issues, 16; blacks, 42, 46; *see also* cases, 95–159; core features, 56, 62; counseling issues in transsexualism, 260–2; cross-cultural influences, 19–21; death of parent, 46; defense against homosexuality, 210; diagnostic issues, 74–6, 81–4; follow up studies, 300–1; hormone treatment, 281–7; incidence, 294; in history, 19–21; overview, 302; parents, 40, 42, 190; prevalence, 92, 297, 308–11; primary transsexualism, 58; psychobiological issues, 144–80; psychological issues, 181, 254; questions, 236; role of father, 199, 230–1,

244. 256; role of mother, 211; and schizophrenia, 238; secondary transsexualism, 59; sex reassignment surgery, 291–301; stability of female transsexualism, 37, 62, 65, 207; theoretical approaches, 208–54; theoretical framework, for, 233–4; true transsexualism, 56, 209; typology, 249–54
transvestism, 54, 55, 167, 208
true self, 241
Turner's syndrome, 173
typology of transsexualism, 249–54
Tyson, P., 194

Uddenberg, N., 42

vagina, 181
Vague, J., 7
Videla, E., 166
virilization, 282
Vogt, J., 30, 284
Volkan, V., 55, 220, 232, 245, 275
Von Bertalanffy, L., 245
voyeurism, 270

Wachtel, S., 177
Walinder, J., 266, 297, 309
Walker, M., 20
Walker, P., 269, 282, 288, 294
Waltz, M., 305
Warner, G., 32
Wechsler Adult Intelligence Scale, 30, 68
Weitzman, E., 218, 245
Westphal, C., 21, 50
wholeness, 221, 226
Wiesemann, H., 173
Winnicott, D., 219, 221, 241
Wolf, E., 226–7
Wollman, L., 308
Wylie, R., 224